Family Businesses in Transition Economies

Léo-Paul Dana • Veland Ramadani
Editors

Family Businesses in Transition Economies

Management, Succession and Internationalization

Editors
Léo-Paul Dana
Montpellier Business School
Montpellier
France

Veland Ramadani
South-East European University
Tetovo
Macedonia

ISBN 978-3-319-14208-1   ISBN 978-3-319-14209-8   (eBook)
DOI 10.1007/978-3-319-14209-8

Library of Congress Control Number: 2015935332

Springer Cham Heidelberg New York Dordrecht London

Printed on acid-free paper

Springer International Publishing AG Switzerland is part of Springer Science+Business Media
(www.springer.com)

*To my late father Albert and my mother
Clemy, gone with the earthquake of 2011*
Léo-Paul Dana

*To my father Ismet and my late mother
Mijasere, whom I miss more and more
everyday*
Veland Ramadani

Foreword

In many ways, this is a remarkable volume. Prior to the collapse of the former Soviet Union, few would have predicted that a topic which has been mainstream in the small business literature for many years would be extended into countries which, prior to 1990, largely viewed private enterprise as an illegal activity. Now, some 25 years after the start of the reform process, we are presented with a volume which examines family business in a different context to that which most of the family business literature addresses.

An emergent literature on family business in transition economies has increasingly become a regular theme in conferences targeted at entrepreneurship scholars from Central and Eastern Europe and countries further East. Many of the issues discussed in these sessions do not appear to be significantly different from those we are familiar with in contemporary family business literature. At the same time, as some of the papers in this volume demonstrate, there are distinctive features. This is to be expected as private business is extended into new conditions. Indeed many argue that this process is an important one for the field in general and not just for researchers specializing in transition and emerging market economies. This is because the concepts and theories used in the field should be robust enough to be applied in a variety of contexts and not just those pertaining in mature market economies on either side of the Atlantic Ocean.

The call for more attention to context has been made by a number of scholars recently, of which Friederike Welter is among the most prominent with her seminal paper on context (Welter, 2011). This growing emphasis on context is important. In the past, the field has arguably often divorced organizations from their contexts or external environment, when clearly balance requires a degree of both. As a result, this volume represents an important addition to the family business literature by emphasizing how, in many ways, family influences cut across cultural, economic, and social boundaries. At the same time, they show certain distinctive features, which are a result of the development path followed by these former centrally planned economies.

A growing recognition of the role of family businesses is an integral part of the study of the growth of private enterprise in Central and Eastern Europe. Now, these former socialist economies, with their growing family business sector, are facing the kind of succession issues which are well familiar in the West. At the same time, distinctive features are associated with the specific conditions pertaining during the transition period. In some of these transition countries, private enterprise was tolerated, even during the Soviet period. This tended not to apply in the former Soviet Republics but in some of the Central and East European countries; Poland is an example. In Poland, during Soviet times, some very small micro enterprises were tolerated in sectors such as food processing, wood and furniture products, clothing, and general engineering.

These private firms were considered as craft-based enterprises during Soviet times. The labeling is important because craft firms were considered to be politically acceptable during the Stalinist period and may, therefore, be considered an integral part of the context of entrepreneurship in those countries where they were allowed to exist. In other words, the term "craft" was interpreted to include some small manufacturing firms that were relatively modern and well equipped and which became a foundation for the development of manufacturing and construction companies during the transformation period. Family ownership was a key feature of these craft-based micro enterprises.

So, to summarize, the emergence of family business sector in these former socialist countries may be viewed as an integral part of the transformation from central planning to a private enterprise-based economy. This change, which took place over a relatively short period of time, represents a specific context for the development of family businesses.

London, UK   David Smallbone
October 18, 2014

Reference

Welter, F. (2011). Contextualising entrepreneurship—conceptual challenges and ways forward. *Entrepreneurship: Theory and Practice, 35*(1), 165–184.

Foreword

In recent years, family businesses in transition economies have drawn immense attention among scholars, in which the transition process has resulted in deep and remarkable changes to the economic, political, and social life (Aidis, Welter, Smallbone, & Isakova, 2007; Dana & Dana, 2003; McKibbin & Pistrui, 1997; Ramadani & Dana, 2013; Ramadani & Schneider, 2013). Anyone interested in transition economies needs to focus much of their attention on family firms. Family firms are extremely prevalent in transition economies; for example, in Asia, more than 70 % of businesses are family owned (Fan, n.d.); it is estimated that 70 % of all Hungarian businesses are family ones and bulk of them are SMEs owned by the first generation (Kadocsa, 2003); in Slovenia, it is estimated that the share of family businesses among small and medium-sized businesses is between 41.11 and 51.79 % (Duh & Belak, 2008); in Croatia, many of businesses are family ones (Galetić, 2002); further, in Czech Republic 80–95 % of SMEs, in Latvia 30 % of SMEs with fewer than 50 employees, in Romania more than half of the SMEs, in Lithuania 92.3 % of SMEs, in Slovak Republic 80–95 %, etc. (Mandl, 2008).

I was therefore very pleased to have the opportunity to see a new book focused on "Family Businesses in Transition Economies," edited by Léo-Paul Dana and Veland Ramadani. This book presents a state-of-the-art work and I am delighted to have been invited to write the foreword of it. The editors have done an excellent job in assembling an important set of research papers on family firms.

Family firms give rise to a number of research questions that are of upmost importance in transition economies for understanding their prevalence, structure, governance, and performance. In emerging and transition economies, typically there are weak protections for minority shareholders, which gives rise to exacerbated agency problems in firm ownership structures (Claessens, Djankov, Fan, & Lang, 2002; Dana, 2010). Moreover, in less well-developed capital markets, there are constraints in terms of the market for professional CEOs. There are pronounced succession problems among family firms (Caselli & Gennaioli, 2011). Succession has been particularly problematic in countries like China due to governmental rules pertaining to the one-child policy (Cao, Cumming, & Wang, 2014; Kamei & Dana, 2012). Issues in succession are particularly important, since ineffective succession gives rise to problems in productivity (Bennedsen, Nielsen, Pérez-González, & Wolfenzon, 2007; Caselli and Gennaioli, 2011) and hence negative overall effects on a country's economic wealth.

The book "Family Businesses in Transition Economies" comprises 16 chapters that provide a consistent outlook of the specificity of family firms' research in transitional economies and challenges it faces. It covers many economies in Eastern Europe and Russia, covering many of these important topics pertaining to family firms, among others. The authors of each chapter introduce new data and provide insights into family firms and economic development into countries that are grossly understudied in academic work. In the first chapter, the editors introduce some of the issues in family firms and explain the organization of the book. The uniqueness of family firms is described in chapter "Context and Uniqueness of Family Businesses". The uniqueness of transition economies is described in chapter "Context and Uniqueness of Transition Economies", and institutional features of transition economies are considered in detail in chapter "Different Features of Transition Economies: Institutions Matter". Specific countries are examined in chapters "To Be or Not to Be in a Family Business: The Case of Eight Countries in South-Eastern European Region", "Management Practices in Bulgarian Family and Non-family SMEs: Exploring "Real" Differences", "Obstacles and Opportunities for Development of Family Businesses: Experiences from Moldova", "Successors' Innovativeness as a Crucial Succession Challenge of Family Businesses in Transition Economies: The Case of Slovenia", "Family Business Succession Risks: The Croatian Context", "The Succession Issues in Family Firms: Insights from Macedonia", "Attributes of Financial Management of Family Companies in the Czech Republic and Slovakia", "Ownership Structure, Cash Constraints and Investment Behaviour in Russian Family Firms", and "Family Businesses Motives for Internationalisation: Evidence from Serbia", including nine European countries in chapter "To Be or Not to Be in a Family Business: The Case of Eight Countries in South-Eastern European Region", Bulgaria (chapter "Management Practices in Bulgarian Family and Non-family SMEs: Exploring "Real" Differences"), Moldova (chapter "Obstacles and Opportunities for Development of Family Businesses: Experiences from Moldova"), Slovenia (chapter "Successors' Innovativeness as a Crucial Succession Challenge of Family Businesses in Transition Economies: The Case of Slovenia"), Croatia (chapter "Family Business Succession Risks: The Croatian Context"), Macedonia (chapter "The Succession Issues in Family Firms: Insights from Macedonia"), Czech Republic and Slovakia (chapter "Attributes of Financial Management of Family Companies in the Czech Republic and Slovakia"), Russia (chapter "Ownership Structure, Cash Constraints and Investment Behaviour in Russian Family Firms"), and Serbia (chapter "Family Businesses Motives for Internationalisation: Evidence from Serbia"). Chapter "Entering New Markets: Strategies for Internationalization of Family Businesses" studies internationalization strategies for family firms in Albania. Chapter "Family Business in Sport Organizations: Western Experiences as Lessons for Transitional Economies" examines sports clubs as family firms. Finally, chapter "Family Businesses in the Trade Sector: An Examination of a Case Study from Kosovo" examines the Albi Group, a case study from Kosovo.

The editors are to be congratulated for assembling a fine set of chapters on such an important topic. I would strongly recommend this book to anyone with an interest in family firms and/or transition economies.

Toronto, ON, Canada   Douglas Cumming
June 18, 2014

References

Aidis, R., Welter, F., Smallbone, D., & Isakova, N. (2007). Female entrepreneurship in transition economies: The case of Lithuania and Ukraine. *Feminist Economics, 13*(2), 157–183.

Bennedsen, M., Nielsen, K., Pérez-González, F., & Wolfenzon, D. (2007). Inside the family firm: The role of families in succession decisions and performance. *Quarterly Journal of Economics, 122*, 647–691.

Cao, J., Cumming, D. J., & Wang, X. (2014). One child policy and family firms in China. *Journal of Corporate Finance,* forthcoming.

Caselli, F., & Gennaioli, N. (2011). *Dynastic management* (NBER Working Paper).

Claessens, S., Djankov, S., Fan, J. P. H., & Lang, L. P. H. (2002). Disentangling the incentive and entrenchment effects of large shareholdings. *Journal of Finance, 57*(6), 2741–2771.

Dana, L. -P. (2010). *When economies change hands: A survey of entrepreneurship in the emerging markets of Europe from the Balkans to the Baltic States.* New York: Routledge.

Dana, L. P., & Dana, T. (2003). Management and enterprise development in post-communist economies. *International Journal of Management and Enterprise Development, 1*(1), 45–54.

Duh, M., & Belak, J. (2008). Special knowledge needs of family enterprises in transition economies: experiences from Slovenia. *Knowledge Management Research and Practice, 6*(3), 187–198.

Fan, J. (n.d.). *Good governance of family-owned businesses is critical to emerging market economies.* Available from: http://www.gcgf.org/wps/wcm/connect/topics_ext_content/ifc_external_corporate_site/global+corporate+governance+forum/news/j_fan_interview [Accessed: June, 10 2014].

Galetić, L. (2002). Characteristics of family firms management in Croatia. *MER Journal for Management and Development, 4*(1), 74–81.

Kadocsa, G. (2003). Research and Development of SMEs at Budapest Tech. *International Jubilee Conference Proceedings* (pp. 307–315). Budapest: BMF.

Kamei, K., & Dana, L. -P. (2012). Examining the impact of new policy facilitating SME succession in Japan: From a viewpoint of risk management in family business. *International Journal of Entrepreneurship and Small Business, 16*(1), 60–70.

Mandl, I. (2008). *Overview of family business relevant issues.* Available from: http://ec.europa.eu/enterprise/entrepreneurship/craft/family_business/family_business_en.htm [Accessed: June 10, 2014].

McKibbin, P., & Pistrui, D. (1997). East meets west: Innovative forms of foreign trade finance between Italian family enterprises and E-merging SMEs in Romania. *Family Business Review, 10*(3), 263–281.

Ramadani, V., & Dana, L. -P. (2013). The state of entrepreneurship in the Balkans: Evidence from selected countries. In V. Ramadani & C. R. Schneider (Eds.), *Entrepreneurship in the Balkans: Diversity, support and prospects* (pp. 217-250). Heidelberg: Springer.

Ramadani, V., & Schneider, C. R. (Eds.) (2013). *Entrepreneurship in the Balkans: Diversity, support and prospects.* Heidelberg: Springer.

Acknowledgment

To the reputable contributors, we would like to thank them to the upmost degree. Their experience, knowledge, research, dedication, and time were generously offered in a restless manner. With their work, the importance and necessity for bringing the book to academic researchers, students, and business owners were highlighted and realized.

To the reviewers, we owe a debt of gratitude to the exemplary individuals of academia in the field of family business who have pursued their passion to better us all. Without their respected and appreciated reviewers, this book would not have the same value emphasizing the crucial aspects of the theoretic and practical insights provided by the contributors.

To the distinguished professors and researchers, David Smallbone and Douglas Cumming, we like to extend a special acknowledgment for their appreciated forewords of the book. Their remarkable ability to address readers with their thoughts and views provides justifiable proof of the significance of this pioneering book of family businesses in transitional economies.

To the editor from Springer, Prashanth Mahagaonkar, and his splendid team, we are grateful for their thoughtful suggestions, support, and encouragement that were offered and well received.

To our families and colleagues, we must express our affectionate thanks. They stood by us since the very first beginning when the idea of this book was launched. Their support and motivation are always irreplaceable and necessary for each of us. We dedicate our gratitude, appreciation, and love for them.

Léo-Paul Dana
Veland Ramadani

Abbreviations

CE	Central European countries
CEE	Central and Eastern Europe
CEO	Chief executive officer
COC	Control of corruption
COMECON	Council for Mutual Assistance
DB	Doing business
EBRD	European Bank for Reconstruction and Development
EC	European Commission
EIB	European Investment Bank
EU	European Union
FB	Family business
FBR	Family Business Review
GDP	Gross domestic product
GE	Government effectiveness
GEM	Global Entrepreneurship Monitor
HRK	The official currency of Croatia
IEFS	Institute of Economy, Finance and Statistics of the Republic of Moldova
IFC	International Finance Corporation
IFI	International Financial Institutions
IT	Information and technology
MDL	The official currency of Moldova
NIE	New Institutional Economics
NPLs	Non-performing loans
OB	Own business
OECD	Organisation for Economic Co-operation and Development
PS	Political stability
RBV	Resource-based view
ROE	Return on equity
ROL	Rule of law

RQ	Regulatory quality
SE	South-Eastern countries
SFF	Small family firms
SMEs	Small and medium-sized enterprises
SOE	State-owned enterprise
UOCQ	Ultimate owner controlling qualification
UOCT	Ultimate owner controlling type
VACC	Voice and accountability
VIF	Variation inflation factor
WB	Western Balkan countries

Contents

List of Contributors

Elena Aculai The National Institute for Economic Research of the Republic of Moldova, Chisinau, Republic of Moldova

Egzona Aliu LEORON Professional Development Institute, Dubai, United Arab Emirates

Přemysl Bartoš Faculty of Management and Economics, Tomas Bata University in Zlín, Zlín, Czech Republic

Jaroslav Belás Department of Enterprise Economics, Faculty of Management and Economics, Tomas Bata University in Zlin, Zlin, Czech Republic

Valerija Bublić Department of Entrepreneurship and Management, VERN' University of Applied Sciences, Zagreb, Croatia

Tullio Buccellato Ernst and Young, Paris, France

Gordana Ćorić Department of Entrepreneurship and Management, VERN' University of Applied Sciences, Zagreb, Croatia

Léo-Paul Dana Montpellier Business School, Montpellier Research in Management, Montpellier, France

Mojca Duh Faculty of Economics and Business, University of Maribor, Maribor, Slovenia

Alain Fayolle EM Lyon Business School, Lyon, France

Gian Fazio School of Slavonic and East European Studies, University College, London, UK

Taki Fiti Faculty of Economics-Skopje, Ss. Cyril and Methodius University, Skopje, Macedonia

Gramos Gashi Albi Group, Prishtina, Republic of Kosovo

Shqipe Gërguri-Rashiti College of Business Administration, American University of Middle East, Kuwait City, Kuwait

Radmila Grozdanić Faculty of Business Economics and Entrepreneurship, Belgrade, Serbia

Roman Hlawiczka Faculty of Management and Economics, Tomas Bata University in Zlín, Zlín, Czech Republic

Frank Hoy Worcester Polytechnic Institute, Worcester, MA, USA

Mária Hudáková Faculty of Special Engineering, University of Žilina, Žilina, Slovakia

Betim Humolli Albi Group, Prishtina, Republic of Kosovo

Marina Letonja GEA College – Faculty of Entrepreneurship, Ljubljana, Slovenia

Predrag Ljubotina GEA College – Faculty for Entrepreneurship, Piran, Slovenia

Saša Petković Faculty of Economics, University of Banja Luka, Banja Luka, Bosnia and Herzegovina

Mirjana Radović-Marković Faculty of Business Economics and Entrepreneurship, Belgrade, Serbia

Veland Ramadani Faculty of Business and Economics, South-East European University, Tetovo, Republic of Macedonia

Vanessa Ratten School of Management, La Trobe Business School, La Trobe University, Melbourne, VIC, Australia

Gadaf Rexhepi Faculty of Business and Economics, South-East European University, Tetovo, Republic of Macedonia

Yulia Rodionova Department of Accounting and Finance, Leicester Business School, De Montfort University, Leicester, UK

Iva Senegović Department of Entrepreneurship and Management, VERN' University of Applied Sciences, Zagreb, Croatia

Ralitsa Simeonova-Ganeva Faculty of Economics and Business Administration, Sofia University St. Kliment Ohridski, Sofia, Bulgaria

Jelena Trivić Faculty of Economics, University of Banja Luka, Banja Luka, Bosnia and Herzegovina

Jaka Vadnjal GEA College – Faculty of Entrepreneurship, Piran, Slovenia

Natalia Vershinina Department of Strategic Management and Marketing, Leicester Business School, De Montfort University, Leicester, UK

Valentina Veverita Small and Medium-Sized Enterprises Development Policies and Liberal Profession Department, The Ministry of Economy, Chisinau, Republic of Moldova

Natalia Vinogradova The National Institute for Economic Research of the Republic of Moldova, Chisinau, Republic of Moldova

Zhelyu Vladimirov Faculty of Economics and Business Administration, Sofia University St. Kliment Ohridski, Sofia, Bulgaria

Desislava Yordanova Faculty of Economics and Business Administration, Sofia University St. Kliment Ohridski, Sofia, Bulgaria

Reviewers

In the pioneering book, editors Dana and Ramadani have compiled the work of 36 leading scholars of family businesses in the transition economies. The research presented in this book is based on multiple studies of around 3,000 family firms located in the transition economies of Albania, Bosnia, Bulgaria, Croatia, Czech Republic, Kosovo, Macedonia, Moldova, Russia, Serbia, Slovakia, and Slovenia. The authors shed light on the unique and distinct contextual opportunities and dilemmas that enterprising families face in each country. Not only is this book a must-read for researchers, educators, students, practitioners, and policy makers interested in family businesses in transition economies, it is perhaps an even more important reading for those operating in other contexts to expand their theoretical perspectives and understand the robustness of their research findings. Kudos to the editors and the authors!

Pramodita Sharma, *Editor, Family Business Review*
Sanders Professor of Family Business, The University of Vermont, USA

In this pioneering book, the authors—all respected scholars and experts in the field of family business—offer a comprehensive overview of state-of-the-art research on family businesses in transitional countries. The book introduces the reader to the richness and uniqueness of this most common type of business organization operating in the challenging environment of Eastern Europe. It addresses highly relevant topics such as the management, succession, financing, and internationalization of family businesses, revealing interesting research findings with significant implications for theory and practice. This book is an indispensable resource for researchers, students, policy makers, entrepreneurs, and anyone who is concerned about the future development and continuity of family businesses in Eastern Europe and beyond.

Vincent Molly, *Professor*
KU Leuven Campus Brussels, Belgium

The editors, Léo-Paul Dana and Veland Ramadani, have done an astonishing compilation of important topics and reputable authors that treat the concept, process, and theoretical achievements in the field of family businesses as one of the strongest economic engines. The book—Family businesses in transitional economies—as a pioneering book that treats these businesses from the perspective of transitional economies will be more than necessary for the academics, for policy makers, and especially for graduate and Ph.D. students, who want to enrich their knowledge on the context, challenges, and activities of family businesses that operate in this region.

Nexhbi Veseli, *Professor,*
South-East European University, Macedonia

There is no doubt that family enterprises make an important contribution to the national and global economies. In world economies, family enterprises represent the majority of all enterprises. The social and economic changes in Eastern Europe ended the period when private enterprises were outlawed and created an opportunity for the rebirth of entrepreneurship and family business development. The micro-and small-to-medium enterprise sectors have been recognized in the transition countries as an engine for economic recovery by creating jobs and fostering the development of an entrepreneurial tradition. This book, edited by Dana and Ramadani, will add to new perspectives about the importance of family business in transition economies. This is the first book to summarize comprehensively and extensively by showing strategy research with a focus on transition economies. The book combines theoretical rigor with up-to-date evidence on a highly relevant topic. It has also a significant value for practitioners and policy makers since it will highlight important factors from transition economies and will discuss important managerial and policy implications.

Mustafa Fedai Çavuş, *Associate Professor*
Osmaniye Korkut Ata University, Turkey

Introduction to "Family Business in Transition Economies"

Léo-Paul Dana and Veland Ramadani

The book—*Family Businesses in Transition Economies*—provides a comprehensive state-of-the-art picture of family businesses that operate in transitional economies; besides a theoretical background, it provides a mixture of empirical evidence that is very likely to offer a brighter view of this field from the perspective of transition countries. The book is a result of long lasting effort and it includes contributions of motivated scholars and experts from different transitional countries and beyond, specially written for the purpose of this book. The volume consists of 16 chapters that are organized into three sections: (1) introductory issues; (2) management, succession and financial issues; and (3) internationalisation and other issues. This introduction gives a brief overview.

The second chapter discusses the "Context and Uniqueness of Family Businesses". Family businesses represent the majority of companies and are an important source of jobs in most countries. Longevity is very important for the family businesses and for economies as a whole. Succession is one of the most difficult decisions for the family business, and one of the most important. When business leadership transitions are not well structured they may cause expensive legal issues leading to the sale or eventual loss of the business. This chapter presents a review of some general, but very important issues, related to family businesses. The purpose of this chapter is not to provide a new model or theory in this field, but just as an introduction to the topics that will be addressed in subsequent chapters of this book. This chapter is contributed by Veland Ramadani and Frank Hoy.

L.-P. Dana
Montpellier Business School, Montpellier Research in Management, Montpellier, France
e-mail: lp.dana@supco-montpellier.fr

V. Ramadani (✉)
Faculty of Business and Economics, South-East European University, Tetovo,
Republic of Macedonia
e-mail: v.ramadani@seeu.edu.mk

© Springer International Publishing Switzerland 2015   1
L.-P. Dana, V. Ramadani (eds.), *Family Businesses in Transition Economies*,
DOI 10.1007/978-3-319-14209-8_1

The third chapter discusses the "Context and Uniqueness of Transition Economies". Transition to a market economy involves profound economic changes, and sometimes—but not necessarily—political change as well. In Europe, economic transition was coupled with political transformation, the resulting context being unprecedented and remaining unique. Central to transition are the cultural assumptions of a social system. Rapid regulatory reform does necessarily lead to rapid or easy transition unless mindset adapts simultaneously. This chapter is contributed by Léo-Paul Dana and Veland Ramadani.

Chapter "Different Features of Transition Economies: Institutions Matter" is written by Jelena Trivić and Saša Petković. Authors noted that main aspects of transition process are liberalization, macroeconomic stabilization, privatization and legal and institutional reforms. Their definition of institutions assumes Douglass North's concept of institutions, which defines institutions as the rules or regulations (humanly devised constraints) that structure political, economic and social interaction while institutional environment comprises institutions (formal and informal ones) and an enforcement mechanism. The subject of this chapter is the analysis of quality of institutions and institutional environment in five Western Balkan countries and their implications on overall standard of living and competitiveness of these countries. In order to measure the quality of institutions, authors used World Governance Indicators. Their results indicate that Western Balkan countries lag significantly behind Central European countries in terms of institutional quality. The widening gap between the standard of living in Western Balkan countries and Central European countries in last 10 years indicates that the crucial problem in Western Balkan countries is the speed of reforms.

Jaka Vadnjal and Predrag Ljubotina contributed the chapter "To Be or Not to Be in a Family Business: The Case of Eight Countries in South-Eastern European Region". In this chapter is addressed the issue of an individual's perception of entrepreneurship and the related factors that influence individual's decision on whether to build a career as an employee, a successor of family business or as an independent entrepreneur, where expectations of student's with family business background were investigated. Some Western and some South-Eastern European were separately analysed population for the purpose of comparative study. The authors' results show important differences between investigated populations. They note that it has been anticipated that differences are caused by historical, cultural and educational backgrounds.

Desislava Yordanova, Zhelyu Vladimirov and Ralitsa Simeonova-Ganeva, authors of the chapter "Management Practices in Bulgarian Family and Non-Family SMEs: Exploring "Real" Differences", investigate the differences in management practices between Bulgarian family and non-family businesses. To detect real rather than sample differences they apply multivariate statistical techniques. The chapter ends with discussion of the empirical findings where authors note that analysis demonstrate that after controlling the size and industry, the investigated family and non-family businesses do not differ significantly with regard to the possession of short or medium-term business plan, adoption of a marketing strategy, exporting, provision and investment in personnel training, introduction of product innovations, registration of trademarks and patents, usage of automatic management information systems, and adoption of quality and safety standards.

The Chapter "Obstacles and Opportunities for Development of Family Businesses: Experiences from Moldova" describes the difficulties of family businesses that are related to the access to different types of resources and other restrictive factors from the external environment. The authors, Elena Aculai, Natalia Vinogradova and Valentina Veverita, observe also the opportunities of the family businesses, arising through cooperation of the efforts and resources of family members, which allows increasing the assets of family businesses and partly compensating the shortcomings of the activity of business support institutes.

The Chapter "Successors' Innovativeness as a Crucial Succession Challenge of Family Businesses in Transition Economies: The Case of Slovenia", a contribution from Marina Letonja and Mojca Duh, aims to broaden our understanding of factors affecting innovativeness of successors in family businesses in transition economies. Reviewing the literature, authors have identified three main constructs as having substantial impact on successors' innovativeness and those are: entrepreneurialism, knowledge transfer and creation, and social capital. They applied a multiple-case study approach and the main research findings of ten cases of Slovenian family businesses are discussed. Authors also developed six propositions that provide a basis for further empirical testing of factor influencing successors' innovativeness and innovation ability of family businesses in transition economies.

In the chapter "Family Business Succession Risks: The Croatian Context", authors Iva Senegović, Valerija Bublić and Gordana Ćorić highlight that family business entrepreneur mainly carries out two types of functions: ownership function and management functions, which bear markedly recognized risks associated with their performance. During the transfer of ownership and leadership in the family businesses, the crucial entrepreneurial and managerial risk is by its nature non-transferable and internally conditioned. Being inevitable in such a situation, additionally burdened with growth, sustainability and innovation imperatives, the risk requires an expert analytical and critical approach by use of all available research methods and techniques for its best estimate. According to the authors, the biggest entrepreneurial and managerial risk lies in the resistance to changes or, in this case, the postponement of ownership and leadership transfer decision-making. Such an approach will only increase the problems unique to family businesses such as the problem of the successor legitimacy and authenticity, rigidity, non-transparent communication related to the transfer planning, etc. On the other hand, a well-led transfer with adequate approach to the associated risks can result in the company transformation into a growing or dynamic venture.

The purpose of the chapter "The Succession Issues in Family Firms: Insights from Macedonia" is to share findings related to succession of family businesses in Republic of Macedonia. In order to gain a better picture of the current situation, problems and perspectives that stand in front of families with respect to succession issue it was conducted a survey. A questionnaire was distributed to the owners of several businesses as well as by e-mail. The questionnaire was distributed to

140 businesses, depending on the size of cities. This chapter is authored by Veland Ramadani, Alain Fayolle, Shqipe Gërguri-Rashiti and Egzona Aliu.

Jaroslav Belás, Přemysl Bartoš, Roman Hlawiczka and Mária Hudáková, authors of the chapter "Attributes of Financial Management of Family Companies in the Czech Republic and Slovakia", aspire to define and compare important attributes of financial management of family businesses in selected regions of the Czech Republic and Slovakia, respectively in Zlin Region (Czech Republic) and Zilina Region (Slovakia). These regions have similar economic parameters and are distant from each other only few kilometers. In this chapter are have been examined these issues: the dependence of financial risks' perception, relationships with commercial banks, the ability to manage financial risks and the level of entrepreneurial optimism depending on company' age, owner's education and company's size. Results of this research prove that it cannot be definitely confirmed but neither rejected that financial risk's perception in Czech and Slovak enterprises is different within a defined groups, i.e., depending on company's age, owner's education and company's size.

The chapter "Ownership Structure, Cash Constraints and Investment Behaviour in Russian Family Firms", contributed by Tullio Buccellato, Gian Fazio, Yulia Rodionova and Natalia Vershinina, investigate the extent to which Russian family firms are liquidity constrained in their investment behaviour and how ownership structure changes the relationship between internal funds and the investment decisions of these firms. Authors estimate a structural financial accelerator model of investment and first test the hypothesis that Russian firms overall and family firms in particular are cash constrained by conducting random-effects estimation. Their results confirm that firms are liquidity constrained when the ownership structure is not included in the econometric specifications. With regards to the ownership structure and the degree of ownership concentration, they found that companies owned by private individuals and families are less cash constrained, which is in agreement with previous literature.

The chapter "Family Businesses Motives for Internationalisation: Evidence from Serbia", contributed by Radmila Grozdanić and Mirjana Radović-Marković attempts to explain resource-seeking internationalization among Serbian family firms, mostly SMEs, by investigating, based on resource dependency theory and the model of entrepreneurial internationalization, whether resource-seeking internationalization can be linked to family businesses' resource deficiencies. It researches whether perceived resource constraints in terms of labor, finance and new technology increase the likelihood of family firms to use internationalization as a means to access or acquire the lacking resources, relative to not internationalizing. By binomial logistic regression analysis method used for the testing in the chapter are elaborated the findings which indicate that perceived lack of skilled labor drives family firms to pursue internationalization as a means for accessing labor and that perceived constraints regarding access to finance are an important determinant for family firms to pursue foreign markets as a means to access capital. These results suggest that perceived constraints in terms of skilled labor and finance are pushing firms to overcome internal resource deficiencies through internationalization, as well as that, these firms which are already internationally active to use their international activity as a means to access or acquire these resources. The findings of the research also support the awareness of the mangers/owners of the family firms of the possibility to use internationalization as a means for overcoming resource constraints, as well as policy makers awareness increase to improve general doing business parameters in the country giving that internationalization could become easier and resources could become more easily transferable across borders.

In the chapter "Entering New Markets: Strategies for Internationalization of Family Businesses", the author Gadaf Rexhepi notes that almost all family businesses face with the problem of their growth after e period of time, especially when they reach its maturity phase they need to enter new markets in order to continue its growth. These and lots of other reason influence family businesses to become part of globalization and follow the trend of most of the successful family businesses in the world who have internationalize their activities. This chapter focuses on the possible strategies that enterprises can use in order to perform in the international markets. The objectives of the study are to examine how to enter in new markets by using the best appropriate strategies in order to achieve competitive advantage in international markets. Regarding these issues, the author conducted an empirical research in 75 family businesses in Albania and final results showed that as the best strategy for the Albanian family businesses for entering in international markets is export strategy.

The chapter "Family Business in Sport Organizations: Western Experiences as Lessons for Transitional Economies" examines family businesses in the sport industry. The author is focused on the reasons why families manage sport organizations in terms of community and location preferences in the context of family business evolution. The chapter ends by stating research and management implications of family owners of sport organizations. The chapter is contributed by Vanessa Ratten.

Chapter "Family Businesses in the Trade Sector: An Examination of a Case Study from Kosovo", authored by Veland Ramadani, Gramos Gashi, Taki Fiti and Betim Humolli, presents a successful story of family business from Kosovo. In this chapter are treated topics such as: history of Albi Group, its business entities, development over the years, governance and succession planning.

The editors and the contributors of this book hope that this collection brings an attractive and noteworthy contribution to the field of family businesses, above all in terms of elucidating the substance of these businesses in specific economies, such are the transitional ones. While transition has proven to be an important topic in academic literature, family business in transition economies have been at the margin of research; yet these are important economic players. Transition economies have not been a focal point of interest in the current literature on family businesses and this book aims to overcome this deficit in our knowledge. Taking into consideration that such a book is not available in the market and no author has treated strictly the above mentioned topics in the perspective of the transitional countries, we trust that this volume shall be very welcomed by regional and international researchers who are interested to know more about family businesses matters in the transitional countries.

Part I
Introductory Issues

Context and Uniqueness of Family Businesses

Veland Ramadani and Frank Hoy

Abstract Family businesses represent the majority of companies and are an important source for the generation of jobs in most countries. Longevity is very important for the family businesses and for economies as a whole. Succession is one of the most difficult decisions for the family business, and one of the most important. When business leadership transitions are not well structured they may cause expensive legal issues leading to the sale or eventual loss of the business. This chapter presents a review of some general, but very important issues, related to family businesses.

Keywords Family businesses • Life-cycle • Succession • Participant in family businesses • Culture

1 Introduction

Family businesses represent the majority of companies and are an important source for the generation of jobs in most countries (Cadbury, 2000; Fattoum & Fayolle, 2009; Hacker & Dowling, 2012; Hoy & Sharma, 2010; Kellermanns, Eddleston, Barnett, & Pearson, 2008, Kuratko & Hodgetts, 2004; Mazzarol, 2006; Ramadani, Fayolle, Gerguri, & Aliu, 2013). Their stability is critical to global economic growth. The importance of these businesses to a country's economy is substantial. Multiple research studies have recorded the predominance of family firms in countries throughout the world. The prevalence of family businesses also documents both the economic and social impact they have (Brigham, 2013). It should be emphasized that not all family businesses are small. In 2006, *Bloomberg Business week* reported that 35 % of companies listed in the Fortune 500 could be classified

V. Ramadani (✉)
Faculty of Business and Economics, South-East European University, Ilinden 335, 1200 Tetovo, Republic of Macedonia
e-mail: v.ramadani@seeu.edu.mk

F. Hoy
Management Department, Worcester Polytechnic Institute, Worcester, MA, USA
e-mail: fhoy@wpi.edu

© Springer International Publishing Switzerland 2015
L.-P. Dana, V. Ramadani (eds.), *Family Businesses in Transition Economies*,
DOI 10.1007/978-3-319-14209-8_2

Table 1 Family business: numbers and facts (statistical history)

Family business constitute	80–98 %	of the business in the worldwide free economy
Family business produces	49 %	of the gross domestic product (GDP) in the United States of America
Family business produces more than	75 %	of the gross domestic product in the most countries worldwide
Family business employs	80 %	workforce in the U.S
Family business employs more than	75 %	of the workforce worldwide
Family business creates	86 %	of new jobs in the U.S.
A total of	37 %	of Fortune 500 companies are family businesses
A total of	60 %	of all public companies in the U.S. are under the control of family businesses
The number of family-owned businesses in the United States is	17 million	
The number of family-owned businesses in the U.S. with revenues greater than 25 million is	35,000	
Performance of family businesses from non-family businesses in the U.S.	6.65 % a year in returns on assets (ROA)	10 % in market value
Performance of family businesses from non-family businesses in Europe	8–16 % per year in Return on equity (ROE)	

Source: Poza (2010)

as family businesses (Perman, 2006; reconfirmed by Fiti & Ramadani, 2013). Some relevant data regarding the significance of family firms are shown in Table 1.

Since family businesses are among the most important contributors to the creation of wealth and generating employment, public policy makers need to give attention to these enterprises to ensure their health, prosperity and longevity (Neubauer & Lank, 1998).

Longevity is very important for the family businesses and for economies as a whole. Succession is one of the most difficult decisions for the family business, and one of the most important (Molly, Laveren, & Deloof, 2010; Ramona, Hoy, Poutziouris, & Steier, 2008; Sareshmukh & Corbett, 2011). When business leadership transitions are not well structured they may cause expensive legal issues leading to the sale or eventual loss of the business (Lipman, 2010; Morris, Williams, Allen, & Avila, 1997).

This chapter presents a review of some general, but very important issues, related to family businesses. The purpose of this chapter is not to provide a new model or theory in this field, but just as an introduction to the topics that will be addressed in subsequent chapters of this book. Numerous reviews of the family business literature are available to scholars and practitioners (De Massis, Sharma, Chua, Chrisman, & Kotlar, 2012; Hoy & Laffranchini, 2014; Zahra & Sharma, 2004). References appearing in this chapter may provide guidance for the reader appropriate to the intent of this book to examine transitional economies.

2 Defining Family Businesses

Family firms constitute the dominant and oldest form of business organizations, and are crucially important in economies (Comi & Eppler, 2014; Zahra, Hayton, & Salvato, 2004). In most countries, family firms play a key role in overall economic development, including workforce engagement. Understanding family firms ranges from small enterprises serving a neighborhood, to large conglomerates that operate in multiple industries and countries (IFC, 2008). Therefore, the definition of a family business is a complex issue. The key component represents the interaction of the family system and business (Chua, Chrisman, & Sharma, 1999; Fattoum & Fayolle, 2009; Hoy & Verser, 1994). The founding editors of *Family Business Review* asked, "What is family business? People seem to understand what is meant by the term *family business*, yet when they try to articulate a precise definition they quickly discover that it is a very complicated phenomenon" (Lansberg, Perrow, & Rogolsky, 1988, p. 1). Hoy and Verser (1994) noted that the editors chose not to define the term family business, instead deciding that the dialogue engendered by *Family Business Review* might help determine the boundaries of the field. The editors expected manuscript submitters to specify what definition they were using so that readers would know how to compare studies. Some of criteria that are often used to define family businesses are presented in Table 2.

The general concept of the family business includes any business in which the bulk of the ownership or control lies in a family, and in which two or more family members are involved directly (Brockhaus, 2004). Family business is a double complex system, comprising business and family. These systems overlap and are both dynamic organisms that develop and change and are both unique with their

Table 2 Criteria used to define family businesses

Definitional criterion	No. of occurrences	Frequency (%)
Ownership	98	79
Management	66	53
Directorship	35	28
Self-identification	19	15
Multiple generations	11	9
Intra-family succession intention	9	7
Total	238	100

Note: Percentages add to more than 100 % because studies typically use multiple criteria
Source: De Massis et al. (2012, p. 13)

particular history, challenges, strengths, weaknesses, opportunities and threats that are exposed. Family members who are involved in the business are part of a system of tasks of business and part of the family system. For this reason, conflicts may occur because each system has its own rules, roles and requirements. Families can have their own style of communication and conflict resolution which can be good for the family but it does not mean that this will be good for resolving business disputes. Entry to the family system is from birth, adoption and marriage, with membership assumed to be permanent; whereas entry into the business system is based on experience and opportunities. Conflicts may arise when the problems from one system are transferred to the other system (Bowman-Upton, 2009; Gashi & Ramadani, 2013).

A definition of family business should determine why it is unique, and this raises the question of "what is unique?" This has nothing to do with the fact that family members own or manage a business. What makes a family business unique is that the model of ownership, governance, and succession management materially affects the objectives, strategies, structure, and the way in which it is formulated, designed and implemented as business activity (Chua et al., 1999; Mandl, 2008).

According to Poza and Daugherty (2013) if a business is to be considered a family business it must meet the following characteristics: (a) ownership control (15 % or higher) by two or more members of the family; (b) strategic influence by family members on the management of the firm, either by being active in management, continuing to create culture, serving as an advisor or board member, or by being an active shareholder; and (c) concern for family relationships; the dream or possibility of continuity across generations. Further to this list of features, Poza and Daugherty add several features: (a) the presence of the family; (b) the overlap of family, management, and ownership, with its zero-sum (win-lose) propensities, which in the absence of growth of the firm, render family business particularly vulnerable during succession; (c) the unique sources of competitive advantage (e.g. a long term investment horizon), derived from the interaction of family, management, and ownership, especially when family unity is high; and (d) the owner's dream of keeping the business in the family (the objective being business continuity from generation to generation). Alderson (2011, p. 6) defines a family business as a "business governed and/or managed in order to form and follow the vision of the business held by a dominant coalition controlled by members of the same family or a small number of families that is potentially sustainable in all generations of the family or families."

Family businesses differ from non-family ones in many ways (Dunn, 1995; Hoy & Sharma, 2010; Jorissen, Laveren, Martens, & Reheul, 2005; Mandl, 2008; Olson et al., 2003). Differences between them, based on a review of many studies, are summarized in Table 3.

From Table 3 it can be seen that in the centre of the firm in family businesses is family, which formally or informally, directly or indirectly influence the firm; their main objectives are both economic and non-economic, respectively sustainability/long-term family income (stability) as well as family satisfaction; their business orientation is satisfaction of internal and external stakeholders (mainly family,

Table 3 Main differences between the family and non-family business

	Family business	Non-family business
Centre of the firm	Family (formally or informally/directly or indirectly influencing the firm)	Owner(s)/managers
Necessary governance	Company and family sphere	Company sphere
Main objective	Economic and non-economic (sustain-ability/long-term family income (stabil-ity) as well as family satisfaction)	Economic (quick profits/growth)
Mindset orientation	Transfer among generations, sustainabil-ity over the life time of the enterprise	Sale of the business, sustainability over the professional life time of the entrepreneur
Competitive strategy	Quality, reputation, long-term relationships	Price
Assets	Financial, social, cultural	Financial
Company climate	Familiness, trust, cohesion, involvement, commitment, engagement, enthusiasm, informality	Business goal orientation, formal-ity, contractual agreements, distance
Business orientation	Satisfaction of internal and external stakeholders (mainly family, clients, employees, local community)	Satisfaction of owners/shareholders
Management style	Value-driven, emotional, goal alignment	Facts-and-Figures-driven, rational, agency control mechanisms
Allocation of profits	Reinvestment into the company	Distribution among owners/shareholders

Source: Mandl (2008, p. 70)

clients, employees, local community); the style of management is value-driven, emotional and goal alignment, they compete on quality, reputation, long-term relationships etc. Alternatively, in the centre of non-family businesses are owner (s) or managers; their main objectives are only economic (quick profits/growth); their business orientation is satisfaction of owners/shareholders; the style of man-agement is facts-and-figures-driven, rational and use agency control mechanisms, etc.

A very important issue raised recently is whether the family business should be "family business" during the whole its life-cycle or not. Mandl (2008) noted that the status of being a family business must not be considered "fixed" (Fig. 1). According to her, there are several businesses that are family businesses over their whole life cycle (Fig. 1a). On the other hand, there are businesses which could be 'transferred' over their life cycle from family business to non-family business and vice-versa. For instance, a business may start as a family business, which is owned and managed by family members, but over the time, property and management due to various reasons may be distributed or transferred to persons outside the family and in the maturity phase, the business will lose the status of being a family business (Fig. 1b). Some businesses could reach the status of being a family business again in their declining phase, if non-family members (owners or managers) withdraw from

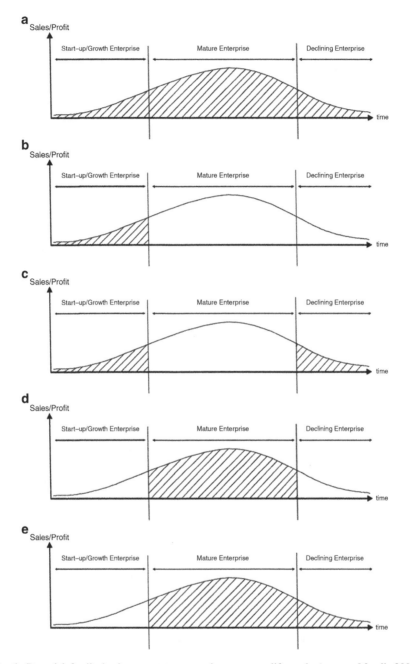

Fig. 1 Potential family businesses status over the company life cycle (source: Mandl, 2008, pp. 14–15). (**a**) Family business status during the whole life cycle. (**b**) Family business status during the start-up/growth phase only. (**c**) Family business status during the start-up/growth and declining phase. (**d**) Family business status in mature phase only. (**e**) Family business status from mature phase onwards

the business and hence, the family power ceases (Fig. 1c). Also, often it could happen that a business is established as a non-family business consisted of the entrepreneur and few non-family members only. Later, when the entrepreneur and his/her children grow, the issue of transfer of business and interest of the second generation to take over the business may occur, which intensifies the role and involvement of the family in the business. After the completion of the transfer phase, two situations can happen: the entrepreneur and his/her family are still involved in the business (Fig. 1e) or they could withdraw from the business and shifting the status of the business from "family" to "non-family" (Fig. 1d).

Based on the variety of definitions introduced in this section, it can be concluded that even today there is not a generally accepted definition for family business (Chua et al., 1999). For the purposes of this book, we follow the path of the editors of *Family Business Review* and rely on chapter authors to clarify what they consider to be family business. So, family business could be defined as a business that is owned and governed by the family, in which are employed some of its members and is based on the assumption that the younger members of the family will set control over the business, following the elder ones.

3   Family Business Categories

According to Gimeno, Baulenas, and Coma-Cros (2010), based on the level of complexity and the degree of structure development, there are five categories of family businesses: captain, emperor, family team, professional family, corporation and family investment group. They have used detailed information about 1,200 Spanish family firms, gathered from FBK Diagnostic. These categories are described below.

- *Captain model.* This model is most commonly found in enterprises ranging from micro to medium in size. The average age of these businesses is 28 years old. In these enterprises, the complexity of family and business is low. Entrepreneurs of these businesses share the ownership with other family members, typically first with spouses or siblings, and later with children. These are so called "founders' businesses" and result from the commitment of one person, usually lasting as long as that person has the authority, interest and energy to lead the business[(Table 4).
- *Emperor model.* Family and business complexity in this model is high. The complexity follows the passing of time. There are two generations working together, but the leading power is in the hands of a person who leads the family and business in the same time. In this model, shares may be owned by several family members from different generations. Average number of shareholders is 5.1. The success or failure of the family business depends largely on the skills of a person with primary discretion over the enterprise. The explanation of the names of the first two models is as follows: a captain is someone who owns a

Table 4 Characteristics of family business categories

Model	Characteristics
Captain	Enterprise managed by the founder
Emperor	Business and family united by a leader
Family team	Extended family working in a small business
Professional family	Few family members are engaged in professional management of a complex business
Corporation	Complex family managing complex business
Family investment group	Families with different complexities jointly invest

Source: Gimeno et al. (2010, p. 60)

simple unit, and an emperor is someone who has power over a wide range of social systems. The difference in complexity between the captain and the emperor models is as result of two factors: the time and resources of family leader. Through the years family complexity increases and at the same time the complexity of the business becomes higher as it grows. Above all, they are differentiated by the resources of the leader. On average level, the "emperor" has more competence as a manager and is more growth-oriented than the "captain."

- *Family team model.* In this model of family business, family complexity is higher than the complexity of the business, while the average number of shareholders is relatively high (6.5 shareholders). Disorders that may arise as a result of the complexity of family seem to be limited because some restrictions are usually in place at this point that apply to family members entering the business—only 36 % of shareholders are engaged in work. But, these restrictions can also be spontaneous as the small size of the firm may force other family members to look for their professional development out the family business. In the future, family complexity can be increased significantly (number of shareholders can be increased to 48 %, respeactively to 9.5 shareholders). This can lead to a dangerous situation for the business, since an existing structure may be faced with the difficulty to absorb this level of complexity. Further development of the structure would be a valid solution, but it can bring a level of resource consumption that may not be obtainable (due to time of leaders, economic resources spent on consultancy, government bodies, etc.). In order to avoid high-risk situations in this model, there are two alternatives for the future: (1) to encourage development creating adequate capacity, and (2) to reduce the number of owners.
- *Professional family model.* This model is opposite to the previous one. Complexity of the business here is significantly higher than the complexity of the family. Businesses of this type are characterized by a high level of growth and development. Growth and development have come from a less personalized structure than the one that typifies the first generation leadership. The family continues involvement in management. In this model there may be a number of family members in managerial positions (average 3), but they behave in a

professional manner. Here family members are oriented towards business operations, possessing a high level of sophistication in management and overall
structure.

- *Corporation model.* This model is among the most developed models—in
  several dimensions. It is characterized with higher complexity, both as a family
  and as a business, and it is the model with the highest average age (61 years) and
  highest level of structure development. The presence of family members in top
  management in some cases is 'circumstantial'. The businesses, which are managed by family members, can easily evolve into businesses managed by
  non-family members.
- *Family investment group.* To have such a model, the family should have a large
  economic surplus. In this model the family realizes joint investment, but does
  not take over the management of business, and the relationship between the
  family and its investment should be different from the family-business relationship. Usually this model appears when the family does not want or is not ready to
  decide on one of the models previously described, and decides to sell the
  business, generating the economic surplus. Then the family decides how they
  will use it.

4 Participants in the Family Business

In general, participants in a family business can be divided into two groups: family
members and non-family members. These groups are shown in Fig. 2. Sharma
(2001, 2004) divides them into internal and external family business members.
Internal members are those who are involved with the business, such as employees,
owners and/or family members. External members are those who are not linked to
the family business, whether through employment, ownership or family membership. Venter, van der Merwe, and Farrington (2012) categorize participants in
family business into four groups: *non-family members* (includes non-family
employees, outside professionals, experts, consultants, advisors, who offer expertise and skills, are part of the management team and assist in strategic business
decisions), *inactive family members* (includes those members who are not being
involved in the family business in terms of interfering in the business decision-
making or disagreements), *the senior generation* (includes parents and their willingness to delegate authority, share important information related to the business
and resign control, as well as ensuring their financial protection after retirement)
and *the incumbent generation* (includes children as active family members being
able to realise their personal ambitions and satisfy their career needs in the context
of the family business). Each participant has personal approaches and ways of
thinking and abilities to put pressure on business and family (Bowman-Upton,
2009; Farrington, 2009; Sharma, 2004; Shuklev & Ramadani, 2012).

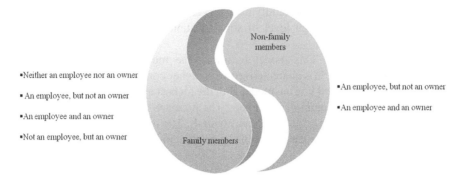

Non-family members

•Neither an employee nor an owner

• An employee, but not an owner

•An employee and an owner

•Not an employee, but an owner

•An employee, but not an owner

•An employee and an owner

Family members

Fig. 2 Participants in the family business (source: based on Bowman-Upton, 2009)

1. Family members

    (a) *Neither an employee, nor an owner*. In this group usually belong children and in-laws. Even though they may not be part of the business, however, have the opportunity to influence and exert pressure on the family that runs the business. For example, children can criticize their parents for spending too much time on business and very little devotion to them. This presents a problem because raises feelings of guilt to parents for not finding time for their children and this can affect business decision making. In-laws may be counted as outsiders, intruders or allies and are usually neglected, ignored and misunderstood. For example, from daughter-in-law is required to support and understand her husband in business activities without a clear understanding of family or business dynamics. It can lead to problems in family or putting her between family confrontations. Sons in-law are in the same situation or difficulties. They can be counted as competitors from the wives' brothers. Sons in-law, although may not be involved in business, they can exert pressure on families and businesses through their wives.

    (b) *An employee, but not an owner*. These members are active in the business, but do not have an ownership position. For this group, there may raise problems of different nature. For example, when compared with those family members who are not employees, but are business owners, raise the feeling of inequity. This situation is often manifested with the words: "while I do all the work, others just stick and reap profits." Or the problem may occur when owners bring decisions without consultation with employees, family members who are not owners. This is manifested by the words: "I deal with daily affairs of the company, knowing how decisions will affect the company's work, while they do not ask me about it at all." Employees, family members generally expect to be treated differently from employees who are not part of the family.

    (c) *An employee and an owner*. The members of this group may have the most difficult position in the enterprise. They must manage effectively with all members involved in both of systems, family and business. As owners, they are responsible for the welfare and business continuity, as well as for daily business activities. They must deal with the concerns of employees that are family members and for those who are not. In this group fall founders, as owners and executive directors.

(d) *Not an employee, but an owner*. This group consists of brothers/sisters and retired relatives. Their main interest is the income/profit provided by the business and everything that might jeopardize this, can be a problem for them. For example, while managers/owners wish to implement development strategies that can spend the wealth and put it in danger, it may encounter resistance from retired relatives who are concerned primarily about dividend or profit from business.

2. Non-family Members

(a) *An employee, but not an owner*. This group of employees often faces with the issues of nepotism and coalition building as a result of family conflicts caused by daily business activities. Family business owners to employees who are not family members and who have little or no option at all for promotion (advancement) should try to uphold their motivation by implementing appropriate policies of recruitment, accepting children of nonfamily employees into the business and minimizing policies that favor family employees over nonfamily employees.

(b) *An employee and an owner*. With the introduction of plans and opportunities for corporate enterprise transformation, this group becomes very important. Employees may become owners during the succession process. In businesses where a successor is selected, partial ownership of the business by its employees can accelerate the cooperation with the new management, because employees will be more interested about the benefits and responsibilities of the business. In situations where the successor is not selected, a part of the business is likely to be sold to employees who are not part of the family, but who have actively participated in its development. The employees in this case will require to be treated as owners, which can be difficult to detect and accept by family members.

5 Family and Business Overlapping

Successful adaptation of family business to the family's demands in one hand, and to business ones, on the other hand, depends on four key components, which are related to each other. They are (Davis & Stern, 2004):

1. Maintaining a proper boundary between family emotional issues and necessary tasks for successful business development and work;

2. Developing of processes and mechanisms for the preparation of the family about its emotional issues solution;
3. Developing a framework of tasks and processes that are tailored to business environment requirements that are not dependent on unresolved family issues;
4. Developing a reasonable structure which contains and motivates organizational cohesion.

Carlock and Ward (2001) described a family business as a scale which should be balanced between the requirements and business opportunities and the needs and desires of the family. The balance between these two 'forces'—business and family—can be achieved based on five variables: (a) *control:* setting in a fair way who will participate or make the decisions; (b) *career:* need to make it possible for family members to be rewarded and promoted based on their performance; (c) *capital:* family members can reinvest without damaging the interests of other family members; (d) *conflict:* conflict must be addressed due to the proximity between business and family; and (e) *culture:* family values have to be used in the development of plans and actions.

The essential problem in the functioning of family enterprises is the institutional overlap of norms in which families and businesses rely. Institutional overlap is shown in Fig. 3. The primary role of the family is to maintain social relations among its members, while the economic function of the company is to produce and provide products and services, the sale of which will generate satisfactory profit. One way to

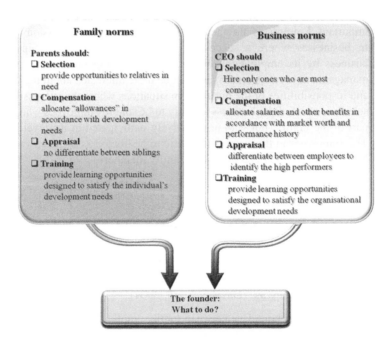

Fig. 3 Institutional overlapping in family businesses (source: based on Lansberg, 1983)

overcome this institutional collision is to acknowledge the decisions, arising as a result of a compromise between contradictory family and business principles. This way of decision-making, however, often results in suboptimal decisions, regarded from management aspects. Family members that work in the family business and fail to align personal goals with those of the business should question their position or status in the business. Also, in family businesses the career path and the training of the family members should be planned (Lansberg, 1983).

A two-dimensional model of two interrelated systems, the family and the business, has driven many research studies. Tagiuri and Davis (1996) introduced the three-circle model, where the dimension of ownership was added. Figure 4 presents the *Three-Circle model of family business*, which shows how individuals can be included in a family business: as family members, as owners and as workers/managers (see also Sharma & Hoy, 2013).

This model represents: family members who are employed and are owners (1); family members who are employed, but are not owners (4); employed in the family business which are not family members (2); employed in a family business who are not family members and are not owners (3); non-family owners (7); family members who are not employed in the family business, but are owners (6), and family members that are not involved in the business (5).

Gersick, Davis, McCollum Hampton, and Lansberg (1997) elaborated on the Three-dimensional model by building a *Three-Dimensional Developmental Model*, which consists of ownership, family and business axes. The ownership axis includes four stages: controlling owner, sibling partnership and consortium of cousins. The family axis includes four stages: young business family, entering the business, working together and passing the baton. And, the business axis goes through the four stages of start-up, growth/formalization and maturity.

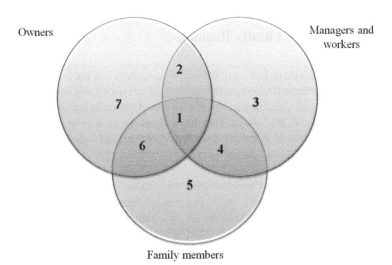

Fig. 4 Three-circle model of family businesses (source: Tagiuri & Davis, 1996, p. 200)

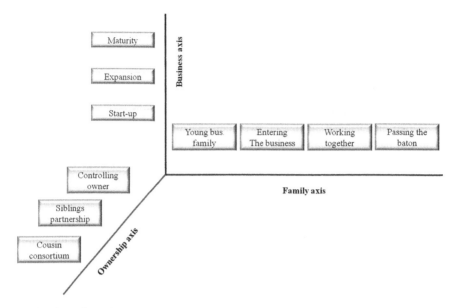

Fig. 5 Three-dimensional development model (source: based on Gersick et al., 1997, p. 17)

This model is presented in Fig. 5. Hoy (2012), in his review of Gersick et al. (1997) *Generation to Generation*, noted that, the Tagiuri and Davis *Three-Circle Model* remains dominant in education and consulting practice, even though in a Google Scholar search, there can be found over twice as many citations for Gersick et al. (1997) as for Tagiuri and Davis (1996).

6   Conflicts in the Family Business

Jehn and Mannix (2001) define conflicts are as "awareness on the part of the parties involved of discrepancies, incompatible wishes, or irreconcilable desires" (p. 238). Sorenson (1999) notes that conflict represents one of the defining characteristics of a family business and this status may have come from highly exposed family disputes in which volatile conflicts destroyed families and businesses. Conflict's sources are different. Major sources of conflicts in family businesses are presented in Table 5.

Clashes between business and family norms cause various types of conflicts. Based on Harvey and Evans (1994), interaction between business, family and external stakeholders creates three levels of conflicts that occur in the family business, presented in Fig. 6. In the first level, there are conflicts that do not occur as a result of interaction between three entities (business, family and external stakeholders) and have no effect on other entities. So, they occur within an entity, for example within the family. In the second level, conflicts arise between two

Table 5 Major sources of conflicts

Major sources of conflicts (in order of most common)	2013 all firms rank	2011 survey rank	2013 Breakdown by firm size			2013 breakdown by generation	
			Small rank	Medium rank	Large rank	1st gen. rank	2nd gen. rank
Future visions, goals and strategy	1	1	1	2	4	2	1
How decision are made	2	n/a	3	4	1	3	2
Managing growth	3	n/a	6	1	3	5	3
Competence of family in the business	4	2	5	3	5	4	5
Financial stress	5	n/a	2	6	7	1	7
Lack of family communication	6	4	4	5	2	6	4
Remuneration	7	6	7	7	10	10	6
Succession-related issues	8	3	10	9	6	7	11
Lack of family/non-family communication	9	5	8	10	8	8	9
Sibling rivalry	10	7	9	8	16	11	8

Source: KPMG (2013, p. 17)

entities collide among themselves. These conflicts are complex. Their sources may be different and when you combine sources among themselves, they become more complex and very difficult to be solved. In the third level, conflicts that occur include all three entities involved in the family business and are among the most complex and difficult to solve.

Harvey and Evans (1994) noted that conflict resolution in the family business depends on the level of conflict, namely by how entities are involved in the respective conflict. The mechanism of first level conflict resolution, when occurring within the family circle, is the ability of the family member. The character of changes is not too significant. The motive for the resolution of conflict comes from inside and the entrepreneur/owner is directly involved in its solution. For this reason it is not necessary supervision during the implementation of the resolution. Conflict resolution is heavier and more complex in the second level, due to the involvement of two entities. The character of changes is transactional. For this, conflict resolution should be undertaken by a group of individuals. It is necessary to supervise the changes that lead to conflict resolution to ensure that they really are resolved. The most complex level of conflict, the third level, involves three entities, business, family and stakeholders. Due to the complexity of these conflicts, it is necessary to engage external consultants to solve them. Entrepreneur/owner will be part of the team along with consultants to resolve conflicts. Due to the involvement of more subjects, supervision is essential and comprehensive.

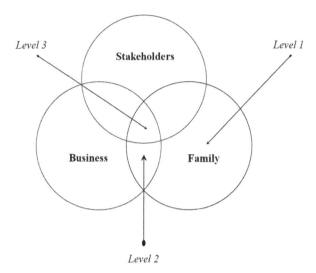

Fig. 6 Conflict levels in family businesses (source: Harvey & Evans, 1994, p. 343)

Regarding conflict resolving issues, Dean (1992) surveyed 234 African American family-owned businesses in Los Angeles and verified that 53 % of them use owner authority to resolve conflicts, 31 % use compromise, 23 % use consensus, and 2 % use mediators.

7 Family Business Culture

Culture represents a way of thinking and understanding during a process of judgment, evaluation and obedience. It is a way of dealing with others. Culture refers to the set of values that are shared by people in a group and have a tendency to continue over time even when group membership changes (Kotter & Heskett, 1992). Family culture can be described as a way family members resolve conflicts and differences, express emotions, and understand reality, separation and loss (Kepner, 2004). Family culture is comprised of four layers: artifacts, values, perspectives, and assumptions (Dyer Jr., 1986; Schein, 1985; Sharpe, 2014). Artifacts are the surface-level aspects of culture, which can be categorized as (Dyer Jr., 1988): physical (type of dresses, cars, company logo, and other emblems used by families); verbal (language, jargon, stories, etc); and behavioral (ceremonies, rituals and other behavioral patterns). Values are broad tendencies, principles, standards and norms that determine what an individual considers to be good or bad (Hoy & Sharma, 2010); they represent those 'forces' what drive behaviour and what lead to confident artifacts within a family's culture (Koiranen, 2002; Sharpe, 2014). Dumas and Blodgett (1999) analysed 50 family business mission statements and identified these values: quality, commitment, trust, social responsibility, honesty, fairness, respect and integrity. A perspective could be defined as a synchronized set of ideas and actions used by family in dealing with different problematic situation (Becker,

Geer, Hughes, & Strauss, 1961). Assumptions are the premises on which a family bases its global views and on which the artifacts, values and perspectives are based (Dyer Jr., 1988).

Family business culture plays an essential role in determining the continuity of success after the first generation. As Dyer Jr. (1988) noted "family business cultures can either contribute to success or be a major stumbling block. To understand and manage the opportunities inherent in family business cultures is not easy, and it is not often done in family firms, but it is essential for leaders who wish to ensure the continuity of their businesses and the well-being of their families" (p. 50). These insights come from the research of more than 40 family businesses.

Family business cultures are categorized differently from different authors. For example, Kets De Vries (as cited in Duh & Belak, 2009) identifies these types of family business cultures: an avoidance culture (an insidious sense of ineffectiveness), charismatic culture (everything depends and goes around the leader), paranoid culture (a persecutory subject matter), bureaucratic culture (very rigid and depersonalized), politicized culture (leadership responsibility is relinquished). Hofstede (1998) classified family business cultures by comparing the degree of individualism versus collectivism, the tendency towards uncertainty avoidance, the bias between masculinity and femininity and the apparent power-distance metric. Dyer Jr. (1988) identified these cultures: paternalistic culture, laissez-faire culture, participative culture and professional culture, which are presented in Table 6 and described below.

Table 6 Characteristics of family culture types

	Paternalistic	Laissez-faire	Participative	Professional
Nature of relationships	Lineal (hierarchical)	Linear	Collateral (group orientation)	Individualistic
Nature of human nature	People are basically untrustworthy	People are good and trustworthy	People are good and trustworthy	People are neither good nor evil
Nature of the truth	Truth resides in the founder family	Truth resides in the founder/family although outsiders are given autonomy	Truth is found in group decision making/ participation	Truth is found in professional rules of conduct
Orientation towards environment	Proactive stance	Harmonizing/proactive stance	Harmonizing/ proactive stance	Reactive/pro-active stance
Universalism/ particularism	Particularistic	Particularistic	Universalistic	Universalistic
Nature of human activity	Doing orientation	Doing orientation	Being-in-becoming orientation	Doing orientation
Time	Present or past orientation	Present or past orientation	Present or future orientation	Present orientation

Source: Dyer Jr. (1988)

Paternalistic culture This type of culture is encountered most often in family businesses investigated in Dyer's empirical research study. This type of culture is used in 80 % of businesses surveyed. In paternalistic cultures, relations between family members are placed in hierarchical order. The leader, who is a member of the family, has full authority and power to make decisions. For this type of culture, the family does not defer too much to external members. Employees have a duty to perform the tasks they receive from family. Paternalistic enterprises are oriented to the past and present.

Laissez-faire culture This type of culture is quite similar to the paternalistic one. It is used by 10 % of businesses surveyed. At laissez-faire culture relations are placed hierarchically, while employees should only realize the goals of the family business. Unlike the first one, at this type of culture, owners have a dose of confidence at employees and give them some freedom in making decisions.

Participative culture This kind of culture is rarely used in family businesses. It is found only in four cases from the total number of businesses surveyed. At the participative culture, relations are equally placed and have a group orientation, while family status and power claim not to be highlighted. Family trusts in the employees and gives opportunity to show their talent. The orientation of this type of culture is toward the present and future.

Professional culture From the business surveyed, only one uses this type of culture. Professional culture enables that business management to be transferred to professional managers, who are not family members. Relations are individualistic, which means that employees focus towards individual achievements. Professional managers have impersonal attitude toward employees, who are evaluated based on their ability to contribute to the growth of company profits.

From this study, the author concluded that the paternalistic culture is the most identified culture in the first generation family businesses. In following generations, more than two-thirds of the paternalistic culture businesses experience cultural changes, respectively the majority become professional culture businesses.

8 Succession Issues

The succession process in family business represents a very complex and important issue (Gashi & Ramadani, 2013; Gersick et al., 1997; Kamei & Dana, 2012). Alan Crosbie (2000) draws a fine analogy between running a family business and flying a plane, where he says: "There is not much danger to anybody when the plane is in the third hour of a transatlantic journey, but at take-off and landing the craft is much more vulnerable to an accident. The point of succession is very much like landing and taking off again. It presents a radically greater threat of danger, than is posed by any of the other periods in the history of the company" (p. 105).

Cadieux and Lorrain (2002) noted what primarily differentiates a family business from a non-family business is the succession process, including capital and management know-how. The succession process represents also a difficult issue in terms of the time needed to prepare the management succession. Poutziouris (2001) noted that "about 30 % of all European enterprises now face business transfer. Moreover, estimates suggest that 30 % of such business transfers will not materialize because failure to plan can be tantamount to planning to fail" (p. 278).

The transfer of the position of the leader does not automatically mean stabilization of the power of the successor. The preparation of the successor for leadership is a process of socialization or development aspect of the succession. The time during socialization should help the successor perform the duty of the leader in a successful manner. The time for learning is also included in this part (Boyatzis & Soler, 2012; Hoy, 2007; Shuklev & Ramadani, 2012). The succession is a function of these independent variables: property, management, successors, leadership, age of the business, complexity of the business, financial performance and proximity of succession. The essence of succession is measured by ranking of the importance of these issues: keeping property in family, keeping control in family, election of successor, conflict resolution between family members, rewarding of family members and finding positions for incompetent family members (Chua et al., 1999). Succession plays a key role in the influence on the desired future of the family business.

Indicators of independent variables for measuring of the importance of keeping the property in family, keeping the control in family, election of successor, conflict resolution between family members, rewarding of family members and finding positions for incompetent members of the family are given in the Table 7.

Longenecker, Moore, and Petty (2000) offered a model of succession that consists of three levels and seven stages. In this model the first level includes introductory activities, which must be performed before the successor enters the

Table 7 Independent variables and indicators

Independent variable	Indicator type	Indicator
Property	Formative	Percentage of property by family
Management	Reflective	Number of family members involved in business and relations between non-family managers towards family members
Successors	Reflective	Number of potential successors, male or female
Leadership	Formative	Percentage of outside members in the board of directors
Business age	Reflective	Age of business and leadership of business through generations
Business complexity	Reflective	Gross income, regional distribution of sales, number of commercial locations and number of full-time employees
Financial performance	Formative	Percentage of 'active' return?
Succession proximity	Formative	Whether the current CEO will retire in the next 10 years

Source: Chua et al. (1999, p. 31)

business. This includes the following phases: pre-business phase, introductory phase and introductory functional. The second level includes activities dealing with the successor's entry in the enterprise as an employee in a regular relationship. Activities relating to the transfer of business leadership to successor constitute the third level. These include the early stages of succession and succession maturity. The stages of this model are treated below:

1. *Pre-business phase*. This is the stage where the potential successor is notified of the business. At this stage, a basis for succession is created that will happen in the coming years. Here, potential successors accompanied by a parent of the business visits the offices and warehouses of the company, and plays with equipment dealing with the business in order to become more familiar with business.
2. *Introductory phase*. This phase includes those experiences that relate to the period before a successor will be of legal age and is willing to join the business part-time. This is the stage where the child is notified with people and other aspects that are directly or indirectly related to the business, such as the introduction of the child to any collaborator or banker.
3. *Introductory functional phase*. This is the stage where the potential successor is employed in the business part-time and during breaks, or after school hours. At this stage the successor is involved in formal education and working in other enterprises. Also at this stage, the successor develops special relationship with the people in the enterprise.
4. *Functional phase*. This is the stage where the successor has completed formal education and is employed full time and indefinitely in the company. Before he/she advances to managerial positions he/she may engage in different jobs within the company as in accountancy or sales, and be fitted with different experiences. This stage for the successor includes granting initial non-managerial tasks.
5. *Advanced functional phase*. At this stage the successor takes on a managerial position that has to do with the management of the workers but not the entire company. He/she may engage in various managerial positions before becoming the general leader of the company.
6. *Early succession phase*. This is the stage when the successor has been named president and general manager of the company. At this stage successor is de jure leader of the enterprise because he/she performs this function with the help of parents.
7. *Mature succession phase*. This phase usually begins 2–3 years after the successor was appointed chairman or general manager of the enterprise. Now, the successor is the de facto leader. But in some cases this does not happen until a parent dies, because for some leaders it can be difficult to leave the business and to give up the management of the enterprise. This is the stage which completes succession.

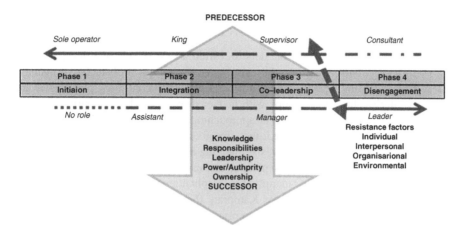

Fig. 7 The process of succession (source: Cadieux & Lorrain, 2002, p. 6)

As it was noted by Dakoumi Hamrouni and Mnasser (2013), Cadieux and Lorrain (2002) completed a synthesis of different academic studies on the process of succession and summarised four phases, as follows (Fig. 7):

1. *Initiation phase.* In this phase, the owner of the family business, respectively the predecessor is master and commander, where he is primarily occupied with the current and total management of the business. In the initial phase the predecessor has the intention of 1 day ceding the business to his or her successor(s), and in this phase there are few chances for the successor(s) to be involved in the business.

2. *Integration phase.* In the second phase the successor will be integrated in the business. During this phase, the successor undergoes an apprenticeship period, where he will have the chance to gain the needed technical knowledge and managerial skills to ensure the continuity and development of the family business.

3. *Joint-management phase.* Here, the successor officially assume his or her title in the business, which means progressive transfer of responsibilities, know-how and authority on the part of the predecessor. In these phase could be created certain tensions between the predecessor and the successor, which are followed by consequences on the activities of the business. To avoid these tensions and conflicts it is necessary to share tasks, duties and competences between the predecessor and the successor.

4. *Disengagement phase.* This is the last phase of the succession process. It is only completed if the predecessor has effectively retired and transferred responsibilities, leadership, authority and ownership to the successor.

In family businesses, continuity transition imposes a wide variety of important changes. Family relationships must be rebuilt, traditional patterns of impact redistributed, and management and ownership structures that have been around for a long time, should open the way for new structures. Among the factors affecting the succession planning process are (Lansberg, 1988; Leach, 2011):

(a) *Founder*—although the founders are often aware of the benefits that come from succession planning, they also face psychological obstacles to manage their exit from the business. A difficult obstacle to continuity planning is the founder's reluctance to cope with his/her death, as to begin continuity planning means that he or she is approaching death. The founders also resist continuity planning because it includes giving up directing the daily business operations. Also, they may resist planning because of the fear that retirement means that they may lose the position and respect in the family, and could lose a significant part of their identity. Or, simply, they think that the successors are not ready yet for this. Ingvar Kamprad, the founder of IKEA (the Swedish enterprise for furniture with cheap prices for the middle-class families, whose wealth is assessed to be 52.5 billion dollars in 2004, being greater than the one of Bill Gates with 46.2 billion dollars) has three sons from the second marriage, Peter being 46, Jonas 43 and Matthias 41 years old. They all work at IKEA. In regards to family business succession, Ingvar Kamprad has once said: "I am proud of my three sons. They are very smart. However, I don't think that anyone of them is ready to lead the company, at least for now" (Shuklev & Ramadani, 2012).

(b) *Family*—in order to understand the reactions of family succession planning, and the reasons why family members may be against planning, it is important to consider the stage of the life cycle in which succession will occur in the family business. Another reason is that the retirement and change of status that comes with it can worsen things. There can be a lack of desire for open discussion about the succession. The younger generation sometimes avoids succession planning because it brings about fear of parental death, separation or abandonment. But, if there is no decision regarding this issue, a lot of problems could appear in the future, as Shi and Dana (2013) noted in their research in Japan, where Yu says: "Succession process planning? Of course it would be useful. It would be better to do it. My father and me, we didn't have such a thing. We could have done better, if we had had someone, consultant or specialist to whom my father and I, we could give our confidence. For us the succession process did not work as we hoped. My grandfather died. And after that, my uncle, Tadashi arranged the things in the family. Just at the moment when we really needed him, he died too. And after that the conflict continued and then my father died. Then, the incidents happened again and again. This was a painful test for me. But I have the impression that it is this kind of test that trains me" (p. 69).

(c) *Managers*—difficulties related to succession planning are not only experienced by the founder and family. Many senior managers are willing to change their relationship from the personal relationship they have with the founders in formal relations with the followers. Managers do not want to limit their autonomy and their impact on the budget, information management systems and personnel.

(d) *Owners* affect succession planning, as the founder provides shares for the purpose of their motivation to be involved in the family business, and these owners do not want to open the issue of succession because they fear they will betray the founder. Fear that the successor would not be the best person to take over the business, is another reason business owners refuse to plan the succession.

(e) *Environment* affects succession planning. These forces consist of suppliers of clients who have grown dependent on the founder as their main contact in the business, and these people know that the founder is the one with whom to talk. They may fear that the successor can terminate those relationships created by the founder.

9 Advantages and Disadvantages of Family Business

According to what was mentioned up to this point, we can identify several advantages and disadvantages of the family business (Shuklev & Ramadani, 2012). The advantages of the family business are:

1. Family members are owners and managers of the business, and ownership is potentially inherited in the future generations. Therefore, the majority of these businesses reinvest their profits in the business;
2. Employment of family members means employment of people who have multiple interests in the success of the business. If problems occur, most probably they will be more worried than an ordinary employee who is not a family member;
3. Family business represents a benefit not only for the family, but for the society as well. A family business, besides employment of family members, provides job opportunities also for other people who have values and capabilities to deal with business;
4. Another advantage can be improvement of relations with customers. It frequently happens that a family business has close familiar or friendly relations with many customers, which guarantees the long-term stability of the business. Customers perceive that the family name on the company is a symbol of trust, i.e. that the family will not want to jeopardize its reputation through poor, unethical or illegal practices.

As all businesses, however, the family business has its disadvantages. Some of them are mentioned below:

1. Family business can be the cause to many problems in family: gambling, anxiety, worries, drug and alcohol abuse, etc. It is in very rare cases that family emotions do not interfere with business practices at some point;

2. Family business managers find it hard not to employ their relatives, even when they do not possess the skills required in the business. Moreover, in many cases these family members have been found to misuse their positions in the business, just because they are part of the family.

Family members, more specifically parents who have spent many years at the top of the business cannot accept the fact that the time has come for them to be replaced by descendants or other family members who will manage the business better and bring something more innovative to the family business.

Besides previous features represented as advantages and disadvantages, researchers have found other features typical to family firms that represent sources for benefits or weaknesses to the owners, and to both family and non-family members. These features include: simultaneous roles, identity feeling, long history, emotional involvement and confusion, specific vocabulary, knowing each-other and shared privacy and the importance of family business. All of these features are presented in Table 8.

Table 8 Advantages and disadvantages of family businesses

Disadvantages	Features	Advantages
Confusive rules and concern. Problems related to family business and property can mix	*Important roles*	Great loyalty to family and business. Fast and effective decision-making
Business objectivity missing. Control provokes nervous feelings. Offenses are expressed to family and business	*Feeling of identity*	Strongly expressed feeling for mission. More objective business decisions
Family members can express their weaknesses. Early disappointment can decrease trust in business relations	*Long history*	Family members can draw relative advantages and complements to their weaknesses. Long tradition can encourage family in hard times
Objective communication missing. Offenses and accusations can complicate business relations. Silent animosity can appear	*Emotional involvement and confusion*	Expression of positive feelings creates loyalty and promotes trust
Can cause emotional reaction and distort in communication, creates conditions for conflict occurrence	*Specific vocabulary*	Provides more effective communication and greater privacy
Can cause relatives to feel over-controlled and cheated	*Knowing each-other and shared privacy*	Improves communication and business decisions that support the business, the owners and the family
Strong rivalry can appear among family members	*Family business importance*	Symbolization of business can develop strong feeling for the mission among employees

Source: Tagiuri and Davis (1996, p. 207)

10 Conclusion

Family businesses in the last decade are seen as vital and economically significant business entities. As a result, this segment has received a lot of attention from academics as a research opportunity. In addition family businesses are also considered as a major source for generation of jobs in most parts of the world. For example, in the United States, around 90 % of businesses are estimated to be owned and managed by families and 95 % in India, Latin America or the Middle East.

Why family businesses are seen and considered as unique is not just because family members own or manage a business. What makes a family business unique is that the model of ownership, governance, and succession management materially affects the objectives, strategies, and structure of a company and the way in which it is formulated, designed and implemented (Chua et al., 1999; Mandl, 2008). The complexity of family businesses arises as a result of the interconnectedness of two separate systems of family and business where each one has different needs and wants, with uncertain boundaries, different roles and different rules.

Based on the level of complexity and degree of development of the structure, there are five categories of family businesses models have been identified (captain, emperor, family team, professional family, corporation, family investment group) with the corporation model being the most developed model with the highest complexity both as a family and as a business.

Family businesses have to be able to show preparedness in terms of managing business and family overlapping, most importantly, trying to balance the requirements and business opportunities and the needs and desires of the family. Research suggests this can be achieved through the five variables of: control, career, capital conflict, culture.

Despite many advantages, family businesses have to deal with several issues and conflicts in addition to standard business concerns. These include generational disputes, sibling rivalries, and succession issues. According to research conducted by KPMG (2013, p. 17), the major sources of conflict are: future visions, goals and strategies, how decisions are made, managing growth, competence of family in business, financial stress, etc. Disputes between business and family norms can cause different conflicts. Interaction between business, family and external stakeholders creates three levels of conflict that occur in the family business with the third level being the most complex and difficult to solve.

Family culture is another vital component to the success of the family business after the first generation. Main types of cultures identified are paternalistic culture, laissez-faire culture, participative culture and professional culture. From a study conducted on 40 family businesses, 80 % of businesses surveyed were characterized by a paternalistic culture, which means the leader, a member of the family, has full authority and power to make decisions and does not trust external members. The least used culture was professional culture, a culture that enables business management to be transferred to professional managers who are not family members (Dyer Jr., 1988).

Succession involves the transfer of the assets, capital, contacts, power, skills, and authority from one generation to the next in a family business. Even though succession is a very important process for the continuity of the business, its success it can be problematic.

To have a smooth transition and a successful succession Longenecker et al. (2000) offered a model of succession that consists of three levels and seven stages. Moreover, succession planning requires a harmonizing personal aspirations and family goals. Therefore, the generation in power must let go and the succeeding generation must desire to be involved in the business (Kamei & Dana, 2012; Shi & Dana, 2013).

The field of family business has only recently received serious scholarly attention. Nevertheless, important contributions have been made. We found theories and models that offer contexts for comprehending distinctions between family and non-family enterprises. Additionally, the results of numerous empirical investigations have identified unique characteristics of family-owned enterprises. More information regarding some of the seminal contributions in this body of literature is reported in Hoy and Laffranchini (2014). Few subjects are as multidisciplinary as family business. Thus, despite the progress, there is much for scholars to study in order to build on what is described in this chapter and to contribute to practice.

References

Alderson, J. K. (2011). *Understanding the family business*. New York: Business Expert Press.

Becker, H. S., Geer, B., Hughes, E. C., & Strauss, A. L. (1961). *Boys in white*. New Brunswick: Transaction Books.

Bowman-Upton, N. B. (2009). *Transferring management in the family-owned business*. Washington, DC: U.S. Small Business Administration.

Boyatzis, E. R., & Soler, C. (2012). Vision, leadership and emotional intelligence transforming family business. *Journal of Family Business Management, 2*(1), 23–30.

Brigham, K. H. (2013). Social and economic impact of family business. In R. L. Sorenson, A. Yu, K. H. Brigham, & G. T. Lumpkin (Eds.), *The landscape of family business*. Cheltenham: Edward Elgar.

Brockhaus, R. H. (2004). Family business succession: Suggestions for future research. *Family Business Review, 17*(2), 165–177.

Cadbury, A. (2000). *Family firms and their governance: Creating tomorrow's company from today's*. London: Egon Zehnder.

Cadieux, L., & Lorrain, J. (2002). Le processus de la succession dans les entreprises familiales: une problématique comportant des défis estimables pour les chercheurs. In *6ème Congrès International Francophone sur la PME*, 24–26 October, Montréal, Canada.

Carlock, R. S., & Ward, J. L. (2001). *Strategic planning for the family business—Parallel planning to unify the family and business*. New York: Palgrave.

Chua, H. J., Chrisman, J. J., & Sharma, P. (1999). Defining the family business by behaviour. *Entrepreneurship: Theory and Practice, 23*(4), 19–39.

Comi, A., & Eppler, M. J. (2014). Diagnosing capabilities in family firms: An overview of visual research methods and suggestions for future applications. *Journal of Family Business Strategy, 5*, 41–51.

Crosbie, A. (2000). *Don't leave it to the children: Starting, building and sustaining a family business*. Dublin: Marino Books.

Dakoumi Hamrouni, A., & Mnasser, K. (2013). Basics factors of success in family-owned businessesfrom second to third generation. *International Journal of Entrepreneurship and Small Business, 18*(1), 57–78.

Davis, P., & Stern, D. (2004). Adaptation, survival, and growth of the family business: An integrated systems perspective. *Family Business Review, 1*(1), 69–84.

De Massis, A., Sharma, P., Chua, H. J., Chrisman, J. J., & Kotlar, J. (2012). *Family business studies: An annotated bibliography*. Cheltenham: Edward Elgar.

Dean, S. M. (1992). Characteristics of African American family-owned businesses in Los Angeles. *Family Business Review, 5*(4), 373–395.

Duh, M., & Belak, J. (2009, June 5–6). Core values, culture and ethical climate in family versus non-family enterprises. In *Proceedings of the 7th international conference on management, enterprise and benchmarking*, Budapest, Hungary, pp. 49–69.

Dumas, C., & Blodgett, M. (1999). Articulating values to inform decision making: Lessons from family firms around the world. *International Journal of Value-Based Management, 12*(3), 209–221.

Dunn, B. (1995). Success themes in Scottish family enterprises: Philosophies and practices through the generations. *Family Business Review, 8*(1), 17–28.

Dyer, W. G., Jr. (1986). *Cultural change in family firms*. San Francisco: Jossey Bass.

Dyer, W. G., Jr. (1988). Culture and continuity in family firms. *Family Business Review, 1*(1), 37–50.

Farrington, S. M. (2009). *Sibling partnerships in South African small and medium-sized family businesses*. Unpublished doctoral thesis, Nelson Mandela Metropolitan University, Port Elizabeth.

Fattoum, S., & Fayolle, A. (2009). Generational succession: Examples from Tunisian family firms. *Journal of Enterprising Culture, 17*(2), 127–145.

Fiti, T., & Ramadani, V. (2013). *Entrepreneurship*. Tetovo: South-East European University (in Albanian language).

Gashi, G., & Ramadani, V. (2013). Family businesses in Republic of Kosovo: Some general issues. In V. Ramadani & R. Schneider (Eds.), *Entrepreneurship in the Balkans: Diversity, support and prospects*. New York: Springer.

Gersick, K. E., Davis, J. A., McCollum Hampton, M., & Lansberg, I. (1997). *Generations to generations: Life cycles of the family business*. Boston: Harvard Business School Press.

Gimeno, A., Baulenas, G., & Coma-Cros, J. (2010). *Family business models: Practical solutions for the family business*. New York: Macmillan.

Hacker, J., & Dowling, M. (2012). Succession in family firms: How to improve family satisfaction and family harmony. *International Journal of Entrepreneurship and Small Business, 15*(1), 76–99.

Harvey, M., & Evans, R. E. (1994). Family business and multiple levels of conflict. *Family Business Review, 7*(4), 331–348.

Hofstede, G. (1998). Attitudes, values and organizational culture: Disentangling the concepts. *Organization Studies, 19*(3), 477–493.

Hoy, F. (2007). Nurturing the interpreneur. *Electronic Journal of Family Business Studies, 1*(1), 4–18.

Hoy, F. (2012). Book review: Keeping the family business healthy: How to plan for continuing growth, profitability, and family leadership; Generation to generation: Life cycles of the family business; and managing for the long run: Lessons in competitive advantage from great family businesses. *Family Business Review, 25*(1), 117–120.

Hoy, F., & Laffranchini, G. (2014). *Managing family business, Oxford bibliographies.* http://www.oxfordbibliographies.com/obo/page/management.

Hoy, F., & Sharma, P. (2010). *Entrepreneurial family firms.* Upper Saddle River, NJ: Pearson Prentice Hall.

Hoy, F., & Verser, T. G. (1994). Emerging business, emerging field: Entrepreneurship and the family firm. *Entrepreneurship: Theory and Practice, 19*(1), 9–23.

IFC. (2008). *Family business governance handbook.* Washington, DC: International Finance Corporation.

Jehn, K. A., & Mannix, E. A. (2001). The dynamic nature of conflict: A longitudinal study of intragroup conflict and group performance. *Academy of Management Journal, 44*(2), 238–251.

Jorissen, A., Laveren, E., Martens, R., & Reheul, A.-M. (2005). Real versus sample-based differences in comparative family business research. *Family Business Review, 18*(3), 229–245.

Kamei, K., & Dana, L.-P. (2012). Examining the impact of new policy facilitating SME succession in Japan: From a viewpoint of risk management in family business. *International Journal of Entrepreneurship and Small Business, 16*(1), 60–70.

Kellermanns, W. F., Eddleston, K. A., Barnett, T., & Pearson, A. (2008). An exploratory study of family member characteristics and involvement: Effects on entrepreneurial behavior in the family firm. *Family Business Review, 21*(1), 1–14.

Kepner, E. (2004). The family and the firm: A co-evolutionary perspective. *Family Business Review, 4*(4), 445–461.

Koiranen, M. (2002). Over 100 years of age but still entrepreneurially active in business: Exploring the values and family characteristics of old Finnish family firms. *Family Business Review, 15*(3), 175–188.

Kotter, J. P., & Heskett, J. L. (1992). *Corporate culture and performance.* New York: Free Press.

KPMG. (2013). *Family business survey 2013: Performers, resilient, adaptable, sustainable.* Melbourne: Family Business Australia.

Kuratko, D. K., & Hodgetts, R. M. (2004). *Entrepreneurship: Theory, process & practice* (6th ed.). Mason, OH: Thomson South-Western.

Lansberg, S. I. (1983). Managing human resources in family firms: The problem of institutional overlap. *Organizational Dynamics, 12*(1), 39–46.

Lansberg, I. S. (1988). The succession conspiracy. *Family Business Review, 1*(2), 119–143.

Lansberg, I. S., Perrow, E. L., & Rogolsky, S. (1988). Family business as an emerging field. *Family Business Review, 1*(1), 1–8.

Leach, P. (2011). *Family businesses: The essentials.* London: Profile Books.

Lipman, F. D. (2010). *The family business guide, everything you need to know to manage your business from legal planning to business strategies.* New York: Macmillan.

Longenecker, J. G., Moore, C. W., & Petty, J. W. (2000). *Small business management: An entrepreneurial emphasis* (11th ed.). Cincinnati: South-Western College.

Mandl, I. (2008). *Overview of family business relevant issues.* Vienna: Austrian Institute for SME Research.

Mazzarol, T. (2006). *Small business management: An applied approach.* Prahran, VIC: Tilde University Press.

Molly, V., Laveren, E., & Deloof, M. (2010). Family business succession and its impact on financial structure and performance. *Family Business Review, 23*(2), 131–147.

Morris, M. H., Williams, R. O., Allen, J. A., & Avila, R. A. (1997). Correlates of success in family business transitions. *Journal of Business Venturing, 12*(5), 385–401.

Neubauer, F., & Lank, A. G. (1998). *The family business: Its governance for sustainability.* London: Macmillan Press.

Olson, P. D., Zuiker, V. S., Danes, S. M., Stafford, K., Heck, R. K. Z., & Duncan, K. A. (2003). The impact of the family and the business on family business sustainability. *Journal of Business Venturing, 18*(5), 639–666.

Perman, S. (2006). Taking the pulse of family business. *Bloomberg Businessweek*, http://www. businessweek.com/stories/2006-02-13/taking-the-pulse-of-family-businessbusinessweek-business-news-stock-market-and-financial-advice.

Poutziouris, Z. P. (2001). The views of family companies on venture capital: Empirical evidence from the UK small to medium-size enterprising economy. *Family Business Review, 14*(3), 277–291.

Poza, E. J. (2010). *Family business* (3rd ed.). Mason, OH: Cengage Learning.

Poza, E. J., & Daugherty, M. S. (2013). *Family business* (4th ed.). Mason, OH: Cengage Learning.

Ramadani, V., Fayolle, A., Gerguri, S., & Aliu, E. (2013). The succession issues in family firms: Evidence from Macedonia. In *5th E-LAB international symposium of entrepreneurship on family entrepreneurship: A new field of research*, EM Lyon Business School, Lyon, France.

Ramona, K. Z., Hoy, F., Poutziouris, P. Z., & Steier, L. P. (2008). Emerging paths of family entrepreneurship research. *Journal of Small business Management, 46*(3), 317–330.

Sareshmukh, S. R., & Corbett, A. C. (2011). The duality of internal and external development of successors: Opportunity recognition in family firms. *Family Business Review, 24*(2), 111–125.

Schein, E. H. (1985). *Organizational culture and leadership: A dynamic view*. San Francisco: Jossey-Bass.

Sharma, P. (2001). Stakeholder management concepts in family firms. In *Proceedings of 12th annual conference of the International Association of Business and Society* (pp. 254–259). Denver, CO: Academy of Management.

Sharma, P. (2004). An overview of the field of family business studies: Current status and directions for the future. *Family Business Review, 17*(1), 1–36.

Sharma, P., & Hoy, F. (2013). Family business roles. In R. L. Sorenson, A. Yu, K. H. Brigham, & G. T. Lumpkin (Eds.), *The landscape of family business*. Cheltenham: Edward Elgar.

Sharpe, A. (2014). Aligning family and business culture: How to create competitive advantage. *Tharawat Magazine, 15*, 16–19.

Shi, H. X., & Dana, L.-P. (2013). Market orientation and entrepreneurship in Chinese family business: A socialisation view. *International Journal of Entrepreneurship and Small Business, 20*(1), 1–16.

Shuklev, B., & Ramadani, V. (2012). *Small business and entrepreneurship*. Tetovo: South-East European University (in Albanian language).

Sorenson, L. R. (1999). Conflict management strategies used by successful family businesses. *Family Business Review, 12*(4), 325–339.

Tagiuri, R., & Davis, J. (1996). Bivalent attributes of the family firm. *Family Business Review, 9*(2), 199–208.

Venter, E., van der Merwe, S., & Farrington, S. (2012). The impact of selected stakeholders on family business continuity and family harmony. *Southern African Business Review, 16*(2), 69–96.

Zahra, S. A., Hayton, J. C., & Salvato, C. (2004). Entrepreneurship in family vs. non-family firms: A resource-based analysis of the effect of organizational culture. *Entrepreneurship Theory and Practice, 28*(4), 363–381.

Zahra, S. A., & Sharma, P. (2004). Family business research: A strategic reflection. *Family Business Review, 17*, 331–346.

Context and Uniqueness of Transition Economies

Léo-Paul Dana and Veland Ramadani

Abstract Transition to a market economy involves profound economic changes, and sometimes—but not necessarily—political change as well. In Europe, economic transition was coupled with political transformation, the resulting context being unprecedented and remaining unique. Central to transition are the cultural assumptions of a social system. Rapid regulatory reform does necessarily lead to rapid or easy transition unless mindset adapts simultaneously.

Keywords Transition • Socialism • Market economy • Shock-therapy • Gradualism • Models of transition

1 Introduction

Transition to a market economy involves profound economic changes and sometimes—but not necessarily—political change as well. In Asia, central economic planning was in some cases replaced by a capitalist economic system, while retaining an existing political system; economies changed paths without governments necessarily changing hands (Dana, 2002). In Europe, transition was more complex as economic change was coupled with political transformation, the resulting context being unprecedented.

Interest in transitional economies grew and much was written about Eastern Europe after the fall of the Iron Curtain. Dana (2010) provided a literature review; early examples include research conducted in Albania (Dana, 1996a), Bulgaria (Dana, 1999a), Croatia (Franicevic, 1999; Martin & Grbac, 1998), the Czech and Slovak Republic (Rondinelli, 1991), the Czech Republic (Dana, 2000d; Sachs, 1993), Estonia (Liuhto, 1996), the Former Yugoslav Republic of Macedonia—

L.-P. Dana (✉)
Montpellier Business School, Montpellier Research in Management, 2300 Avenue des Moulins, Montpellier, France
e-mail: lp.dana@supco-montpellier.fr

V. Ramadani
Faculty of Business and Economics, South-East European University, Ilinden 335, 1200 Tetovo, Republic of Macedonia
e-mail: v.ramadani@seeu.edu.mk

© Springer International Publishing Switzerland 2015
L.-P. Dana, V. Ramadani (eds.), *Family Businesses in Transition Economies*,
DOI 10.1007/978-3-319-14209-8_3

FYROM (Dana, 1998b), Hungary (Hisrich & Fulop, 1995; Hisrich & Vecsenyi, 1990; Noar, 1985), Latvia (Peng, 2000), Moldova (Dana, 1997b), Poland (Arendarski, Mroczkowski, & Sood, 1994; Sachs, 1993; Zapalska, 1997), Russia (Ahmed, Robinson, & Dana, 2001; Bruton, 1998; Hisrich & Gratchev, 1993; Robinson, Ahmed, Dana, Latfullin, & Smirnova, 2001), Slovakia (Dana, 2000d; Ivy, 1996), and the Ukraine (Ahmed, Dana, Anwar, & Beidyuk, 1998). Researchers also examined the economies of former Soviet allies, including Angola (Gray & Allison, 1997), Cuba (Dana, 1996c), and Mozambique (Dana, 1996b).

Others have researched transition in Asia. Brown and Zasloff (1999) and Dana (1999d) provided renditions of transition in Cambodia. Among the early accounts of transition in China are Beamish (1993), Chau (1995), Chow and Tsang (1995), Dana (1998a, 1999c), Dandridge and Flynn (1988), Fan, Chen, and Kirby (1996), Lombardo (1995), Overholt (1993), Peng (2000), Shirk (1993), Siu and Kirby (1995), Wei (2001), and Williams and Li (1993). Dana (1997a) focused on entrepreneurship in Kazakhstan and Dana (2000a) on the Kyrgyz Republic. Lasch and Dana (2011) compared the context for entrepreneurship in the Kyrgyz Republic with that in Uzbekistan. Dana (2002, 2007) examined entrepreneurship in Myanmar. Dana (1995b) focused on Laos. Dana (1994a, 1994b), Peng (2000) and Tan and Lim (1993) reported on Vietnam.

Despite many differences among nations in transition, economies experiencing such radical change shared a unique context, and this is the subject of this chapter, which is divided into four sections. Following the introduction, the process and strategies of transition are discussed in the second, respectively third section. In the fourth, models of transition are presented. Economic activities in formal and parallel transitional economies are discussed in the fifth section. The closing sections provide some reflections from the transition process and highlight that beside regulatory reform, transition also involves mindset.

2   The Fall of the Berlin Wall: The Transition Started

On November 9, 1989, The Berlin Wall was torn down—an emblematic event of the downfall of the Communist Bloc. This event formally marked the beginning of the transition process from administrative/command economies to market economies, from socialism to capitalism, or from public to private ownership. The collapse of the Wall indicated a process that "changed the course of history in Europe, while at the same time presenting enormous challenges for the countries involved" (Smallbone & Welter, 2009, p. 11). This process included political and economic transitions, that were projected to invigorate each-other and their execution was seen as a *sine qua non* for catching-up and integration with flourishing countries in Western Europe (Gowan, 1995; Oreskovic, 2012; Smallbone & Welter, 2001, 2009; Sokol, 2001; Tridico, 2013).

As shown in Fig. 1, the *political transition* includes political liberalization, free elections and democratization. This kind of transition was launched in order to

Fig. 1 Transition 'model' scenario (source: Sokol, 2001)

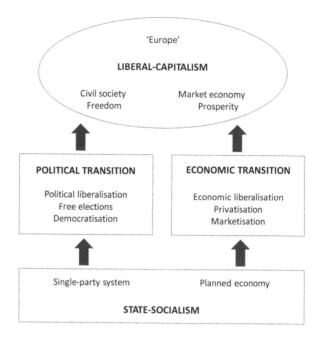

replace the single-party system with liberal democracy and civic society. Political transition was followed by different problems, such as: political partition and instability, problematic establishment of democratic institutions, appearance and development of nationalist/separatist and radical movements, threats to individual and minority rights, etc. (Brown, 1994; Sokol, 2001).

Economic *transition* is related to the turning of a centrally planned economy into a functioning market economy. This transition includes economic liberalization (where central administration of prices is replaced by market mechanisms, which involves better market opportunities as well as higher levels of competition), privatization and the creation of market institutions. This kind of transition goes through three phases, where each of them has specific characteristics (Blanchard, 1997; Fischer, Sahay, & Vegh, 1996; Gerry & Li, 2010; Svejnar, 2002; Tridico, 2013; Wei, 1997):

(a) *The chaotic phase*. This phase is characterized by so called 'vacuum power', where authorities (power groups) and policymakers choose to modify the existing system and, consequently, to apply new policies. This is the phase during which legal or illegal organizations emerge in order to take advantage of the chaotic situation and criminal groups make use of the vacuum power to create and start up their own (illegal) businesses. In addition, in these circumstances can be seen the growth of informal economic network which can lead to the development of "black and gray" economic activities. This was mainly experienced between 1989 and 1990. It should be emphasized that several former socialist countries i.e. Poland and Hungary had undergone reform processes in the 1980s which lead to shaping the developments that occurred during the 1990s.

(b) *The stabilization phase*. Usually, in this phase a macroeconomic stabilization program is implemented. This phase is recognized by implementation of radical policies that are needed to change the system and develop the market economy. During the stabilization phase governments should build appropriate institutions—essential for further and sustainable economic growth. This phase was much debated in former socialist countries when deciding about the 'best potential' market economy model, during the period between 1990 and 1992.

(c) *The consolidation phase*. This phase is characterized by expansion and execution of the policies regarding institutional changes. This phase involves social and economic changes, adjustment of behavior and mind-set of economic agents, social norms, and formal structure of the society. During the consolidation phase the institutions are essential, "the experience of transition shows that the policies. . .that are not grounded in adequate institutions may not deliver successful outcomes" (Roland, 2001, p. 30). The role and importance of institutions in transition economies are broadly discussed in Tridico (2013), Murrell (2006); Fadda (2002), Lissowska (2001) and Roland (2001, 2003).

In general, as Tridico (2013) noted, countries whose chaotic phase was too deep are still facing too many difficulties; countries that did not realize suitable macro-stabilization policies are still facing macroeconomic unbalances; and those that had a complex consolidating phase are characterized by a fragile institutional framework.

Transition at the firm level entails shifting from public to private sector ownership. This process goes either through direct privatization of the state owned enterprises or through the creation of entirely new enterprises. How quickly the transformation process is taking place can be measured by the speed of new business creation, the profiles of the entrepreneurs and their created businesses, the obstacles they face and the extent to which these businesses are able to grow (Smallbone & Welter, 2001).

3   Strategies of Transition

A strong debate between academics and policy-makers on a transition strategy of former socialist economies was developed. This debate continues nowadays, even though a period of 25 years has passed since the collapse of the socialism in Central and Eastern Europe and the former Soviet Union. Two main transition strategies were proposed: shock-therapy and gradualism (Dehejia, 2003; Katz, 1995; Marangos, 2003; Sachs, 1990). Dana (2000d) showed how two neighboring countries, the Czech Republic and Slovakia each adopted their respective model; the

Czech Republic rushed into shock-therapy while Slovakia adopted gradualism. According to Roland (2003), *the shock-therapy* was obviously dominant in the beginning of the transition process in former socialist economies, it was promoted by international financial organizations and has been supported and legitimated by famous economists from the best universities in the world; on other hand, *the gradualism*, or as he called it, '*the evolutionary-institutionalist perspective*' was a minority approach in the beginning of transition process, but increased its support over time in the light of the transition experience. The debate among researchers with respect to the transition strategies is broadly discussed in Iwasaki and Suzuki (2014).

Shock-therapy consists of radical and wide-ranging economic reforms, in which macroeconomic stabilization, the liberalization of domestic trade and prices, and profound institutional restructuring are launched at about the same time and implemented as fast as possible (Aslund, 2007; Dehejia, 2003; Sachs, 1990; Turley & Luke, 2010; Williamson, 1990). Shock-therapy was seen as a strategy for rapid break with the past and a rapid introduction of the entire economic reforms simultaneously (Havrylyshyn, 2007; Lipton & Sachs, 1990). Regarding the questions, why the transition process should be executed very quickly, shock-therapists emphasize the following reasons (Iwasaki & Suzuki, 2014, p. 7):

(a) Strong demand from the international community, calling for the deterrence of backsliding into the Cold War period;
(b) Survival strategy for reformers who face off against pro-communist opposing forces; and
(c) The necessity of cultivating a middle class that will proactively support democracy and a market economy. In other words, the shock-therapists tend to stress political reasoning to justify their debate attitude toward a transition strategy.

Here should be noted that shock-therapy indicates a "policy philosophy that demands prompt and parallel implementations of the reform packages advocated by the Washington Consensus" (Iwasaki & Suzuki, 2014, p. 4). The Washington Consensus was a common understanding of international financial institutions, International Monetary Fund and World Bank, and American think-tanks to solve the structural balance of payment problems, since many socialist countries suffered from severe macroeconomic imbalances, such as a disparity between supply and demand, trade deficits and high foreign debt (Lenger, 2008). The main aspects of Washington Consensus are presented in Table 1. Shock-therapy is also called radicalism or the big-bang approach.

Gradualism, as a transition strategy, consists of non-radical economic reforms, where macroeconomic stabilization, market and trade liberalization and restructuring of institutions are not launched at the same time. These reforms are implemented at a slower tempo and sometimes are even interrupted (Aghion & Blanchard, 1994; Svejnar, 1989). Supporters of gradualism were unified against the shock-therapists in criticizing radicalism's "speed-before-quality," "haphazard," and "unrealistic" approach (Iwasaki & Suzuki, 2014). Within gradualism were identified different approaches: slow-paced gradualism, eclectic gradualism, step-by-step gradualism and institutional gradualism (Fig. 2).

Table 1 Washington Consensus aspects

Policy type	1–2 years	2–5 years	5+ years
Macroeconomic stabilization	Implementation	Continuation	Continuation
Price and market reform	Implementation	Continuation	Continuation
Trade stabilization	Implementation	Continuation	Continuation
Labor market reform	Preparation	Implementation	Continuation
Financial reform	Preparation	Implementation	Continuation
Small privatization	Implementation	Implementation	Continuation
Private sector development	Implementation	Implementation	Continuation
Large privatization and governance	Preparation	Implementation	Continuation
Legal aspects	Implementation	Continuation	Continuation
Institutional reforms	Implementation	Continuation	Implementation
Unemployment insurance	Implementation	Continuation	Continuation

Source: Based on Fischer and Gelb (1991)

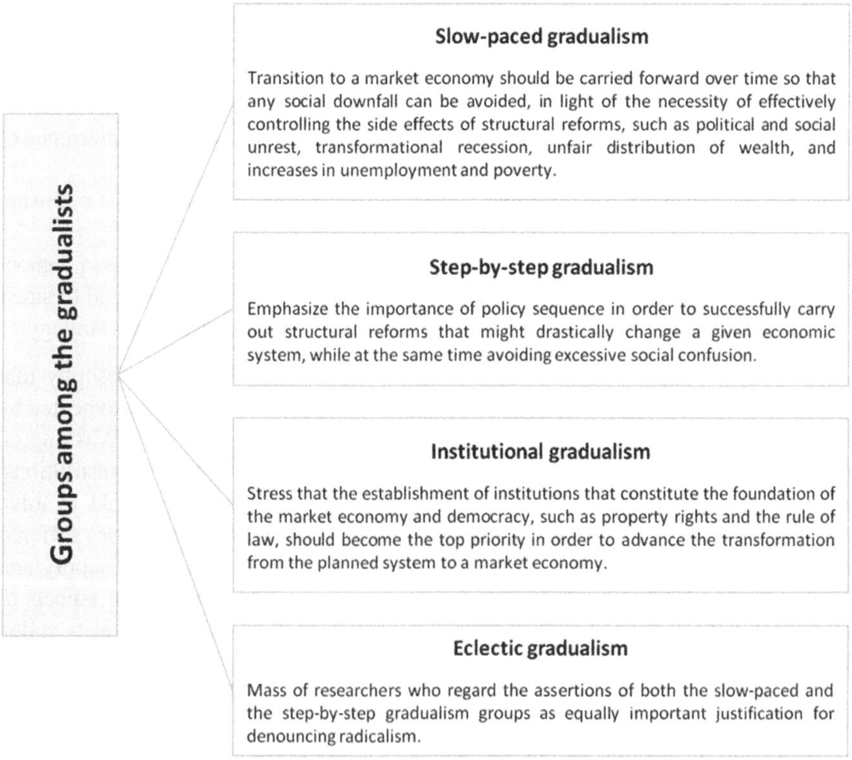

Slow-paced gradualism

Transition to a market economy should be carried forward over time so that any social downfall can be avoided, in light of the necessity of effectively controlling the side effects of structural reforms, such as political and social unrest, transformational recession, unfair distribution of wealth, and increases in unemployment and poverty.

Step-by-step gradualism

Emphasize the importance of policy sequence in order to successfully carry out structural reforms that might drastically change a given economic system, while at the same time avoiding excessive social confusion.

Institutional gradualism

Stress that the establishment of institutions that constitute the foundation of the market economy and democracy, such as property rights and the rule of law, should become the top priority in order to advance the transformation from the planned system to a market economy.

Eclectic gradualism

Mass of researchers who regard the assertions of both the slow-paced and the step-by-step gradualism groups as equally important justification for denouncing radicalism.

Groups among the gradualists

Fig. 2 Gradualists' approaches (source: based on Iwasaki & Suzuki, 2014)

In the literature can be identified different arguments supporting these two transitional strategies. According to Wei (1997), and as discussed by Lenger (2008) and Havrylyshyn (2007) the main arguments why the shock-therapy should be supported are, as follows: (1) the shock-therapy provides a critical scale of privatized sector in the economy and the privatized firms will be efficient; (2), the shock-therapy may increase the credibility of a reform; (3) the gradualist strategy gives time to reform opponents to organize themselves and thus create large opportunities for rent-seeking by both old and new elites; (4) in the context of price reforms, a gradual reform is undesirable because it may induce an inter-temporal speculation; (5) if any reform program needs mutual agreement, sequential plans may not work, owing to time-inconsistency; and (6) the shock-therapy brings the benefits more quickly. Wei (1997) provides also some supportive arguments for the gradualism, such as: (1) gradualism may evade excessive costs, particularly for the government budget; (2) gradualism avoids an extreme decrease in living standards as the start of the reform; (3) gradualism tolerate 'trial-and-error' and mid-course adjustment; (4) gradualism helps government to gain incremental authority; (5) gradualism is politically more sustainable than shock-therapy.

Some of the countries that have chosen shock-therapy strategy were Czechoslovakia, Poland and Russia (see detailed discussions in Dana, 2010), whereas the gradual strategy was chosen by Hungary, Lithuania, Romania and Slovenia (*see* Table 2).

The main differences between shock-therapy and gradualism can be summarized as follows (Havrylyshyn, 2007):

- Shock-therapist worried that delays in stabilization and liberalization Estonia, result in huge rent-seeking and opposition to, and perhaps reversal of, reforms.
- Shock-therapist agreed on the need for institutional modifications but not necessarily in advance of reforms.
- Gradualists feared that moving too fast would cause greater social costs and pain for the population.
- Gradualists proposed that market institutions have to come before liberalization and privatization to ensure maximum efficiency gains.

Table 2 Transition countries grouped by transition strategies

Sustained shock therapy	Aborted shock-therapy	Advance start/steady progress	Gradual reforms	Limited reforms
Poland	Albania	Croatia	Azerbaijan	Uzbekistan
Czech Republic	Macedonia	Hungary	Armenia	Turkmenistan
Slovakia	Bulgaria	Slovenia	Kazakhstan	Belarus
Latvia	Kyrgyzstan		Tajikistan	
Lithuania	Russia		Ukraine	
Estonia			Georgia	
			Romania	

Source: Based on Havrylyshyn (2007), Lenger (2008), and Neuhoff (2004)

A crucial difference in both strategies is the attitude toward uncertainty regarding the outcome of reforms. Shock-therapy strategy, based on the Washington Consensus underlines that the economics of reforms is well understood and these reforms should be implemented with the trust that the efficiency gains will be harvested. Here is accentuated American or European capitalism, which has been proven to be more successful than socialism, and in this case, the transition will be simply a matter of copying better models. In contrast, the gradualism stress the aggregate uncertainty of transition outcomes, which means that the entire economic reform outcomes may range from very positive to very negative, or differently said, success is by no means guaranteed (Roland, 2003). A simplified presentation of the transition strategies are summarized in Table 3.

Table 3 A simplified presentation of the transition strategies

	Shock-therapy (Washington Consensus view)	Gradualism (evolutionary-institutionalist perspective)
1. The Political economy of reforms and reform strategies		
Attitude towards uncertainty	Insistence on sure efficiency gains; faith in societal engineering	Insistence on aggregate uncertainty; skepticism toward societal engineering
Political economy emphasis	Use window of opportunity to create irreversibility	Ensure continuous and growing support for reforms
View of partial reforms	Create rents that block further reform progress	Depends on sequencing: can either create momentum or stall reform process
View of reform complementarities	Of absolute importance. Necessity to jumpstart the market economy by simultaneous introduction of all main reforms	Very important but comprehensiveness of initial reforms not necessary provided initial reforms can create momentum for further reforms. Transitional institutions can develop and evolve gradually toward more perfect institutions
Main support group for reforms	Owners of privatized enterprises	Middle class and new private sector
Focus of reforms	Liberalization, stabilization, privatization	Create institutional underpinnings of markets to encourage strong entrepreneurial entry
Attitude toward institutional change	Emphasis on adoption of laws	Comprehensive: legal and financial change, law enforcement, reform of organization of government, development of self-enforcing social norms
Attitude toward initial conditions	Create tabula rasa conditions by breaking existing communist state structure	Use existing institutions to prevent economic disruption and social unrest while developing new institutions

(continued)

Table 3 (continued)

	Shock-therapy (Washington Consensus view)	Gradualism (evolutionary-institutionalist perspective)
2. Allocative changes		
Main view of markets and liberalization	Markets will develop spontaneously provided government does not intervene; supply and demand as focus of analysis	Importance of institutional underpinnings needed to enhance market growth: minimum legal and contracting environment, law enforcement, political stability, building of business networks and long term partnerships; contracting agents and their institutional environment as unit of analysis
Main attitude toward inefficient state-owned enterprises (SOE's)	Aggressive closing down	Containment and politically feasible downsizing. Rely on evolutionary development of private sector to shrink state sector
Main view of government	Weaken it as much as possible to prevent intervention in markets	Role of government in law enforcement and in securing property rights
3. Governance changes		
Focus of privatization	Fast transfer of ownership in private hands via mass privatization to break government power and jumpstart market economy. Faith on market to ensure efficient resale	Emphasis on organic development of private sector. Emphasis on sales to outsiders to achieve efficient transfer of ownership from the start
Main emphasis of government reform	Main emphasis is shrinking the size of government	Reform in the organization of government so as to align as much as possible the interests of government bureaucrats with the development of markets
Hardening budget constraints	Exogenous policy choice that depends on political will	Endogenous outcome of institutional changes

Source: Based on Roland (2003, p. 28)

In the literature on transition strategies can be identified a group of researchers who belong neither to the shock-therapists, nor to the gradualists. They belong to the so called *neutralism*. They state that these two strategies "are not intrinsically paradoxical to each other, but rather are mutually alternative options; therefore, neither of the two can always be superior to the other theoretically and practically" (Iwasaki & Suzuki, 2014, p. 9). According to 'neutralists', policy-makers have three alternatives: (a) They can choose either shock-therapy or gradualism, depending on the actual country's state and conditions (case-based situation); (b) They can make a combination of both, and (c) Switching between the two at different stages of transition (Islam, 1993; McMillan & Naughton, 1992; Papapanagos & Sanfey, 2003).

4   Models of Transition

Several models of transition can be identified in the literature. These include: the Yugopluralist model; *Perestroika* restructuring by decree; the *Përsëritje* model (Dana, 1996a), and Asian models of gradual transition (Dana, 2002), including the *Doi-Moi* model (Dana, 1994a, 1994b). These models will be now discussed.

4.1   The Yugopluralist Model

This model of transition (Dana, 1994d) was identified in former Yugoslavia—the name given, in 1929, to the Kingdom of Serbs, Croats, and Slovenes. As the name implies, this was a multicultural country. Jordan (1970) summarized: "Yugoslavs use two alphabets, embrace three religious faiths, speak three main languages and numerous other tongues" (p. 592).

This state had been created in 1918, with the fusion of lands that had been on opposing sides during the Great War. The nature of pluralism, in Yugoslavia, eventually led to the demise of the federation, and this resulted in the independence of Bosnia-Herzegovina, Croatia, the Former Yugoslav Republic of Macedonia (FYROM), and Slovenia. Montenegro remained united with Serbia, together forming the Federal Republic of Yugoslavia. Of all the Yugoslav republics, only Slovenia and Croatia were selected for the enlargement waves of the European Union (Slovenia in May 2004 and Croatia in July 2013).

In Yugoslavia, the transition process was initiated at the local level. This resulted in an economic model to Yugoslavia, and a function of its pluralism—Yugopluralist model (Dana, 1994d). After Tito's death, loosely federated Yugoslavia became an example of fragmented pluralism (an unstable state of socio-economic pluralism from which a society can shift, sometimes by force, to another form of pluralism, or even away from pluralism altogether, towards "ethnic cleansing"). Had ethno-cultural differences been eroded, and cultures interacted in a mainstream arena, then fragmented pluralism in Yugoslavia would have shifted towards melting pot pluralism (a form of socio-economic pluralism, where people, from different cultures, share activities in a secular mainstream arena, the expression of cultural differences tends to be limited to private life). If the ethnic groups had accepted the authority of a strong political unit, then the result would have been structural pluralism (involves a society with different cultures that do not share a secular mainstream arena. In such a case, there is minimal interaction across cultures). In contrast, the Yugopluralist model decentralized power to the communes, and the authority of the federal government faded. The lack of a common interest resulted in a fragmented economy, and cultural differences contributed to regional disparities, leading to the collapse of Yugoslavia.

Yugoslavia was among the first in Eastern Europe to move in the direction of a market economy (Dana, 1994d). Until 1964, artisans were allowed to employ a maximum of three crafts-persons. The number of employees permitted was increased to five in 1965, and to ten in 1983. In 1988, the Enterprise Law permitted the private ownership of firms. While the pace of privatization was slow, many managers opted to create their own spin-off firms. As well, unemployed people created their own jobs. Yet, entrepreneurs faced numerous problems, including exponential inflation that began escalating that year. In 1989, despite weak demand and soaring unemployment, inflation reached 2,700 (*The Economist*, 1990).

Yugoslavia, under communist rule, had traditionally limited local consumption in order to boost exports. Entering the 1990s with a current account surplus, Yugoslavia no longer needed to stifle domestic demand. Augmented wages in 1990 gave Yugoslav consumers unprecedented purchasing power, creating opportunities for entrepreneurs identifying consumer needs and catering to incipient demand.

Until 1989, Austrians had shopped for bargains, in Yugoslavia. In 1990, for the first time, Yugoslavs crossed into Austria for less expensive products. The introduction of the "new dinar" (worth 10,000 dinars) was central to the restructuring of the economy in 1990. The new dinar resulted in stable prices for the first time in several years; this made a fundamental difference in entrepreneurs' abilities to plan. Furthermore, whereas exchange control under the traditional communist regime made the dinar non-convertible, the new dinar was made convertible and pegged to the German currency, which reached an all-time high relative to the U.S. dollar in 1990. Most relevant for entrepreneurs was the fact that for the first time they could easily import sophisticated machinery for automation.

Another significant reform taking place under the Yugopluralist model was that of having a formal debt swap program, something absent in all other Eastern European countries except Poland. Hard currency was raised abroad and leveraged into favorable terms in Yugoslavia, using debt-for-equity swaps and counter-trade as well as cash. The Conti Trade Services Corporation, for example, packaged investments for the Emerging Eastern Europe Fund consisting of capital ($75 million in 1990) that was raised in England and administered by Tyndall Holdings PLC. This allowed returns on a modernized factory to be significant. The first Yugoslavian debt-equity swap was engineered by the First National Bank of Chicago. Conversion of a thrice-restructured Yugoslavian debt, held by the bank, resulted in the construction of a luxury Hyatt Hotel in Belgrade.

The fact that Yugoslavia was inviting foreign investment also resulted in good import/export and joint venture opportunities for entrepreneurs both in and outside Yugoslavia. By late 1990, there were already 40 joint ventures in Yugoslavia. Most of these were in the beer industry. After a decade of evolution under decentralized federalism of the Yugopluralist Model, by 1990, Yugoslavia had a benignly weak central government. The economy was still planned but firms were doing most of their planning with their local party leader rather than with Belgrade. Trade among the Yugoslav republics decreased, and few firms had branches outside the republics in which they were based. Although Serbia still wanted a federation, economic reality of the Yugopluralist Model was that the Yugoslav republics were behaving as separate countries. With cultural heterogeneity among six republics, five ethnic groups, Catholics, Serbian Orthodox, Greek Orthodox and different groups of

Muslims, one cannot expect them to think alike or to agree on a common policy for entrepreneurship. Danforth (1990) wrote, "Civil war is discussed daily in every republic" (p. 103).

4.2   The Perestroika Model[1]

This model was identified in former Union of Soviet Socialist Republics (USSR). The Union of Soviet Socialist Republics (Soviet Union) was created in December 1922, as the centrally planned successor to the Russian Empire. Covering most of the land that once comprised the Russian Empire, this country was the world's largest, covering 8,649,821 square miles. This is equal to a sixth of the earth's land surface.

In 1922, the original Soviet Union consisted of four republics. At its peak, the Soviet Union consisted of 15 republics: Armenia, Azerbaijan, Byelorussia (later known as Belarus), Estonia, Georgia, Kazakhstan, Kirghizia (later known as the Kyrgyz Republic), Latvia, Lithuania, Moldavia (later known as Moldova), Russia, Tajikistan, Turkmenistan, the Ukraine, and Uzbekistan. The Soviet Union bordered 12 countries: Afghanistan, China, Czechoslovakia, the Democratic People's Republic of Korea (North Korea), Finland, Hungary, Iran, Mongolia, Norway, Poland, Romania, and Turkey.

In 1985, Mikhail Gorbachev came into power and announced that the Soviet Union was entering a new period of its history. He responded to a deepening economic crisis by introducing *perestroika*, which means, "rebuilding" or "changing." He admitted that in the previous 20 years industrial production had declined while corruption increased. (For discussions of corruption, see Glinkina, 1998; and Shleifer & Vishny, 1993). Thanks to *perestroika*, over 60 co-operative and commercial banks sprung up across the Soviet Union. As well, *glasnost* (openness) was about to change the mindset. (The root of the word *glasnost* is *golos* (voice), which is also the root of the word for voting, *golosova*t.)

In contrast to transition in the Yugoslav federation, *perestroika* entails change dictated by a central government. Involving transition by decree (Dana, 1994d, 2010), its objective is to completely restructure an economy. Although Russia had neither a long history of capitalism, nor a culture that traditionally valued entrepreneurship, perestroika legislation abruptly decreed a change in the economic system of the state, phasing out communism in favor of capitalism. It was felt that the expedient liberalization of prices and privatization of state firms would lead to rapid transition. Variants of this model have met different levels of success across the Union of Soviet Socialist Republics (USSR) and among member countries of the Council for Mutual Assistance (COMECON).

Despite the existence of some problems, with the monumental changes brought about by *perestroika*, several elements of the former centralized economic system were altered forever. Some of the most important changes included:

---

[1] Source: Based on Dana (2010).

(i) The reduction or elimination of subsidies to unprofitable state enterprises;
(ii) The introduction of competition within the system, often from outside the country;
(iii) The breakdown of *Gosnab* (the centralized or "state" supply system) to all enterprises;
(iv) The elimination of *Gosplan* (the centralized or "state" planning of the economy); and
(v) The introduction of market forces.

These changes, and others, have had a profound impact on the Russian people, their economy, their standard of living, and their outlook on life. Yet, these reforms were insufficient, as constituent republics of the Soviet Union wanted more autonomy. In March 1990, Estonia and Lithuania pushed for independence from the Soviet Union. Lithuania declared its independence in March 1990. Latvia declared its independence in May 1990. Uzbekistan declared its laws sovereign, in June 1990. Byelorussia and Moldavia declared sovereignty, in July 1990, followed by Turkmenistan, in August. In August 1990, Tajikistan declared its laws supreme over Moscow's. Kazakhstan declared sovereignty in October 1990. Georgia declared independence in March 1991. In August 1991, Soviet warships blockaded the harbor at Tallinn, the Estonian capital.

A drawback of rapid transition by decree is that it can destabilize a country, generating unemployment and social problems. When, in 1990, the German Democratic Republic (East Germany) rushed into transition, its unemployment skyrocketed immediately from almost nil in June, to 200,000 following economic unification in July and possibly over 2,000,000 after political unification in October (Dana, 1994c).

Rapid transition can be a shock to society, and this approach has been referred to as "shock policy" (Dana, 2000a). President Karimov of Uzbekistan used the term "shock therapy." Peng (2000) described this as the "big bang approach." Upon gaining its independence, Uzbekistan established policies that were clearly opposed to such shock therapy; it opted instead for gradual transition.

4.3 The Përsëritje Model

This model is that of Albania, a Balkan country that covers 11,101 square miles, bordering the Adriatic Sea, the Former Yugoslav Republic of Macedonia, Greece, and Serbia and Montenegro. Albanians are divided into two dialect groups; Gheg is prevalent in the north and Tosk, the official dialect, in the south. After several decades of centralized planning, and a policy of isolationism, Albania adopted the *Përsëritje* model of transition, which was considered by the Bretton Woods institutions among the most successful transforming countries of Eastern Europe. Yet, this country remains among Europe's poorest, as crime is a major player in Albania. This model is analyzed in detail in Dana (1996a, 2010).

The *Përsëritje* model of transition increased the scope for small business, while introducing liberal reforms. In 1992, huge prairie fields of the Albanian agricultural system were privatized. By 1994, there were 420,000 self-employed farmers, with private holdings averaging 1.4 hectares. Since 1995, the sale and purchase of agricultural land has been permitted. Today, over half of Albania's GDP is derived from agricultural activities, a sector employing about half of the working population, directly on the farm, or indirectly at the markets.

4.4 Models of Gradual Transition

While governments in Eastern Europe formally denounced communism and officially embraced democracy, free press and the values of a free-market economy, transition in Asia involves models of its own. Unlike the situation prevailing in much of Eastern Europe, in Cambodia and in other states that abandoned communist ideology in favor of capitalism, using the big bang approach—which proclaimed immediate transition to capitalism—China implemented a model of gradual transition, tolerating private enterprise as a complement to the centrally planned state sector, but not as a replacement; entrepreneurship in China was introduced by the government as a supplement to the socialist economy (Dana, 2002). While the *guoying qiye*—literally, state-run enterprise—is the Chinese term to describe a collective enterprise, the *siying qiye* is defined as a private enterprise owned by entrepreneurs and providing employment for eight or more people. Smaller firms, with fewer than eight people are referred to as *getihu*. Despite its success, in June 2001, China's Prime Minister Zhu Rongji declared that he was slowing down transition in China, due to difficulties created by economic reform (Dana, 2002, 2014). Within these models belong and so called *doi-moi* model. This model was identified in Vietnam. The Vietnamese word *doi-moi* literally means 'renovation'. Until the 1980s, Vietnam had an economic policy that conformed to the command system. Leaders at the national level made centralized decisions about local production, often without knowledge of local conditions. Produce raised or goods manufactured in one locality were shipped to the central level and then distributed back to the localities, creating huge inefficiencies and losses, due to mold, rats and slippage. Manufacturing was very limited because the French colonialists concentrated on extracting raw materials and emphasized neither industry nor infrastructure. Manufacturing equipment that did exist was old and rusty. In addition, the US-led embargo, which started in 1964, prevented people and firms in Vietnam from legally replacing industrial parts patented in the United States. In the same year, Vietnam launched *Doi-Moi*, which laid the path to a free-market economy, personal freedom, and openness to the West. This model is compatible with restoring the prestige of the ruling Communist party of Vietnam and no major political reform is implied here. Based on this model, the government affirmed its commitment to free enterprise within the context of socialism. The result is gradual transition involving complementarities between state firms operating under a system of centralization, and the small business sector operating independently (Dana, 2014). Kruft and Sofrova (1997) emphasized the gradualism.

5 Economic Activities in Formal and Parallel Transitional Economies

Where governments have clung on to socialist ideology, there tends to be a large sector of the economy that is state-controlled, and it operates alongside the traditional bazaar and the more modern firm-type sector. It is useful, therefore, to distinguish among these very distinct sectors of economic activity, which co-exist in the transitional economies (see Dana, 2002; Smallbone & Welter, 2001). The bazaar, the state-controlled planned sector, and the firm-type sector are components of the formal economy, some of the features of which are summarized in Table 4.

Readers are likely to be most familiar with the firm-type sector, an economic institution that involves a mode of commercial activity such that industry and trade take place primarily within a set of impersonally defined institutions. In this sector of the economy, the decision space is occupied by product attributes; the buyer and seller are secondary, if not trivial, to the transaction decision as the interaction between the buyer and the product is deemed more important than that between the buyer and the seller (Dana, 2000b, 2010). It is assumed that profit-maximizing transactions will occur based on rational decision-making, rather than the nature of personal relationships. The focus is on impersonal considerations, as described in Weber's (1924) thesis. Competition takes place between sellers, who engage in segmentation, in order to partition the market into like-groups of predictable consumers. Prices are tagged, reflecting market forces. While Western marketing

Table 4 Contrasting sectors of the formal economy

The firm-type sector	The bazaar	State-controlled planned sector
Product and impersonal transaction	Personal relationships	Focus on bureaucracy
By target market—demographic, geographic, etc.	By producer and the type of good being sold	Segmentation not considered
Indicated by the vendor, with the view of covering expenses, making a desired profit and providing the desired image for the product	Negotiated, often starting off from an unreasonable price, either unusually high from the vendor's side or low from the buyer's side	Prices are dictated by the state
An activity that takes place among sellers, competing for clients	Tension between buyer and seller competing to influence price	Competition is deemed unnecessary, as the state declares a monopoly

Source: Based on Dana (2014)

principles (Gronroos, 1989) apply to this sector, market-orientation is linked to the maturity of the industrialization process.

In contrast, the bazaar is a social and cultural system, a way of life and a general mode of commercial activity, in which interpersonal relationships are central to recruitment, retention, promotion, and purchasing decisions and nepotism often takes priority over merit (Dana, 2000b). The price and the level of service quality reflect the relationship between the buyer and the seller. In this scenario, consumers do not necessarily seek the lowest price or the best quality (Dana, 2010). An individual gives business to another with whom a relationship has been established, to ensure that this person will reciprocate. Reciprocal preferential treatment reduces transaction costs. The multiplicity of small-scale transactions, in the bazaar, results in a fractionalization of risks and therefore of profit margins; the complex balance of credit relationships is carefully managed, as described by Geertz (1963). Prices in the bazaar are negotiated, as opposed to being specified by the seller. In contrast to the firm-type sector, in which the primary competitive stress is between sellers, the sliding price system of the bazaar results in the primary competitive stress being between buyer and seller (Parsons & Smelzer, 1956). The lack of information results in an imperfect market and with few exceptions, such as basic food staples, retail prices are not indicated; rather, these are determined by negotiations. The customer tests price levels informally, before bargaining begins. It is often the buyer who proposes a price, which is eventually raised. Firms in the bazaar are not perceived as rivals of one another. There is minimal—if any—brand differentiation among merchants. Vendors do not necessarily seek to optimize monetary gain. Economic rationality is not an issue.

In transitional economies, state firms are remnants of the communist model—a doctrine first published in German (Marx and Engels, 1848), in Russian in 1882, and in English in 1888. This model assumed that a central office was in the best position to balance supply and demand. The focus of the state-controlled planned sector is thus neither on transactions nor on relationships, but rather on the state bureaucracy.

When the state produces everything, centralization rules out competitors. Barriers to trade, coupled with an import-substitution policy, ensure that competition is not a factor. Since demand exceeds supply, marketing is not necessary and segmentation need not be considered. Prices are a function of the government's bureaucracy. Dalgic (1998) reported on an empirical study, which found that state-owned firms had much less of a market orientation, than did private companies.

In addition, the parallel economy includes informal economic activity; internal economic activity with no transaction; covert economic activity; and fictitious economic activity (*see* Table 5). Prior to transition, the lack of a legal market economy led to shortages. Survival strategies often involved the emergence of entrepreneurs in the parallel economy, where inefficient regulations could be circumvented. According to Grossman (1977), this underground activity increased the overall efficiency of resource allocation under central planning. A mindset evolved, equating efficiency with the evasion of regulation.

Table 5 Economic activities in parallel economy

Economic activity	Status	Example
Informal entrepreneurship	Not always 'in the books'	Selling artwork
Subsistence self-employment	No commercial transaction	Subsistence farming
Covert economic activity	Illegal transaction	Unauthorized selling of drugs
Fictitious economic activity	Speculative transactions	Foreign devil company

Source: Based on Dana, Etemad and Wright (2008); Mason, Dana, and Anderson (2009); and Ramadani and Dana (2013)

Transition was characterized by economic and regulatory reform, and some laws took immediate effect. Human mind-set, however, takes time (Dana, 2010). Hence mind-set in transition economies was often slower than the pace of regulatory framework (North, 1990). As a result, new problems came to be associated with transition. As a consequence of their experience under central planning, many people equated entrepreneurship with the avoidance of communist law (Dana, 2010).

When new regulations were introduced to usher in a market economy, it was still tempting to circumvent business law. As noted by Feige and Ott (1999), during transition, evasion and non-compliance with new rules renders them ineffective. Where economic reform has been faster than the ability of people to adapt, inertia has delayed actual transition. Štulhofer (1999) used the term *"cultura inertia"* as many people distrusted banks and even the state.

This unique context made the parallel sector very attractive, avoiding red tape as well as taxation. In transitional economies that lack developed market institutions, it is common to have a high proportion of underground activities. This is no surprise, considering the low initial role of legitimate private enterprise, coupled with a high degree of liberalization, and hindered by the lack of macro-stability in the absence of a sufficiently developed legal framework.

The size of the parallel economy and the level of corruption vary greatly across Eastern Europe. Johnson, Kaufmann, and Shleifer (1997) estimated that the unofficial economy was 15 % in Poland, compared with 50 % in Russia and the Ukraine. Johnson, Kaufmann, McMillan, and Woodruff (2000) reported that Russia and the Ukraine had higher levels of unofficial business and corruption than was visible in Poland, Romania and Slovakia. Johnson et al. (2000) reported that 90 % of their Russian and Ukrainian respondents said it was normal to pay bribes, while in Slovakia only 40 % said the same; in Poland and Romania, the percentage was 20 %. As illustrated in Table 5, forms of economic activities in the parallel economy may be informal, internal, covert or fictitious.

Informal economic activity can take the form of an impromptu stall or itinerant vending (De Soto, 1989; Morris & Pitt, 1995; Peattie, 1987; Portes, Castells, & Benton, 1989; Rosser, Rosser, & Ahmed, 2000; Sanders, 1987; Tokman, 1978). Unrecorded cash sales circumvent taxation as well as regulation. The law is often bent, but authorities generally tolerate the sector. A relevant discussion from Dana (1992) is presented concisely by Chamard and Christie (1996). Johnson, Kaufmann, and Zoido-Lobaton (1998) discuss discretion in the sector.

Internal subsistence activity (Cole & Fayissa, 1991) is often necessary, as a means to adapt to rapid reform. Whereas McClelland (1961) defined the word "entrepreneur" as an individual who has "some control over the means of production and produces more than he can consume in order to sell (or exchange) it" (p. 65), internal subsistence activity refers to that which is consumed internally rather than sold. Thus, this category of economic activity is described as internal, because it does not involve an external exchange; no business transaction takes place. Wealth is created, but nothing is sold for profit; that which is created is consumed or saved for personal use. Internal subsistence activity includes subsistence agriculture, and subsistence fishing. Both are legal, but involve no market transaction external to the producer. While internal economic activity exists—as an activity of choice—even amid the most advanced and industrialized backdrop (Dana, 1995a), for some people in transitional economies, this is the only strategy for survival. In Moldova, for example, where prices have escalated while pensions have not, retired professionals have been growing food that they otherwise could not afford.

Covert economic activity involves business transactions, which are illegal, and therefore conducted in a covert way, in order to avoid punitive measures from law-enforcing authorities (Fadahunsi & Rosa, 2002; Feige & Ott, 1999; Haskell & Yablonsky, 1974; Henry, 1978). Since the liberalization of the marketplace has facilitated organized crime, many entrepreneurs have set up businesses that sell children into the sex trade. This is a growing issue in Eastern Europe, as young women are being enticed into prostitution (see Jacobs, 2002), as a means to a "better future." While Cantillon (1755) referred to self-employed prostitutes as entrepreneurs, today's covert activities include large-scale trans-national trafficking of human beings. Officials estimate that each year, 100,000 people become enslaved prostitutes against their will.

Fictitious economic activity has been created to facilitate circumvention of the law; this "implies speculative transactions and different kinds of swindles with a view to receiving and transferring money, including contrived rent-seeking (Glinkina, 1998, p. 102)." As it shown in Dana (2002), much of this has been taking place in Vietnam, where "foreign devil" companies have been used to set up fictitious economic activity.

6   Twenty-Five Years Later: Reflections

The world has celebrated the 25th Anniversary of Berlin Wall downfall and starting the transition process of former socialist countries—an event fueled by expectations and hopes for a better life. Reflecting upon this event from today's perspective arise a lot of questions: Did the transition meet the expectations? Whether the defined aims and goals are really accomplished? Were there formulated clear strategies and approaches on how these countries will deal with the new circumstances? Did the transition process started too early and found them unprepared? Do the people live better after the transition? Did the people of these countries expected too much? Is still present the nostalgia for the past? What we have learnt from the transition?... and too many other questions, which are or still waiting to be answered.

On May 6–7, 2014, in Budapest, Hungary was organized a 2-day symposium, entitled *'Transition in Perspective'*. It was organized by Peterson Institute for International Economics and School of Public Policy at Central European University. The aim of the symposium was to assess the lessons learnt from the transition process and 'builds' a road ahead. Some of conclusions from this symposium are summarized as follows (Aslund, 2014):

- In terms of economic performance can be concluded that the overall transition was a success since each sub-region has increased its share of the global economy;
- Avoiding rent seeking and gradualism was seen as the key for success to ensuring a parallel movement political and economic reforms;
- The most crucial part of the transition process was the privatization of *all* state-owned enterprises;
- The privatization process still remains a sensitive and controversial matter, for instance Russia and Hungary stand out as examples of the fragility of the post-socialist transition and the fact that privatization can be reversed.
- It was concluded that the European Union and the International Monetary Fund are important tools, however, they cannot do the job on their own;
- There is still a clear division between the Central and East European countries that have or are on that track to become members of the EU and the former Soviet republics, which are far more corrupted;
- An important issue was the disrupting of the old communist elites, who were corrupted by their hypocrisy of obedience to an ideology that nobody believed in. A part of them, especially in Russia and Bulgaria, has turned out to be the secret police, being the least transparent, the most lawless, the most ruthless, and also the most international.
- During the transition process a positive impact of a strong civil society and national cohesiveness was emphasized;
- Poland and Estonia were accentuated as the greatest economic and political successes seen from today's perspective;
- Even though Hungary and Poland were recognized as reform leaders in the 1990s, since 2001 these countries have regressed;
- Although Slovakia was delayed in economic reforms in the 1990s, however, it managed to catch up by adopting reforms in 2003–2004, producing the highest economic growth in Central and Eastern Europe in 2000–2010;
- It was emphasized that Georgian Rose Revolution in 2003 contributed greatly to improvement; some improvement was experienced in Moldova while adjusting to the European Union.

Although in the first years of transition, most of transition countries were experiencing very disordered and uneven economic performance, however, in

L.-P. Dana and V. Ramadani

Table 6 GDP/per capita in transition economies (1989–2013)

Country Name	1989	1990	1991	1999	2000	2007	2008	2012	2013
Albania	723	639	349	1.105	1.193	3.639	4.423	4.406	4.652
Armenia	–	637	589	597	621	3.079	3.917	3.354	3.505
Azerbaijan	–	1.237	1.209	574	655	3.851	5.575	7.394	7.812
Bulgaria	2.450	2.377	1.268	1.611	1.579	5.581	6.917	7.022	7.296
Bosnia and Herzegovina	–	–	–	1.249	1.436	3.950	4.802	4.396	4.656
Belarus	–	1.705	1.747	1.210	1.273	4.736	6.377	6.722	7.575
Croatia	–	5.185	4.026	5.068	4.862	13.372	15.694	13.159	13.530
Czech Republic	–	3.787	2.783	6.045	5.734	17.524	21.708	18.690	18.861
Estonia	–	–	–	4.132	4.063	16.405	17.786	16.887	18.478
Georgia	–	1.611	1.310	629	692	2.318	2.920	3.529	3.602
Hungary	2.783	3.186	3.288	4.714	4.543	13.535	15.365	12.560	–
Kazakhstan	–	1.647	1.512	1.130	1.229	6.771	8.514	12.120	13.172
Kyrgyz Rep.	–	609	576	258	280	722	966	1.178	1.263
Kosovo	–	–	–	–	1.088	2.736	3.303	3.567	3.816
Lithuania	–	2.841	2.777	3.113	3.267	12.102	14.775	14.172	–
Latvia	2.884	2.796	2.549	3.049	3.309	13.073	15.464	13.947	–
Moldova	–	972	835	321	354	1.231	1.696	2.047	2.230
Macedonia	–	2.225	2.342	1.806	1.748	3.892	4.686	4.548	4.851
Montenegro	–	–	–	–	1.610	5.946	7.336	6.514	7.126
Poland	2.166	1.694	2.187	4.340	4.477	11.157	13.886	12.721	13.432
Romania	1.790	1.651	1.254	1.584	1.662	8.170	9.949	8.437	9.499

Russia Fed.	3.429	3.485	3.427	1.331	1.772	9.145	11.700	14.091	14.612
Serbia	–	–	–	2.338	809	5.277	6.498	5.294	5.935
Slovak Rep.	1.852	2.211	2.474	5.550	5.330	15.649	18.201	16.893	
Slovenia	–	8.699	6.339	11.250	10.045	23.441	27.015	22.059	
Tajikistan	–	496	468	178	139	523	709	953	1.037
Turkmenistan	854	881	848	551	645	2.607	3.919	6.798	7.987
Ukraine	1.597	1.570	1.490	636	636	3.069	3.891	3.873	3.900

Source: World Bank (2014)

general, it can be concluded that they perform better today than before 1989 (de Arriba Bueno, 2010). Almost each of them has increased its GDP/per capita, i.e. only five countries have not reached their GDP per capita level of 1990 as yet (Aslund, 2014). These countries are Macedonia, Kyrgyzstan, Moldova, Tajikistan and Ukraine (Wyplosz, 2014). The pace of GDP/per capita in transition economies is presented in Table 6.

Good protection of property rights, effective execution of contracts and the law is directly related to fostering and development of the economic activities. The protection of property rights remains to be a real challenge for transitional economies. According to Smallbone and Welter (2009) protection of property rights includes "freedom from bribery, extortion, racketeering and corruption, which are conditions still faced in countries such as Ukraine, Russia and Belarus" (p. 15). Based on International Property Rights Index 2013, from 131 analyzed countries, the most of transition countries are ranked in the 'second part' of the list. For example, Moldova is ranked on 119th place, Albania, Ukraine and Georgia on 112th place, Bosnia And Herzegovina and Serbia on 107th place, Russia, Kazakhstan and Azerbaijan on 102st place, etc. (Di Lorenzo, 2013). Even that in some countries in transition, such as Estonia, Slovakia, Czech Republic, Poland, Bulgaria and Romania, is identified a slight progress (Di Lorenzo, 2013), the judicial system is still inefficient and subject to political influence (Ramadani, 2013; Ramadani & Schneider, 2013; Gerguri, Rexhepi, & Ramadani, 2013).

As it was noted in the conclusions of the above mentioned symposium, the privatization of state-owned enterprises was among the most important, but in meantime, the most contentious aspect of the transition process. Nowadays, the privatization process remained controversial, raising concerns about fairness, justice, and trust for the reason that a lot of state-owned enterprises have been handed to oligarchs and insiders in most of the countries, especially in Russia and Hungary (Aslund, 2014). Here should be mentioned that each country has applied different privatization methods (Bennett, Estrin, Maw, & Urga, 2004; Djankov & Murrell, 2002). For example, Bulgaria, Lithuania and Czech Republic have applied mass privatization method through distribution of exchangeable vouchers for shares throughout the population; Albania, Macedonia, Romania, Slovenia and Croatia have used manager-employee buyouts (MEBOSs), selling the property to groups of managers and workers of state-owned enterprises; Hungary, Slovak Republic, Estonia, Latvia applied the direct sales approach, where enterprises were sold one by one to foreign investors, etc. (see Table 7).

Nowadays, different researchers come up with different conclusions regarding privatization in transition economies. Megginson and Netter (2001) and Nellis (1999) provide a thorough overview of the economic effects of privatization in concluding that this process contributed to the improvement of enterprise performance and restructuring, believing that foreign ownership had an excessive impact on it. In addition, it was noted that in countries with weak institutions, privatization led to reverse outcomes, respectively instead of better financial results and increased efficiency it resulted in stagnation and the decapitalisation of enterprises. Privatization also created a big gap between the rich (a minority of politically

Table 7 Privatization methods

Country	Primary method	Secondary method
Czech Republic	Mass	Direct sales
Slovak Republic	Direct sales	Mass
Slovenia	MEBOs	Mass
Hungary	Direct sales	MEBOs
Poland	Direct sales	MEBOs
Estonia	Direct sales	Mass
Latvia	Direct sales	Mass
Lithuania	Mass	Direct sales
Bulgaria	Direct sales	Mass
Romania	MEBOs	Direct sales
Albania	MEBOs	Mass
Croatia	MEBOs	Mass
Macedonia	MEBOs	Direct sales

Source: Bennett et al. (2004)

well-connected people) and the large part of the poor population. (Rohać, 2013). Thus, privatization in former socialist countries did not provide the expected outcomes however, it was a process that must have taken place.

Long administrative and bureaucratic procedures represent a serious obstacle of doing business. Fiti and Ramadani (2013) noted high correlation between the administrative and bureaucratic procedures (expressed by the number of necessary procedures and required days for starting a new business) and corruption—the more procedures, the more opportunities for corruption. Regarding this issue, most of transition countries have marked significant improvements—most of them are in a better position comparing to some European Union (EU) countries, such as Spain, Greece and Malta (Doing Business, 2014). If we see the Doing Business ranking list, from the group of transition countries, in Top five countries are ranked: Georgia (8th place), Lithuania (17th), Estonia (22nd), Latvia (24th) and Macedonia (25th). Here should be pointed that the introduction of the so-called one-stop system contributed significantly to shortening the procedures and timeframe to start a new business.

According to reports of the EBRD (2005, 2013), although in transition countries there was a certain reduction of corruption in its three basic forms of existence: *bribe tax* (as a percentage of total sales of enterprises), *kickback tax* (as a percentage of the value of contracts in the form of additional and unofficial payments to ensure receipt of contracts) and *bribery frequency* (as percentage of respondents who said they accepted to pay bribes in customs, tax administration etc.), it still presents a serious problem. Shkolnikov and Nadgrodkiewicz (2010) stated that high-level scandals continue to blow up elsewhere. For example, corruption continues to devour Bulgaria and Romania, and for this reason they have been subjected to strong criticism from EU, who decided to withhold Bulgaria's development funds; in the Czech Republic, officials from Defense Ministry were accused of corruption in connection with commissioning overpriced public contracts; in Hungary, the nation was shocked when the government admitted to lying about economic performance in order to win elections, in Poland have been identified many cases of excessive pressure of private interests on legislation; etc. Transparency International Corruption Perceptions Index 2013 shows that countries in transition are mostly ranked in positions from middle to high corrupted countries (Transparence International, 2014). For instance, from 175 analyzed countries, Turkmenistan and Uzbekistan are ranked on 168th place (highly corrupted countries), Ukraine on 144th place, Russia on 127th place, Belarus on 123rd place, Albania on 166th place, etc. In slightly better positions are ranked Estonia (28), Poland (38) and Hungary (47). Therefore, it is necessary for state institutions to undertake more concrete and stringent measures in this direction, that would result in cutting lengthy court procedures, simplifying complicated procedures for obtaining various permits, facilitating the introduction and transfer of new technologies, consistently protecting intellectual property etc. This can increase the rate of entry of new small and medium enterprises and enterprises with high growth potential, as well as the interest of potential investors to invest money, expertise and time (Ramadani, 2013; Ramadani, Dana, Gerguri, & Tašaminova, 2013; Ramadani, Gerguri, Rexhepi, & Abduli, 2013; Smallbone & Welter, 2001).

Although progress is evidenced in almost all spheres of economic and politic life, nostalgia for the past in post-socialist countries still remains strong—most of the people feel that new system didn't achieve to realize the expected and hoped results (Dana, 2010; de Arriba Bueno, 2010; Ellman, 2012; Pusca, 2007). Different surveys that were conducted in post-socialist countries can confirm this. For instance, in Hungary, 70 % of the people who were already adults at the time of the Berlin Wall fall are dissatisfied with the transformations in the political system; in Bulgaria, around 60 % of citizens believe they lived better under communism; in Poland, 44 % of people have positive thoughts about former communist rule—the numbers go higher among the elderly, 54 % (Shkolnikov & Nadgrodkiewicz, 2010). Anelia Beeva, a Bulgarian girl around 30s once stated: "[Before] we went on holidays to the coast and the mountains, there were plenty of clothes, shoes, and food. And now the biggest chunk of our incomes is spent on food. People with university degrees are unemployed and many go abroad" (Mudeva, 2009). Even though a lot of weaknesses and obstacles occurred during the transition process however, transition has had a lot of positive impact on the development of many post socialist countries.

7   Conclusion

This chapter has focused on the transition process from administrative and command economies to market ones, from socialism to capitalism, or from public to private ownership. Transition from a planned to a market economy in post-socialist countries, beside economic transformation, also entails the culture of capitalism, other values, different institutions, property rights, costs and time (Tridico, 2013).

The contribution of this chapter is related with two very important issues of transition. Firstly, in this chapter are presented several transition strategies and models that have been implemented in different post-socialist countries; secondly, in this chapter for the first time in the literature are presented various reflections 25 years after the fall of Berlin Wall. Two strategies were employed: Shock therapy and gradualism. Shock-therapy was seen as a strategy for rapid break with the past and a rapid introduction of the entire economic reforms simultaneously (Havrylyshyn, 2007; Lipton & Sachs, 1990). Reforms were mainly related to macroeconomic stabilization, market and trade liberalization and restructuring of institutions. Gradualism consists of non-radical economic reforms that were implemented at a slower rhythm and sometimes were even interrupted (Svejnar, 1989; Aghion & Blanchard, 1994). In this chapter are also presented several transition models, such as: the Yugopluralist model (Dana, 1994d, 2010); *Perestroika* restructuring by decree; the *Përsëritje* model (Dana, 1996a), and Asian models of gradual transition, including the *Doi-Moi* model (Dana, 1994a, 1994b). Each of them has its advantages and its drawbacks. Success is also influenced by historical experience, cultural values and other factors.

The authors present evidence demonstrating that policy-makers, educators and managers should keep in mind that the success of a policy or program or strategy in the West does not guarantee equal success elsewhere. For this reason, it is crucial to avoid trans-locating these from one environment to a different one. Transition is process-driven, and this dictates the understanding of people and their culture (Dana, 2002).

Although the West has provided a lot of efforts and funding to transitional economies, and economic and political system has been greatly improved in recent years, complaints are often heard about the problems arising from transition. Outsiders often fail to realize that transition to a market economy requires more than efforts and funding. Transition also involves mindset. Whether or not transition is taking place gradually or rapidly, alongside political reform or in its absence, the mindset of people often holds on to perceptions of former times. Business takes place between people, and the interaction between the parties does not take place in a vacuum, but rather it is part of a social system, as discussed by Hakansson (1982).

Central to transactions are the cultural assumptions of a social system. In the West, these are implicit because it is assumed that everyone knows about them; marketing takes place in the context of a firm-type economy. In transitional economies, contextual factors must not be ignored. As discussed by Huntington (1996), globalization has not led to a single world culture.

References

Aghion, P., & Blanchard, J. O. (1994). On the speed of transition in Central Europe. In S. Fischer & J. J. Rotemberg (Eds.), *NBER macroeconomics annual* (Vol. 9, pp. 283–320). Cambridge: MIT Press.

Ahmed, Z. U., Dana, L.-P., Anwar, S. A., & Beidyuk, P. (1998). The environment for entrepreneurship and International Business in the Ukraine. *Journal of International Business and Entrepreneurship, 6*(2), 113–130.

Ahmed, Z. U., Robinson, B. R., & Dana, L.-P. (2001). A U.S. entrepreneur in Moscow. *Entrepreneurship and Innovation, 2*(1), 51–58.

Arendarski, A., Mroczkowski, T., & Sood, J. (1994). A study of the redevelopment of private enterprise in Poland: Conditions and policies for country growth. *Journal of Small Business Management, 32*(3), 40–51.

Aslund, A. (2007). *How capitalism was built: The transformation of Central and Eastern Europe, Russia, and Central Asia.* New York: Cambridge University Press.

Aslund, A. (2014). Transition in perspective: 25 years after the fall of communism. Available at: http://blogs.piie.com/realtime/?p=4312 (Accessed: August 22, 2014).

Beamish, P. (1993). The characteristics of joint ventures in the People's Republic of China. *Journal of International Marketing, 1*(2), 29–48.

Bennett, J., Estrin, S., Maw, J., & Urga, G. (2004). Privatisation methods and economic growth in transition economies. CEPR Discussion Paper, No. 4291.

Blanchard, O. (1997). *The economics of post-communist transition.* New York: Oxford University Press.

Brown, J. F. (1994). *Hopes and shadows: Eastern Europe after communism.* Harlow: Duke University Press/Longman.

Brown, M., & Zasloff, J. J. (1999). *Cambodia confounds the peacemakers, 1979-1998.* Ithaca: Cornell University Press.

Bruton, G. D. (1998, January). Incubators and small business support in Russia. *Journal of Small Business Management, 36*(1), 91–94.

Cantillon, R. (1755). *Essai sur la Nature du Commerce en Général* (translated into English in 1931, by Henry Higgs, London: MacMillan). London: R. Gyles.

Chamard, J., & Christie, M. (1996). Entrepreneurship education programs: A change in paradigm is needed. *Entrepreneurship, Innovation, and Change, 5*(3), 217–226.

Chau, S. S. (1995). The development of China's private entrepreneurship. *Journal of Enterprising Culture, 3*(3), 261–270.

Chow, K. W. C., & Tsang, W. K. E. (1995). Entrepreneurs in China: Development. *Functions and Problems, International Small Business Journal, 1,* 63–77.

Cole, W. E., & Fayissa, B. (1991). Urban subsistence labor force: Towards a policy-oriented and empirically accessible taxonomy. *World Development, 19*(7), 779–789.

Dalgic, T. (1998). Dissemination of market orientation in Europe. *International Marketing Review, 15*(1), 45–60.

Dana, L.-P. (1992). Entrepreneurship, innovation and change in developing countries. *Entrepreneurship, Innovation, and Change, 1*(2), 231–242.

Dana, L.-P. (1994a). A Marxist mini-dragon? Entrepreneurship in today's Vietnam. *Journal of Small Business Management, 32*(2), 95–102.

Dana, L.-P. (1994b). Economic reform in the New Vietnam. *Current Affairs, 70*(11), 19–25.

Dana, L.-P. (1994c). Entrepreneurship, innovation and change in Former East Germany: An ethnographic account. *Entrepreneurship, Innovation, and Change, 3*(4), 393–401.

Dana, L.-P. (1994d). The impact of culture on entrepreneurship, innovation, and change in the Balkans: The Yugopluralist model. *Entrepreneurship, Innovation, and Change, 3*(2), 177–190.

Dana, L.-P. (1995a). Entrepreneurship in a Remote Sub-Arctic Community: Nome, Alaska. *Entrepreneurship: Theory and Practice, 20*(1), 57–72.

Dana, L.-P. (1995b). Small business in a non-entrepreneurial society: The case of the Lao People's Democratic Republic (Laos). *Journal of Small Business Management, 33*(3), 95–102.

Dana, L.-P. (1996a). Albania in the twilight zone: The *Perseritje* model and its impact on small business. *Journal of Small Business Management, 34*(1), 64–70.

Dana, L.-P. (1996b). Small business in Mozambique after the war. *Journal of Small Business Management, 34*(4), 67–71.

Dana, L.-P. (1996c). The last days of the Compañero model in Cuba. *Entrepreneurship, Innovation, and Change, 5*(2), 127–146.

Dana, L.-P. (1997a). Change, entrepreneurship and innovation in the Republic of Kazakhstan. *Entrepreneurship, Innovation, and Change, 6*(2), 167–174.

Dana, L.-P. (1997b). Stalemate in Moldova. *Entrepreneurship, Innovation, and Change, 6*(3), 269–277.

Dana, L.-P. (1998a). Small business in Xinjiang. *Asian Journal of Business and Information Systems, 3*(1), 123–136.

Dana, L.-P. (1998b). Waiting for direction in the Former Yugoslav Republic of Macedonia (FYROM). *Journal of Small Business Management, 36*(2), 62–67.

Dana, L.-P. (1999a). Bulgaria at the crossroads of entrepreneurship. *Journal of Euromarketing, 8*(4), 27–50.

Dana, L.-P. (1999c). Entrepreneurship as a supplement in the People's Republic of China. *Journal of Small Business Management, 37*(3), 76–80.

Dana, L.-P. (1999d). *Entrepreneurship in Pacific Asia: Past, present and future.* Singapore: World Scientific.

Dana, L.-P. (2000a). Change and circumstance in Kyrgyz markets. *Qualitative Market Research, 3*(2), 62–73.

Dana, L.-P. (2000b). *Economies of the Eastern Mediterranean Region: Economic miracles in the making.* Singapore: World Scientific.

Dana, L.-P. (2000d). The hare and the tortoise of Former Czechoslovakia: Small business in the Czech and Slovak Republics. *European Business Review, 12*(6), 337–343.

Dana, L.-P. (2002). *When economies change paths: Models of transition in China, the Central Asian Republics, Myanmar, and the Nations of Former Indochine Française.* Singapore: World Scientific.

Dana, L.-P. (2007). *Asian models of entrepreneurship—From the Indian Union and the Kingdom of Nepal to the Japanese Archipelago: Context, policy and practice.* Singapore: World Scientific.

Dana, L.-P. (2010). *When economies change hands: A survey of entrepreneurship in the emerging markets of Europe from the Balkans to the Baltic States.* New York: Routledge.

Dana, L.-P. (2014). *Asian models of entrepreneurship: From the Indian Union and Nepal to the Japanese Archipelago: Context, policy and practice.* New Jersey: World Scientific.

Dana, L.-P., Etemad, H., & Wright, R. W. (2008). Toward a paradigm of symbiotic entrepreneurship. *International Journal of Entrepreneurship and Small Business, 5*(2), 109–126.

Dandridge, T. C., & Flynn, D. M. (1988). Entrepreneurship: Environmental forces which are creating opportunities in China. *International Small Business Journal, 6*(3), 34–41.

Danforth, K. C. (1990, August). A house much divided. *National Geographic, 178*(2), 92–123.

de Arriba Bueno, R. (2010). Assessing economic transition in Eastern Europe after twenty years. *Transformations in Business and Economics, 9*(20), 42–63.

De Soto, H. (1989). *The other path: The invisible revolution in the third world.* New York: Harper and Row.

Dehejia, V. H. (2003). Will gradualism work when shock therapy doesn't? *Economics and Politics, 15*(1), 33–59.

Di Lorenzo, F. (2013). *2013 Report: International Property Rights Index.* Washington, DC: Americans for Tax Reform Foundation/Property Rights Alliance.

Djankov, S., & Murrell, P. (2002). Enterprise restructuring in transition: A quantitative survey. *Journal of Economic Literature, 40*(3), 739–779.

EBRD. (2005). *Transition report.* London: European Bank for Reconstruction and Development.

EBRD. (2013). *Transition report: Stuck in transition?* London: European Bank for Reconstruction and Development.

Ellman, M. (2012). *What did the study of transition economies contribute to mainstream economics?* (RRC Working Paper Special Issue No. 2). Kunitachi: Hitotsubashi University.

Fadahunsi, A., & Rosa, P. (2002). Entrepreneurship and illegality: Insights from the Nigerian cross-border trade. *Journal of Business Venturing, 17*(5), 397–429.

Fadda, S. (2002). *Does the change of economic institutions require a change in value?* (Working Paper no. 28). Rome: University Roma Tre.

Fan, Y., Chen, N., & Kirby, D. (1996). Chinese peasant entrepreneurs: An examination of township and village enterprises in Rural China. *Journal of Small Business Management, 34* (4), 72–76.

Feige, L. E., & Ott, K. (Eds.). (1999). *Underground economies in transition: Unrecorded activity, Tax, Corruption and Organized Crime*. Aldershot: Ashgate.

Fischer, S., & Gelb, A. (1991). The process of socialist economic transition. *Journal of Economic Perspectives, 5*(4), 91–105.

Fischer, S., Sahay, R., & Vegh, C. A. (1996). Stabilization and growth in transition economies: The early experience. *Journal of Economic Perspectives, 10*(2), 45–66.

Fiti, T., & Ramadani, V. (2013). *Entrepreneurship*. Tetovo: Southeast European University (in Albanian language).

Franicevic, V. (1999). Political economy of the unofficial economy: The state and regulation. In E. L. Feige & K. Ott (Eds.), *Underground economies in transition: Unrecorded activity, Tax, Corruption and Organized Crime* (pp. 117–137). Aldershot: Ashgate.

Geertz, C. (1963). *Peddlers and princes: Social development and economic change in two Indonesian Towns*. Chicago: University of Chicago Press.

Gerguri, S., Rexhepi, G., & Ramadani, V. (2013). Innovation strategies and competitive advantages, *modern economics: Problems, trends. Prospects, 8*(1), 10–26.

Gerry, C., & Li, C. (2010). Consumption smoothing and vulnerability in Russia. *Applied Economics, 42*(16), 1995–2007.

Glinkina, S. P. (1998). The ominous landscape of Russian corruption. *Transitions, 5*(3), 16–23.

Gowan, P. (1995). Neo-liberal theory and practice for Eastern Europe. *New Left Review, 213*, 3–60.

Gray, K., & Allison, M. (1997). Microenterprise in a post-emergency environment. *Small Enterprise Development, 8*(4), 34–40.

Gronroos, C. (1989). Defining marketing: A market-oriented approach. *European Journal of Marketing, 23*(1), 52–60.

Grossman, G. (1977). The second economy of the USSR. *Problems of Communism, 26*(5), 25–40.

Hakansson, H. (Ed.). (1982). *International marketing and purchasing of industrial goods: An interaction approach*. Chichester: Wiley.

Haskell, M. R., & Yablonsky, L. (1974). *Crime and delinquency*. Chicago: Rand McNally.

Havrylyshyn, O. (2007). Fifteen years of transformation in the post-communist world: Rapid reformers outperformed gradualists. *Development Policy Analysis, 4*, 1–17.

Henry, S. (1978). *The hidden economy: The context and control of borderline crime*. London: Martin Robertson.

Hisrich, D. R., & Fulop, G. (1995). Hungarian entrepreneurs and their enterprises. *Journal of Small Business Management, 33*(3), 88–94.

Hisrich, D. R., & Gratchev, M. V. (1993). The Russian entrepreneur. *Journal of Business Venturing, 8*(6), 487–497.

Hisrich, D. R., & Vecsenyi, J. (1990). Entrepreneurship and the Hungarian transformation. *Journal of Managerial Psychology, 5*(5), 11–16.

Huntington, S. P. (1996). *The clash of civilization and the remaking of world order*. New York: Simon and Schuster.

Islam, S. (1993). Russia's rough road to capitalism. *Foreign Affairs, 72*(2), 57–66.

Ivy, R. L. (1996). Small scale entrepreneurs and private sector development in the Slovak Republic. *Journal of Small Business Management, 34*(4), 77–83.

Iwasaki, I., & Suzuki, T. (2014). *Radicalism versus gradualism: A systematic review of the transition strategy debate* (RRC Working Paper No. 45). Kunitachi, Tokyo: Hitotsubashi University.

Jacobs, T. (2002). Sex trade scars Baltic women. *Baltic Times, 7*(302), 1–2.

Johnson, S., Kaufmann, D., McMillan, J., & Woodruff, W. (2000). Why do firms hide? Bribes and unofficial activity after communism. *Journal of Public Economics, 76,* 495–520.

Johnson, S., Kaufmann, D., & Shleifer, A. (1997). The unofficial economy in transition. *Brookings Papers on Economic Activity, 2,* 159–239. Cf2014.

Johnson, S., Kaufmann, D., & Zoido-Lobaton, P. (1998). Regulatory discretion and the unofficial economy. *American Economic Review, 88*(2), 387–392.

Jordan, R. P. (1970). Yugoslavia: Six republics in one. *National Geographic, 137*(5), 589–633.

Katz, S. (1995). Some key development issues for transitional economies-East and West. In S. F. Naya & J. L. H. Tan (Eds.), *Asian transitional economies: Challenges and prospects for reform and transformation.* Singapore: Institute of Southeast Asian Studies.

Kruft, A. T., & Sofrova, A. (1997). The need for intermediate support-structures for entrepreneurship in transitional economies. *Journal of Enterprising Culture, 5*(1), 13–26.

Lasch, F., & Dana, L.-P. (2011). Contrasting contexts for entrepreneurship: Capitalism by Kyrgyz Decree compared to gradual transition in Uzbekistan. *Journal of Small Business and Entrepreneurship, 24*(3), 319–327.

Lenger, A. (2008). Big-bang versus gradualism? Towards a framework for understanding institutional change in Central and Eastern Europe. Available at: https://www.wipo.uni-freiburg.de/dateien/tagungen/reformen/alexander_lenger_big-bang_versus_gradualism.pdf (Accessed: August 26, 2014).

Lipton, D., & Sachs, J. (1990). Creating a market economy in Eastern Europe: The case of Poland. *Brookings Papers on Economic Activity, 21*(1), 75–148.

Lissowska, M. (2001). *Institutional change in transition countries—Constraints and path dependency.* Warsaw: Warsaw School of Economics.

Liuhto, K. (1996). The transformation of the enterprise sector in Estonia. *Journal of Enterprising Culture, 4*(3), 317–329.

Lombardo, G. A. (1995). Chinese entrepreneurs: Strategic adaptation in a transitional economy. *Journal of Enterprising Culture, 3*(3), 277–292.

Marangos, J. (2003). Was shock therapy really a shock? *Journal of Economic Issues, 37*(4), 943–966.

Martin, J. H., & Grbac, B. (1998). Smaller and larger firms' marketing activities as a response to economic privatization: Marketing is alive and well in Croatia. *Journal of Small Business Management, 36*(1), 95–99.

Mason, A. M., Dana, L. P., & Anderson, R. B. (2009). A study of enterprise in Rankin Inlet, Nunavut: where subsistence self-employment meets formal entrepreneurship. *International Journal of Entrepreneurship and Small Business, 7*(1), 1–23.

Marx, K., & Engels, F. (1848). *Manifest der Kommunisitischen Partei.* London: J.E. Burghard.

McClelland, D. C. (1961). *The achieving society.* Princeton, NJ: D. Van Nostrand.

McMillan, J., & Naughton, B. (1992). How to reform a planned economy: Lessons from China. *Oxford Review of Economic Policy, 8,* 130–142.

Megginson, W. L., & Netter, J. M. (2001). From state to market: A survey of empirical studies on privatisation. *Journal of Economic Literature, 39*(2), 321–389.

Morris, H. M., & Pitt, F. L. (1995). Informal sector activity as entrepreneurship: Insights from a South African township. *Journal of Small Business Management, 33*(1), 78–86.

Mudeva, A. (2009, November 8). Special report: In Eastern Europe, people pine for socialism. Reuters, http://www.reuters.com/article/idUSTRE5A701320091108 (Accessed: August 26, 2014).

Murrell, P. (2006). Institutions and transition. In L. Blume & S. Durlauf (Eds.), *The New Palgrave: A dictionary of economics* (2nd ed.). Basingstoke: Macmillan.

Nellis, J. (1999). *Time to rethink privatization in transition economies?* (IFC Discussion Paper No. 38). Washington, DC: World Bank.

Neuhoff, F. (2004). *Eastern Europe-convergence and transition.* Berlin: Humboldt University.

Noar, J. (1985). Recent small business reforms in Hungary. *Journal of Small Business Management, 23*(1), 65–72.

North, D. (1990). *Institutions, institutional change, and economic performance*. Cambridge: Harvard University Press.

Oreskovic, R. (2012). Economic transition in the Czech Republic and Hungary: Twenty years later. Available at: http://econ.as.nyu.edu/docs/IO/28042/EconomicTransition.pdf (Accessed: August 21, 2014).

Overholt, W. H. (1993). *The rise of China: How economic reform is creating a new superpower*. New York: Norton.

Papapanagos, H., & Sanfey, P. (2003). Emigration and the optimal speed of transition. *Review of International Economics, 11*(3), 541–554.

Parsons, T., & Smelzer, N. (1956). *Economy and society*. Glencoe, IL: Free Press.

Peattie, L. (1987). An Idea in good currency and how it grew: The informal sector. *World Development, 15*(7), 851–860.

Peng, M. W. (2000). *Business strategies in transition economies*. Thousand Oaks: Sage.

Portes, A., Castells, M., & Benton, L. A. (Eds.). (1989). *The informal economy: Studies in advanced and less developed countries*. Baltimore: John Hopkins University Press.

Pusca, A. (2007). Shock, therapy, and post-communist transitions. *Alternatives, 32*(3), 341–360.

Ramadani, V. (2013). Entrepreneurship and small business in Republic of Macedonia. *Strategic Change, 22*(7/8), 485–501.

Ramadani, V., & Dana, L.-P. (2013). The state of entrepreneurship in the Balkans: Evidence from selected countries. In V. Ramadani & C. R. Schneider (Eds.), *Entrepreneurship in the Balkans*. Berlin: Springer.

Ramadani, V., Dana, L.-P., Gerguri, S., & Tašaminova, T. (2013). Women entrepreneurs in the Republic of Macedonia: Waiting for directions. *International Journal of Entrepreneurship and Small Business, 19*(1), 95–121.

Ramadani, V., Gerguri, S., Rexhepi, G., & Abduli, S. (2013). Innovation and economic development: The case of FYR of Macedonia. *Journal of Balkan and Near Eastern Studies, 15*(3), 324–345.

Ramadani, V., & Schneider, C. R. (Eds.). (2013). *Entrepreneurship in the Balkans*. Berlin: Springer.

Robinson, P. B., Ahmed, Z. U., Dana, L.-P., Latfullin, R. G., & Smirnova, V. (2001). Towards entrepreneurship and innovation in Russia. *International Journal of Entrepreneurship and Innovation Management, 1*(2), 230–240.

Rohać, D. (2013). What are the lessons from post-communist transitions? *Economic Affairs, 33*(1), 65–77.

Roland, G. (2001). Ten years after . . . Transition and economics. *IMF Staff Papers, 48*, 29–52.

Roland, G. (2003). *Transition: An evolutionary-institutionalist perspective*. USA: University of California.

Rondinelli, D. A. (1991). Developing private enterprise in the Czech and Slovak Federal Republic. *Columbia Journal of World Business, 26*, 26–36.

Rosser, J. B., Jr., Rosser, M., & Ahmed, E. (2000). Income inequality and the informal economy in transition economies. *Journal of Comparative Economics, 28*, 156–171.

Sachs, J. (1990, January 13). What is to be done? *The Economist*, 23–28.

Sachs, J. (1993). *Poland's jump to the market economy*. Cambridge: MIT.

Sanders, R. (1987). Toward a geography of informal activity. *Socio-Economic Planning Sciences, 24*(4), 229–237.

Shirk, S. (1993). *The political logic of economic reform in China*. Berkeley, CA: University of California Press.

Shkolnikov, A., & Nadgrodkiewicz, A. (2010). The fall of the Berlin wall: Twenty years of reform in Central and Eastern Europe. *Caucasian Review of International Affairs, 4*(1), 73–81.

Shleifer, A., & Vishny, R. W. (1993). Corruption. *Quarterly Journal of Economics, 108*(3), 599–617.

Siu, W.-S., & Kirby, A. D. (1995). Marketing in Chinese small business: Tentative theory. *Journal of Enterprising Culture, 3*(3), 309–342.

Smallbone, D., & Welter, F. (2001). The distinctiveness of entrepreneurship in transition economies. *Small Business Economics, 16*(4), 249–262.

Smallbone, D., & Welter, F. (2009). *Entrepreneurship and small business development in post-socialist economies*. London: Routledge.

Sokol, M. (2001). Central and Eastern Europe a decade after the fall of state-socialism: Regional dimensions of transition processes. *Regional Studies, 35*(7), 645–655.

Štulhofer, A. (1999). Between opportunism and distrust: Socio-cultural aspects of the underground economy in Croatia. In L. E. Feige & K. Ott (Eds.), *Underground economies in transition: Unrecorded activity, tax, corruption and organized crime* (pp. 43–63). Aldershot: Ashgate.

Svejnar, J. (1989). A framework for the economic transformation of Czechoslovakia. *PlanEcon, 5*(52), 1–18.

Svejnar, J. (2002). *Assistance to the transition economies: Were there alternatives?* (William Davidson Institute Working Paper). Ann Arbor: University of Michigan.

Tan, C. L., & Lim, T. S. (1993). *Vietnam: Business and investment opportunities*. Singapore: Cassia.

The Economist. (1990, June 23). Yugoslavia, p. 103.

Tokman, V. E. (1978). Competition between the informal sectors in retailing: The case of Santiago. *World Development, 6*(9), 1187–1198.

Transparence International. (2014). Transparency International Corruption Perceptions Index 2013. Available at: http://www.ey.com/Publication/vwLUAssets/EY-Transparency-International-Corruption-Perceptions-Index-2013/$FILE/EY-Transparency-International-Corruption-Perceptions-Index-2013.pdf (Accessed: August 26, 2014).

Tridico, P. (2013). Values, institutions and models of institutional change in transition economies after the fall of Berlin Wall. *Challenge, 56*(3), 6–27.

Turley, G., & Luke, P. J. (2010). *Transition economics: Two decades on*. London: Routledge.

Weber, M. (1924). *The theory of social and economic organization*. New York: Free Press.

Wei, S. J. (1997). Gradualism versus big bang: speed and sustainability of reforms. *Canadian Journal of Economics, 30*(4), 1234–1247.

Wei, L. (2001). Incentive systems for technical change: The Chinese system in transition. *International Journal of Entrepreneurship and Innovation Management, 1*(2), 157–177.

Williams, E. E., & Li, J. (1993). Rural entrepreneurship in the People's Republic of China. *Entrepreneurship, Innovation, and Change, 2*(1), 41–54.

Williamson, J. (Ed.). (1990). *Latin American adjustment: How much has happened?* Washington, DC: Institute for International Economics.

World Bank. (2014). *Understanding regulations for small and medium-size enterprises*. Washington, DC: International Bank for Reconstruction and Development/The World Bank.

World Bank. (2014). GDP per capita (current US$). Available at: http://data.worldbank.org/indicator/NY.GDP.PCAP.CD (Accessed: September 8, 2014).

Wyplosz, C. (2014). Twenty-five years later: Macroeconomic aspects of transition. Available at: http://graduateinstitute.ch/files/live/sites/iheid/files/sites/international_economics/shared/international_economics/prof_websites/wyplosz/Papers/Transition%20June%202014.pdf (Accessed: August 24, 2014).

Zapalska, A. (1997). A profile of woman entrepreneurs and enterprises in Poland. *Journal of Small Business Management, 35*(4), 76–82.

Different Features of Transition Economies: Institutions Matter

Jelena Trivić and Saša Petković

Abstract Process of transition is most simply defined as a process which includes moving from centrally planned to market oriented economy. There is no uniqueness about which countries are transitional ones, as their geographical, cultural, economic and overall social context disables forming of one unique sample that would fit in every analysis. The main aspects of transition process are liberalization, macroeconomic stabilization, privatization and legal and institutional reforms. Our definition of institutions assumes Douglass North's concept of institutions which defines institutions as the rules or regulations (humanly devised constraints) that structure political, economic and social interaction while institutional environment comprises institutions (formal and informal ones) and an enforcement mechanism. The quality of institutions in this chapter is measured by World Governance Indicators. The subject of this chapter is the analysis of quality of institutions and institutional environment in five Western Balkan countries and analysis of implications of institutional environment on overall standard of living and competitiveness of these countries. Our results indicate that Western Balkan countries lag significantly behind Central European countries in terms of institutional quality. The widening gap between the standard of living in Western Balkan countries and Central European countries in last 10 years indicates that the crucial problem in Western Balkan countries is the speed of reforms.

Keywords Institutions • Transition • Western Balkans • Central Europe • World Governance Indicators

1 Introduction

In the recent economic history, transition countries represent a useful laboratory to assess changes of economic systems from one type to another (Estrin, Hanousek, Kocenda, & Svejnar, 2009). According to Joseph Stiglitz (1999) the last century has been marked by two great economic experiments. The first one is the emergence of

J. Trivić (✉) • S. Petković
Faculty of Economics, University of Banja Luka, Majke Jugovica 4, 78000 Banja Luka, Bosnia and Herzegovina
e-mail: jelena.trivic@efbl.org; sasa.petkovic@efbl.org

© Springer International Publishing Switzerland 2015
L.-P. Dana, V. Ramadani (eds.), *Family Businesses in Transition Economies*,
DOI 10.1007/978-3-319-14209-8_4

the Soviet Union in 1917, and the second is the moving back from centrally planned economies, in which state ownership prevailed, to a market economy where private ownership prevails. As Ramadani and Dana (2013, p. 218) state: "Transitional economies provide a particularly fascinating backdrop for the development of entrepreneurship".

There is no uniqueness about which countries are transitional ones, as their geographical, cultural, economic and overall social context disables forming of one unique sample that would fit in every analysis. Due to their size, different methods of transition and achieved results, many authors put their attention on Russia and China, especially in the first years of transition. Central European countries such as Poland, Czech Republic, Slovakia, Slovenia, Hungary as well as Baltic states, came into the focus of research while approaching and entering the EU, which also occurred in Bulgaria and Romania in 2007 and in Croatia in 2013. Bosnia and Herzegovina, Macedonia, Serbia and Montenegro are rarely found in samples of cross-country analysis of transition economies. Slovenia was the only ex-Yugoslavian country that was very often included in researches, while in case of Croatia the situation is different. Probably the most used examples of transition economies are those included in Transition Report of *European Bank for Research and Development* which in 2013 included 34 very different countries and group of countries (EBRD, 2013).[1]

As we will show, the heart of transitional process is *institutional building*. In this paper institutions are defined as "the rules of the game" according to Douglas North's and New Institutional Economics' definition.

The subject of this paper is the analysis of quality of institutions in five Western Balkan (WB) countries compared to five Central European (CE) countries that serve as a benchmark. Our *scope* is to determine how far are Western Balkan countries from the Central European countries in terms of institutional quality and in that context our scope is to determine what kind of implications it has for overall standard of living in all analyzed countries. We test the *hypothesis* that better institutions or better institutional environment is highly correlated and thus inter-related with economic development and that these two influence each other. Our results indicate that Western Balkan countries lag significantly behind Central European countries in terms of institutional quality. Institutions, as the rules by which the game on the market is played, are far from good in WB countries compared to CE countries and thus there are very huge differences in the average standards of living between these two samples. The widening gap between the standard of living in five WB countries and five CE countries in last 10 years indicates that the crucial problem in WB countries is the speed of reforms.

---

[1] Even if analyzed by many authors as an example of unique transitional country, progress in transition is not assessed in China by Transition Reports, as it would require individual analysis due to its size and special path of reforms.

2 Transition Process: Some Key Aspects

2.1 Defining Transition and Transition Process

Process of transition is most simply defined as a process which includes moving from centrally planned to market oriented economy. More precise definition says that transition process is the "reform process in countries that have made the decision to move from a planned socialist system to a private market economy, one in which private ownership predominates and most resources are allocated through markets" (Fischer & Gelb, 1991, p. 91). It also requires interplay of the economics and politics, i.e. reform process is reformation of the both in its essence (Murrell, 1996). Process of transition means social, economic and political transformation in ex communist countries (Petković & Berberović, 2013, p. 14).

What are the main aspects of transition process which more or less prevailed in all transition countries? According to IMF (2000) and some authors (Fischer & Gelb, 1991; Havrylyshyn & Wolf, 1999; Žarković, 2012) these are the following:

1. Liberalization
2. Macroeconomic stabilization
3. Privatization
4. Legal and institutional reforms

As Kolodko (1999, p. 2) claims: "A market economy requires not only liberal regulation and private ownership, but also adequate institutions". Similarly, Dana and Dana (2003, p. 52) claim that transition process is a function of all causal variables including culture, historical experience, and government policy.

2.2 Shock Therapy vs. Gradualism

There are in general two opposed strategies of transition from socialism to capitalism: a "big bang" or shock therapy approach and gradualist approach (Roland, 2002, p. 29).

Advocates of the big bang approach argued for fast macroeconomic stabilization, price liberalization and dismantling institution of old communist system, the process that Svejnar (2002) called reforms of "Type I". The essence of this kind of reforms was to adopt programs as fast as possible. In countries of the Central Europe where reforms started in 1990, transition process was mostly of "big bang" type (Roland & Verdier, 1999). After these countries experienced sharp initial fall in output, economic recovery followed and they relatively quickly moved towards European Union membership. The most characteristic examples of this type of reforms are Czech Republic and Poland in Central Europe and Russia. Probably the most famous practitioner of "big bang" approach in many ex socialist countries was Jeffrey Sachs. Big bang approach in Poland, according to

Jeffrey Sachs himself, was a success story "despite huge controversy, deep fears, and great intellectual and political debates" (Sachs, 2012). Afterwards, Sachs was invited to advise Russian reforms although Sachs himself never regarded Russian reform to be shock therapy. By some authors Russia has suffered from "shock without therapy" (Roland & Verdier, 1999, p. 2). After the collapse of Russian economy in early years of transition, Sachs resigned in January 1994.

The essence of gradualist approach ("Type II" approach) was the need for precise sequencing of reforms where reforms were regarded as incremental process (Roland, 2002, p. 29). The often cited example of good performed gradualist approach was the case of China which can be regarded as a type of gradualist approach *per se*. Transition of Type II approach included enforcement of laws, institutional building and regulations that support a market oriented economy (Svejnar, 2002). After assessing the experience of transition in countries of Central and Eastern Europe, Former Soviet Union countries and China, many authors tried to explain why gradualist approach gave better results than big bang approach at least in initial stages of transition (Popov, 2007; Roland, 2000; Stiglitz, 1999; Svejnar, 2002). Although, Central European countries which based their reforms more or less on "big bang" approach found ways for economic recovery and good institutional arrangements.

2.3   When Transition Ends?

In that context, one can reasonably ask a question "When transition ends?". This question depends on "terminal point" (Svejnar, 2002). According to the World Bank (2002) this terminal point occurs when historical productivity discrepancies in old, restructured and new enterprises disappear. Regarding the achieved per capita income that signifies the end of transition, in publication of World Bank the answer is indirect. It depends "on the success of disciplining the old sector and encouraging the new one" (World Bank, 2002, p. 19). In the book "When Transition is over?" of Anett Brown from 1999, several authors also tried to answer this question. Some of the authors thought that this was unanswerable question (Lavigne, 1999) but also indirectly answered that for CEE countries transition is over when they enter the EU (Lavigne, 1999). Some other authors as Kornai (1999) pointed three very precise indicators that implied the end of transition. These are: (1) the communist party no longer has monopoly power; (2) the private sector accounts for dominant part of the GDP, (3) and the market is the dominant coordinator of economic activities. Svejnar (2002, p. 26) offered his own view on transition end, which happens when these states substitute central planning by a market and when they achieve sustainable and sufficient economic growth that allows them to interact with the advanced economies without substantive protectionism. For countries like Poland, Czech Republic, Slovakia, Hungary and Slovenia, in 1999 Kornai predicted transition to be over when they enter EU. At least for these countries it seems that transition is completed, although there are some EU countries such as Croatia, Bulgaria and Romania where transition is far from over. In countries that started transition few years after 1990s such as other Balkan countries, the process is also still ongoing and the question is still open, although transition process is not at the heart of economic debate as it was in 1990s.

3 Institutions and Institutional Quality as a Cornerstone of Transition Process

3.1 Defining Institutions

Discussion about gradualism and shock therapy leads to the discussion on how important is the role of *institutions* for the transition, as one of its element. The most used definition of institutions assumes Douglass North's concept of institutions. According to North (1990, p. 3) institutions are the rules, regulations (humanly devised constraints) that structure political, economic and social interaction; they consist of both: formal rules (constitution, laws, property rights) and informal constraints (sanctions, taboos, customs, tradition and codes of conducts). The purpose of the rules and conventions is to define the rules by which the game is played, monitored and enforced. Organization or individuals are entities which devise and implement these institutions. Institutional environment in that sense comprises institutions (formal and informal ones) and an enforcement mechanism (Tešić, 2010, p. 103).

Similarly, using the definition within New Institutional Economics (NIE), World Bank (1998, p. 11) defines institutions as formal and informal rules and their enforcement mechanisms that shape the behavior of individuals and organizations in the society.

"Deeper" determinants of economic growth, beside physical and human capital accumulation and technological change, also include institutions (Rodrik, Subramanian, & Trebbi, 2002, p. 2). Many other authors, based primarily on the North's definition of institutions, explored their role in economic performances and proved positive relationship between institutional development and growth (Acemoglu, Johnson, & Robinson, 2004; Acemoglu & Robinson, 2010; Dollar & Kraay, 2003; Eicher & Leukert, 2009; Hall & Jones, 1998; Knack & Keefer, 2005; La Porta, de Silanes, Schleifer, & Vishny, 1998).

While exploring the role of institutions in economic development, Hall and Jones (1998, p. 2) coined a new term—*social infrastructure*, which includes institutions and government policies that determine economic environment within which individuals accumulate skills, and firms accumulate capital and produce output.

3.2 Institutions in Transition Economies: Some Theoretical Issues

Economists of NIE were not at the heart of debate in the early years of transition. Murrell (2003) explored usage of NIE postulates in the process of transition, and concluded that the main reason why institutions were not regarded as crucial factor of transition was the assumption that development of institutional framework was slow and could not contribute to transition process in the short-run. But after some time, more and more authors started to analyze institution building in transition economies and to relate the quality of institution with the progress in reforms (Campos, 2000; Efendic, Pugh, & Adnett, 2010; Fischer & Sahay, 2004; Kolodko, 1999; Murrell, 2003; Popov, 2007; Roland, 2002; Svejnar, 2002).

Kolodko (1999) blames Washington consensus for neglecting the significance of institutional building in transition economies. Aware of the fact that institutions change very slowly, he finds that they have very strong influence on economic performance. According to him, institutional framework is the most important element of the long-run growth, and "unlike certain liberalization measures, institution building by its nature must be a gradual process" (Kolodko, 1999, p. 225).

Arguing that International Financial Institutions (IFIs) were well conscious of the need for institutional development in transition economies, Fischer and Sahay (2004) tried to prove that IFIs made many efforts in helping to build institutions. Beside debate of the role of IFIs in transition economies, they have also admitted the crucial role of institutions for the transition process.

One of the main conclusions of the authors who explored the role of institutions in transition economies is that institutions do change over time (Campos, 2000). Analyses of transition economies proved on experiment that institutions are not a static factor of economic growth and development, and that there is an ample room for policy choices in attempt to create good institutional framework (Kolodko, 2002; Murrell, 2003).[2]

3.3 Measuring Institutions and Data Sources

But, what constitutes these "rules of the game", i.e. institutions?

Maybe the best way to answer the previous question is to see how we can measure institutions across countries; by which data and variables. There are several data sources and indicators used in empirical work as measures of institutions:

---

[2] Douglas North, the Nobel laureate who defined institutions and institutional change, referred to the role of institutions and their importance for transition economies in his annual lecture for UNU/WIDER (North, 1997).

1. *World Governance Indicators*, developed by Kaufmann et al. (2010) and supported by the World Bank, composed of six variables: voice and accountability, political stability, government effectiveness, regulatory quality, rule of law and control of corruption. Governance Indicators are used by Beck and Laeven (2005), Murrell (2003);
2. *International Country Risk Guide* developed by the Political Risk Service in 1980 which monitors political, economic and financial risk. Some of the variables include measures of institutional quality such as Government Repudiation of Contracts, Risk of Expropriation, Corruption, Law and Order, and Bureaucratic Quality. These are used for example by Knack and Keefer (1995), Campos (2000), Hall and Jones (1998), La Porta et al. (1998);
3. *Index of Economic Freedom* developed by the Heritage Foundation;
4. *Economic Freedom of the World* developed by the Fraser Institute;
5. *Corruption Perception Index* developed by the Transparency International.

For measuring institutional change in transition economies, authors usually use EBRD's Transition Reform indicators which measure structural and institutional reform compared to the developed market economies (Efendic et al., 2010). According to them, Transition Indicators are the best proxies of institutional change in these economies, as transition in its essence is a process of transformation from centrally planned towards market oriented economies, while Campos (2000), the World Bank (1994, 1998) and Streeten (1996) put emphasize on *governance* as a proxy of overall institutional quality in the analysis of institutional quality.

4   Quality of Institutions in Western Balkan Countries Compared to Central European Countries

4.1   Unit and Methods of Analysis

The sample includes two different groups of countries: five Western Balkan countries—*Albania, Bosnia and Herzegovina, Croatia, Macedonia and Serbia*, and five countries of CEE—*Czech Republic, Hungary, Poland and Slovakia* plus *Slovenia*. We choose two samples of culturally and geographically close countries which all belong to European continent and all aspire to become members of EU or they already are. Thus they share or will share the same systems, attitudes and values. In the first sample, transition is far from over, while in the second it could be regarded as finished. Regardless the fact that Croatia became a member of EU, we put it with Western Balkans as the membership happened very recently. For CEE as Kornai (1999) suggested, transition ended by entering EU a decade ago.

Institutions are measured by World Governance Indicators Database (2014) which indicates quality of *Governance* in certain country. Kaufman, Kraay, and Mastruzzi (2010, p. 4) define *Governance* as traditions and institutions by which authority in a country is exercised which includes the process by which governments are selected, monitored and replaced, the capacity of the government to effectively formulate and implement sound policies and the respect of citizens and the state for the institutions that govern economic and social interactions among them. Each variable of six indicators goes from -2.5 to 2.5 where lower value indicates lower result.

The goal of the research is to determine what Western Balkans can learn from the experience of CEE countries, and how far they are from CEE countries in the sense of institutional building. Moreover, we will determine the nature and strength of relationship between quality of institutions and economic development measured by GDP per capita in PPP[3] by method of correlation in both samples of countries. Quality of institutions will also be put in relation with competitiveness of countries measured by the Global Competitiveness Index.

4.2   Results and Discussion

Figure 1 shows averaged movement of the first element of institutional framework *Voice and Accountability (VACC)* which "captures perceptions of the extent to which a country's citizens are able to participate in selecting their government, as well as freedom of expression, freedom of association, and a free media" (World Governance Indicators, 2014).[4]

It is obvious that WB countries lag extremely behind CEE countries but the closing of averages through time is evident. The difference in 1996 was around 1.6 points in absolute value while in 2012 it was around 0.8, which is twice less.

Figure 2 shows averaged movement of the second element of institutional framework *Political Stability (PS)* which "measures perceptions of the likelihood that the government will be destabilized or overthrown by unconstitutional or violent means, including politically-motivated violence and terrorism" (World Governance Indicators, 2014).

As for the previous parameter, the difference is substantive but again, with closing tendency. The difference in 1996 was around 1.55 and in 2012 it was 1.1.

Figure 3 shows averaged movement of the third element of institutional framework *Government Effectiveness (GE)* which "captures perceptions of the quality of public services, the quality of the civil service and the degree of its independence from political pressures, the quality of policy formulation and implementation, and the credibility of the government's commitment to such policies" (World Governance Indicators, 2014).

The tendency of closing the averages of WB to CEE countries is again evident but substantive space in quality of government effectiveness still exists. The difference in 1996 was 0.95 points in absolute value while in 2012 it was 0.45.

---

[3] PPP stands for Purchasing Power Parity.

[4] All tables with data for following figures can be found in Appendices (Tables 1, 2, 3, 4, 5, 6, and 7).

Fig. 1 Comparison of voice and accountability between averages in WB and CEE countries (source: World Governance Indicators Database, 2014)

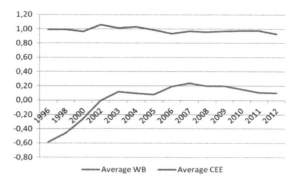

Fig. 2 Comparison of political stability between averages in WB and CEE countries (source: World Governance Indicators Database, 2014)

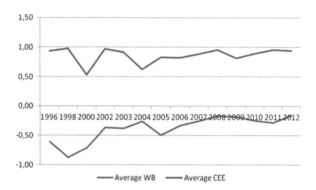

Fig. 3 Comparison of government effectiveness between averages in WB and CEE countries (source: World Governance Indicators Database, 2014)

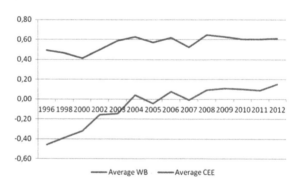

Figure 4 shows averaged movement of the fourth element of institutional framework *Regulatory Quality (RQ)* which "captures perceptions of the ability of the government to formulate and implement sound policies and regulations that permit and promote private sector development" (World Governance Indicators, 2014).

The difference of Regulatory Quality in average in WB countries is far away from CEE countries in average, and the difference in 2012 was 0.75 in absolute value.

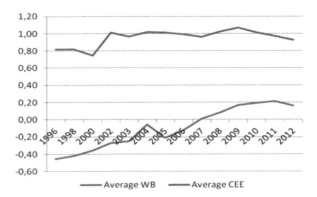

Fig. 4 Comparison of regulatory quality between averages in WB and CEE countries (source: World Governance Indicators Database, 2014)

Figure 5 shows averaged movement of the fifth element of institutional framework *Rule of Law (ROL)* which "captures perceptions of the extent to which agents have confidence in and abide by the rules of society, and in particular the quality of contract enforcement, property rights, the police, and the courts, as well as the likelihood of crime and violence" (World Governance Indicators, 2014).

Maybe the most important variable of institutional quality *Rule of Law* shows the signs of improvement in WB but the difference still remains. In absolute value it was 1 point in 2012 which is relatively 20 % less on the scale from −2.5 to 2.5.

Figure 6 shows averaged movement of the last element of institutional framework *Control of Corruption (COC)* which "reflects perceptions of the extent to which public power is exercised for private gain, including both petty and grand forms of corruption, as well as capture of the state by elites and private interests" (World Governance Indicators, 2014).

Corruption is regarded as the most important informal institution especially in transition countries (Bevan & Estrin, 2004).

Finally, in Fig. 7 we show average of all six indicators of institutional quality measured by World Governance Indicators from 1996 to 2012 for WB countries and for CEE countries in average.

In average, WB countries lag significantly behind CEE countries. It is also evident that they are approaching but the difference is still clear amounting 0.8 points on the scale from −2.5 to 2.5.

Having in mind these differences between WB and CEE countries, considering institutional quality in these countries, we are also interested in evaluating the relationship between institutional quality and economic development in all ten countries of our interest. The rationale behind this is to evaluate importance of institutions for *standard of living* of the citizens in the countries of interest. Correlation between quality of institutions estimated by average of six World Governance Indicators and Economic Development measured by GDP per capita in PPP in international dollars is shown in Diagram 1. Variables of institutional quality include average in 3 years period from 2010 to 2012 while GDP/pc is average in 3 years with 1 year in advance (from 2011 to 2013) in each country. The rationale for this is the assumption that institutions will have the impact on economic development in subsequent time.

Fig. 5 Comparison of rule of law between averages in WB and CEE countries (source: World Governance Indicators Database, 2014)

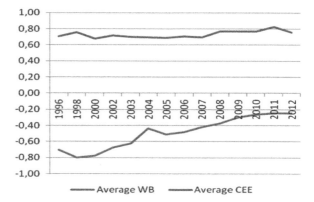

Fig. 6 Comparison of control of corruption between averages in WB and CEE countries (source: World Governance Indicators Database, 2014)

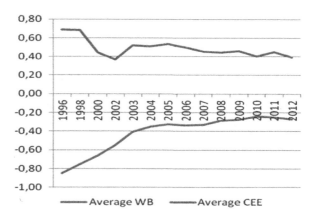

Fig. 7 Comparison of average of six indicators of governance between averages (source: World Governance Indicators Database, 2014)

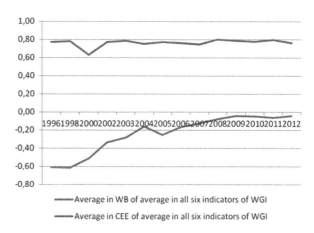

Diagram 1 Relation between institutional quality and GDP/pc in PPP (source: World Governance Indicators Database, 2014; IMF World Economic Outlook, 2014)

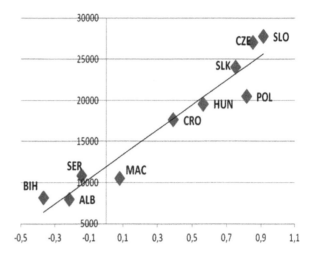

Correlation coefficient of 0.96 shows strong and positive relationship between these two variables in last 3 years. We used average from last 3 years in order to avoid some extremes that could happen in 1 year for both indicators. The results shown in this diagram are expected as institutional quality and economic development are interrelated and influence each other. It is logical to expect that more developed countries will have better institutional quality, and vice versa, but the strength of relationship is astonishing. For correlation of 0.96 we can say that it shows very strong correlation which means that these two variables move together almost perfectly in each country.

An interesting analysis using the same method of correlation can be done for the relationship between institutional quality measured in the same way as for previous diagram and competitiveness level of these countries which is estimated each year in the Global Competitiveness Report. Data for Global Competitiveness Index which show competitiveness level of certain country range from 1 to 7 with higher value indicating better result. For institutions we use 3-year averages from 2010 to 2012 and for competitiveness level averages from 2011 to 2013, for each country.

As in the previous diagram, the correlation is positive and strong. Correlation coefficient is 0.89 indicating a strong positive correlation although not as strong as between institutions and economic development. The results shown in Diagram 2 are expected as institutional quality and competitiveness level are also interrelated but the strength of relationship is again astonishing.[5]

We saw that institutions are highly correlated with GDP/pc in all ten countries. This means that countries with better institutions can easily provide better life for their citizens.

The main problem for WB is shown in the next Diagram. Even if *average* of institutional quality in WB are closing to *average* in CEE in last 10 years, the gap

---

[5] Data for Diagram 1 and Diagram 2 are in Appendices in Table 8.

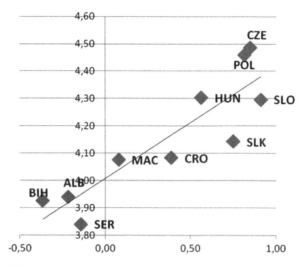

Diagram 2 Relation between institutional quality and competitiveness level (source: World Governance Indicators Database, 2014; The Global Competitiveness Index Data Platform, 2014)

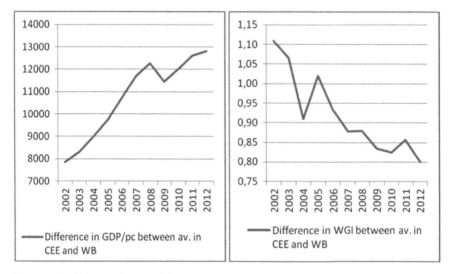

Diagram 3 Widening absolute difference in GDP/pc (*left side*) and shrinking absolute difference in WGI (*right side*) between averages in WB and CEE (source: IMF World Economic Outlook Database, 2014; World Governance Indicators Database, 2014)

between *average* GDP/pc in CEE countries and *average* GDP/pc in WB countries is widening in the last 10 years.[6]

What Diagram 3 indicates is that for WB the speed of reforms is a crucial problem. Since they have not caught the "transition train" in time, it seems that WB

---

[6] Data for Diagram 3 are in Appendices in Table 9.

countries are now indeed "stuck in the transition". The progress they are maybe making is not enough to catch even the countries of New Europe regarding the standard of living in these countries. Too much time has been wasted, and the world now is changing much faster than it was 25 years ago.

5 Conclusions and Implications

Defining and examining the basic characteristics and achievements of reform process in transition countries is indeed a difficult task. Not only because there is no uniqueness about which countries are in transition, but also because the transition process began nearly 25 years ago in most of the countries, and it is still unclear when it will end.

Theoretical background especially stresses the importance of institutional building in transition economies. All transition countries are doomed to gradualist approach as the essence of every reform is building of good institutions. The pure reform of the market without building of institutional environment is meaningless. This was a fundamental error that many transition countries made. Adequate institutional environment provides a framework in which companies, individuals and organizations can operate freely and in which transaction costs are kept to a minimum.

The aim of this study was to examine the position of the Western Balkan countries in the transition process. We compared the quality of institutions measured by six indicators of governance in five Western Balkan countries with five countries of Central Europe which served as a benchmark. Our comparative analysis showed that Western Balkan countries in average still significantly lag behind Central European countries in terms of institutional quality and governance. In that sense, they have a lot work to do in reforms of institutions and the primary task is to improve the rule of law as one of the most important institution of the market system.

It was shown that there is a strong and positive correlation in all ten countries between economic development and institutions and between competitiveness and institutions. This indicates that institutions, defined as the rules of the game, create essential framework for economic growth and development of any nation. Even Tomaš (2013, p. 116) is right when says that today there is more democracy and more market economy than ever before particularly in Bosnia and Herzegovina, we conclude for all five Western Balkan countries in our sample, that progress in transition is far from complete and plenty of job had been left undone, especially in Bosnia and Herzegovina due to its complicated political structure.

Future research might consider the following questions: (1) What can WB countries gain from their European perspective? (2) What is the importance of institutions for overall business infrastructure? and finally (3) Which institutions are crucial for SMEs sector and entrepreneurial development?

Appendices

Table 1 Voice and accountability

Country/territory	1996	1998	2000	2002	2003	2004	2005	2006	2007	2008	2009	2010	2011	2012
Albania	−0.76	−0.45	−0.32	−0.04	0.06	0.03	0.03	0.05	0.09	0.16	0.13	0.11	0.07	0.01
BiH	−0.18	−0.13	−0.25	−0.20	0.14	0.12	0.18	0.16	0.10	−0.03	−0.04	−0.13	−0.22	−0.14
Croatia	−0.16	−0.34	0.47	0.51	0.58	0.64	0.43	0.44	0.48	0.43	0.44	0.43	0.46	0.48
Macedonia, FYR	−0.50	−0.32	−0.43	−0.22	−0.04	−0.14	−0.08	0.13	0.25	0.18	0.15	0.09	−0.01	0.00
Serbia	−1.32	−1.03	−0.73	−0.05	−0.14	−0.17	−0.17	0.18	0.28	0.25	0.32	0.27	0.25	0.17
Average WB	−0.58	−0.46	−0.25	0.00	0.12	0.10	0.08	0.19	0.24	0.20	0.20	0.16	0.11	0.10
Czech Republic	1.00	0.91	0.68	0.98	0.97	0.95	0.88	0.93	0.96	1.00	1.02	1.00	0.99	0.93
Hungary	1.01	1.08	1.16	1.16	1.13	1.14	1.16	1.02	1.04	0.96	0.90	0.90	0.82	0.72
Poland	1.01	1.06	1.06	1.07	0.97	1.00	0.90	0.76	0.84	0.92	1.01	1.03	1.03	1.06
Slovak Republic	0.63	0.68	0.81	0.97	0.92	0.96	0.92	0.92	0.93	0.91	0.86	0.89	0.97	0.96
Slovenia	1.32	1.22	1.10	1.12	1.08	1.09	1.07	1.07	1.06	1.01	1.05	1.04	1.05	0.98
Average CEE	0.99	0.99	0.96	1.06	1.01	1.03	0.99	0.94	0.97	0.96	0.97	0.97	0.97	0.93

Source: World Governance Indicators Database (2014) and calculation of authors

Table 2 Political stability

Country/territory	1996	1998	2000	2002	2003	2004	2005	2006	2007	2008	2009	2010	2011	2012
Albania	-0.43	-0.66	-0.65	-0.39	-0.33	-0.45	-0.49	-0.49	-0.20	-0.03	-0.05	-0.19	-0.29	-0.16
BiH	-0.64	-0.63	-0.59	-0.25	-0.44	-0.03	-0.47	-0.42	-0.60	-0.51	-0.65	-0.70	-0.84	-0.54
Croatia	-0.18	-0.04	0.15	0.53	0.52	0.64	0.43	0.54	0.59	0.55	0.59	0.58	0.60	0.58
Macedonia, FYR	-0.63	-0.88	-0.78	-1.12	-1.03	-0.90	-1.18	-0.74	-0.43	-0.30	-0.29	-0.49	-0.58	-0.44
Serbia	-1.15	-2.19	-1.70	-0.60	-0.61	-0.56	-0.77	-0.56	-0.61	-0.56	-0.49	-0.44	-0.30	-0.22
Average WB	-0.60	-0.88	-0.71	-0.37	-0.38	-0.26	-0.50	-0.33	-0.25	-0.17	-0.18	-0.25	-0.28	-0.16
Czech Republic	1.04	0.81	0.26	0.95	0.85	0.63	0.91	1.01	0.98	1.01	0.88	0.96	1.10	1.04
Hungary	0.91	1.12	0.82	1.18	1.11	0.81	0.98	0.96	0.72	0.72	0.52	0.67	0.74	0.67
Poland	0.72	0.74	0.22	0.65	0.54	0.11	0.34	0.33	0.64	0.86	0.90	0.99	1.06	1.03
Slovak Republic	0.81	1.08	0.57	0.85	0.91	0.54	0.85	0.76	1.01	1.07	0.88	1.02	0.96	1.06
Slovenia	1.21	1.13	0.79	1.21	1.15	1.03	1.05	1.06	1.07	1.12	0.90	0.83	0.94	0.92
Average CEE	0.94	0.98	0.53	0.97	0.91	0.62	0.83	0.82	0.89	0.96	0.82	0.89	0.96	0.94

Source: World Governance Indicators Database (2014) and calculation of authors

Table 3 Government effectiveness

Country/territory	1996	1998	2000	2002	2003	2004	2005	2006	2007	2008	2009	2010	2011	2012
Albania	-0.80	-0.69	-0.83	-0.57	-0.61	-0.44	-0.63	-0.46	-0.38	-0.35	-0.24	-0.27	-0.20	-0.28
BiH	-1.26	-1.08	-0.86	-0.97	-0.77	-0.57	-0.72	-0.60	-0.81	-0.59	-0.70	-0.73	-0.76	-0.47
Croatia	0.07	0.06	0.31	0.34	0.38	0.47	0.48	0.56	0.47	0.57	0.61	0.63	0.56	0.70
Macedonia, FYR	0.62	0.62	0.62	0.97	0.89	0.91	0.97	1.08	0.90	1.01	0.89	0.91	0.93	0.92
Serbia	-0.92	-0.85	-0.85	-0.55	-0.62	-0.17	-0.31	-0.20	-0.22	-0.19	-0.04	-0.05	-0.10	-0.11
Average WB	**-0.46**	**-0.39**	**-0.32**	**-0.16**	**-0.15**	**0.04**	**-0.04**	**0.08**	**-0.01**	**0.09**	**0.11**	**0.10**	**0.09**	**0.15**
Czech Republic	0.84	0.94	0.96	1.02	0.96	0.90	0.80	0.88	0.72	0.71	0.68	0.67	0.68	0.62
Hungary	-0.62	-0.62	-0.78	-0.50	-0.33	-0.13	-0.28	-0.10	-0.20	-0.02	-0.09	-0.15	-0.11	-0.07
Poland	0.78	0.67	0.60	0.49	0.55	0.49	0.48	0.42	0.40	0.48	0.52	0.64	0.62	0.66
Slovak Republic	0.57	0.54	0.57	0.57	0.68	0.91	0.94	0.92	0.74	0.87	0.86	0.83	0.83	0.83
Slovenia	0.89	0.79	0.73	0.90	1.07	0.97	0.92	0.98	0.94	1.19	1.16	1.03	0.99	1.02
Average CEE	**0.49**	**0.46**	**0.41**	**0.50**	**0.59**	**0.63**	**0.57**	**0.62**	**0.52**	**0.65**	**0.63**	**0.60**	**0.60**	**0.61**

Source: World Governance Indicators Database (2014) and calculation of authors

Table 4 Regulatory quality

Country/territory	1996	1998	2000	2002	2003	2004	2005	2006	2007	2008	2009	2010	2011	2012
Albania	-0.42	-0.19	-0.26	-0.25	-0.47	-0.16	-0.30	-0.09	0.07	0.15	0.25	0.23	0.24	0.17
BiH	-0.70	-0.82	-0.48	-0.56	-0.48	-0.19	-0.49	-0.42	-0.26	-0.16	-0.10	-0.10	-0.04	-0.06
Croatia	-0.16	-0.10	-0.04	0.30	0.48	0.54	0.49	0.38	0.46	0.49	0.55	0.55	0.52	0.44
Macedonia, FYR	-0.25	-0.14	-0.12	-0.20	-0.19	-0.04	-0.19	-0.02	0.12	0.22	0.26	0.28	0.33	0.35
Serbia	-0.74	-0.85	-0.89	-0.65	-0.60	-0.44	-0.55	-0.45	-0.34	-0.29	-0.12	-0.02	0.03	-0.08
Average WB	**-0.45**	**-0.42**	**-0.36**	**-0.27**	**-0.25**	**-0.06**	**-0.21**	**-0.12**	**0.01**	**0.08**	**0.17**	**0.19**	**0.22**	**0.16**
Czech Republic	1.02	0.92	0.73	1.19	1.18	1.08	1.12	1.11	1.03	1.16	1.33	1.30	1.21	1.06
Hungary	0.88	1.01	1.07	1.31	1.12	1.18	1.11	1.21	1.19	1.19	1.08	1.02	1.03	0.97
Poland	0.65	0.68	0.73	0.75	0.72	0.81	0.81	0.71	0.77	0.82	0.95	0.99	0.94	0.96
Slovak Republic	0.52	0.44	0.54	0.94	0.96	1.16	1.18	1.14	1.03	1.12	1.06	1.00	1.00	1.03
Slovenia	1.03	1.05	0.66	0.86	0.87	0.86	0.83	0.78	0.80	0.83	0.91	0.75	0.68	0.61
Average VG	**0.82**	**0.82**	**0.75**	**1.01**	**0.97**	**1.02**	**1.01**	**0.99**	**0.96**	**1.02**	**1.07**	**1.01**	**0.97**	**0.93**

Source: World Governance Indicators Database (2014) and calculation of authors

Table 5 Rule of law

Country/territory	1996	1998	2000	2002	2003	2004	2005	2006	2007	2008	2009	2010	2011	2012
Albania	-0.93	-1.20	-1.24	-0.92	-0.88	-0.76	-0.81	-0.73	-0.70	-0.64	-0.53	-0.44	-0.49	-0.57
BiH	-0.26	-0.64	-0.64	-0.67	-0.69	-0.49	-0.56	-0.50	-0.48	-0.41	-0.36	-0.37	-0.35	-0.23
Croatia	-0.61	-0.34	0.01	-0.17	-0.05	0.05	0.09	-0.05	0.04	0.08	0.14	0.17	0.18	0.21
Macedonia, FYR	-0.41	-0.48	-0.66	-0.63	-0.56	-0.25	-0.37	-0.56	-0.46	-0.37	-0.27	-0.29	-0.26	-0.24
Serbia	-1.28	-1.33	-1.34	-0.97	-0.94	-0.74	-0.91	-0.56	-0.50	-0.53	-0.44	-0.40	-0.32	-0.39
Average WB	**-0.70**	**-0.80**	**-0.78**	**-0.67**	**-0.62**	**-0.44**	**-0.51**	**-0.48**	**-0.42**	**-0.37**	**-0.29**	**-0.26**	**-0.25**	**-0.24**
Czech Republic	0.84	0.84	0.60	0.83	0.84	0.74	0.82	0.84	0.86	0.89	0.94	0.93	1.02	1.01
Hungary	0.83	0.79	0.85	0.93	0.89	0.89	0.83	0.96	0.92	0.89	0.76	0.75	0.74	0.60
Poland	0.67	0.76	0.65	0.63	0.51	0.40	0.42	0.35	0.37	0.51	0.60	0.66	0.75	0.74
Slovak Republic	0.15	0.18	0.29	0.24	0.33	0.50	0.52	0.52	0.45	0.57	0.50	0.53	0.57	0.46
Slovenia	1.05	1.22	1.01	0.96	0.95	0.92	0.86	0.87	0.88	0.98	1.06	0.98	1.04	0.98
Average VG	**0.71**	**0.76**	**0.68**	**0.72**	**0.70**	**0.69**	**0.69**	**0.71**	**0.70**	**0.77**	**0.77**	**0.77**	**0.83**	**0.76**

Source: World Governance Indicators Database (2014) and calculation of authors

Table 6 Control of corruption

Country/territory	1996	1998	2000	2002	2003	2004	2005	2006	2007	2008	2009	2010	2011	2012
Albania	−1.09	−1.01	−0.82	−0.86	−0.77	−0.67	−0.75	−0.81	−0.66	−0.55	−0.49	−0.49	−0.65	−0.72
BiH	−0.35	−0.28	−0.49	−0.35	−0.30	−0.31	−0.20	−0.29	−0.38	−0.36	−0.37	−0.32	−0.31	−0.30
Croatia	−0.82	−0.72	−0.21	0.25	0.16	0.20	0.14	0.09	0.08	−0.04	−0.10	−0.03	0.01	−0.04
Macedonia, FYR	−0.96	−0.67	−0.66	−0.88	−0.66	−0.49	−0.44	−0.37	−0.35	−0.17	−0.10	−0.06	−0.04	0.02
Serbia	−1.03	−1.08	−1.12	−0.91	−0.47	−0.48	−0.38	−0.28	−0.35	−0.30	−0.31	−0.29	−0.25	−0.31
Average WB	**−0.85**	**−0.75**	**−0.66**	**−0.55**	**−0.41**	**−0.35**	**−0.33**	**−0.33**	**−0.33**	**−0.28**	**−0.28**	**−0.24**	**−0.25**	**−0.27**
Czech Republic	0.65	0.55	0.08	0.36	0.44	0.38	0.46	0.30	0.23	0.27	0.33	0.26	0.30	0.23
Hungary	0.58	0.65	0.69	0.52	0.60	0.65	0.62	0.61	0.56	0.38	0.34	0.25	0.32	0.28
Poland	0.54	0.67	0.55	0.33	0.38	0.11	0.22	0.17	0.19	0.35	0.37	0.41	0.49	0.59
Slovak Republic	0.36	0.25	0.15	−0.10	0.31	0.39	0.49	0.40	0.30	0.30	0.23	0.24	0.24	0.07
Slovenia	1.32	1.30	0.77	0.72	0.86	1.02	0.89	1.02	0.98	0.91	1.02	0.85	0.90	0.81
Average VG	**0.69**	**0.68**	**0.45**	**0.37**	**0.52**	**0.51**	**0.54**	**0.50**	**0.45**	**0.44**	**0.46**	**0.40**	**0.45**	**0.39**

Source: World Governance Indicators Database (2014) and calculation of authors

Table 7 Average of six indicators of institutional quality

Country/territory	1996	1998	2000	2002	2003	2004	2005	2006	2007	2008	2009	2010	2011	2012
VACC	−0.58	−0.46	−0.25	0.00	0.12	0.10	0.08	0.19	0.24	0.20	0.20	0.16	0.11	0.10
PS	−0.60	−0.88	−0.71	−0.37	−0.38	−0.26	−0.50	−0.33	−0.25	−0.17	−0.18	−0.25	−0.28	−0.16
GE	−0.46	−0.39	−0.32	−0.16	−0.15	0.04	−0.04	0.08	−0.01	0.09	0.11	0.10	0.09	0.15
RQ	−0.45	−0.42	−0.36	−0.27	−0.25	−0.06	−0.21	−0.12	0.01	0.08	0.17	0.19	0.22	0.16
ROL	−0.70	−0.80	−0.78	−0.67	−0.62	−0.44	−0.51	−0.48	−0.42	−0.37	−0.29	−0.26	−0.25	−0.24
COC	−0.85	−0.75	−0.66	−0.55	−0.41	−0.35	−0.33	−0.33	−0.33	−0.28	−0.28	−0.24	−0.25	−0.27
Average all 6 averages—WB	**−0.61**	**−0.62**	**−0.51**	**−0.34**	**−0.28**	**−0.16**	**−0.25**	**−0.17**	**−0.13**	**−0.08**	**−0.05**	**−0.05**	**−0.06**	**−0.04**
VACC	0.99	0.99	0.96	1.06	1.01	1.03	0.99	0.94	0.97	0.96	0.97	0.97	0.97	0.93
PS	0.94	0.98	0.53	0.97	0.91	0.62	0.83	0.82	0.89	0.96	0.82	0.89	0.96	0.94
GE	0.49	0.46	0.41	0.50	0.59	0.63	0.57	0.62	0.52	0.65	0.63	0.60	0.60	0.61
RQ	0.82	0.82	0.75	1.01	0.97	1.02	1.01	0.99	0.96	1.02	1.07	1.01	0.97	0.93
ROL	0.71	0.76	0.68	0.72	0.70	0.69	0.69	0.71	0.70	0.77	0.77	0.77	0.83	0.76
COC	0.69	0.68	0.45	0.37	0.52	0.51	0.54	0.50	0.45	0.44	0.46	0.40	0.45	0.39
Average all 6 averages—CEE	**0.77**	**0.78**	**0.63**	**0.77**	**0.78**	**0.75**	**0.77**	**0.76**	**0.75**	**0.80**	**0.78**	**0.78**	**0.80**	**0.76**

Source: World Governance Indicators Database (2014) and calculation of authors

Table 8 Three years average of institutional quality, GDP/pc and competitiveness level in the Western Balkans and Central European Economies

Country/ territory	Overall institutional quality (average 2010, 2011, 2012)	GDP/pc PPP international dollars (average 2011, 2012, 2013)	Competitiveness level (average 2011, 2012, 2013)
Albania	−0.218	7,991.315	3.940
BiH	−0.366	8,150.586	3.927
Croatia	0.391	17,678.714	4.083
Macedonia, FYR	0.079	10,539.068	4.077
Serbia	−0.142	10,843.902	3.840
Czech Republic	0.849	27,043.467	4.487
Hungary	0.563	19,575.442	4.303
Poland	0.813	20,507.835	4.460
Slovak Republic	0.750	24,037.894	4.143
Slovenia	0.911	27,800.035	4.297

Source: World Governance Indicators Database (2014); IMF World Economic Outlook Database (2014); The Global Competitiveness Index Data Platform and calculation of authors

Table 9 Absolute difference in GDP/pc and absolute difference in WGI between averages in Western Balkans and Central European Economies

Country/territory	2002	2003	2004	2005	2006	2007	2008	2009	2010	2011	2012
Albania	4,444	4,768	4,993	5,376	5,833	6,312	6,876	7,131	7,454	7,774	7,997
Bosnia and Herzegovina	4,924	5,175	5,571	6,044	6,601	7,196	7,757	7,602	7,764	8,031	8,127
Croatia	12,421	13,350	14,188	15,254	16,506	17,818	18,553	17,417	17,270	17,665	17,618
FYR Macedonia	6,328	6,622	7,050	7,600	8,211	8,926	9,539	9,505	9,877	10,336	10,465
Serbia	6,474	6,786	7,598	8,315	8,911	9,679	10,288	10,044	10,309	10,725	10,722
Average GDP pc WB	**6,918**	**7,340**	**7,880**	**8,518**	**9,212**	**9,986**	**10,603**	**10,340**	**10,535**	**10,906**	**10,986**
Average all six WGI indicators—WB	**−0.34**	**−0.28**	**−0.16**	**−0.25**	**−0.17**	**−0.13**	**−0.08**	**−0.05**	**−0.05**	**−0.06**	**−0.04**
Czech Republic	17,047	18,049	19,476	21,180	23,294	25,195	26,243	25,045	25,877	26,916	27,000
Hungary	13,616	14,469	15,740	16,967	18,208	18,732	19,309	18,166	18,660	19,394	19,497
Poland	11,072	11,737	12,698	13,568	14,863	16,306	17,481	17,893	18,796	19,843	20,562
Slovak Republic	12,694	13,553	14,642	16,060	17,903	20,298	21,867	20,895	22,024	23,308	24,142
Slovenia	19,449	20,409	21,843	23,434	25,494	27,894	29,403	26,979	27,452	28,145	27,837
Average GDP pc CEE	**14,776**	**15,643**	**16,880**	**18,242**	**19,952**	**21,685**	**22,861**	**21,796**	**22,562**	**23,521**	**23,808**
Average all six WGI indicators—CEE	**0.77**	**0.78**	**0.75**	**0.77**	**0.76**	**0.75**	**0.80**	**0.78**	**0.78**	**0.80**	**0.76**
Difference in WGI between av. in CEE and WB	*1.11*	*1.06*	*0.91*	*1.02*	*0.93*	*0.88*	*0.88*	*0.83*	*0.83*	*0.86*	*0.80*
Difference in GDP/pc between av. in CEE and WB	*7,857*	*8,303*	*9,000*	*9,724*	*10,740*	*11,699*	*12,258*	*11,456*	*12,027*	*12,615*	*12,822*

Source: World Governance Indicators Database (2014); IMF World Economic Outlook Database (2014)

References

Acemoglu, D., Johnson, S., & Robinson, J. (2004). *Institutions as the fundamentals cause of long-run growth* (NBER Working Paper 10481). Cambridge.

Acemoglu, D., & Robinson, J. (2010). The role of institutions in growth and development. *Review of Economics and Institutions, 1*(2). doi:10.5202/rei.v1i2.1, ISSN:2038-1379.

Beck, T., & Laeven, L. (2005). *Institution building and growth in transition economies* (World Bank Policy Research Working Paper 3657).

Bevan, A., & Estrin, S. (2004). The determinants of foreign direct investment into European transition economies. *Journal of Comparative Economics, 32*, 775–787.

Brown, A. N. (1999). Introduction. In A. N. Brown (Ed.), *When is transition over?* (pp. 1–12). Kalamazoo, MI: W.E. Upjohn Institute for Employment Research.

Campos, N. (2000). *Context is everything: Measuring institutional change in transition economies* (Policy Research Working Paper 2269). World Bank.

Dana, L. P., & Dana, T. (2003). Management and enterprise development in post-communist economies. *International Journal of Management and Enterprise Development, 1*(I), 45–54.

Dollar, D., & Kraay, A. (2003). *Institutions, trade, and growth* (Policy Research Working Paper). The World Bank Development Research Group.

EBRD. (2013). *Transition report 2013, stuck in transition*. London: European Bank for Reconstruction and Development.

Efendic, A., Pugh, G., & Adnett, N. (2010). Institutions and economic performance: System GMM modelling of institutional effects in transition. On-line publication: AAB-RIINVEST University in Pristina, Kosovo. Available at: http://www.riinvestinstitute.org/pdf/Efendic_et_al.pdf

Eicher, T., & Leukert, A. (2009). Institutions and economic performance: Endogeneity and parameter heterogeneity. *Journal of Money, Credit and Banking, 41*(1), 197–219. doi:10.1111/j.1538-4616.2008.00193.x.

Estrin, S., Hanousek, J., Kocenda, E., & Svejnar, J. (2009). *Effects of privatization and ownership in transition economies* (Working Paper 4881). The World Bank Development Economics Department.

Fischer, S., & Gelb, A. (1991). The process of socialist economic transformation. *Journal of Economic Perspectives, 5*(4), 91–105.

Fischer, S., & Sahay, R. (2004). *Transition economies: The role of institutions and initial conditions*. IMF. Preliminary Draft.

Hall, R., & Jones, C. (1998). *Why do some countries produce so much more output per worker than others* (NBER Working Paper 6564). Cambridge.

Havrylyshyn, O., & Wolf, T. (1999). Determinants of growth in transition countries. *IMF Finance and Development, 36*(2), 12–15.

International Monetary Fund. (2000). *Transition economies: An IMF perspective on progress and prospects* (Issue Briefs 00/08).

Kaufman, D., Kraay, A., & Mastruzzi, M. (2010). *The worldwide governance indicators methodology and analytical issues* (Policy Research Working Papers 5430). World Bank.

Keefer, P., & Knack, S. (2005). Social capital, social norms and the new institutional economics. In C. Ménard & M. Shirley (Eds.), *The handbook of the new institutional economics* (pp. 701–726). Dordecht, The Netherlands: Springer.

Knack, S., & Keefer, P. (1995). Institutions and economic performance: Cross country test using alternative institutional measures. *Economics and Politics, 7*(3), 208–227.

Kolodko, G. W. (1999). Transition to a market economy and sustained growth. Implications for the post-Washington consensus. *Communist and Post-Communist Studies, 32*, 233–261.

Kołodko, G. W. (2002). *Globalization and catching-up in transition economies*. Rochester: University of Rochester Press.

Kornai, J. (1999). Reforming the welfare state in postsocialist economies. In A. Brown (Ed.), *When is transition over?* (pp. 99–114). Kalamazoo, MI: W.E. Upjohn Institute for Employment Research.

La Porta, R., de Silanes, F. L., Schleifer, A., & Vishny, R. (1998). *The quality of government* (NBER Working Paper 6727). Cambridge.

Lavigne, M. (1999). What is still missing? In A. Brown (Ed.), *When is transition over?* (pp. 13–38). Kalamazoo, MI: W.E. Upjohn Institute for Employment Research.

Murrell, P. (1996). How far has the transition progressed? *Journal of Economic Perspectives, 10*, 25–44.

Murrell, P. (2003). Institutions and firms in transition economies. Draft prepared as a chapter of the Handbook of new institutional economics.

North, D. (1990). *Institutions, institutional change and economic performance.* Cambridge: Cambridge University Press.

North, D. (1997, March). The contribution of the new institutional economics to an understanding of the transition problem. In *1st Annual lecture UNU WIDER.*

Petković, S., & Berberović, S. (2013). *Ekonomika i upravljanje malim i srednjim preduzećima.* Banja Luka: Ekonomski fakultet.

Popov, V. (2007). Shock therapy versus gradualism reconsidered: Lessons from transition economies after 15 years of reforms. *Comparative Economic Studies, 49*, 1–31.

Ramadani, V., & Dana, L. P. (2013). The state of entrepreneurship in the Balkans: Evidence from selected countries. In V. Ramadani & R. C. Schneider (Eds.), *Entrepreneurship in the Balkans.* Berlin: Springer.

Rodrik, D., Subramanian, A., & Trebbi, F. (2002). *Institutions rule: The primacy of institutions over geography and integration in economic development* (NBER Working Paper 9305). Cambridge.

Roland, G. (2000). *Transition and economics: Politics, markets, and firms.* Cambridge, MA: MIT Press.

Roland, G. (2002). The political economy of transition. *Journal of Economic Perspectives, 16*(1), 29–50.

Roland, G., & Verdier, T. (1999). *Law enforcement and transition* (Working Paper No. 262). William Davidson Institute.

Sachs, J. (2012, March) What I did in Russia, Personal website. http://jeffsachs.org/2012/03/what-i-did-in-russia/

Stiglitz, J. (1999). Whiter reform, ten years of the transition. Key note address. In *World Bank annual conference on development economics.*

Streeten, P. (1996). Governance. In M. G. Quibria & J. M. Dowling (Eds.), *Current issues in economic development. An Asian perspective* (pp. 27–66). Oxford: Oxford University Press.

Svejnar, J. (2002). Transition economies: Performance and challenges. *The Journal of Economic Perspectives, 16*(1), 3–28.

Tešić, J. (2010). Institutional environment and foreign direct investment in the Western Balkans. In S. Milford & I. Tarosy (Eds.), *The Western Balkans—Lessons from the past and future prospects: A view from the Danube Region.* Institute for the Danube Region and Central Europe and IDResearch Ltd.

Tomaš, R. (2013). Causes of slow and inefficient transition of economy of Bosnia and Herzegovina and possibilities for its improvement. *Poslovna izvrsnost,* god. VII, br. I. Ekonomski fakultet Zagreb, pp. 99–119.

World Bank. (1994). *Governance. The World Bank's experience.* Washington, DC.

World Bank. (1998). *Beyond the Washington consensus: Institutions matter.* Washington, DC.

World Bank. (2002). *Transition the first ten years analysis and lessons for Eastern Europe and the former Soviet Union.* Washington, DC.

Žarković, V. (2012). *Privatizacija u Centralnoj i Istocnoj Evropi.* Banja Luka: Ekonomski fakultet.

Data sources

The Global Competitiveness Index Data Platform. http://www.weforum.org/issues/competitive ness-0/gci2012-data-platform/

World Governance Indicators Database, February 2014. Official web page http://info.worldbank. org/governance/wgi/index.aspx#home

World Economic Outlook Database, International Monetary Fund. http://www.imf.org/external/ pubs/ft/weo/2013/02/weodata/index.aspx

Part II
Management, Succession and Financial Issues

To Be or Not to Be in a Family Business: The Case of Eight Countries in South-Eastern European Region

Jaka Vadnjal and Predrag Ljubotina

Abstract Family businesses account for a major share of small-sized firms in several economies. Taking into account the global economic situation this trend is expected to continue. With the goal of better understanding the process of transferring the business to the next generation, which ensures a long-term success, expectations of student's with family business background were investigated. This particular research addresses the issue of an individual's perception of entrepreneurship and the related factors that influence individual's decision on whether to build a career as an employee, a successor of family business or as an independent entrepreneur. Some Western and some South-Eastern European were separately analysed population for the purpose of comparative study. The results show important differences between investigated populations. It has been anticipated that differences are caused by historical, cultural and educational backgrounds. This challenging area is raising a lot of sub-questions for possible future research.

Keywords Family business • Succession • Independence • Career decisions

1 Introduction

In the search for more entrepreneurs in the sense of restructuring of the economy, career choices intentions of young people and possible parallel motives to become entrepreneurs are intensively investigated topics in contemporary research in entrepreneurship and broadly in social science. A number of studies conducted among students investigate student's career choice intention after leaving the college or university. Different pieces of research go into exploration of various personal and psychological characteristics and emotions that influence the career choice decision within the context of the social environment. Intentional founders for example, strive for independence and have high levels of innovation and self-fulfillment motives (Fisher, Reuber, & Dyke, 1993; Kolvereid, 1996; Krueger, 2003).

J. Vadnjal (✉) • P. Ljubotina
GEA College – Faculty for Entrepreneurship, Kidričevo nabrežje 2, 6330 Piran, Slovenia
e-mail: jaka.vadnjal@gea-college.si; predrag.ljubotina@gea-college.si

© Springer International Publishing Switzerland 2015
L.-P. Dana, V. Ramadani (eds.), *Family Businesses in Transition Economies*,
DOI 10.1007/978-3-319-14209-8_5

Despite of these findings, there is gap for some deeper understanding of career choice of successors of family business which are traditionally in most cases expected to join their parents' business and to take it over in some undefined time horizon (Miller, Steier, & LeBreton-Miller, 2003). Those are important and often hard decisions which have to be done no later but after their studies. However, this decision is preferred to be made even before so, the choosing of studies is already in the line with the needs of the business. The group of young people with family business background has in comparison to their colleagues, even harder situation to decide because of the following three options they have: (1) find a job elsewhere, (2) establishing their own business or (3) taking on the role of a successor in the family business. Another argument which definitely supports the need for similar surveys is the fact that, when speaking about succession intention, there is often a huge gap between expectations of potential successor and expectations of a parent, family business owner. Some evidence shows, the expectations of their parents that children will continue family business are three times more frequent comparing to possible successor (Tan, Wong, & Choong, 2013), which confirms the idea of the large gap between the viewpoints of the two generations.

So far, there have been no measuring instruments developed in the research literature that would deal directly with this topic (Birley, 2002). Given the world-wide economic and social relevance provided by family businesses, understanding entrepreneurial motives and attitudes among students, potential successors, is of crucial importance to secure long term sustainability of family firms (Astrachan & Shanker, 2003). Taking into consideration this paradigm, the research including ten countries in Western Europe was carried out (Zellweger, Philipp, & Halter, 2011) with an ambition to fill the revealed gap by investigating the determinants of career choice intentions of students with family business background.

A similar survey among students of the South-Eastern (from her after SE) European universities was conducted. The aim of the study of the research results was to replicate the mentioned study and to provide mutual benchmarking of the results and, on this basis to show the compared situation of the SE and Western Europe. The main purpose of the research work was to enable an insight into the motives of potential successors for their career decisions and moreover, on this basis propose measures to family business founders, guidance counselors and educational organizations responsible for facilitating the process of transition between generations of the family business.

Assuming that there are differences between European west and east which are historically driven, it can be assumed that this fact could influence young generation and their perception of family business and entrepreneurship in general. The main ambition of the study was to perform a survey among students at universities of selected SE European countries and to find these differences between the three groups of students.

2 Literature Review

Examining antecedents for career choice intentions is based on theory of planned behavior (Ajzen, 1991; Fishbein & Ajzen, 1975). In several pieces of research it is pointed out that perceived behavioral control has a major significant impact on career intent of antecedents in family business (Krueger, Reilly, & Carsrud, 2000). Behavioral control by itself consists from locus of control, which deals with external factors that may have impact on behavior, and self-efficacy, which takes into account person's internal or intrinsic factors. To obtain credible and reliable results both parameters need adequate measurement (Ajzen, 2002). An individual can possess high level of internal locus of control, but at the same time doubt on really being capable of performing a specific task (Bandura, 1997). Self-efficiency is affected by performance and locus of control by life experiences (Dyal, 1984). Self-efficacy in the context of this particular research lays in the conviction that an individual is able to execute a certain type of behavior (Bandura, 1994). In accordance with these claims and reference research of career choice intentions of students with family business background (Zellweger et al., 2011) it can be expected that higher level of internal locus of control will result with higher level of preference of founding a new business compared with succession intention.

Self-efficacy parameter provides information about the ease or difficulty of performing the intended behavior (Ajzen, 2002). Family firms and parents as role models may well be an important source of entrepreneurial self-efficacy (Davidsson, 1995). Consequently, it determines the strength of a belief that an individual is capable of successfully performing the intended task or behavior (Chen, Greene, & Crick, 1998). High levels of self-efficacy reinforce efforts for achievement and promote quick recovery from failure (Bandura, 1997). High level of self-efficacy contributes to the probability of establishing a new company and to create products and networks (Stinchcombe, 1965). As personal motives are important for career choice decision, two additional parameters were measured. Theory of planned behavior assumes that if the outcome of behavior is expected to satisfy an individual motive, the probability of performing that behavior will be higher. Independence and innovation are described as two highly important factors (Carter et al., 2003).

Independence motive expresses one's desire for freedom (Schein, 1978). The innovation motive on the other hand stands for an individual's intention of accomplishing something completely new (Carter et al., 2003). Among the most frequent reasons why offspring intends to succeed the family firm is to be in control and to be the boss. This leads to the conclusion that succession intention is also related to the independence motive (Vadnjal, 2008). Thus, it can be expected that founding a new business best accomplishes and satisfies the independence motive. Consequently, this gives the offspring an opportunity to be completely free and to fulfil his or her dreams. It is expected that the independence motive is least accomplished with the decision for employee career (hired labor force), which places succession in the position of somehow middle choice.

Our last investigated career intent driver is innovation motive, which has a great influence on career motives of founder entrepreneurs (Carter et al., 2003). Originality and open mind are important influencing factors for starting a new business (Bird, 1988). Founders tend to search for new solutions to problems and new products, organization models or market opportunities (Baker, Miner, & Eesley, 2003). In this context it is expected the future career of a founder (of own business) to be more preferable than the succession career. The employee career was expected to be on the last place when speaking about innovation motive due to the fact that it gives least possibilities for originality in all aspects.

For the purpose of comparison and benchmarking the four hypotheses are kept identical as in reference study (Zellweger et al., 2011).

H1: Higher level of internal locus of control results in preferring founding intention to the succession, and the succession to the employment (Ajzen, 2002; Bandura, 1997).

H2: Higher level of self-efficiency results in preferring founding intention to the succession, and the succession to the employment (Chen et al., 1998; Davidsson, 1995).

H3: Higher level of independence motive results in preferring founding intention to the succession, and the succession to the employment (Carter et al., 2003; Vadnjal, 2008).

H4: Higher level of innovation motive results in preferring founding intention to the succession, and the succession to the employment (Baker et al., 2003; Bird, 1988).

3 Methodology and Sampling

We use multinomial logistic regression as a method for data analysis. The method is selected based on the fact that the dependent variable is categorical, with three possible outcomes. The effects of the independent variables on each of the outcomes are compared to a central category which is in all hypotheses the succession intention so, it has been used it also as a reference category for multinomial logistic regression (Gregory, Rutherford, Oswald, & Gardiner, 2005). Students were asked to declare how they see their career intention (1) within 5 years from the completion of their studies and (2) after that period. The possibilities were three: an employee, a successor or a founder.

There are four independent values: locus of control, self-efficacy, independence motive and innovation motive. In addition to these, two control variables were used, gender and feelings towards family business. In order to measure each independent value a set of questions was used and for each question a Likert six point scale ranging from "very unimportant" to "very important". Six-point scale was utilized in order to avoid neutral decisions.

Benchmarking study was conducted on 36,451 students which participated in survey on college entrepreneurship conducted in 2006 (Zellweger et al., 2011). 9,904 (27.2 %) of them had family business background and 5,363 (14.7 %) students did indicate their career choice. 609 (1.7 %) students intended to follow their parent's footsteps in family firm, while 1,808 (5.0 %) would start a new business and 2,946 (8.1 %) planned to become employees.

The data for this study were collected at four Slovenian faculties (24.5 % of the total number of respondents) and nine faculties from SE European countries: Serbia (13.6 %), Macedonia (6.4 %), Bosnia and Hercegovina (5.6 %), Bulgaria (8.7 %), Croatia (14.1 %), Albania (22.0 %) and Romania (5.1 %). The research was conducted in the spring semester of 2012. In all countries 2,218 students were involved in total, coming from very different fields of studies: approximately half of them were business students while others were future engineers (mechanical, chemistry, and metallurgy), language school students and social science students. 996 of them had family business background which represented for 44.9 % of the whole sample. In all participating countries, the sampling approach was an opportunistic one: responses were collected in classrooms as a part of the study process, being aware that this approach will in the end result in possible biases of responding and limited generalizability of findings. The respondent's structure is shown in Table 1.

The dependent variable in the model (Y) is categorical with three possible dimensions which suggested multinomial logistic regression model as the most suitable statistical method (Gregory et al., 2005). Linear regression model was used specified as:

$$Y = A0 + B1*X1 + B2*X2 + B3*X3 + B4*X4 + \varepsilon \qquad (1)$$

Y is observed categorical value of dependent variable, A0 is the population intercept, Bi is the partial regression slope parameter and ε is the error associated with prediction for Y. In this model there are four predictors (Xi) and four regression weights (Bi).

It is assumed that no pairs of predictors are correlated to such an extent as to either cause the singularity of the correlation matrix, or to destabilize the estimation of model parameters (population intercept, partial regression slopes). Since all Pearson correlations are well below the 0.60 cut-off, there was indication of

Table 1 Respondent's structure

Number surveyed		2,218	
Family business background		996	44.9 %
Gender	Male	635	63.8 %
	Female	361	36.2 %
Family entrepreneurs	Father	488	49.0 %
	Mother	107	10.7 %
	Both	401	40.3 %

Source: Own research 2012

multicollinearity. To support this claim variation inflation factor (VIF) was calculated for both groups of students. All VIF factors were bellow 1,3 which is well
below the suggested maximal cut-off of 10.0 (Hair, Black, Babin, & Anderson,
2009) or 5.0 suggested with more conservative approach (Daniel, 2011). All VIF
factors were between 1.0 and 1.3 which is close to ideal value of 1.0.

4 Findings

Table 2 reports the results of multinomial regression analysis for three groups of
students with succession intention as reference category. The Western European
data are taken from the reference survey (Zellweger et al., 2011).

4.1 Locus of Control

The results show that students with higher level of internal locus of control will
more likely select employment than succession intention in both regions. On the
other hand students in SE Europe will more likely decide for new business than for
succession. In Western European countries there is no noticeable difference
between the two categories. In SE European countries the opposite result are
identified. Opposing finding for the locus of control for students from east deserves
further investigation. Higher level of internal locus of control should result with
more desire for control according to some previous findings (Krueger, 2003). It may

Table 2 Multinomial logistic regression coefficients

		Western Europe (2011)		SE Europe (2012)	
		B	Exp(B)	B	Exp(B)
Employed	Locus	0.198	1.219	0.069	1.071
	Self-efficacy	−0.154	0.857	−0.548	0.578
	Independence	−0.898	0.407	0.096	1.100
	Innovation	0.039	1.040	0.205	1.227
	Gender	0.140	1.150	0.298	1.347
	Feelings	−1.257	0.285	0.280	1.323
New business	Locus	0.014	1.014	−0.069	0.934
	Self-efficacy	0.108	1.114	−0.214	0.808
	Independence	0.173	1.189	0.343	1.409
	Innovation	0.327	1.387	0.419	1.520
	Gender	−0.152	0.859	0.743	2.103
	Feelings	−0.970	0.379	−0.104	0.901

Source: Zellweger et al. (2011), own research 2012

be suspected that a more collectivist rather that individualist culture prevents in SE Europe prevents locus of control to take place as it does elsewhere.

4.2 Self-Efficacy

In the case of self-efficacy in the SE European region the hypothesis can be partly confirmed. It can be observed that SE students will more likely select succession of family business than employment or new start-up. The main difference comparing to the reference study is that students will more likely choose a career of a founder than a succession of a family business. The reason for higher level of preference to family business succession may lie in the fact that family business have not had long tradition in the SE European countries and may still be felt as "the best thing which can happen in an individual's life and professional career" thus, a critical view on this is still being missed.

4.3 Independence Motive

In the case of independence motive the hypothesis can be confirmed completely for Western students. There is a different result from SEE students, where it can be observed that students with higher levels of independence motivation will more likely select employment before succession of family business. It has been suspected that the reason for this difference lays in the fact that entrepreneurship in still a very young perspective in SE Europe which means that entrepreneurs are still mostly founders of their family firms because transition processes on the next generation has not really become yet. Majority of (family) businesses are still owned and managed by the first generation. Potential successors find it too difficult to be creative and to realize their own vision due to the fact that it is almost impossible to change anything in the business practice and strategy while parents are still active in the family firm.

4.4 Innovation Motive

In the Western countries it can be observed that there is no noticeable difference between the two possibilities when about succession versus employment options are discussed. In SE region the hypothesis can be completely confirmed. This difference may have to do with the fact, that in countries with longer tradition, several family businesses often already are managed and owned by second or even third generation of the family. Thus, Western European family businesses are generally more mature in some later life-cycle stage which may lead to a conclusion that skills to tackle managerial and ownership issues prevail from innovativeness which is more significant for start-ups and businesses in their earlier stages.

4.5 Hypothesis Confirmation

In Table 3 an overview of our results compared to results of the reference survey in Western European countries in the context of the hypotheses is presented. For both regions two columns are shown each representing one of two statements in each hypothesis. The meaning of symbols is as following: SE/EM stands for the first part of each hypothesis meaning that respondents expressed preference for self-employment (including both: starting own business or continuing family business) over the employment somewhere else. Thus, if hypothesis is confirmed, this is signed with "+" symbol. On the other hand, OB/FB stands for preference of establish own business comparing to succeeding a family business. Again, if hypothesis is confirmed, this is signed with "+" symbol.

4.6 Control Variables

Control variables show considerable differences between genders. In the east, male students compared to female are more likely to found a new business than to choose the career in family firm. In Western region is completely opposite. Discussing employment intention with succession intention, male students compared to female from both regions prefer employment over the succession career, although it should be noted that the difference is very low and it cannot be supported that gender has no impact on the decision.

Positive exposure towards family business results with higher likelihood of preferring the succession career to both alternatives in Western Europe. In SE Europe students with positive feelings about family firm will prefer employment to succession and succession to new company. Obviously, the gender and positive

Table 3 Hypothesis results in all regions

Hypothesis	West		East	
	OB/FB	SE/EM	OB/FB	SE/EM
1-Locus	0	–	+	–
2-Self-efficacy	+	+	–	+
3-Independence	+	+	+	+
4-Innovation	+	0	+	+

Note: *OB* own business, *FB* family business, *SE* self-employed including OB and FB, *EM* employee
Source: Zellweger et al. (2011), own research 2012

feelings have considerable influence on students when they are choosing their career path and that this influence is different in the two regions.

4.7 Dependant Variable

In both studied regions student's career choices were analyzed and compared. SE European students were very determined about their career choice within the time leg of 5 years. For the period more than 5 years after completion of studies more students did not make their decision yet. The large number of students selected employment as their career path for the period immediately after completing the studies and new start-up after that period. This can lead us to possible conclusion that students need more entrepreneurial knowledge and experience before starting their entrepreneur careers. On the other hand, the number of students which selected a career of a successor was relatively stable in time period which suggests that once they are determined for this career path, they don't expect changes. The findings are illustrated on Fig. 1.

5 Discussion and Implications

By explicitly investigating students with family business background in SE European countries and comparing the results with Western region, the study makes some important observations and contributions to understanding the differences between the economies with longer capitalistic tradition and those where this was interrupted for several decades because of the changes in political systems after the World War II. Students with higher levels of internal locus of control will

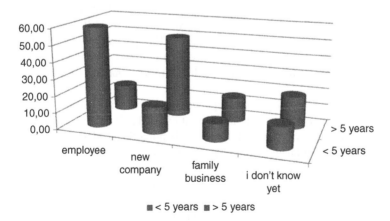

Fig. 1 Career choice within 5 years after study and after. Source: Own research 2012

choose employment or new start-up rather than succession of family firm. This finding may lead into conclusion that off-springs perceive family firm as an environment which imposes decisions and visions. Persons with high level of internal locus of control feels that they are decision makers since they know that only they influence the way the events unfold. They feel that family firm is an obstacle which prevents them to shape their own path. Potential successors experience long time exposure to family environment on one side and family business on the other side. Students raised in a family business environment are affected by the parent's absence from family life due to their intensive engagement in business matters. Presumably an off-spring from a family business may be more exposed to this effect in his/her time of adolescence. From early childhood they have to compete for parent's time and attention. Parents as role models have great impact on future entrepreneurial tendencies of their off-springs. Exaggeration in the sense of parent's succession expectations could have substantial negative influence on children with high level of internal locus of control. Consequently potential successor will choose different career path, which gives him/her more control under events.

Individuals with high levels of self-efficacy will choose succession compared to new business. Family business already operates. It does have its own operational problems, but on the other hand, all problems can be better controlled due to the fact that the company has a stabile organization. Product is well known, workflow is consistent and markets are developed at least at some level. This offers the opportunity to be very effective on selected specific field of work in family firm. New start-up on the other hand, has a lot of variables which usually have negative influence on effectiveness. In all regions high levels of self-efficacy mean that students will select one of both entrepreneurial careers before employment. It can be generally postulated, that students which have family business background and have high level of self-efficacy, will choose a career path which allows them to make profit directly.

Self-efficacy is also linked with independence motive to some extent. Environment with a lot of co-workers has high demands for constant activity coordination and adaptations. This is typical for employment career path. It has been suspected that political and economic instability in SE Europe has great influence on the results. Existing economic situation forces individuals with high level of self-efficacy to stay in family business which offers maximal stability on micro economic level.

Individual with high level of independence motive will still choose one of two entrepreneurial career paths, but in different order. Their first selection is starting a new business which is expected. It is obviously not influenced with the environment since results are similar in both analyzed regions. New company offers maximum of opportunities for independence. The fact that family business already exists and offers more stability obviously does not outperform the desire for independence. Staying in family firm means dependence. Negative influence of parent's expectations could have an important role in this group of individuals since each attempt of influence is understood as a restriction.

Student with high detected level of innovation motive prefer career in their own company compared to family business. This is the expected result. Innovative individual will maximize his innovation potential only if he/she has absolute control over the environment. Students are also not so decisive when choosing between employment and succession. In the two regions there is no noticeable difference. Stability of existing family firm which was mentioned before, has a negative connotation in this case. Stability means that all major business parameters are defined. For an innovative individual this fact can be easily understood as a limitation for introducing new ideas.

In SEE region family firms are still in majority managed by the first owner. Firms are in the first generation of their life-cycle which usually claims the rights for success. These owners mostly possess lover levels of formal education and don't have adequate business knowledge, they rely exclusively on experience, gathered in quite different economic environment and they often reject all changes. Off-springs seem to be on the opposite side. They have new ideas and usually they are better educated which usually generates conflicts. This is why family firms should have a very clear vision of introducing an off-spring to the business. Parents should be aware of their role in early stage of upbringing. In the early years they should spend enough time with children. Later on they should always allocate enough time for sharing positive information about the business with off-springs and avoid negative feelings all the times. In the last stage, children should be slowly introduced to the business by taking care about small tasks at first, which will later become more and more demanding. At the end, it is a parent's responsibility to develop the sense of belonging and commitment with their potential successors.

Broadly-based international pieces of research have demonstrated that less than half potential successors are prepared to take the responsibility and continue family business (Stavrou, 1999). Reason for succession intention are more entrepreneurial than family driven. The important factors are desire to realize own ambitions and independence motive (Vadnjal, 2008). A young person can reach this goal in number of different ways, one of which is a succession career. This is where formal educational system plays an important role by pointing out strengths and weaknesses of different career opportunities. On the other hand, the findings of this study suggest that implications may, both for education and training and professional work with family businesses, go beyond the traditional paradigms on succession planning which in most cases includes the training and preparation of possible successor(s). On the other hand, traditional approach does not suggest much an option for off-springs which show entrepreneurial ambitions but would for different reasons prefer not to continue the family business tradition but go on their own. Both teachers and professionals should become able to open a family business the insight to somehow third way which is supporting family businesses to start their own spin-offs from family holding companies.

The educational system should offer more entrepreneurial knowledge and experience since some surveys proof that entrepreneurial knowledge has positive influence on entrepreneurial aspirations (Vadnjal, Jelovac, & Damjan, 2010). The existing system gives students a lot of facts but very little creativity. In SE Europe entrepreneurship still has some negative connotations which may be the consequence of the present political situation as well as historical reasons. It is very important to change this attitude and to create a positive entrepreneurial environment which will offer knowledge and opportunities for getting experience. The fact that family businesses constitute a substantial part of the existing European companies and have a significant role to play in future strength of the European economy, specific actions should be undertaken to shape the environment in favor of family business.

A serious limitation of this study that has awareness of the authors is relatively low number of students included in the survey which resulted with quite some non-significant parameter values and possible biases which have not been separately tested. Also number of siblings and their birth order was not considered in the study which also may have an impact on individual career decision. Considering the opportunistic approach, samples used in the survey were not coincidental and adequately balanced between countries.

References

Ajzen, I. (1991). The theory of planned behavior. *Organizational Behavior and Human Decision Processes, 50*(2), 179.

Ajzen, I. (2002). Perceived behavioral control, self-efficacy, locus of control, and the theory of planned behavior. *Journal of Applied Social Psychology, 32*, 1–20.

Astrachan, J. H., & Shanker, M. C. (2003). Family businesses' contribution to the U.S. economy: A closer look. *Family Business Review, 16*(3), 211–219.

Baker, T., Miner, A. S., & Eesley, D. T. (2003). Improvising firms: bricolage, account giving and improvisational competencies in the founding process. *Research Policy, 32*(2), 255–276.

Bandura, A. (1994). Self-efficacy. In V. S. Ramachaudran (Ed.), *Encyclopedia of human behavior* (Vol. 4, pp. 71–81). New York: Academic Press.

Bandura, A. (1997). *Self-efficacy: the exercise of control.* New York: W.H. Freeman.

Bird, B. (1988). Implementing entrepreneurial ideas: The case of intention. *Academy of Management Review, 13*(3), 442.

Birley, S. (2002). Attitudes of owner-managers' children towards family and business issue. *Entrepreneurship Theory and Practice, 26*(3), 5–19.

Carter, N., Gartner, W. B., Shaver, K. G., & Gatewood, E. J. (2003). The career reasons of nascent entrepreneurs. *Journal of Business Venturing, 18*, 13–39.

Chen, C. C., Greene, P. G., & Crick, A. (1998). Does entrepreneurial self-efficacy distinguish entrepreneurs from managers? *Journal of Business Venturing, 13*(4), 295–316.

Daniel, D. J. (2011). Multiple linear regression using SPSS. University of Montana.

Davidsson, P. (1995). Determinants of entrepreneurial intentions. In *RENT IX Workshop*, Piacenza. http://eprints.qut.edu.au/2076/1/RENT_IX.pdf (20.11.2012).

Dyal, J. A. (1984). *Cross-cultural research with the locus of control construct. V Lefcourt, Herbert M. Research with the locus of control construct* (pp. 209–306). San Diego: Academic Press.

Fischer, E. M., Reuber, R., & Dyke, L. (1993). A theoretical overview and extension of research on sex, gender, and entrepreneurship. *Journal of Business Venturing, 8*(2), 151–168.

Fishbein, M., & Ajzen, I. (1975). *Belief, attitude, intention, and behavior. An introduction to theory and research.* New York: Addison-Wesley. http://people.umass.edu/aizen/f&a1975.html (15.1.2013).

Gregory, B. T., Rutherford, M. W., Oswald, S., & Gardiner, L. (2005). An empirical investigation of the growth cycle theory of small firm financing. *Journal of Small Business Management, 43* (4), 382–392.

Hair, J. F., Black, W., Babin, B., & Anderson, R. E. (2009). *Multivariate data analysis.* Englewood Cliffs, NJ: Prentice Hall.

Kolvereid, L. (1996). Prediction of employment status choice intentions. *Entrepreneurship Theory and Practice, 21*(1), 47.

Krueger, N. (2003). The cognitive psychology in entrepreneurship. In Z. J. Acs & D. B. Audretsch (Eds.), *Handbook of entrepreneurship research: An interdisciplinary survey and introduction.* New York: Springer.

Krueger, N. F., Jr., Reilly, M. D., & Carsrud, A. (2000). Competing models of entrepreneurial intentions. *Journal of Business Venturing, 15*(5–6), 411–432.

Miller, D., Steier, L., & LeBreton-Miller, I. (2003). Lost in time: intergenerational succession, change, and failure in family business. *Journal of Business Venturing, 18*(4), 513–531.

Schein, E. H. (1978). *Career dynamics: matching individual and organizational needs.* Reading, MA: Addison-Wesley Longman.

Stavrou, E. (1999). Succession in family business: exploring the effect of demographic factors on offspring intentions to join and take over the business. *Journal of Small Business Management, 37,* 43–61.

Stinchcombe, A. L. (1965). Social structure and organizations. In J. G. March (Ed.), *Handbook of organizations* (Rand McNally sociology series, pp. 142–193). Chicago: Rand McNally.

Tan, B. I., Wong, K. L., & Choong, C. K. (2013, May 29–31). TQM and family owned business: Performance and sustainability. In *Proceedings of 2013 international conference on technology innovation and industrial management*, Phuket.

Vadnjal, J. (2008). Development and growth orientation of family and non-family businesses. *Economic and Business Review, 10*(3), 197–218.

Vadnjal, J., Jelovac, D., & Damjan, J. (2010). Vpliv šole in okolja na odnos odraslih srednješolcev do podjetništva. *Andragoška spoznanja, 1,* 23–34.

Zellweger, T., Sieger, P., & Halter, F. (2011). Should I stay or should I go? Career choice intentions of students with family business background. *Journal of Business Venturing.* doi:10.1016/j.jbusvent.2010.04.001 (20. 6. 2011).

Management Practices in Bulgarian Family and Non-family SMEs: Exploring "Real" Differences

Desislava Yordanova, Zhelyu Vladimirov*, and Ralitsa Simeonova-Ganeva

Abstract Family businesses constitute an important part of the economies in Central and Eastern Europe. However, there is a lack of understanding about differences between family and non-family businesses in this context. This study investigates differences in management practices between Bulgarian family and non-family SMEs. To detect real rather than sample differences we apply multivariate statistical techniques that controls for the effects of a number of contextual variables as recommended by Jorissen et al. (Family Business Review 18(3):229–246, 2005). The chapter ends with discussion of the empirical findings and research and practical implications.

Keywords Family businesses • Non-family businesses • Differences • Small and medium-sized enterprises • Bulgaria

1 Introduction

Family businesses play an increasing role in the growth-oriented economies in Central and Eastern Europe (CEE) (Pistrui, Welsch, & Roberts, 1995 cited in Donckels & Lambrecht, 1999:171). In one of the first studies on family business in the Balkans, Poutziouris, O'Sullivan, and Nicolescu (1997) noted that family business activity in Bulgaria was in the foundation phase. More than 15 years after the Poutziouris et al.'s (1997) research, the role of family businesses in the Bulgarian economy has increased significantly. The survey on family business in Bulgaria conducted in 2010 by the National Statistical Institute and initiated by the Association of the Family Business revealed that family businesses represent 42 % of all enterprises.[1] They employ 28.3 % of the workforce in the private sector. The

---

* University of Surrey, Marie-Curie Fellowship, FP7-2012, GA No. 327405.

[1] http://www.fbn-bulgaria.org/bg/news/59/17/nad-42-ot-kompaniite-v-blgariya-sa-familni, Accessed: 20.01.2012.

D. Yordanova (✉) • Z. Vladimirov • R. Simeonova-Ganeva
Faculty of Economics and Business Administration, University "St. Kliment Ohridski", 125 Tsarigradsko Shose Blvd., bl.3, 1113 Sofia, Bulgaria
e-mail: d_yordanova@abv.bg; jeve@feb.uni-sofia.bg; rganeva@gmail.com

turnover of family businesses is about 20 % of total turnover of Bulgarian enterprises, while the amount of investments in fixed assets of family businesses are 16 % of all investments in the country. Family businesses provide more than 17 % of the total amount of products and services produced by the Bulgarian enterprises.

Although entrepreneurship in the transition economies in Central and Eastern Europe has attracted some research attention, the role of family business is largely neglected (Pistrui, Welsch, & Roberts, 1997). In Bulgaria a few empirical studies investigate family businesses (e.g. Davidkov & Yordanova, 2013; Pelov, 2005; Todorov, 2011; Yordanova, 2010, 2011, 2012; Yordanova & Davidkov, 2011). The research on family businesses in former socialist countries in general is very scarce because private business ownership was not a legal activity during the period of central planning (Duh, Tominc, & Rebernik, 2009). The Bulgarian family firms have appeared as separate legal entities as a result of the profound political and socio-economic changes after 1989. Due to those specific historical circumstances, they differ in some aspects such as age, growth plans and involvement in international business operation from family businesses in other countries (Yordanova, 2013). Research findings about family businesses in other contexts may not be applicable to economies in Central and Eastern Europe due to differences in institutional environments, historic development, culture, resources, entrepreneurial role models, etc.

The research exploring the differences between family and non-family businesses constitutes one of the basic fields of family business research (Gallo, Tapies, & Cappuyns, 2004). Chua, Chrisman, and Steier (2003) emphasized the importance of discovering and explaining differences in behaviour and performance between family and non-family businesses for the development of a theory of the family firm. Identifying differences in management practices between family and non-family businesses has important theoretical and practical implications. There is lack of understanding about differences between family and non-family businesses in the transition economies in Central and Eastern Europe. Most research on this topic has been conducted in other contexts (for example Coleman & Carsky, 1999; Cromie, Stephenson, & Monteith, 1995; Daily & Dollinger, 1992; Daily & Thompson, 1994; Donckels & Fröhlich, 1991; Gallo, 1995; Gudmundson, Hartman, & Tower, 1999; Jorissen, Laveren, Martens, & Reheul, 2005; Naldi, Nordqvist, Sjoberg, & Wiklund, 2007; Reid, Morrow, Kelly, Adams, & McCartan, 2000; Short, Payne, Brigham, Lumpkin, & Broberg, 2009; Smyrnios & Odgers, 2002; Teal, Upton, & Seaman, 2003; Westhead, 1997; Westhead & Cowling, 1997).

This study investigates differences in management practices between Bulgarian family and non-family SMEs. To detect real rather than sample differences we apply multivariate statistical techniques that controls for the effects of a number of contextual variables as recommended by Jorissen et al. (2005). This approach allows for addressing the methodological concerns expressed in the literature about the methodological appropriateness of some comparative studies of family and non-family businesses (Jorissen et al., 2005; Westhead, 1997; Westhead & Cowling, 1997, 1998). The focus on SMEs is due to the fact that the great majority of both family and non-family businesses in Bulgaria are SMEs. The paper is structured as follows. The next section describes the context of the research. The following section includes a theoretical framework that discusses the nature of family business and different theoretical perspectives that help to explain differences between family and non-family businesses. The forth section contains testable hypotheses derived from the outlined theoretical arguments and past empirical findings. In the fifth section, the research methodology is described. The following section outlines the main empirical findings. Finally, the conclusions, limitations, practical implications and future research recommendations are discussed.

2   The Context of the Research

In the ex-communist countries in Central and Eastern Europe including Bulgaria, entrepreneurship was not always a legal activity (Tkachev & Kolvereid, 1999). Until recently, the economies of these countries were based on large state-owned industrial enterprises using mass production methods and relatively inflexible production processes, producing for geographically restricted markets (McMillan & Woodruff, 2002; Smallbone, Welter, Isakova, & Slonimski, 2001; Tkachev & Kolvereid, 1999). Private business was practically eliminated in these countries (Manolova, Carter, Manev, & Gyoshev, 2007) and when existent was part of the grey economy (Smallbone & Welter, 2001). The unprecedented reforms aimed at the democratization of the society and the liberalization of the economy resulted in the legalization of the private ownership (Tkachev & Kolvereid, 1999) and prompted the emergence of small privately-owned firms in transition economies. During the transition period, entrepreneurship became an important factor for the transition from centrally-planned to market economy (McMillan & Woodruff, 2002). The specific environmental conditions encouraged the coexistence of various forms of entrepreneurship in transition economies such as informal economic activity, covert economic activity, and internal economic activity with no transaction (Dana & Dana, 2003).

In 1989 Bulgaria started profound political, economic and social reforms. After more than a decade of reforms, the economy of Bulgaria was recognized as a functioning market economy by the European Union in 2002. It has experienced rapid economic growth in recent years, even though its income level remains the lowest within the European Union (Eurostat, 2012). The preparation of the accession of Bulgaria to the European Union exercised a positive influence on the environment for enterprise development. In 2007, after fulfilling economic and political criteria, Bulgaria joined the European Union. Since 2001, Bulgaria has managed to attract considerable amounts of foreign direct investment. During the financial crisis of 2007–2010, Bulgaria marked a decline in its economy in 2009, but quickly restored its positive growth in 2010 (Eurostat, 2012).

Despite the steady economic growth in the recent past, Bulgaria still remains one of the least developed countries in the European Union. As indicated by the World Bank's reports Doing Business for 2006–2010 Bulgaria has achieved a significant improvement in its business environment. Since 2011 the country stepped back in this classification and in most EU countries it is easier to do business than in Bulgaria. In terms of Global Competitiveness Index, Bulgaria lags behind the majority of the EU member states. Problematic aspects of competitiveness of the country include corruption, access to financing, inefficient government bureaucracy, policy instability, etc. Despite the recognition of the importance of entrepreneurship for the economy by the Bulgarian governmental authorities during the transition period, there were several major obstacles to entrepreneurship development including political uncertainty, energy issues, lack of management skills, problematic financing, volatile currency, the impact of inflation, deflation and taxation on entrepreneurship, infrastructure deficiencies, and stigma associated with entrepreneurship (Dana, 1999; Ramadani & Dana, 2013; Ramadani & Schneider, 2013).

During the last 5 years the Bulgarian SME sector registered relatively stable performance in terms of size, industry structure, employment contribution, share of exporters, competitiveness, and integration into European and world business networks (Simeonova-Ganeva et al., 2012, 2013). The low share of exporters, low competitiveness, and low integration into European and world business networks can be attributed to the large share of microenterprises (Simeonova-Ganeva et al., 2012, 2013). Most microenterprises lack professionalism (Todorov, 2006) and make significant contribution to the family budget of the owner(s), but not to the development of innovations in the economy. The adaptation of the Bulgarian SMEs to the European requirements and global economy is a slow and painful process. The average labour productivity in the Bulgarian SMEs is significantly lower than the average in the European Union. These enterprises are involved predominantly in activities with low value added. The adoption of professional management practices such as innovation and quality management are rarely implemented by these enterprises. The main factors that foster the modernization of Bulgarian SMEs are:

• The external influence from the EU through regulations;
• The internal influence exerted by the subsidiaries of multinational companies operating in Bulgaria.

In summary, during the last decade the Bulgarian economy has achieved macroeconomic stability and growth. Various measures were implemented in order to improve the environment for doing business. However, the Bulgarian economy is characterized by very low competitiveness in comparison with the other European Union member states. The reasons for the low competitiveness of the Bulgarian economy can be found at both macro-economic and micro-economic levels. At micro-economic level, management practices are a critical factor for achieving higher competitiveness of the Bulgarian companies and increasing their ability to cope with diverse challenges that they face in the global economy (Vladimirov, 2011b).

3   Theoretical Background

3.1   The Nature of Family Business

There is no common agreement among scholars and practitioners about the meaning of the term family business. Although there is no widely accepted family firm definition (Westhead & Cowling, 1998), various studies have detected that family firms differ from otherwise similar organizations because of the critical role that family members play in business processes at many levels (Chua, Chrisman, & Sharma, 1999; Davis & Harveston, 1998). Churchill and Hatten (1987) highlighted two distinctive characteristics of family businesses: involvement of family members in the business and non-market-based transfers of power between family members. In contrast to non-family employees and managers, family members involved in the business are connected emotionally to each other in their family life and therefore have interrelated roles and obligations in the business and in the family. The non-market-based transfer of power between family members derives from the biological reality of human life cycle and family ties. Chua et al. (1999) suggested that family firms were businesses "governed and/or managed with the intention to shape and pursue the vision of the business held by a dominant coalition controlled by members of the same family or a small number of families in a manner that is potentially sustainable across generations of the family or families".

Chrisman, Chua, and Litz (2003) suggested that the following elements were essential in defining the family firm:

- The intention to maintain family control;
- Unique, synergistic resources arising from family involvement;
- A vision held by the family for transgenerational value creation;
- The pursuit of the vision.

Based on the degree of family involvement, Shanker and Astrachan (1996) established three definitions of family business: a broad, inclusive definition, a middle definition, and a tight or narrow definition. The broadest and most inclusive definition suggests little direct family involvement. The family has some degree of effective control of the strategic direction of the business. The family business is intended to remain in the family. The middle definition suggests some family involvement. The founder or her/his descendent runs the business and the family has legal control of voting stock. The third or narrow definition suggests a significant family involvement. At least two family members have a significant management responsibility in the family business. The family is directly involved in both management and ownership of the business. Multiple generations of the family have been involved in the business.

Chrisman, Chua, and Sharma (2005) identified two approaches in the literature to defining the family business: components-of-involvement approach and essence approach. The components-of-involvement approach treats family involvement as a necessary condition in order to define a firm as family business. Following this approach, the definitions of family business use a combination of the components of a family's involvement in the business: ownership, governance, management, and transgenerational succession. The essence approach is more restrictive and treats family involvement only as a necessary condition in order to define a firm as family business. According to this approach family business status is associated with specific behaviours and distinctiveness stemming from the family involvement including: (1) family's influence on the firm strategy; (2) family's intention to keep control over the business; (3) family firm behaviour; and (4) unique, inseparable, synergistic resources and capabilities arising from family involvement and interaction (familiness).

In their famous three-circle model Tagiuri and Davis ([1982] 1996) depicted the family business as a system consisting of three overlapping but distinctive sub-systems: ownership, family, and business. Gersick, Davis, Hampton, and Lansberg (1997) add the development over time to the three-circle model of Tagiuri and Davis ([1982] 1996). They describe family businesses according to different stages of development of ownership, family, and business sub-systems and show how and why family businesses change over time.

3.2 Understanding Differences Between Family and Non-family Firms

A number of theoretical frameworks have been used in the literature to explain the observed differences between family and non-family businesses (Jorissen et al., 2005). All these explanations point to the significant influence of the business family on the family firms.

Agency theory studies agency relationships in which one party (agent) acts on behalf of another party (principal). Agency theory deals with potential problems of agency relationships, which may arise from differences between the principal and the agent in relation to goals and interests, information and attitudes toward risk. The costs incurred for the control of these agency problems are called agency costs. According to the agency theory the observed differences between family and non-family firms may be a result of the overlapping ownership and management relationships in family firms, which leads to lower need to monitor opportunistic managerial behaviour and thus reduces agency costs in family firms (Jorissen et al., 2005). In family firms the interests of owners and top managers are aligned to a greater extent than in non-family firms, because one or several family members, who are tied emotionally and tend to act in the interest of the family, usually occupy these positions. This allows for better control of agency problems and reduces monitoring costs in family firms in comparison with non-family firms. Previous research suggests that two fundamental forces differentiate agency costs in family and non-family firms: altruism and the tendency for entrenchment (Chrisman et al., 2005).

System theory plays an important role in understanding the complex world of family businesses and helped to unify the field of family business studies (Distelberg & Sorenson, 2009). It attempts to explain the interrelation between the family and the business systems in family firms. There are various contradictions between the values, norms, and principles that operate in the family system and the business system, which interfere with the effective management in family businesses especially when family business matures and develops more complex organizational forms (Lansberg, 1983). According to Tagiuri and Davis ([1982] 1996) family businesses possess several unique inherent attributes deriving from the overlap between the family and the business (simultaneous roles, shred identity, lifelong common history, emotional involvement, private language, mutual awareness, privacy, and the symbolic meaning of the company), which may affect their success or failure. Kets de Vries (1994) outlined a number of advantages (long-term orientation, family culture, greater independence of action, greater resilience in hard times, greater flexibility and quicker decision-making, and knowledge of the business) and disadvantages (low access to capital markets, confusing organization, nepotism, paternalism, the overflow of family conflicts into the business, financial strain by unproductive family members, and succession problems) of family businesses stemming from the interrelation between the family and the business. These specific characteristics, advantages and disadvantages, and contradictions between the family and the business systems in family firms may provide an explanation for the observed differences between family and non-family firms (Jorissen et al., 2005).

The Resource-Based View of the Firm (RBV) assumes that strategic formulation and competitive advantage are dependent on the resources and capabilities of the firm (Barney, 1991). One of the principal insights of the resource-based view is that not all resources are of equal importance or possess the potential to be a source of sustainable competitive advantage (Barney, 1991). The RBV helps to identify specific resources and capabilities that lead to establishing sustainable competitive advantage in family firms (Habbershon & Williams, 1999; Habbershon, Williams, & MacMillan, 2003). Family firms possess a unique bundle of resources ("familiness") because of the systematic interaction between the business, the family and its members, which may help the family firm to acquire a competitive advantage (Habbershon & Williams, 1999). Sirmon and Hitt (2003) identified five family-specific resources with the potential to generate competitive advantages: human capital, social capital, survivability capital, patient financial capital, and governance structure. They argue that family and non-family firms differ in the way they evaluate, acquire, shed, bundle, and leverage these resources. Carney (2005) identifies three specific propensities of the governance structure of family firms: parsimony, personalism, and particularism. These characteristics provide advantages in cost leadership strategies especially in scarce environments, aid the creation of social capital, and facilitate opportunistic entrepreneurship (Carney, 2005). Family businesses may also face some disadvantages such as the ability to make appropriate shedding decisions about resources, which may influence negatively their performance (Sirmon & Hitt, 2003). The specific characteristics, advantages and disadvantages of family firms may explain the observed differences in other firm characteristics and behaviours between family and non-family firms.

4 Literature Review and Hypotheses

The analysis reported in the previous section suggests that there are important theoretical reasons behind the argument that family and non-family firms differ in relation to adopted management practices. This section provides an overview of the comparative research on management practices in family and non-family businesses and contains the hypotheses of the study.

The empirical evidence about strategic and business planning is controversial. Several studies indicate that there are no differences between family and non-family businesses in relation to the use of (formal) strategic and business planning (Donckels & Fröhlich, 1991; Reid & Adams, 2001). According to the agency theory, the overlapping ownership and management relationships in family firms, which leads to lower need to monitor opportunistic managerial behaviour (Jorissen et al., 2005), may be associated with less formal strategy and business planning in family firms in comparison with non-family firms. Several empirical studies confirm that strategic planning and business planning is less prevalent in family firms than in non-family firms. Chaganti and Schneer (1994) examine the link between owner-manager's mode of entry and management patterns and report that family firms tend to avoid long-range operations planning in comparison with the rest of the companies. Smith (2007) perform industry-based analysis of a large sample of family and non-family SMEs and find that family SMEs in several industries are less likely to produce a formal strategic or business plan than non-family SMEs. In the internationalization process family businesses are less likely to use formal strategic of business plan than non-family businesses (Graves & Thomas, 2006). After controlling for demographic sample differences, Jorissen et al. (2005) find that family firms rely to a lesser extent to short-term formal planning than do non-family firms. Using matched sample methodology, Westhead (1997) find that family firms make significantly less use of planning systems than non-family firms. Fiegener, Brown, Prince, and File (1996) report that CEOs in family firms rate strategic planning less important in successor preparation than CEOs in non-family firms. Managers in family firms give less importance to strategic planning as a competitiveness factor than managers in non-family firms (de Lema & Duréndez, 2007). There are differences in the attitudes of key individuals that formulate marketing strategies between family and non-family firms in relation to risk (Spence & Crick, 2006). Therefore we suggest that:

H1: Family firms are less likely to have short or medium-term business plan than non-family firms.
H2: Family firms are less likely to have marketing strategy than non-family firms.

The Resource-Based View of the Firm (RBV) is powerful and unifying theoretical framework in international business research (Peng, 2001). The RBV highlights the importance of firm resources and capabilities for internationalization. Some resources including technology, brands, culture, or managerial capabilities may be critical for establishing competitive advantage over local firms in their own markets (Fernández & Nieto, 2005). Family firms may experience resource constraints, which may prevent them from internationalizing their business activities. Family businesses often lack managerial capabilities (Austrian Institute for SME Research, 2008; Gallo & Pont, 1996; Kets de Vries, 1994). The managerial capabilities of family firms lag behind those of non-family firms as they internationalize their business activity (Graves & Thomas, 2006). They tend to avoid external financing (Austrian Institute for SME Research, 2008) and to report more financial difficulties (Chittenden, Hall, & Hutchinson, 1996; James, 1999). Family firms are more reluctant to take risks than non-family firms and tend to have local business focus (Austrian Institute for SME Research, 2008; Donckels & Fröhlich, 1991; Naldi et al., 2007). Empirical research comparing family and non-family businesses demonstrates that family businesses are less export oriented than non-family businesses (Donckels & Fröhlich, 1991; Fernández & Nieto, 2005; Jorissen et al., 2005). Therefore, we suggest that:

H3: Family firms are less likely to export than non-family firms.

The various contradictions between the values, norms, and principles that operate in the family system and the business system may interfere with the effective human resource management in family businesses (Lansberg, 1983). Donckels and Fröhlich (1991) report that family firms are less likely to be concerned with employees' participation in ownership and decision-making and their self-fulfillment than non-family firms. In family firms, the needs of family members employed in the business are approached in terms of individual career development, while the training needs of non-family employees are considered as firms-specific human resource development issues (Matlay, 2002). The possibility of non-family managers improving their managerial competence may be considered as a threat by family firms, in which the owning family is managerially active (Loan-Clarke, Boocock, Smith, & Whittaker, 1999). Drawing upon System theory, we argue that these specific characteristics and practices in family firms may explain possible differences in the adoption of human resource management policies and practices between family and non-family firms and particularly the relatively limited concern of family businesses for employee training (Kotey & Folker, 2007). Empirical evidence confirms that family firms tend to provide less training to employees and invest less in training than non-family firms (Cromie et al., 1995; Kotey & Folker, 2007; Loan-Clarke et al., 1999; Reid & Adams, 2001). We suggest the following hypotheses:

H4: Family firms are less likely to provide training to employees than non-family firms.
H5: Family firms are less likely to invest in training than non-family firms.

Drawing upon system theory we suggest that family influence defined as the overlap between the "family system" and the "business system" (König et al., 2013) impacts innovation in family firms. The interaction between the business and the family leads to inertia, which can represent a barrier to a family business' capacity to innovate (Webb, Ketchen, & Ireland, 2010). Family ownership is negatively associated with R&D investments (Block, 2012; Chen & Hsu, 2009; Munari, Oriani, & Sobrero, 2010; Muñoz-Bullón & Sanchez-Bueno, 2011) and innovation activities (Chin, Chen, Kleinman, & Lee, 2009; Czarnitzki & Kraft, 2009). Family firms differ from non-family businesses in respect to product innovation strategies and organization of the product innovation process (De Massis, Frattini, & Lichtenthaler, 2013; De Massis, Frattini, Pizzurno, & Cassia, 2013). The higher long-term orientation of family firms may lead to different rate of disruptive innovations of family businesses in comparison with non-family businesses (Zellweger, 2007; Zellweger, Nason, & Nordqvist, 2012). Family firms may be reluctant to collaborate in innovative projects in order to preserve their socioemotional wealth (De Massis et al., 2012). Previous research suggests that families' concern with socioemotional preservation affects negatively expenditures on formal R&D activity, engagement in open innovation activities, and radical or explorative innovation outputs (Block, Miller, Jaskiewicz, & Spiegel, 2013; Chrisman & Patel, 2012; Classen, Van Gils, Bammens, & Carree, 2012). Family firms tend to show preferences for exploitative versus explorative innovations (Patel & Chrisman, 2013), incremental versus radical innovations (Block et al., 2013; Nieto, Santamaria, & Fernandez, 2013) and process versus product innovations (Classen, Carree, Van Gils, & Peters, 2013). Family firms may lack resources and capabilities necessary for creating and registering intellectual property. Khan (2012) finds that family firms do not venture out into producing their own brands due to the additional marketing spending associated with branding and lack of knowledge on how to create brands. Therefore, we propose the following hypotheses:

H6: *Family firms are less likely to introduce product innovations than non-family firms.*

H7: *Family firms are less likely to have trademarks and registered patents than non-family firms.*

According to agency theory the overlapping ownership and management relationships in family firms leads to lower need to monitor opportunistic managerial behaviour (Jorissen et al., 2005) and thus reduces the need to implement management information systems (MIS). Empirical evidence suggests that family firms tend to use less MIS than non-family firms including control systems (Daily & Dollinger, 1992, 1993; de Lema & Duréndez, 2007), formal appraisal systems (Cromie et al., 1995), planning systems and formal MIS (Westhead, 1997), variable reward systems (Jorissen et al., 2005; Reid et al., 2000). Small companies have weaker resources to adapt to the IT and bear higher risks during its adoption (Riemenschneider, Harrison, & Mykytyn, 2003). The use of these technologies in small firms is still insufficient (Beekhuyzen, Hellens, & Siedle, 2005), mainly because it requires significant changes in business models and communication channels (Buhalis & Law, 2008, p. 619). Family firms tend to be inward looking, conservative and resistant to change (Aronoff & Ward, 1997; Sharma, Chrisman, & Chua, 1997). A major impediment to new technology adoption in small firms is the lack of finance and internal expertise (Wang & Ahmed, 2009). Small family firms often experience financial difficulties (Chittenden et al., 1996; James, 1999). Therefore, we argue that:

H8: Family firms are less likely to use automatic MIS than non-family firms.
H9: Family firms are less likely to use internet in their business activities than non-family firms.

Quality certification is considered as a factor that could affect the strategic behaviour of the firm (de Lema & Duréndez, 2007). Despite the benefits of quality management for small firms (Kalleberg & Leicht, 1991; Upton, Teal, & Felan, 2001), these firms are reluctant to accept quality standards (Taylor & Taylor, 2004). Limited internal resources such as time, expertise, information, training, or financial resources represent serious obstacles for small firms to implement quality initiatives (Beheshti & Lollar, 2003; Bertolini, Rizzi, & Bevilacqua, 2007; Hendricks & Singhal, 2000; Taylor, 2001; Vladimirov, 2011a; Walker, Pritchard, & Forsythe, 2003; Yapp & Fairman, 2006). Empirical research demonstrates that family firms are less likely to possess quality certification than non-family firms (de Lema & Duréndez, 2007). Thus, we suggest that:

H10: Family firms are less likely to use quality and safety standards than non-family firms.

5   Research Methodology

The sample used in this study is composed of 300 Bulgarian SMEs. It was obtained through a national representative survey of the Bulgarian small and medium-sized enterprises. The survey was conducted for the preparation of the annual report "Analysis of the Situation and Factors for Development of SMEs in Bulgaria 2011–2012: Economic Recovery and Competitiveness" (Simeonova-Ganeva et al., 2012) and was financed by the Bulgarian Small and Medium-Sizes Promotion Agency. The sample design includes random selection within clusters, as each cluster is defined by three criteria: region of economic planning, size of enterprise by number of employees and field of activity. The information was obtained through a combination between a personal interview in the respondent's office and a telephone interview in the period February–March 2012. The interview length was 30 min and the questionnaire was composed of 45 questions about the use of various management practices, the characteristics of the enterprise, the characteristics of the owner-manager, and the succession planning in family SMEs.

Table 1 Characteristics of the sample firms

Characteristic	%
Size	
Micro-enterprises	74.3
Small enterprises	13.7
Medium-sized enterprises	12
Family business status	
Yes	31
No	69
Sector	
Trade	28.7
Manufacturing	24
Services	40.7
Other	6.6

Source: Authors

The sample is dominated by micro-enterprises (Table 1), which represent more than 74 % of all enterprises. Small enterprises account for 13.7 % of the studied enterprises, while the rest of the sample is composed of medium-sized enterprises. More than 30 % of the sample firms are family businesses. The studied enterprises operate mainly in the service sector (40.7 %), trade sector (28.7 %), and manufacturing sector (24 %).

The dependent variables in this study are dichotomous (Table 2). They express the likelihood that the company has implemented a certain management practice (code 1) or has not implemented that practice (code 0).

The available definitions of family business in the literature emphasize two important elements: family ownership or ownership control and family involvement in the company's management (Chua et al., 1999; Churchill & Hatten, 1987; Donckels & Fröhlich, 1991; Handler, 1989; Lansberg, 1988; Shanker & Astrachan, 1996; Sharma et al., 1997). For the purposes of this study a company is coded as a family business if it meets two conditions. First, members of one family group own the majority of the firm ownership. Second, family members are involved in the management of the company. The independent variable FAMILY is a binary variable and indicates whether the company is a family business (code 1) or not (code 0). Approximately 83 % of the studied family businesses are still owned and managed by their founder.

The study employs several control variables. The variable SIZE indicates the firm size measured as a number of employees. The variable TRADE takes value 1 if the company operates mainly in the trade sector and value 0 otherwise. The variable MANUFACTURING takes value 1 if the company is involved mainly in manufacturing activities and value 0 if not.

A logistic regression model is employed to deal explicitly with dichotomous dependent variables (Greene, 1997). In this case logistic regression is a more robust method since according to Greene (1997), Hair, Anderson, Tathan, and Black (1998), and Maddala (1983):

Table 2 Variables in the study

Variable	Description
BUS_PLAN	1 = the company has a short or medium-term business plan, 0 = otherwise
M_STRATEGY	1 = the company has a marketing strategy, 0 = otherwise
EXPORT	1 = the company has exported products and/or services during the last year, 0 = otherwise
TRAINING	1 = the company has provided training to employees during the last year, 0 = otherwise
INVEST_TR	1 = the company has invested in training during the last year; 0 = otherwise
INNOVATION	1 = the company has introduced a new or improved product during the last year, 0 = otherwise
TRADE_MARKS	1 = the company has a registered trade mark, 0 = otherwise
PATENTS	1 = the company has registered a patent, 0 = otherwise
MIS	1 = the company has implemented an automatic MIS, 0 = otherwise
WEBSITE	1 = the company has a website; 0 = otherwise
ONLINE_SALES	1 = the company provides a possibility for online orders or sales; 0 = otherwise
ONLINE_PAYMENT	1 = the company provides a possibility for online payment; 0 = otherwise
E_SIGNATURE	1 = some of the managers in the company possess an electronic signature; 0 = otherwise
STANDARDS	1 = the company has implemented quality and/or safety standards, 0 = no
FAMILY	1 = the company is a family business; 0 = no
SIZE	Number of employees
TRADE	1 = the company operates predominantly in the trade sector; 0 = otherwise
MANUFACTURING	1 = the company operates predominantly in the manufacturing sector; 0 = otherwise

Source: Authors

1. The dependent variable needs not to be normally distributed;
2. Logistic regression does not assume a linear relationship between the dependent and the independent variables;
3. The dependent variable needs not to be homoscedastic for each level of the independent variable(s);
4. Normally distributed error terms are not assumed;
5. Independent variables can be categorical;
6. It does not require independent variables to be interval or unbounded.

The application of non-parametric techniques is adequate when the independent variables are predominantly categorical. The use of the maximum likelihood approach is recommended when sample selection bias is possible (Nawata, 1994). Binary logistic regression provides a framework that indicates if and how well independent variables can adequately predict the use of the studied management practice (Greene, 1997). The estimated binary logistic models take the following form:

$$Prob\ (management\,practice) = 1 \ / \ \left(1 + e^{-Z}\right) \tag{1}$$

where, $Z = f\,(X_i, C)$, i.e. a linear combination of independent variables (X_i) and a constant (C).

The research hypotheses will be supported if regression analysis provides an acceptable accuracy of classification of cases and of goodness of fit measures. In addition, the impact of explanatory variables should be statistically significant at least at the 10 % level (two-tailed test) with the predicted sign. Wald statistics will be used to estimate the significance of the independent variables. Data analyses are performed with the statistical package SPSS version 20.

6 Empirical Findings

In this section, we estimate several logistic regression models to examine real differences between adopted management practices in family and non-family businesses in our sample of 300 Bulgarian SMEs. The model chi-square and the percentage of cases correctly classified were employed to determine whether the estimated models fitted correctly (Table 3). The VIF values for the two regressors in all regressions in Table 3 have been calculated. These values (not shown) indicate that there are no serious multicollinearity problems, as they are all well within acceptable limits (less than 1.3). Table 3 contains estimated coefficients, standard errors, Wald's statistics, and goodness of fit measures of the estimated models.

The variable FAMILY has no statistically significant impact on the dependent variable BUS_PLAN when firm size and sector are accounted for. The hypothesis H1 is rejected. SMEs that operate mainly in the manufacturing sector are significantly more likely to have short or medium-term business plan than the rest of the sample firms.

The regression model using M_STRATEGY as a dependent variable reveals that there are no statistically significant differences in the likelihood of implementing a marketing strategy between the studied family and non-family SMEs. The hypothesis H2 is rejected. SMEs that operate predominantly in the manufacturing or trade sectors are significantly less likely to have implemented a marketing strategy than other SMEs.

In relation to exporting there are no statistically significant differences between the sample family and non-family SMEs. Therefore, the hypothesis H3 is rejected. All control variables have significant and positive influence on the likelihood of exporting. Larger companies and companies that operate mainly in the manufacturing or trade sectors are significantly more likely to export products and/or services than the rest of the studied SMEs.

Table 3 Logistic regression of management practices associated with family or non-family firms

Dependent variables	Independent variables and goodness of fit measures	B	St. error	Wald
BUS_PLAN	FAMILY	−0.005	0.261	0.000
	SIZE	0.004	0.003	2.195
	TRADE	0.094	0.278	0.114
	MANUFACTURING	0.824**	0.326	6.386
	Constant	−0.002	0.190	0.000
	Model Chi-square	12.597**		
	Overall % correct predictions	57%		
M_STRATEGY	FAMILY	−0.117	0.284	0.169
	SIZE	−0.002	0.003	0.716
	TRADE	−0.672**	0.315	4.551
	MANUFACTURING	−1.193***	0.329	13.142
	Constant	1.469***	0.232	40.072
	Model Chi-square	17.383***		
	Overall % correct predictions	69.1%		
EXPORT	FAMILY	−0.012	0.421	0.001
	SIZE	0.019***	0.004	27.582
	TRADE	1.049**	0.506	4.293
	MANUFACTURING	1.786***	0.475	14.132
	Constant	−3.201***	0.414	59.651
	Model Chi-square	70.078***		
	Overall % correct predictions	88.9%		
TRAINING	FAMILY	−0.226	0.260	0.759
	SIZE	0.008***	0.003	7.971
	TRADE	−0.283	0.283	0.998
	MANUFACTURING	−0.329	0.312	1.110
	Constant	−0.128	0.189	0.459
	Model Chi-square	12.089**		
	Overall % correct predictions	59.1%		
INVEST_TR	FAMILY	−0.106	0.293	0.130
	SIZE	−0.012***	0.003	16.375
	TRADE	−0.011	0.317	0.001
	MANUFACTURING	0.312	0.361	0.745
	Constant	1.214***	0.217	31.158
	Model Chi-square	19.598***		
	Overall % correct predictions	73.2%		
INNOVATION	FAMILY	−0.106	0.290	0.133
	SIZE	0.009***	0.003	9.800
	TRADE	0.457	0.315	2.105
	MANUFACTURING	0.895***	0.327	7.505
	Constant	−1.346***	0.224	35.977
	Model Chi-square	25.642***		
	Overall % correct predictions	70.1%		

(continued)

Table 3 (continued)

Dependent variables	Independent variables and goodness of fit measures	B	St. error	Wald
TRADE_MARKS	FAMILY	−0.364	0.426	0.733
	SIZE	0.010***	0.003	12.574
	TRADE	0.785*	0.465	2.846
	MANUFACTURING	1.169**	0.453	6.647
	Constant	−2.697***	0.356	57.467
	Model Chi-square	27.597***		
	Overall % correct predictions	85.9%		
PATENTS	FAMILY	−0.145	0.505	0.082
	SIZE	0.003	0.004	0.462
	TRADE	0.120	0.550	0.048
	MANUFACTURING	0.408	0.553	0.544
	Constant	−2.695***	0.376	51.321
	Model Chi-square	1.510		
	Overall % correct predictions	92.6%		
MIS	FAMILY	−0.306	0.339	0.817
	SIZE	0.011***	0.003	14.687
	TRADE	−0.859	0.392	4.803
	MANUFACTURING	−0.239	0.366	0.426
	Constant	−1.204***	0.222	29.501
	Model Chi-square	24.710***		
	Overall % correct predictions	78.5%		
WEBSITE	FAMILY	−0.882***	0.275	10.285
	SIZE	0.011***	0.003	10.348
	TRADE	−0.273	0.293	0.872
	MANUFACTURING	−0.137	0.321	0.182
	Constant	−0.045	0.192	0.054
	Model Chi-square	31.016***		
	Overall % correct predictions	57.9%		
ONLINE_SALES	FAMILY	−0.577**	0.292	3.897
	SIZE	0.004	0.003	2.572
	TRADE	−0.251	0.304	0.680
	MANUFACTURING	−0.367	0.335	1.198
	Constant	−0.549***	0.197	7.794
	Model Chi-square	8.656*		
	Overall % correct predictions	69%		
ONLINE_PAYMENT	FAMILY	−0.738**	0.287	6.622
	SIZE	0.002	0.002	0.797
	TRADE	−0.384	0.299	1.651
	MANUFACTURING	−0.314	0.323	0.949
	Constant	−0.268	0.192	1.941
	Model Chi-square	10.910**		
	Overall % correct predictions	65%		

(continued)

Table 3 (continued)

Dependent variables	Independent variables and goodness of fit measures	B	St. error	Wald
E_SIGNATURE	FAMILY	−0.874***	0.274	10.157
	SIZE	0.048***	0.014	12.815
	TRADE	−0.242	0.300	0.651
	MANUFACTURING	−1.025***	0.355	8.349
	Constant	0.472**	0.216	4.784
	Model Chi-square	55.201***		
	Overall % correct predictions	67.4%		
STANDARDS	FAMILY	−0.321	0.294	1.187
	SIZE	0.042**	0.017	5.724
	TRADE	−0.177	0.315	0.316
	MANUFACTURING	0.461	0.423	1.192
	Constant	0.819***	0.239	11.753
	Model Chi-square	27.203***		
	Overall % correct predictions	76.2%		

Source: Authors
$*p < 0.1$; $**p < 0.05$; $***p < 0.01$

In the area of personnel training, our results indicate that family business status affects neither the likelihood of training provision nor the likelihood of investment in training. The hypotheses H4 and H5 are rejected. The variable SIZE influences positively the probability of training provision and negatively the probability of investment in training. Larger companies are more likely to have provided training to their employees during the last year, but smaller companies are more likely to have invested in personnel training during the same period.

As can be seen in Table 3, being a family business is not a significant predictor of the likelihood of introducing product innovations and registering intellectual property rights. Thus, the hypotheses H6 and H7 are rejected. Firm size and sector tend to influence significantly the likelihood of introducing product innovations and registering trade marks. Larger companies and companies in the manufacturing sector are more likely to have introduced a new or improved product during the last year. Smaller companies and companies that do not operate in the trade or manufacturing sector are less likely to have a registered trade mark. However, none of the independent variables employed in the study is found to affect the probability of registering a patent.

The probability of adoption of automatic MIS does not depend on the family business status and the sector. The hypothesis H8 is rejected. Family and Non-family businesses are equally likely to adopt automatic MIS. The variable SIZE appears as a significant predictor of the adoption of automatic MIS. Larger companies are more likely to adopt automatic MIS than smaller companies in the studied sample of Bulgarian SMEs.

Family SMEs are significantly less likely to use internet in their business activities than non-family SMEs in the sample. The variable FAMILY affects negatively the likelihood of having a website, online orders or sales, online payments, and electronic signature of managers. The hypothesis H9 cannot be rejected. Larger SMEs are more likely to have a website and an electronic signature of some of their managers than the rest of the sample SMEs. The companies that operate mainly in the manufacturing sector are less likely to have an electronic signature of some of their managers than SMEs operating in other sectors.

There are no significant differences in relation to quality and safety certification between family and non-family SMEs in the sample. These two groups of companies are equally likely to implement quality and safety standards. The hypothesis H10 is rejected. The smaller companies are less likely to implement such standards than larger companies in the sample.

7   Discussion and Conclusions

The shift from centrally planned economy to market economy in the countries in Central and Eastern Europe has led to the emergence of a large number of privately owned small and medium-sized enterprises including family businesses. SMEs play important role for the economic recovery in transition countries by contributing to the development entrepreneurial tradition and employment (Duh et al., 2009; McMillan & Woodruff, 2002). SMEs in transition economies face diverse challenges in the global economy (Szabó et al., 2010; Vladimirov, 2011b). Therefore, it is of the utmost importance to gain understanding of the management practices in both family and non-family SMEs in this context, because the adopted management practices determine firms' competitiveness in both local and international markets.

The present research is among the incipient investigations that attempts to compare management practices in family and non-family firms in a sample from a Central and Eastern European country. The proposed hypotheses are guided by previous theoretical and comparative empirical research on family business. In response to the methodological concerns expressed in the literature about the methodological appropriateness of some comparative studies of family and non-family businesses (Jorissen et al., 2005; Westhead, 1997; Westhead & Cowling, 1997, 1998), this study utilizes multivariate statistical techniques that control for the effects of a number of contextual variables as recommended by Jorissen et al. (2005). This approach allows for detecting real rather than sample differences between the studied family and non-family businesses (Jorissen et al., 2005).

The empirical findings of the present study support Jorissen et al.'s (2005) and Smith's (2007) conclusion that there are fewer "real" differences between family and non-family businesses than it was claimed in previous empirical research. The analysis demonstrates that after controlling for size and industry, the investigated family and non-family SMEs do not differ significantly with regard to the possession of short or medium-term business plan, adoption of a marketing strategy, exporting, provision and investment in personnel training, introduction of product innovations, registration of trade marks and patents, usage of automatic management information systems, and adoption of quality and safety standards. The significant similarities between family and non-family SMEs in this study may be explained with the specific historical circumstances associated with the emergence and development of private enterprises in transition economies. Both family and non-family businesses have established and operated in an environment characterized by a high degree of turbulence and uncertainty due to profound political, economic, and social changes in transition countries during the last 25 years and the integration of some of these countries into the European Union. SMEs and family businesses in this context tend to be relatively young (Duh et al., 2009; Yordanova, 2013). Duh et al. (2009) emphasize that transition economies in Central and Eastern Europe are dominated by first-generation family businesses that are still managed by their aging founder. Similar to Duh et al. (2009), in this study more than 80 % of the studied family SMEs are controlled by the first generation. Another reason for the similarities found in the studied sample may be that it is composed of SMEs. Smith (2007) argues that agency problems and effects may be stronger in larger family and non-family firms. The separation of ownership and control may be more pronounced in large non-family firms than in non-family SMEs (Smith, 2007), which in this respect are similar to family SMEs.

The only significant differences between family and non-family SMEs are related to the use of internet applications. Family SMEs are significantly less likely to have a website and electronic signature of managers and to provide an opportunity for online orders, sales, and payments. These findings may be explained with the greater lack of resources in family businesses such as finance and internal expertise in comparison with non-family businesses. Previous research suggests that the lack of finance and internal expertise is a major barrier to new technology adoption in small firms is (Wang & Ahmed, 2009). Family firms tend to have local business focus (Austrian Institute for SME Research, 2008) and therefore they may not be aware of the need and the benefits of using internet applications. Family firms tend to be inward looking, conservative, risk averse and resistant to change (Aronoff & Ward, 1997; Donckels & Fröhlich, 1991; Naldi et al., 2007; Sharma et al., 1997) and thus they may be reluctant to implement new technologies and to introduce the required changes in business models and communication channels (Buhalis & Law, 2008).

This research confirms previous evidence that firm size is the dominant independent variable that explains the managerial differences among SMEs rather than the family business status (Smith, 2007). Firm size appears as a significant determinant of the majority of the studied management practices. Larger SMEs in the studied sample are more likely to export products or services, provide personnel training, introduce product innovations, register trade marks, use internet applications and automatic management information systems, and adopt quality and safety standards, while smaller SMEs are more likely to invest in personnel training.

Major methodological advantages of this research are the use of a national representative sample of Bulgarian SMEs and multivariate statistical techniques that control for the effects of a number of contextual variables. However, the present study has several limitations that should be discussed. First, data was collected through a self-reported survey and thus may be subjected to cognitive biases and errors. Second, a number of other contextual variables, which are not included in the analysis, may be related to the adoption of the studied management practices in the sample companies. Third, the findings may be influenced by specific features of the Bulgarian cultural and institutional environment and therefore may not be applicable to other transition or mature economies.

In order to enhance the understanding about management practices in family and non-family companies operating in different contexts, future research needs to examine the following aspects. The management practices examined were limited to those covered in the database. Future research should investigate similarities and differences in the adoption of other management practices related to strategy, marketing, finance, human resource management, quality management, etc. Future research should also examine to what extent the findings of this study can be generalized to both large and small and medium-sized family and non-family firms operating in different contexts. A longitudinal analysis should complement the findings in this research in order to identify changes in the adopted management practices in different life-cycle stages in both family and non-family businesses.

The empirical results of the study advance our knowledge about management in family and non-family businesses in a transition context and have several practical implications. Policy makers, loan institutions, risk capitalists, job candidates, clients and other business partners should try to avoid stereotyped attitudes toward family businesses. Our findings refute one of the most widespread believes that family businesses are less professional than non-family businesses. We fail to detect differences in the adoption of a wide variety of management practices between the studied family and non-family firms. Firm size should be used as a more reliable indicator of the adoption of professional management practices than the family business status. The greater use of internet by small family firms should be encourage and supported because it was acknowledged that internet usage can help small companies gain a competitive advantage against their competitors (Poon & Swatman, 1995). From a pedagogical perspective, education and training in the field of family business management should emphasize that family and non-family businesses are not universally different. In some contexts, some types of family businesses may exhibit characteristics and behaviours similar to those of non-family businesses.

References

Aronoff, C. E., & Ward, J. L. (1997). *Preparing your family business for strategic change* (Family business leadership series, Vol. 9). Marietta, GA: Business Owner Resources.

Austrian Institute for SME Research. (2008). *Overview of family business relevant issues*. Final report, Vienna.

Barney, J. (1991). Firm resources and sustained competitive advantage. *Journal of Management, 17*, 99–120.

Beekhuyzen, J., Hellens, L., & Siedle, M. (2005). Cultural barriers in the adoption of emerging technologies. In *Proceedings of HCI International 2005*.

Beheshti, H. M., & Lollar, J. G. (2003). An empirical study of US SMEs using TQM. *TQM and Business Excellence, 14*(8), 839–847.

Bertolini, M., Rizzi, A., & Bevilacqua, M. (2007). An alternative approach to HACCP system implementation. *Journal of Food Engineering, 79*(4), 1322–1328.

Block, J. H. (2012). R&D investments in family and founder firms: An agency perspective. *Journal of Business Venturing, 27*, 248–265.

Block, J., Miller, D., Jaskiewicz, P., & Spiegel, F. (2013). Economic and technological importance of innovations in large family and founder firms: An analysis of patent data. *Family Business Review, 26*, 180–199.

Buhalis, D., & Law, R. (2008). Progress in information technology and tourism management: 20 years on and 10 years after the internet—The state of the eTourism research. *Tourism Management, 29*(4), 609–623.

Carney, M. (2005). Corporate governance and competitive advantage in family-controlled firms. *Entrepreneurship Theory and Practice, 29*(3), 249–265.

Chaganti, R., & Schneer, J. (1994). A study of the impact of owner's mode of entry on venture performance and management patterns. *Journal of Business Venturing, 9*, 243–246.

Chen, H. L., & Hsu, W. T. (2009). Family ownership, board independence, and R&D investment. *Family Business Review, 22*, 347–362.

Chin, C. L., Chen, Y. J., Kleinman, G., & Lee, P. (2009). Corporate ownership structure and innovation: Evidence from Taiwan's electronics industry. *Journal of Accounting Auditing Finance, 24*(1), 145–175.

Chittenden, F., Hall, G., & Hutchinson, P. (1996). Small firm growth, access to capital markets and financial structure: Review of issues and an empirical investigation. *Small Business Economics, 8*(1), 59–67.

Chrisman, J. J., Chua, J. H., & Litz, R. (2003). Discussion: A unified systems perspective of family firm performance: An extension and integration. *Journal of Business Venturing, 18*, 467–472.

Chrisman, J. J., Chua, J. H., & Sharma, P. (2005). Trends and directions in the development of a strategic management theory of the family firm. *Entrepreneurship Theory and Practice, 29*(5), 555–575.

Chrisman, J. J., & Patel, P. (2012). Variations in R&D investments of family and non-family firms: Behavioral agency and myopic loss aversion perspectives. *Academy of Management Journal, 55*, 976–997.

Chua, J. H., Chrisman, J. J., & Sharma, P. (1999). Defining the family business by behavior. *Entrepreneurship Theory and Practice, 23*, 19–39.

Chua, J., Chrisman, J., & Steier, L. (2003). Extending the theoretical horizons of family business research. *Entrepreneurship Theory and Practice, 27*(4), 331–338.

Churchill, N. C., & Hatten, K. J. (1987). Non-market based transfers of wealth and power. A research framework for family business. *American Journal of Small Business, 11*(3), 51–64.

Classen, N., Carree, M., Van Gils, A., & Peters, B. (2013). Innovation in family and non-family SMEs: An exploratory analysis. *Small Business Economics*. doi:10.1007/s11187-0139490-z. Advance online publication.

Classen, N., Van Gils, A., Bammens, Y., & Carree, M. (2012). Accessing resources from innovation partners: The search breadth of family SMEs. *Journal of Small Business Management, 50*, 191–215.

Coleman, S., & Carsky, M. (1999). Sources of capital for small family-owned businesses: Evidence from the national survey of small business finances. *Family Business Review, 12* (1), 73–85.

Cromie, S., Stephenson, B., & Monteith, D. (1995). The management of family firms: An empirical investigation. *International Small Business Journal, 13*(4), 11–34.

Czarnitzki, D., & Kraft, K. (2009). Capital control, debt financing and innovative activity. *Journal of Economic Behavior and Organization, 71*, 372–383.

Daily, C. M., & Dollinger, M. J. (1992). An empirical examination of ownership structure in family managed and professionally managed firms. *Family Business Review, 5*(2), 117–136.

Daily, C., & Dollinger, M. (1993). Alternative methodologies for identifying family- versus non-family-managed businesses. *Journal of Small Business Management, 31*, 79–90.

Daily, C. M., & Thompson, S. S. (1994). Ownership structure, strategic posture and firm growth: An empirical examination. *Family Business Review, 7*, 237–249.

Dana, L. P. (1999). Bulgaria at the crossroads of entrepreneurship. *Journal of Euromarketing, 8*(4), 27–50.

Dana, L. P., & Dana, T. (2003). Management and enterprise development in post-communist economies. *International Journal of Management and Enterprise Development, 1*(1), 45–54.

Davidkov, T., & Yordanova, D. (2013). The effect of entrepreneurial orientation on performance in Bulgarian enterprises: An empirical investigation. *Annuare de l'Universite de Sofia "St. Kliment Ohridski", Faculte des Sciences Economiques et de Gestion, 11*, 113–124.

Davis, P. S., & Harveston, P. D. (1998). The influence of family on the family business succession process: A multi-generational perspective. *Entrepreneurship Theory and Practice, 22*(3), 31–53.

de Lema, D. G. P., & Duréndez, A. (2007). Managerial behaviour of small and medium-sized family businesses: An empirical study. *International Journal of Entrepreneurial Behaviour and Research, 13*(3), 151–172.

De Massis, A., Frattini, F., & Lichtenthaler, U. (2012). Research on technological innovation in family firms: Present debates and future directions. *Family Business Review, 26*(1), 10–31

De Massis, A., Frattini, F., Pizzurno, E., & Cassia, L. (2013). Product innovation in family versus nonfamily firms: An exploratory analysis. *Journal of Small Business Management.* [Online] Wiley Online Library. Available from: http://onlinelibrary.wiley.com/doi/10.1111/jsbm.12068. Accessed 24 Feb 2014.

De Massis, A., Frattini, F., & Lichtenthaler, U. (2013). Research on technological innovation in family firms present debates and future directions. *Family Business Review, 26*(1), 10–31

Distelberg, B., & Sorenson, R. L. (2009). Updating systems concepts in family businesses: A focus on values, resource flows, and adaptability. *Family Business Review, 22*(1), 65–81.

Donckels, R., & Fröhlich, E. (1991). Are family businesses really different? European experiences from STRATOS. *Family Business Review, 4*(2), 149–160.

Donckels, R., & Lambrecht, J. (1999). The re-emergence of family-based enterprises in east central Europe: What can be learned from family business research in the western world? *Family Business Review, 12*(2), 171–188.

Duh, M., Tominc, P., & Rebernik, M. (2009). Growth ambitions and succession solutions in family businesses. *Journal of Small Business and Enterprise Development, 16*(2), 256–269.

Eurostat. (2012). *Europe in figures. Eurostat yearbook 2012.* Luxembourg: Publications Office of the European Union.

Fernández, Z., & Nieto, M. J. (2005). Internationalization strategy of small and medium-sized family businesses: Some influential factors. *Family Business Review, 18*(1), 77–89.

Fiegener, M., Brown, B., Prince, R., & File, M. (1996). Passing on strategic vision: Preferred modes of successor preparation by CEOs of family and non-family businesses. *Journal of Small Business Management, 34*(3), 15–26.

Gallo, M. A. (1995). The role of family business and its distinctive characteristic behavior in industrial activity. *Family Business Review, 8*(2), 83–97.

Gallo, M. A., & Pont, C. G. (1996). Important factors in family business internationalization. *Family Business Review, 9*(1), 45–59.

Gallo, M., Tapies, J., & Cappuyns, K. (2004). Comparison of family and nonfamily business: Financial logic and personal preferences. *Family Business Review, 17*, 303–318.

Gersick, K. E., Davis, J. A., Hampton, M., & Lansberg, I. (1997). *Generation to generation: Life cycles of the family business*. Boston: Harvard Business School Press.

Graves, C., & Thomas, I. (2006). Internationalization of Australian family businesses: A managerial capabilities perspective. *Family Business Review, 19*(3), 207–224.

Greene, W. (1997). *Econometric analysis*. London: Prentice-Hall International.

Gudmundson, D., Hartman, E. A., & Tower, C. B. (1999). Strategic orientation: Differences between family and nonfamily firms. *Family Business Review, 12*(1), 27–39.

Habbershon, T. G., & Williams, M. L. (1999). Resource-based framework for assessing the strategic advantages of family firms. *Family Business Review, 12*, 1–15.

Habbershon, T. G., Williams, M. L., & MacMillan, I. C. (2003). A unified systems perspective of family firm performance. *Journal of Business Venturing, 18*, 451–465.

Hair, F. J., Anderson, E. R., Tathan, L. R., & Black, C. (1998). *Multivariate data analysis* (5th ed.). Upper Saddle River, NJ: Prentice Hall.

Handler, W. C. (1989). Methodological issues and considerations in studying family businesses. *Family Business Review, 2*(3), 257–276.

Hendricks, K. B., & Singhal, V. R. (2000). *The impact of total quality management (TQM) on financial performance: Evidence from quality award winners*. Ontario and Atlanta. Accessed September 20, 2006, from www.comatech.be/nl/uk/artic1es.php-l0k

James, H. S. (1999). What can the family contribute to business? Examining contractual relationships. *Family Business Review, 12*(1), 61–71.

Jorissen, A., Laveren, E., Martens, R., & Reheul, A. (2005). Real versus sample-based differences in comparative family business research. *Family Business Review, 18*(3), 229–246.

Kalleberg, A. L., & Leicht, K. T. (1991). Gender and organizational performance: Determinants of small business survival and success. *Academy of Management Journal, 34*(1), 136–161.

Kets de Vries, M. F. (1994). The dynamics of family controlled firms: The good and the bad news. *Organizational Dynamics, 21*(3), 59–71.

Khan, T. R. (2012). Family businesses that produce counterfeits: What is stopping them from creating their own brand? *Procedia Economics and Finance, 4*, 304–311.

König, A., Kammerlander, N., & Enders, A. (2013). The family innovator's dilemma: How family influence affects the adoption of discontinuous technologies by incumbent firms. *Academy of Management Review, 38*(3), 418–441.

Kotey, B., & Folker, C. (2007). Employee training in SMEs: Effect of size and firm type—Family and nonfamily. *Journal of Small Business Management, 45*(2), 214–238.

Lansberg, I. (1983). Managing human resources in family firms: The problem of institutional overlap. *Organizational Dynamics, 12*(1), 39–46.

Lansberg, I. (1988). The succession conspiracy. *Family Business Review, 1*, 119–143.

Loan-Clarke, J., Boocock, G., Smith, A., & Whittaker, J. (1999). Investment in management training and development by small businesses. *Employee Relations, 21*(3), 296–311.

Maddala, G. (1983). *Limited dependent and qualitative variables in econometrics*. New York: Cambridge University Press.

Manolova, T., Carter, N., Manev, I., & Gyoshev, B. (2007). The differential effect of men and women entrepreneurs' human capital and networking on growth expectancies in Bulgaria. *Entrepreneurship Theory and Practice, 31*(3), 407–426.

Matlay, H. (2002). Training and HRD strategies in family and non-family owned small businesses: A comparative approach. *Education and Training, 44*(8/9), 357–369.

McMillan, J., & Woodruff, C. (2002). The central role of entrepreneurs in transition economies. *Journal of Economic Perspectives, 16*(3), 153–170.

Munari, F., Oriani, R., & Sobrero, M. (2010). The effects of owner identity and external governance systems on R&D investments: A study of western European firms. *Research Policy, 39*, 1093–1104.

Muñoz-Bullón, F., & Sanchez-Bueno, M. J. (2011). The impact of family involvement on the R&D intensity of publicly traded firms. *Family Business Review, 24*, 62–70.

Naldi, L., Nordqvist, M., Sjoberg, K., & Wiklund, J. (2007). Entrepreneurial orientation, risk taking, and performance in family firms. *Family Business Review, 20*, 33–47.

Nawata, K. (1994). Estimation of sample selection bias models by the maximum likelihood estimator and Heckman's two-step estimator. *Economics Letters, 45*(1), 33–40.

Nieto, M., Santamaria, L., & Fernandez, Z. (2013). Understanding the innovation behavior of family firms. *Journal of Small Business Management.* doi:10.1111/jsbm.12075. Advance online publication.

Patel, P., & Chrisman, J. (2013). Risk abatement as a strategy for R&D investments in family firms. *Strategic Management Journal.* doi:10.1002/smj.2119. Advance online publication.

Pelov, T. (2005). Development of family business through cooperation. *Economic Alternatives, 1.* Available at http://alternativi.unwe.bg/alternativi/index.php?nid=1

Peng, M. W. (2001). The resource-based view and international business. *Journal of Management, 27*(6), 803–829.

Pistrui, D., Welsch, H. P., & Roberts, J. S. (1995). Entrepreneurship, the family, and enterprise development in transforming economies: A Romanian perspective. In A. J. Haahti (Ed.), *Entrepreneurship and economic development* (pp. 147–162). Tampere: University of Tampere, School of Business Administration.

Pistrui, D., Welsch, H. P., & Roberts, J. P. (1997). The [re]-emergence of family businesses in the transforming Soviet Bloc: Family contributions to entrepreneurship development in Romania. *Family Business Review, 10*(3), 221–237.

Poon, S., & Swatman, P. (1995). The internet for small businesses: An enabling infrastructure for competitiveness. In *Proceedings of the fifth Internet Society conference*, Hawaii (pp. 221–231).

Poutziouris, P., O'Sullivan, K., & Nicolescu, L. (1997). The [re]-generation of family-business entrepreneurship in the Balkans. *Family Business Review, 10*(3), 239–261.

Ramadani, V., & Dana, L.-P. (2013). The state of entrepreneurship in the Balkans: Evidence from selected countries. In V. Ramadani & C. R. Schneider (Eds.), *Entrepreneurship in the Balkans: Diversity, support and prospects* (pp. 217–250). New York: Springer.

Ramadani, V., & Schneider, C. R. (2013). *Entrepreneurship in the Balkans: Diversity, support and prospects.* New York: Springer.

Reid, R., & Adams, J. (2001). Human resource management—A survey of practices within family and non-family firms. *Journal of European Industrial Training, 25*, 310–320.

Reid, R., Morrow, T., Kelly, B., Adams, J., & McCartan, P. (2000). Human resource management practices in SMEs: A comparative analysis of family and nonfamily businesses. *Journal of the Irish Academy of Management, 21*(2), 157–181.

Riemenschneider, C. K., Harrison, D. A., & Mykytyn, P. P., Jr. (2003). Understanding IT adoption decisions in small business: Integrating current theories. *Information and Management, 40*(4), 269–285.

Shanker, M. C., & Astrachan, J. H. (1996). Myths and realities: Family businesses' contribution to the US economy—A framework for assessing family business statistics. *Family Business Review, 9*(2), 107–119.

Sharma, P., Chrisman, J. J., & Chua, J. H. (1997). Strategic management of the family business: Past research and future challenges. *Family Business Review, 10*(1), 1–36.

Short, J. C., Payne, G. T., Brigham, K. H., Lumpkin, G. T., & Broberg, J. C. (2009). Family firms and entrepreneurial orientation in publicly traded firms: A comparative analysis of the S&P 500. *Family Business Review, 22*(1), 9–24.

Simeonova-Ganeva, R., Vladimirov, Z., Ganev, K., Panayotova, N., Dimitrova, T., Davidkova, T., et al. (2013). *A study of entrepreneurship and the prospects for innovations development in SMEs (2012-2013).* Bulgarian Small and Medium Enterprises Promotion Agency, Ministry of Economy, Energy and Tourism, INSIGHT: Noema & Sigma Hat, Sofia.

Simeonova-Ganeva, R., Vladimirov, Z., Ganev, K., Panayotova, N., Dimitrova, T., Yordanova, D., et al. (2012). *Analysis of the situation and factors for development of SMEs in Bulgaria 2011-2012: Economic recovery and competitiveness.* Bulgarian Small and Medium Enterprises Promotion Agency, Ministry of Economy, Energy and Tourism, Noema, Sofia.

Sirmon, D. G., & Hitt, M. A. (2003). Managing resources: Linking unique resources, management, and wealth creation in family firms. *Entrepreneurship Theory and Practice, 27*(4), 339–358.

Smallbone, D., & Welter, F. (2001). The distinctiveness of entrepreneurship in transition economies. *Small Business Economics, 16*(4), 249–262.

Smallbone, D., Welter, F., Isakova, N., & Slonimski, A. (2001). The contribution of small and medium enterprises to economic development in Ukraine and Belarus: Some policy perspectives. *MOCT-MOST, 11*, 253–273.

Smith, M. (2007). "Real" managerial differences between family and non-family firms. *International Journal of Entrepreneurial Behaviour and Research, 13*(5), 278–295.

Smyrnios, K., & Odgers, J. (2002). An exploration of owner and organizational characteristics, and relational marketing and opportunity search variables associated with fast-growth family versus nonfamily firms. In *Proceedings of the Family Business Network 13th annual world conference*, Helsinki, Finland (pp. 239–256). Lausanne, Switzerland: FBN.

Spence, M., & Crick, D. (2006). A comparative investigation into the internationalization of Canadian and UK high-tech SMEs. *International Marketing Review, 22*(5), 524–548.

Szabó, A., Yordanova, D., Kristi, D., Dejan, E., Szabó, Z., Gál, M., et al. (2010). The impact of the economic crises on SMEs in selected CEE countries. *ERENET Profile, V*(3), 6–29.

Tagiuri, R., & Davis, J. A. ([1982] 1996). Bivalent attributes of the family firm. *Family Business Review, 9*(2), 199–208.

Taylor, E. (2001). HACCP in small companies, benefit or burden. *Food Control, 12*(4), 217–222.

Taylor, E., & Taylor, J. Z. (2004). Using qualitative psychology to investigate HACCP implementation barriers. *International Journal of Environmental Health Research, 14*(1), 53–63.

Teal, E. J., Upton, N., & Seaman, S. L. (2003). A comparative analysis of strategic marketing practices of high-growth U.S. family and non-family firms. *Journal of Developmental Entrepreneurship, 8*(2), 177–195.

Tkachev, A., & Kolvereid, L. (1999). Self-employment intentions among Russian students. *Entrepreneurship and Regional Development, 11*(3), 269–280.

Todorov, K. (2006). Bulgarian entrepreneurship in united Europe: Challenges and opportunities. In: *Yearbook of UNWE* (pp. 77–100)

Todorov, K. (2011). *Business entrepreneurship. Part I: Foundations. Starting up a new business.* Sofia: BAMDE.

Upton, N., Teal, E. J., & Felan, J. T. (2001). Strategic and business planning practices for fast growth family firms. *Journal of Small Business Management, 39*, 60–72.

Vladimirov, Z. (2011a). Implementation of food safety management system in Bulgaria. *British Food Journal, 113*(1), 50–65.

Vladimirov, Z. (2011b). *Global challenges to small and medium-sized enterprises.* Sofia: University Press "St. Kliment Ohridski", 257 p.

Walker, E., Pritchard, C., & Forsythe, S. (2003). Hazard analysis critical control point and prerequisite programme implementation in small and medium size food businesses. *Food Control, 14*(3), 169–174.

Wang, Y., & Ahmed, P. K. (2009). The moderating effect of the business strategic orientation on eCommerce adoption: Evidence from UK family run SMEs. *Journal of Strategic Information Systems, 18*, 16–30.

Webb, J., Ketchen, D., & Ireland, R. D. (2010). Strategic entrepreneurship within family-controlled firms: Opportunities and challenges. *Journal of Family Business Strategy, 1*(2), 67–77.

Westhead, P. (1997). Ambitions, external environment and strategic factor differences between family and non-family companies. *Entrepreneurship and Regional Development, 9*(2), 127–158.

Westhead, P., & Cowling, M. (1997). Performance contrasts between family and non-family unquoted companies in the UK. *International Journal of Entrepreneurial Behaviour and Research, 3*(1), 30–52.

Westhead, P., & Cowling, M. (1998). Family firm research: The need for a methodological rethink. *Entrepreneurship Theory and Practice, 23*(1), 31–56.

Yapp, C., & Fairman, R. (2006). Factors affecting food safety compliance within small and medium-sized enterprises: Implications for regulatory and enforcement strategies. *Food Control, 17*(1), 42–51.

Yordanova, D. (2010). Succession in Bulgarian family firms. An explanatory investigation. In A. Surdej & K. Wach (Eds.), *Managing ownership and succession in family firms* (pp. 110–120). Warsaw: Scholar Publishing House.

Yordanova, D. (2011). Entrepreneurial orientation in family and non-family firms: Evidence from Bulgaria. *International Journal of Economic Sciences and Applied Research, 4*(1), 185–203.

Yordanova, D. (2012). Development and selection of successors in family firms: Evidence from Bulgaria. In *Annual book of Sofia University "St. Kliment Ohridski"* (Vol. 10, pp. 91–103). Faculty of Economics and Business Administration.

Yordanova, D. (2013). *Entrepreneurial orientation in Bulgarian family and non-family enterprises: Determinants and links with performance and internationalization.* Sofia: Avangard Prima Press.

Yordanova, D., & Davidkov, T. (2011). Determinants of entrepreneurial orientation: Evidence from Bulgaria. In G. Chobanov, J. Plöhn, & D. Schellhaass (Eds.), *Towards a knowledge based society in Europe* (Vol. 3). Frankfurt am Main: Peter Lang.

Zellweger, T. (2007). Time horizon, costs of equity capital, and generic investment strategies of firms. *Family Business Review, 20*, 1–15.

Zellweger, T., Nason, R., & Nordqvist, M. (2012). From longevity of firms to transgenerational entrepreneurship of families: Introducing family entrepreneurial orientation. *Family Business Review, 25*, 136–155.

Obstacles and Opportunities for Development of Family Businesses: Experiences from Moldova

Elena Aculai, Natalia Vinogradova, and Valentina Veverita

Abstract The chapter examines the processes of formation and development of small family enterprises, as in Moldova, the family business is created and developed mainly as micro and small enterprises. Since the activity of family businesses is not legally regulated and is not considered by the statistics in the Republic of Moldova, primarily the results of surveys and interviews with entrepreneurs, conducted by the authors during the realization of international projects and studies carried out in the National Institute for Economic Research of the Academy of Sciences of Moldova in the period 2001–2013 served the basis for writing this material. The chapter describes the barriers for family businesses, conditioned by their access to certain types of resources and other limiting factors from the external environment. Simultaneously, additional opportunities of the family SMEs are observed, arising through cooperation of the efforts and resources of family members, which allows increasing the assets of family businesses and partly compensating the shortcomings of the activity of business support institutes.

Keywords Family business • Small and medium-sized enterprises • Obstacles and opportunities for development of enterprises • Transition countries

1 Introduction

The scale of family businesses in economically developed countries can hardly be overestimated: in the OECD countries family run businesses account on average 85 % of all businesses and 90 % of businesses from the U.S. are family controlled (Barbera & Moores, 2011, p. 954). Family business is seen as a competitive

E. Aculai (✉) • N. Vinogradova
The National Institute for Economic Research of the Republic of Moldova, Chisinau, Republic of Moldova
e-mail: eaculai@yandex.com; natalia.vinogradova01@gmail.com

V. Veverita
Small and Medium-Sized Enterprises Development Policies and Liberal Profession Department, The Ministry of Economy of the Republic of Moldova, Chisinau, Republic of Moldova
e-mail: valentina.veverita@mec.gov.md

© Springer International Publishing Switzerland 2015
L.-P. Dana, V. Ramadani (eds.), *Family Businesses in Transition Economies*,
DOI 10.1007/978-3-319-14209-8_7

advantage in the long term, compared to non-family businesses (Heck et al., 2006, pp. 81–82). Thus, studies regarding the family controlled firms on the CAC40 and the S&P500 showed that family businesses have a better performance that exceeds the one of the non-family firms. The results of another study carried out in the U.S. show that return on investment is 25 % higher in family businesses (Kenyon-Rouviez & Ward, 2005, p. 2).

Family business also plays a significant role in emerging market relations in the modern period (Belak, Duh, Uršič, & Belak, 2005; Donckels & Lambrecht, 1999). First, the family businesses, along with other groups of enterprises contribute to the economic development of the regions by creating added value, providing jobs, attracting investment and so on. Secondly, family businesses contribute to the development of entrepreneurial potential and self-realization of business owners and also to the establishment of the middle class, providing social, economic and political stability of society in the long term.

The activity of family businesses is not legally regulated and is not considered by statistics in the Republic of Moldova. This article examines the small-scale family businesses, because, according to the authors, the family business in Moldova is created and developed mainly on micro and small enterprises.

Moldova stands among the countries with emerging market economy where the companies during all stages of their activities face many barriers. Problems appear to be relatively more difficult for micro and small enterprises, including the family type ones. The article describes the barriers for family businesses, conditioned by their access to certain types of resources and other limiting factors from the external environment. Simultaneously, additional opportunities of the family SMEs are observed, arising through cooperation efforts and resources of family members, which allow increasing the assets of family businesses, and partly compensating the shortcomings of the activity of business support institutes.

The results of surveys and interviews with employers served the basis for the research. They were conducted by the authors during the realization of international projects and studies carried out in the National Institute for Economic Research of the Academy of Sciences of Moldova, in the period 2001–2013. Besides, the data from the National Bureau of Statistics of the Republic of Moldova, Registration Chamber of the Republic of Moldova, the National Bank of Moldova, the results of other studies were also used.

2 Short Review of Economic Development of the Republic of Moldova in the Transition Period

The Republic of Moldova is a small country in southeastern Europe with the population of 3.5 million people and the territory of 33,846 km^2, situated between Romania and Ukraine. Until 1991, Moldova was one of the 15 republics of the Soviet Union. Since the late 1980s, and especially, since the early 1990s, Moldova has suffered significant changes both in political and economic spheres (Hensel & Gudim, 2004, pp. 89–102).

First, in 1991, Moldova declared its withdrawal from the USSR and the creation of the Republic of Moldova as an independent state. This was accompanied by rupture of closer economic ties of Moldovan enterprises (primarily, related to the military-industrial complex) with those from other former Soviet Republics; as well as by loss of a huge Soviet market. The situation was aggravated by the territorial conflict. The territory in the eastern part of the Republic of Moldova, which had a considerable industrial potential, has been severed from the official state. In 1992, it declared the political sovereignty and up to now it is beyond the control of the Moldovan government authorities.

Second, the country began the transition from a planned administrative economic system to the market economy. Unlike many countries in Central and Eastern Europe, in Moldova there was practically no private property to the early 1990s. Therefore, the transformation of the economy of the Republic of Moldova took place on several directions simultaneously:

– Transition from the planned administrative economy to the demand-oriented market economic relations based on economic freedom principles,
– Change of predominant ownership form in the economy: from the absolute monopoly of state ownership to the development of various forms of ownership, primarily, the private one (Mclindon, 1996, p. 115),
– Changing the size of economic entities from mainly large enterprises to small and medium-sized enterprises.

The mentioned political and economic reforms in the country have been accompanied by deep economic crisis, which was more profound than in neighboring countries. For instance, the fall of GDP in Moldova was so severe, that it still is only 59.5 % of GDP from 1989 (data from 2011) (Institute of Economy, Finance and Statistics of the Republic of Moldova, 2012b, p. 12).

The changes in politics, economics and the society led to the entrepreneurship's development. So as any private entrepreneurship was regarded as criminal activity in the first half of the 1980s (Efimov & Frolov, 1964, pp. 20–22), during the second half of the 1980s, the entrepreneurship based on personal labor of citizens and their family members (Law on self-employment, 1986), as well as in the form of cooperatives with the possibility to use of hired labor (Law on Cooperation in the USSR, 1988) has been legalized. These legal instruments have played a positive role as the people in Moldova could purchase a modest experience of entrepreneurship. This experience proved to be useful to them after 1991, when large state-owned enterprises were closed and thousands of people lost their jobs and livelihoods (Aculai & Veverita, 2012, pp. 74–83). Significant difficulties in the enterprises' creation (Smallbone & Welter, 2001, pp. 249–262) and the absence of the effective state support led to the fact that many officially registered businesses did not work, while the "parallel economy", included informal and internal systems of enterprise, has developed (Dana & Dana, 2003; Ramadani & Dana, 2013). "Shuttle traders", selling cheap goods imported from the neighboring countries, as well as

people who grew food on small plots of land by own labor were typical represen-
tatives of the Moldovan business at the initial stage of transition to the market
economy (Dana, 1997, pp. 269–277). A large part of them were so called forced
entrepreneurs, for whom entrepreneurship was the only way to feed their own
families (Aculai, 2013, pp. 28–40).

Since 1992, the legal framework regulating business in the modern Republic of
Moldova has began to be shaped (the Law on entrepreneurship and enterprises, the
first Law on support and protection of small business, etc. have been adopted). State
Programmes of small business development began to be elaborated and
implemented; the State Fund for Entrepreneurship Support was established. Thus,
there was developing the legislative and institutional framework, which to a certain
extent contributed to the establishment and development of entrepreneurship.

3   The Characteristics of Entrepreneurship in Present

Today, more than 160,000 companies are registered in Moldova, among which the
most are of such legal forms as limited liability companies (51.3 %) and individual
entrepreneurs (physical persons), (39.6 %) (see Fig. 1).

The vast majority of Moldovan enterprises are of private ownership of citizens
(89.8 %); 4.3 % are in foreign ownership and 4.1 %—in mixed ownership.
Currently, only 1.8 % of all enterprises are in the state (public) property (Fig. 2).

Trading is the most common activity in Moldova, while 40.4 % of the enterprises
being involved in this activity; industrial enterprises account for 10.2 %, construction—5.5 %. Agriculture includes 5.0 % of enterprises (excluding farms).

On average, one Moldovan enterprise employs 10.3 persons and the annual
turnover per 1 company accounted for 4.2 million MDL (about 232,000 EUR) in
2012; the average annual profit before taxation for one enterprise accounted for

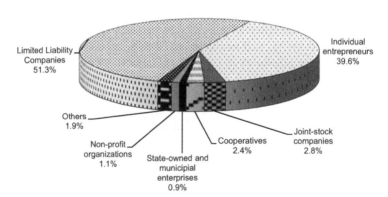

Fig. 1 Registered enterprises by legal forms, as to January, 1, 2014 (%) (source: State Chamber of
Registration of the Republic of Moldova, 2014)

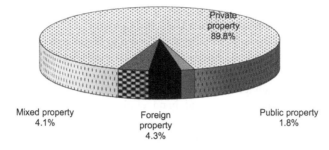

Fig. 2 Total enterprises by forms of ownership, 2012 (%) (source: National Bureau of Statistics of The Republic of Moldova, 2014)

92.9 thousand MDL (5,000 EUR), while 51 % of enterprises have finished the 2012 financial year with a loss.

A legal framework is established in the Republic of Moldova, which determines the basis for creation and activity of enterprises. Support directions for priority groups of enterprises, in particular related to the SMEs sector are also provided.

4   Family Business in Moldova: Preferential Development Within the Framework of Micro and Small Enterprises

The legal basis of entrepreneurial activity in the Republic of Moldova is established in the Law on Entrepreneurship and Enterprises 1992, which defines the possible legal forms of business, the specifics of their establishment, development and liquidation. But the mentioned law, as well as other legal acts of Moldova does not give a definition of family businesses and does not consider them as special organizational and legal forms of business. Accordingly, there is no statistics to identify and analyze a group of family-owned businesses.

According to the authors, the family business in the Republic of Moldova is developing mainly in the framework of micro and small enterprises. This conclusion is made due to the following circumstances:

First, we must consider the peculiarities of formation of private business in Moldova in the 1990s. During this period, private enterprises were established mainly in two ways. First of all, by creating from scratch and often forced of micro enterprises in order to receive the minimum subsistence income; these enterprises were characterized by limited capacities. As evidenced by interviews conducted by the authors in the framework of international projects, some of these enterprises were created by combining efforts and resources of family members. One of the typical histories about the creation and activity of the family business, related to the 'forced' business is presented in Box 1.

Box 1. Forced business in owners' declining years

Two pensioners, husband and wife were forced to organize a family business in 1996. The amount of their pensions was two times lower than the monthly utility bills.

Following the advice of a relative, spouses rented a retail space in the market and began selling second hand clothes, imported in the form of humanitarian aid from abroad. Previous activities of the spouses had nothing to do with trade, so they had in old age to learn the skills of trade for the first time.

Business was not officially registered. Initial costs were covered from their own modest savings.

The main purpose of the business at all stages was 'to survive' with no ambition or focus on growth. Both husband and wife, being elderly, gladly would have left this heavy business (both physically and mentally), if there was another source of income.

Source: INTAS (2001–2003, Case 18).

Another way of establishing private business was the privatization of large-scale state enterprises. The privatization method used in Moldova was based on providing every citizen the right to own a certain amount of national property, which was confirmed by a special document named patrimonial voucher. This document was not legally able to be sold or transferred to another person, so the accumulation of capital of large enterprises in the hands of one family was impossible. In subsequent years, during the process of redistribution of capital, some families may have had large stakes in individual companies, but these kinds of data are not published in statistics and these facts and are unknown for the public; we believe there were just few of such cases.

Secondly, it makes sense to pay attention to some of the characteristics of family relations in Moldova. In the traditional model of Moldovan family the dominant role belongs to the man. This is confirmed by the results of the households' survey, according to which the role of the head of the family belongs to the man in 62.7 % of households from urban areas and 74.5 % of rural households (National Bureau of Statistics of the Republic of Moldova, 2013a). In addition, the Republic of Moldova still keeps a non-uniform distribution of responsibility for housework between men and women. Cooking, washing, cleaning, shopping and even childcare are primarily on the women's responsibility. Thus, according to calculations made by Colesnicova (2012) in 2008, women from urban areas spent a day by 2.2 more time on housework than men. This gap was even greater in rural areas—by 3.3 times (Colesnicova, 2012, p. 108).

Different roles of women and men in family life are reflected in their participation in the business: 72.5 % of all entrepreneurs from Moldova are men, despite the fact that the proportion of men in the economically active population is much lower and accounts for 50.6 % (Table 1).

Table 1 Gender distribution of the various population groups (%)

	Entrepreneurs	Economically active population	Total population
Total, including:	100.0	100.0	100.0
Men	72.5	50.6	48.1
Women	27.5	49.4	51.9

Source: Based on Aculai (2009, p.13)

The presence of gender differences in society, family and business is confirmed in interviews by entrepreneurs, especially women. For example, an entrepreneur that has a small trading company, noted that the main qualities required for business, such as: responsibility, ability to make decisions and take risks are inherent mostly for men. Women are not accustomed to be leaders, because they were not prepared for this during their childhood (INTAS, 2001–2003, Case 4). Another business-woman who was leading business with her husband, related about the establishment of her entrepreneurial career as follows: "A woman finds more difficult to search for finance for the start of her own business. It is hard to overcome the stereotypes of society. At first, I was asked whose daughter was I. We normally think that every entrepreneur woman has a man behind her" (MyBusiness.md, 2013a).

These circumstances suggest that, if the owner and manager of the medium/large enterprise is a man, then, taking into account the traditional distribution of gender roles in the family, he would mainly accept his wife to be engaged in housework and raising children rather than work. Such views belong more to older people, but it should be noticed that the average age of the entrepreneur in Moldova is quite high being equal to 45 years old (Aculai, 2009, p. 17). In the opposite situation, when a woman acts as owner and manager of a medium/large business, it is more likely that she will attract her spouse into business. But this situation is observed relatively less, because, according to the National Bureau of Statistics, the proportion of women entrepreneurs in medium enterprises is 2.3 times lower than the corresponding share of men, and in large enterprises these figures vary by three times (Table 2).

Overprotection by parents of their adult children represents another specificity of family relationships inherent for Moldova. Traditionally, many parents try to 'extend the childhood' of their children, supporting them financially and after reaching adult age. For example, during one interview, entrepreneurs (husband and wife) told that one of the purposes of their business was to support their student daughters, one of whom lived with her parents, and the other—in neighboring Romania (INTAS, 2005–2007, Case 05). However, it was not supposed that student daughters could also participate in the family business.

Thirdly, it is important to note the adverse conditions of the business environment in Moldova, which persist throughout the period of economic reforms. Unfavorable business environment in condition of a low GDP per capita creates preconditions for the reproduction and expansion of a group of entrepreneurs who build their business forcedly under highly limited resources. In this situation, entrepreneurs believe that it is important to use the help of family members in the business—wives, parents, especially at the initial stage of business. In some cases, the subsequent development of a business can be successful. An example is presented in Box 2.

Table 2 Distribution of enterprises by size and by sex of entrepreneurs (%)

	Total	Including	
		Men	Women
Total including by number of employees:	100.0	100.0	100.0
0–9 persons (micro)	71.5	67.8	79.4
10–49 persons (small)	22.1	24.5	17.2
50–249 persons (medium)	5.4	6.6	2.9
250+ (large)	1.0	1.2	0.4

Source: Aculai (2009, p. 31)

Box 2. Family business grows: Moldovan embroidery kits are in demand in 27 countries

Anatol Luca and his wife Marina are former dancers from the Moldovan legendary folk dance ensemble "Joc". During their dance career they embroidered national costumes for the stage for several times, not knowing that this ancient craft in a few years will become the foundation of their family business.

In the early 1990s, it became clear that income from dancing was not enough to support and feed a family. Anatol decided to start a business selling haberdashery. Embroidery kits imported from Romania were one of the most in demand products in his stores. But these products were constantly going up in price and their imports became unprofitable. So, the couple decided to establish their own production of embroidery kits under the brand name "Luca-S". The production process was organized in their garage, where at the beginning Marina was working herself, and afterwards she was helped by a hired employee. The production was started with less expensive and simpler embroidery kits for children. Later, after ordering a special computer program in England, which developed the scheme of embroidery and the necessary range of colors, they moved towards production of more complex plots.

Family business of Anatol and Marina Luca began to grow. The cramped workroom in the garage was not enough and the couple rented a room for production. In parallel they began to attend specialized exhibition in Russia and Ukraine, where they found distributors for their products. In 2010, the company decided to enter the international market and went to the most prestigious in Europe exhibition of products for needlework in Cologne. Participation in the exhibition, despite the high costs brought success. The couple returned home with several contracts signed with the French, British and German partners. Over the past few years they built relations and began exporting products already in 27 countries, including Australia, China and Vietnam.

Source: Based on Mybusiness.Md (2013b).

Table 3 Entrepreneurs opinion on business environment changes (%)

Years	Change trends of the business environment		
	Better	Worse	No changes
2011–2013	17.7	46.9	35.4
2009–2011	20.4	32.0	47.6

Source: based on National Institute for Economic Research of the Republic of Moldova (2013); Institute of Economy, Finance and Statistics of the Republic of Moldova (2011)

In recent years, the Moldovan entrepreneurs are quite critical regarding the business climate in the country. The survey of them showed that in 2011–2013, according to the majority of respondents, the business environment has deteriorated. Thus, more respondents, than earlier mention about the deterioration of the environment in the recent 2 years (Table 3).

The above circumstances allow the authors to conclude that family businesses in Moldova are primarily connected to the *SME sector*, especially to the smallest size enterprises—micro and small.

5　Profile of the SME Sector in the Republic of Moldova

In the Republic of Moldova statistics keeps records about 49.4 thousand enterprises belonging to the SME sector, which accounts for 97.6 % of the total enterprises in the country. SMEs employ 57.7 % of the employees; produce 34.5 % of sales revenues and 23.0 % of the net profit. SMEs' share in GDP is 29.5 % (National Institute for Economic Research of the Republic of Moldova, 2013).

SMEs sector, in accordance with the legislation (The Republic of Moldova. Law on Support of Small and Medium-sized Enterprises Sector No. 206-XVI, 2006) consists of micro, small and medium-sized enterprises, the criteria for which are shown in Table 4.

Micro enterprises, possessing the most limited resources dominate in the structure of the SME sector, their share accounts for 77.5 % (see Fig. 3).

The potential of the SMEs sector in Moldova is quite limited: the average number of employees per one SME is 6.1 persons, at 1 micro enterprise—2.4 persons. Assets of one SME (according balance sheets of enterprises in 2012) amounted to 332.3 thousand MDL, or 20.8 thousand EUR (according to exchange rate at the date of December 29, 2012), including long-term assets—110.8 thousand MDL (or 6,000, 9,000 EUR) (National Bureau of Statistics of the Republic of Moldova, 2013b).

The Government recognizes the importance of SMEs for the economic and social development of the country therefore develops and implements policies that support this sector. To this end, the Law on support of small and medium-sized enterprises sector 2006 has been adopted; the Strategy of development of SMEs sector 2012 as well as several state programs have been developed and implemented.

Table 4 Quantitative criteria of SMEs in Republic of Moldova

Category of the enterprise according to its size	Number of employed persons	Gross profit, thousand EUR[a]	Balance sheet assets, thousand EUR[a]
Micro	1–9	<160.4	<160.4
Small	10–49	<1,336.9	<1,336.9
Medium	50–249	<2,673.8	<2,673.8

Source: The Republic of Moldova. Law on Support of Small and Medium-sized Enterprises Sector No. 206-XVI (2006)
[a]Calculated considering EURO exchange rate equal to 18.7 MDL, on March 7, 2014

Fig. 3 The structure of SME sector in the Republic of Moldova in 2012, % of total number of enterprises (source: based on National Bureau of Statistics of The Republic of Moldova, 2014)

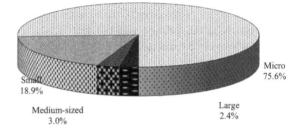

Public policy development on the SMEs sector is carried out by the Ministry of Economy of Moldova, in particular—Small and Medium-Sized Enterprises Development Policies and Liberal Profession Department. The state agency—the Organization for Development of Small and Medium Enterprises (ODIMM) is responsible for the implementation of policy in this area. Credit Guarantee Fund works within ODIMM, and provides loan guarantees to SMEs. At the regional level, the economic policy, including measures to support SMEs is implemented by economic departments under the public administration of districts.

Despite the existence of laws and implementation of a number of state programs and the work of institutions providing services to the SME sector, the business environment is not favorable in the country. For small-sized enterprises, including family ones, with limited resources, the negative impact of the business environment sometimes is relatively more important than for large firms. On the other hand, the question arises: is it possible to assume that the type of interactions in family businesses is an additional chance for them to survive and develop?

6 Limited Access of SMEs to the Resources and Family Businesses Opportunities

The limited access to resources represents a serious problem for the Moldovan SMEs. Results of the survey of entrepreneurs, carried out in 2012, showed that the barriers associated with funding sources (73.3 % of respondents) and human

Table 5 Enterprises problems related to access to resources

Problems	% of respondents that pointed on the problem[a]
Financial resources	73.3
Human resources	45.9
Equipment, technology	33.3
Raw materials	19.3
Real estate	11.1
Information	6.7
Others	3.7
No problems	4.4

Source: Institute of Economy, Finance and Statistics of the Republic of Moldova (2012a)
[a]Respondents had the opportunity to point out any number of problems

resources (45.9 % of respondents) are the most significant. The complete list of SMEs problems, stipulated by limited access to resources is presented in Table 5.

Family relations that are traditionally close in the Moldovan society, especially in rural areas often help in overcoming these problems. A typical example is that of a 39 year-old entrepreneur with a family, including two children, who maintain close relations with parents, brothers and sisters who live nearby, considering them a part of his family. Although he has an enough successful business (production of milk and dairy products), sometimes he asks for support from family and gets it in the form of labor, money or advice. Entrepreneur is sure that he would not have succeeded without their help (INTAS, 2001–2003, Case 11).

Difficult access to finance occupies the first place in all surveys conducted by the authors since 1997. This was indicated by 70–95 % of the respondents in different years (taking into account that they had the ability to mark all the existing problems). Specifying the reasons for difficult access to financial resources, entrepreneurs mention a high interest rate for the credit and the significant cost of its processing (82.8 % of respondents); the complexity of the procedure for obtaining credits (38.3 %) and lack of collateral (31.3 %) (Institute of Economy, Finance and Statistics of the Republic of Moldova, 2012a). Insufficiency of finances is exacerbated by the low income of citizens (in 2012, the average monthly disposable income per person in Moldova was only 1,508.8 MDL (80.7 EUR), as well as there are small amounts of deposits per 1 citizen of Moldova, which were 816 MDL (43.6 EUR) at the end of 2012.

The problem of access to finance is particularly important for micro enterprises whose owners had no previous business experience. In such circumstances, private funds of entrepreneurs and of their families are often the main sources of financial resources, which may be provided in the form of a loan or participation in the authorized capital of the enterprise. As a result, the union of family members' capital represents a real possibility of additional accumulation of financial assets for business establishment and development. In particular, the immediate family (spouses, parents) of the entrepreneur helps him/her gratuitously (INTAS, 2001–2003, Cases 4, 11, 13). More distant relatives can provide money as interest-free loans (INTAS, 2001–2003, Case 11), or at a certain percentage (INTAS, 2001–2003, Case 4). Entrepreneurs prefer more often relatives' credits than a bank loan that requires guarantee, which is not available at the stage of business formation (INTAS, 2001–2003, Case 4). In addition, relatives' credit is available in more affordable and flexible terms; for example, it is possible to postpone repayment of the loan, if necessary, without the imposition of penalties.

Additional benefits of combining of funds in family businesses is that family members are involved in business together and are considering the advisability of investing directions, respectively, increases the overall interest and responsibility for the results of business activities.

The second important problem of Moldovan SMEs, connected with the limited access to resources is associated with the <u>personnel</u>. In 2012, 45.9 % of respondents indicated on its importance, and this figure is increasing in recent years. Businesses face, first of all, such problems as the lack of professional qualification of employees (57.8 % of respondents, who reported on the existence of such a problem) and the complexity of the search of workers with the needed specialties (37.8 % of respondents). The complexity of the personnel's selection is caused by the outflow of skilled workers and professionals, and in general, of the most active people outside the country, as in Moldova it is difficult to find jobs with the desired level of remuneration. Another reason to cause difficulty in recruiting is the lack of institutions working in the labor market. On the other hand, many Moldovan entrepreneurs, especially small ones in order to search and recruit staff, use mainly informal sources (relatives, friends, former colleagues) without applying to employment centers and recruitment agencies.

The possibility to use the labor of family members in the interests of business represents, sometimes, a possible solution for the personnel problem. At the same time, "some family members work in the family business permanently, while others help if it is necessary" (INTAS, 2001–2003, Case 11). For example, one interviewed entrepreneur was helped by her husband who was a PhD, scientific researcher of the Academy of Sciences of Moldova during the establishment of her business by working her personal driver (INTAS, 2001–2003, Case 12). Benefits of using family members in the business are fairly obvious: members of the family business are more motivated, they can work for lower wages, often even without payment. They have more confidence because, as a rule, family members will not create an alternative business.

Negative characteristics of the use of family labor in the business (regardless of whether they are owners or not) can be informal employment, with the result that there are no contributions to the social fund, medical insurance and subsequently the pension.

Mutual assistance in the framework of the family business partly countervails the difficulties in relations with various government institutions. For example, in one interview, an entrepreneur confessed he did not know the details of the registration of the enterprise, as one of his "relatives" was engaged in this process and did it quickly for him (INTAS, 2001–2003, Case 11).

An important feature of the family business is the possibility of succession. For example, one of the surveyed entrepreneurs engaged in linguistic teaching pays her granddaughter education in foreign languages, hoping to eventually bring the girl to her business, and then—to transfer the business to her (INTAS, 2001–2003, Case 9).

Concomitant conditions that favor the development of the family business also include the support from those family members who assume the major share of the household works. This is especially important if the main role in the business belongs to a woman. For example, one interviewed entrepreneur specifically stressed the attention that her pensioner mother's help in childcare is a very important factor, which gives confidence in the health of children and frees up time for business (INTAS, 2001–2003, Case 10).

7 External Environmental Conditions and Their Impact on Family Businesses

The presence of an unfavorable business environment and the negative trends of its change are a serious barrier, causing the need for shady financial flows and thereby contributing to the maintenance of the informal economy. This increases the already existing great burden that lies on the entrepreneur and the stress associated with doing business, resulting in less time remaining to maintain his/her health and personal development, as well as to communicate with family members and friends. As a result, the entrepreneur has often no desire to transfer business, weighed down by serious challenges to their descendants. Simultaneously, a number of young people prefer to go abroad in search of employment or emigration. Not surprisingly, the average age of the Moldovan entrepreneur is 45 years old (Aculai, 2009, p. 17).

Simultaneously unfavorable business environment (primarily limited access to financial resources, lack of the personnel with the required specialties) may partly contribute to the formation of family businesses, but only in those cases when it comes to "forced" entrepreneurs. For example, an elderly father of two daughters who lost their jobs proposed them the idea of making the business of textile products for homes and offices. He invested some money in the statutory capital of the company, paid its registration and space renovation. He began working at the company as an accountant, but even when the business "grew up", he continued to help his daughters-entrepreneurs by financing the working capital. As a result, his daughters could financially support their families, and also got a taste for entrepreneurship (INTAS, 2001–2003, Case 16).

Labor migration, which is a characteristic feature of the modern economy of Moldova, although largely has a negative impact on the economic prospects of the country (the destruction of families, migration of young people, young children left without parents in the care of other relatives), but in a sense, is able to impact positively on the development of family businesses. Funds earned abroad can be invested in the development of their own business in their country. These kinds of businesses were established in the early 2000s as activities that did not require significant financial investments and complex management decisions. For example, in transport services when a minibus to transport passengers within the country was bought due the money earned from abroad (INTAS, 2001–2003, Cases 17, 29). But because the entrepreneurial spirit of the citizens of Moldova is underdeveloped, a relative big part of the money earned abroad until recently, were invested in real estate purchase or were spent on consumption. From 700,000 of our citizens who work abroad according to the statistics, only 7 % invest their money in the business in Moldova, while only 2 % open a new business from scratch here (Mybusiness. Md, 2014).

The state programme "PARE 1 + 1" is implemented in order to facilitate the process of investing resources of migrant workers in private business in the country. In the framework of this program, the government provides training to returned migrant workers or members of their families and then irrevocable financing in the amount of 200,000 MDL (10.7 thousand EUR) with the condition that to every one MDL invested from remittances, one MDL from the Programme will be added. For example, young entrepreneurs Valentina and Vasile Mihailov received a grant for the production of products of sheep wool based on knitwear under the state programme in 2011. They started with the production of woolen slippers, and since 2012, in addition to room shoes, spouses began to sew faux fur products: jackets, coats, blankets, belts and more. Today, 17 positions are already produced within their factory (Mybusiness.Md, 2014).

Changing the institution of the family, at least the traditional family model for Moldova—reducing the number of marriages, later marriage for both men and women, as well as a large number of divorces (which constitute 44 % of the number of marriages in 2012 compared with 32 %—in 1990), reduce the confidence in a partner, which may limit the development of the family business.

Illustration is the case when the divorce of spouses-business owners put enough successful development of the family business under the threat of bankruptcy (Box 3).

Box 3. Marital relations crisis as a threat to family business

In 1994, Petru and his wife Janna who lost their jobs due to staff cuts at the state factory founded a small family company making knitted products. The main reason for the creation of business was the search for income-generating possibilities in order to feed themselves and their three children. Initially, both contributed equally to the business. From time to time, they were assisted by their children and other relatives. As the enterprise grew, more management duties were performed by Janna, and in 1999 she became the general manager.

The company grew, reaching the medium size according to Moldovan legislation, and the brand became recognizable in the country. Petru, while still continuing to work at the enterprise, set up another business with friends, but did not managed to contribute any income to the family.

After a few years, the relationship between spouses got worse and during the divorce, the husband's demands regarding the division of property brought the company almost to the bankruptcy. Janna succeeded to improve the situation in the company, opened new stores of selling products, but the time was lost and new strong competitors managed to capture a significant market share.

Source: Based on Aculai, Vinogradova, and Welter (2008, pp. 93–94).

Some family businesses operating in Moldova are established within the framework of cross-border cooperation with neighboring countries—Romania and Ukraine. The presence of shared history, culture, language of Moldovan citizens with the cross-border population of neighboring countries contributed significantly for the establishment of such relations. It is important to take into account the relative ease of crossing the border: Ukraine (due to visa-free travel) and Romania—as many Moldovan citizens have dual citizenship (Moldovan and Romanian). The main feature of family businesses involved in cross-border cooperation are the expanding of boundaries of the family outside the country. For example, during some regular trips to Romania in order to visit the student daughter, a Moldovan entrepreneur was able to start a business related to the import of goods from Romania (INTAS, 2005–2007, Case 16). Another entrepreneur got married with a Romanian citizen and got the main help from his Romanian relatives—the family of his wife, who became a kind of representative of that business in Romania (INTAS, 2005–2007, Case 08). Geographic expansion of family businesses is expanding opportunities for their development, especially that the domestic market of Romania and Ukraine is much wider and the economic potential is higher than in the Republic of Moldova.

8   Some Conclusions

- Despite the fact that the establishment of a legally family business in Moldova is not regulated, the family business has been developing for more than 20 years.
- Formation of a family business is predominantly within the framework of micro and small enterprises, especially among the "forced" entrepreneurs.
- The characteristics of the family business in Moldova are currently due to: a relatively short period of time since the revival of private entrepreneurship in the late 1980s of the twentieth century; preserving elements of traditional family model and transfer of family relations in relations within the business; unfavorable business environment.
- Barriers to the family business are due to the general problems of SMEs, as well as the specific features of family businesses.
- At the same time, the family business does not only create barriers, but also provides additional opportunities for its development, partly compensating for the lack of resources, especially financial and personnel.
- Development of family businesses facilitates them to obtain the necessary business services in the context of the lack of infrastructure institutions.
- Opportunities for family businesses could grow significantly due to the regulation of these groups of companies.

References

Aculai, E. (2009). *Conditions for enterprise creation and development: Gender analysis.* [Online] UNDP, UNIFEM. Chisinau: Nova Imprim SRL. Available from: http://undp.md/presscentre/ 2009/Statistics_24Dec/block_Bussines_ENG_29-03-2010_NEW.pdf [Accessed: 15 February 2014].

Aculai, E., & Veverita, V. (2012). Legislation on small and medium-sized enterprises' support in the Republic of Moldova: Retrospective and present. *Economie si Sociologie, 2,* 74–83.

Aculai, E., Vinogradova, N., & Welter, F. (2008). How to be successful in an adverse business environment: Knitwear Factory in Moldova. In R. Aidis & F. Welter (Eds.), *Innovation and entrepreneurship: Successful Start-ups and Businesses in Emerging Economies* (pp. 89–104). Cornwall: Edward Elgar/MPG Books.

Aculai, E. (2013). Basic characteristics and specificities of SMEs in emerging market countries (in Romanian). *Economie şi Sociologie, 3,* 66 pp. Supplementary edition.

Barbera, F., & Moores, K. (2011). Firm ownership and productivity: A study of family and non-family SMEs. *Small Business Economics, 40*(4), 953–976.

Belak, J., Duh, M., Uršič, M., & Belak, J. (2005). *The importance of family enterprises for the development of less developed regions.* [Online] Prague. Available from: http://www.agris.cz/ Content/files/main_files/59/137575/belak.pdf. [Accessed: 1 March 2014].

Colesnicova, T. (2012). *Gender equality regulation in the sphere of employment in the Republic of Moldova.* Chisinau: Ed. Complex of IEFS.

Dana, L.-P. (1997). Stalemate in Moldova. *Entrepreneurship, Innovation, and Change, 6*(3), 269–277.

Dana, L.-P., & Dana, T. (2003). Management and enterprise development in post-communist economies. *International Journal of Management and Enterprise Development, 1*(1), 45–54.

Donckels, R., & Lambrecht, J. (1999). The re-emergence of family-based enterprises in East Central Europe: What can be learned from family business research in the western world? *Family Business Review, 12*(2), 171–188.

Efimov, M., & Frolov, E. (1964). Responsibility for private entrepreneurial activities and commercial mediation (in Russian). *Sovetskaya yustizia, 18*, 20–22.

Heck, R. K. Z., Danes, S. M., Fitzgerald, M. A., Haynes, G. W., Jasper, C. R., Schrank, H. L., et al. (2006). The family's dynamic role within family business entrepreneurship. In P. Z. Poutziouris, K. X. Smyrnios, & S. B. Klein (Eds.), *Handbook of research on family business*. Northampton, MA: Edward Elgar.

Hensel, S., & Gudim, A. (2004). Moldova's Economic Transition: Slow and Contradictory. In A. Lewis (Ed.), *The EU and Moldova. On a fault-line of Europe* (pp. 89–102). London: Federal Trust.

Institute of Economy, Finance and Statistics of The Republic of Moldova. (2011). *Analiza formelor existente de organizare a dialogului dintre Î}\\^{I}{MM şi organele administraţiei publice, identificarea mecanismelor de consolidare a acestui dialog la diferite nivele de administrare*. Scientific Report/Aculai, E. et al. Chisinau: IEFS.

Institute of Economy, Finance and Statistics of The Republic of Moldova. (2012a). *Evaluarea posibilităţilor şi formelor preferenţiale de parteneriat social între Î}\\^{I}{MM şi organele administraţiei publice, dezvoltarea responsabilităţii sociale a întreprinderilor*. Scientific Report/Aculai, E. et al. Chisinau: IEFS.

Institute of Economy, Finance and Statistics of The Republic of Moldova. (2012b). *Prognozarea şi monitorizarea indicatorilor macroeconomici ai Republicii Moldova (pentru perioada 2013-2015)*. Scientific Report/Chistruga, M., Olarescu, Z. et al. Chisinau: IEFS.

INTAS. (2001–2003). Female Entrepreneurship in Transition Economies: The Example of Ukraine, Moldova and Uzbekistan (contract no. INTAS 00-0843)/F.Welter (coordinator).

INTAS. (2005–2007). Cross-border cooperation and partnership in selected NIS countries and the consequences of EU-enlargement: Fostering entrepreneurship in the Ukraine, Belarus and Moldova (contract no. INTAS 04-79-6991)/D. Smallbone (coordinator).

Kenyon-Rouviez, D., & Ward, L. (2005). *Family business: Key issues*. New York: Macmillan.

Mclindon, M. P. (1996). *Privatization and capital market development: Strategies to promote economic growth*. London: Praeger.

Mybusiness.Md. (2013a). *Арина Даниска: опытом и достижениями нужно делиться.* [Online] Available from: http://mybusiness.md/categories/item/1098-arina-daniska-opytom-i-dostizhenijami-nuzhno-delitsja [Accessed: 15 February 2014].

Mybusiness.Md. (2013b). *Полмира вышивает по-молдавски...* [Online] Available from: http://mybusiness.md/categories/item/1207-polmira-vyshivaet-po-moldavski [Accessed: 15 February 2014].

Mybusiness.Md. (2014). *Vasilini—популяризатор австралийского мериноса в Молдове.* [Online] Available from: http://mybusiness.md/categories/item/1348-vasilini-populjarizator-avstralijskogo-merinosa-v-moldove [Accessed: 15th February 2014].

National Bureau of Statistics of The Republic of Moldova. (2013a). *Household budget survey in the Republic of Moldova for 2012*. Unpublished.

National Bureau of Statistics of The Republic of Moldova. (2013b). *Generalized balance sheet of micro enterprises for 2012*. Unpublished.

National Bureau of Statistics of The Republic of Moldova. (2014). Statistical databank. [Online] Available from: http://statbank.statistica.md/pxweb/Database/EN/databasetree.asp. [Accessed: 1 March 2014].

National Institute for Economic Research of the Republic of Moldova. (2013). *Cercetarea procesului de creare a parteneriatului public-privat, identificarea factorilor, evaluarea formelor şi direcţiilor de dezvoltare a acestuia*. Scientific Report/Aculai, E. et al. Chisinau: INCE.

Ramadani, V., & Dana, L.-P. (2013). The state of entrepreneurship in the Balkans: Evidence from selected countries. In V. Ramadani & R. C. Schneider (Eds.), *Entrepreneurship in the Balkans*. Berlin: Springer.

Smallbone, D., & Welter, F. (2001). The distinctiveness of entrepreneurship in transition economies. *Small Business Economics, 16*, 249–262.

State Chamber of Registration of the Republic of Moldova. (2014). *Statistics data*. [Online] Available from: http://www.cis.gov.md/content/6 [Accessed: 15 February 2014].

The Republic of Moldova. Law on Entrepreneurship and Enterprises No. 845, 1992. (1994). Chisinau: Monitor of Parliament, No. 2.

The Republic of Moldova. Law on Support of Small and Medium-sized Enterprises Sector No. 206-XVI, 2006. (2006). Chisinau: Official Monitor No. 126-130/605.

The Republic of Moldova. Strategy for Development of Small and Medium-sized Enterprises for 2012-2020. (2012). Chisinau: Official Monitor No. 198-204.

Welter, F., Smallbone, D., Aculai, E., Rodionova, N., & Vinogradova, N. (2003). *Female entrepreneurship in transition economies: The example of Ukraine, Moldova and Uzbekistan (2001-2003)*. National Report on Survey Data for Moldova (INTAS-2000-00843). Essen: Rheinisch-Westfalisches Institut fur Wirtschaftsforschung.

Successors' Innovativeness as a Crucial Succession Challenge of Family Businesses in Transition Economies: The Case of Slovenia

Marina Letonja and Mojca Duh

Abstract This contribution aims to broaden our understanding of factors affecting innovativeness of successors in family businesses in transition economies. In-depth literature review was conducted and three main constructs were identified as having considerable impact on successors' innovativeness and that are: entrepreneurialism, knowledge transfer and creation, and social capital. We applied a multiple-case study approach and the main research findings of ten cases of Slovenian family businesses are discussed. We developed six propositions that provide a basis for further empirical testing of factor influencing successors' innovativeness and innovation ability of family businesses in transition economies.

Keywords Family business • Succession • Founder • Successor • Innovativeness • Social capital • Tacit knowledge • Knowledge transfer • Transition economy • Slovenia

1 Introduction

While family businesses and succession have become an interesting subject of research in the recent years, and since 1990 the interest in the field has grown (Chirico, 2008), the question of smaller family firms (SFF) ability for innovation processes remains relatively unexplored (Chrisman, Chua, & Sharma, 2003). SME's, innovation marketing and excellent research systems are drivers of innovation growth in EU. SFF represent an important share in the structure of all firms; over 70 % of all firms worldwide, according to Mandl (2008). Thus increase of their

M. Letonja
GEA College – Faculty of Entrepreneurship, Dunajska cesta 156, 1000 Ljubljana, Slovenia
e-mail: marina.letonja@gmail.com

M. Duh (✉)
Faculty of Economics and Business, University of Maribor, Razlagova 14, 2000 Maribor, Slovenia
e-mail: mojca.duh@uni-mb.si

© Springer International Publishing Switzerland 2015
L.-P. Dana, V. Ramadani (eds.), *Family Businesses in Transition Economies*,
DOI 10.1007/978-3-319-14209-8_8

innovativeness is crucial for development of EU and Slovenia, which is one of the innovation followers with a below average performance, as an innovative society.

In our contribution we study SFF on a case of transitional economy in Slovenia. Although Slovenia, from a legal prospective is not in transition anymore, we believe, that from economic-development aspect it can be viewed as a transitional economy. Transition from this aspect means a transition from a routine to an innovative economy and society, which Slovenia has not achieved yet. This is a reason why we claim that Slovenia is still in transition (e.g., Bekö & Jagrič, 2011).

Very little is known on how SFF in transition economies face the challenges of succession. Owners/managers of SFF, mostly founders, practically have no experience in managing the succession process, as there is no tradition in these economies. Institutional support in a form of consulting and training is lacking as well and SFF are seldom subject of political or only occasionally public discussion (Duh, 2008). Our research focuses on the transition of SFF to the next generation as a potential for innovation processes in SFF in a transition economy. We explore innovativeness of the next generation and its importance for innovativeness and long-term sustainable development of SFF due to the fact that competitivness and long-term success are crucially determined by continuous innovation of products, processes as well as by social innovation. Our study aims at investigating crucial factors affecting innovativeness of successors in SFF in a transition economy. Therefore, the main research questions, which we address in our contribution, are: *Which factors strengthen or weaken innovativeness of the next generation in SFF in a transition economy? Why and how transfer of experiential knowledge (tacit knowledge shared through common experiences), routine knowledge (tacit knowledge routinized and embedded in actions and practice) and social capital of founder affect innovativeness of successors? Why and how entrepreneurialism and academic knowledge on the field of entrepreneurship affect innovativeness of successors?*

We conducted in-depth literature review and applied multiple-case study approach in the process of searching answers to our resarch questions. We conducted case studies of ten SFF. We limit our research on leadership succession which is found to be "one of the most challenging tasks in an organizational life" (Zahra & Sharma, 2004, p. 334). Our research addresses only inter-generational family succession, since research findings indicate that a majority of family enterprises' leaders have been found to be desirous of retaining family control past their tenure (e.g., Le Breton-Miller, Miller, & Steier, 2004). Due to strong presence of SFF in many Central and Eastern European post-socialist countries, we believe that our research findings could be of importance for academics, professionals and owners/managers of SFF in these countries.

This contribution is divided into four sections. Following the introduction section, the theoretical background is discussed in the second section. In the third section, methodology and findings with propositions are presented. The concluding section highlights the most important findings, future research directions and implications for owners and/or managers of family businesses.

2 Theoretical Background

2.1 Transition in Slovenia

Slovenia lies at the crossroads of commercial routes from the Southwest to the Southeast of Europe, and from Western Europe to the Near East. With approximately a population of two million living in a vastly diverse territory of 20,000 square kilometers it is a relatively small country. It is young country since it became independent state after the collapse of the Socialist Federal Republic of Yugoslavia in 1990. Slovenia has entered European Union (EU) in May 2004 as the most advanced of all transition economies in Central and Eastern Europe.

Since 1990 Slovenia has undergone a threefold transition: (1) transition from a socialist to a market economy, (2) transition from a regional to a national economy, and (3) transition from being a part of Yugoslavia to becoming an independent state and a member of the EU (Mrak, Rojec, & Silva-Jáuregui, 2004). The transition to the market economy from the former socialist economy with social and state ownership in Slovenia was closely associated with the development of small and medium-sized enterprises (SMEs). The legal bases for the development of private SMEs were the Law on Enterprises (1988) and the Law on Craft (1988). The first law opened opportunities for the development of the private entrepreneurial sector, and the second law reduced obstacles for the development of the craft sector, especially limitations on employment in craft enterprises. Even though Slovenia's macro-economic environment was traditionally not very supportive to entrepreneurship (Ramadani & Dana, 2013), the number of SMEs increased dramatically since the 1990s. In the year 2010 there were 126.965 enterprises in Slovenia, of which 99.8 % were micro (enterprises with 0–9 employees), small (enterprises with 10–49 employees) and medium-sized (enterprises with 50–249 employees) enterprises. Only 0.2 % of all enterprises in Slovenia had more than 250 employees, however providing 30 % of the nation's jobs. The same percentage of jobs (30 %) is provided by micro enterprises. The size structure of enterprises and the employment share in Slovenia is comparable to the one in EU-27, whereas there are big differences in value added per employee. Value added per employee in EU-27 is 47,080 € and 29,840 € in Slovenia indicating that Slovenian enterprises considerably lag behind EU-27 average value added per employees (Močnik, 2012). Recent economic crisis has reduced a number of employees in Slovenian enterprises. In the time period 2008–2010 a number of employees has been reduced for 16.6 % in large enterprises, and for 4.9 % in SMEs. Contrary, micro enterprises increase a number of employees (1.6 % growth rate) (Širec, 2012).

Several researches ascertain that Slovenia is not in transition anymore when looking from legal perspective (e.g., Bekö & Jagrič, 2011). However, when looking from economic-development perspective Slovenia can still be viewed as a transitional economy since a transition from a routine to an innovative economy and society has not been finished yet. In many cases economic reforms have been faster than the change in mindset and the ability of people to adapt thereby delaying a transition (e.g., Dana & Dana, 2003). Recent GEM (Global entrepreneurship monitor) research for Slovenia show that a gap still exist between the respect people exhibit towards entrepreneurship as a profession and their belief that entrepreneurship is a good career choice (Rebernik et al., 2014). In authors' opinion not enough effort has been devoted in society for transforming the declared respect of individuals for entrepreneurship as a profession into their actual decision to pursue an entrepreneurial career. Besides necessary creation of normal business environment in Slovenia, the efforts should be made to raise people's awareness that entrepreneurship can be a good career path which allows a good work-life balance.

2.2   Family Business Succession and Its Specifics in Slovenia

One of the major problems family businesses encounter is the transfer of ownership and management to the next family generation (e.g., Sharma, Chrisman, & Chua, 2003). Research findings indicate that only 30 % of family enterprises survive to the second generation because of unsolved or badly solved succession to the next family generation, and many enterprises fail soon after the second generation takes control (Morris, Williams, Allen, & Avila, 1997). The low survival rates could be explained by research findings showing that family enterprises have become more conservative and less innovative over time (e.g., Donckels & Fröhlich, 1991), and second generation family businesses often fail due to inaction and reluctance to seek out new business opportunities (Ward, 1997). Dyck, Mauws, Starke, and Mischke (2002) suggest that succession can represent a strategic opportunity in rapidly growing firms or firms in emerging and dynamic markets which are facing changing managerial needs.

We believe that the survival of family firms across generations depends on their ability to renew through innovation. The realization of effective succession, and firm's innovation and competitiveness in the succeeding generation depends to great extent on the preparation of the competent leader and enhancement of his/her innovativeness. The exploration of family business's succession as a process of strategic renewal by enhancing successor's innovativeness is of special importance for transition economies among which we still encounter Slovenia (as explained in previous section). According to some research results there are between 40 and 52 % (Duh & Tominc, 2005) or even 60–80 % of SFF in Slovenia (e.g., Glas, Herle, Lovšin Kozina, & Vadnjal, 2006), contributing 30 % of the GDP (Vadnjal, 2006) and the majority of them being in the first family generation (Duh, 2008). Recently the subject of discussion has become the problem of transferring family firms to the next generation. Namely, SFF established in 1990s, are approaching the critical phase of transferring firms to the next generation. Owners/managers of SFF, mostly founders, practically have no experience in managing process of succession, as there is no tradition of succession in Slovenia and similar is true for other transition countries. Since Slovenia is one of the innovation followers with a below average performance, the enhancement of innovativeness of successors and their firms is of crucial importance for the future of Slovenia as innovative society.

2.3 Successors' Innovativeness

Innovativeness refers to "a firm's tendency to engage in and support new ideas, novelty, experimentation, and creative processes that may result in new products, services, or technological processes" (Lumpkin & Dess, 1996, p. 142). In family firms, innovativeness is regarded as a highly important dimension of entrepreneurial orientation for long-term performance, together with autonomy and pro-activeness (Nordqvist, Habbershon, & Melin, 2008). According to our belief entrepreneurs are not managers, but innovators, therefore succession should contribute to enhancement of the level of entrepreneurship, rather than efficiency. More than production and ability to produce at the lowest costs, it is important that successors have entrepreneurial education and enough knowledge for innovation ability. According to Steier (2001) innovation ability of firms is complemented by social capital, which is defined as a stock of resources and abilities in a network of relationships between firms and/or people and it encourages cooperative behavior, thereby facilitating the development of new forms of association and innovative organization.

In our study we are exploring three constructs and that are entrepreneurialism (i.e., entrepreneurial competences of successors), knowledge transfer and creation, and social capital, and their impact on successors' innovativeness.

2.3.1 Entrepreneurialism

Entrepreneurialism stands for entrepreneurial competencies, which are according to Ganzaroli, Fiscato, and Pilotti (2006): attitude toward problem solving, attitude toward entrepreneurship, social relationships, attitude toward risk, attitude toward negotiation, attitude toward team working, creativity, technical knowledge and competence, marketing knowledge and competence, administrative knowledge and competence, working commitment, communication skills, motivating skills. This definition coincides, although not entirely, with the description of factors, leading to innovation at the individual level as proposed by Litz and Kleysen (2001).

In our research we propose entrepreneurial competences as crucial for development of innovative capabilities of successors. We follow Ganzaroli et al. (2006) and their definition of factors, contributing to the formation of entrepreneurial competences: working experience outside the SFF, family context (i.e., familiness) and formal education (i.e., in entrepreneurship).

2.3.2 Knowledge Transfer and Creation

The processes of creating new and using existent knowledge are of crucial importance for fostering innovations in organizations. Nonaka, Toyama, and Konno
(2000) see organizations as entities which create knowledge continuously through
so called SECI process (i.e., socialization, externalization, combination, and inter-
nalization), which is central to the organizational knowledge creation theory aiming
at explaining organizational creativity, change and innovation.The concept of
knowledge conversion is based on one of the most recognized typology of knowledge which differentiates between explicit and tacit (implicit) knowledge (e.g.,
Nonaka & von Krogh, 2009). In family business literature the transfer of tacit
knowledge from predecessor to successor and successor's training to assume the
top management functions have been found to be key processes in developing and
protecting knowledge and guaranteeing the continuity of the family business since
family firms often "maintain their own ways of doing things—a special technology
or commercial know-how that distinguish them from their competitors" (Cabrera-
Suárez, De Saa-Pérez, & García-Almeida, 2001, p. 38). However, many authors
suggest that successors have not only to acquire knowledge from the members of
previous generation, but also add new knowledge and diverse perspectives
(Cabrera-Suárez et al., 2001; Chirico, 2008; Kellermanns & Eddelston, 2004)
since fast changing environment "requires raising potential successors who add
future value to the firm by seeking new opportunities and fostering entrepreneurship" (García-Álvarez, López-Sintas, & Gonzalvo, 2002, p. 202). For this reason,
different research studies address early exposure to a family business (e.g., Gersick,
Davis, McCollom Hampton, & Lansberg, 1997), apprenticeship (Chirico, 2008; Le
Breton-Miller et al., 2004), the role of mentoring in family firms (Boyd, Upton, &
Wircenski, 1999), involvement of the next-generation family members in decison-
making and strategic planning (Mazzola, Marchision, & Astrachan, 2008) and team
working, as well as knowledge accumulation by learning-by- doing (Chirico, 2008).

2.3.3 Social Capital

Social capital complements innovation ability of firms (Steier, 2001), and firms
derive social capital from their embeddedness in the overall structure of a network
and from their embeddedness in different relationships within a network (Uzzi,
1997). According to Light and Dana (2013) social capital that involves relationship
of mutual trust and the norm of recipocity facilitate entrepreneurship only when
supportive cultural capital exists. Social capital has also been explained as an
internal phenomenon as "some aspect of social structure that facilitates certain
actions of individuals within the structure" (Coleman, 1990, p. 302) and thus
internal social capital. The complexity of social capital relates to many issues that
can exist within the family firm, including "norms, values, cooperation, vision,
purpose, and trust" (Pearson, Carr, & Shaw, 2008).

Nahapiet and Ghoshal (1998) proposed three distinct dimensions of social capital: a structural dimension, a cognitive dimension and a relational dimension. According to Inkpen and Tsang (2005) structural dimension involves the pattern of relationships between network actors. It concerns the configuration of linkages among units or firms and the extent of centrality in social networks; a cognitive dimension reflects the shared purpose and meaning created through lasting relationships within the organization or group; and a relational dimension represents the trust, obligations, and commitments that result from the personal relationships that are created through the structural and cognitive dimensions.

3 Method

3.1 Case Study Approach

The research questions and the field development level on the topic researched induced us to adopt a qualitative empirical research approach. We used a multiple-case study approach (e.g., Yin, 2003), which has been widely accepted in family business research (e.g., Chirico, 2008). Multiple cases "permit replication logic where each case is viewed as an independent experiment that either confirms or does not the theoretical background and the new emerging insights" (Chirico, 2008, p. 435). Although there is no ideal number of cases, Eisenhardt (1989) believes that between four and ten cases is best in order to increase rigor. We selected ten cases from the database which authors of the paper have been creating for many years.

3.2 Data Collection

We selected ten cases of family firms in the size class of micro, small and medium sized family firms (from 0 to 249 employees). Namely, many micro enterprises face the problem of transferring ownership and management to the next generation. This is why we talk SFF. Limitation for the sample was that founder of the firm is employed in a firm, still owns a firm or is active in the firm, although retired, and that next generation is involved in a firm. For the purpose of our research we defined a family firm as the one in which a founder (i.e., an owner/manager) considers the business as a family one. Research was geographically limited to Slovenia.

The authors conducted personal interviews with a founder and a successor since they are very well qualified to elaborate on it and since there might be significant differences in perceptions between founders and successors (e.g., Zahra & Sharma, 2004). In all cases interviews took place at premises of a company during the working days. It is believed the timing and place of the interview did not influence on the readiness and openness to reveal data and information.

Our sample consists of ten SFF (two micro, four small, four medium-sized firms). They employ minimum eight workers (total of 657, average of 66), 39 family members. The geographical dispersion of the sample is favorable, as our selected cases cover all Slovenian regions. The average age of the SFF is 23.4 years. Most of SFF (five) report medium, two high and three low technological complexity of a firm. Eight successors are employed in their SFF. The average age of the successors is 29.7 years. The involved firms have 18 successors and 10 potential successors.

3.3   Data Analysis

We built ten extensive case studies and interviews of two respondents from each firm allowed us to compare the answers given by them. When analysing cases we were guided by a theoretical framework created from existing literature. Conceptual insights that emerged from cases helped us to refer to the existing literature to develope and enrich these insights. We conducted cross-case comparisons in order to refine emerging insights (e.g., Chirico, 2008). Interpretation and propositions were refined in several iterations before finalizing them. Data analysis was conducted applying a combination of deductive and inductive methods.

3.4   Findings with Development of Propositions

In this section we discuss findings and provide propositions for the future research arising from our case studies analysis. Our research is exploratory and thus seeks to stimulate further work focusing on innovativeness of the next generation and innovative performance of SFF in transitional economies.

3.4.1   Innovativeness of SFF and Their Successors

Our research revealed that although most founders report constant development of new products, services, processes, in order to remain competitive in their industry, only four have protected know–how, one of them has registered six and one eight patents on his name, two founders report over five registered patents on the name of the company. One founder has protected brand. Three successors are developing new processes and services with their parent. Successors all report constant development activities, seven report up to ten own developments of new solutions, especially in IT, improvements of existing services and processes, simplifications, which lead to cost reduction. They are less involved into development of new products. This is result of their non-technical formal education (only one successor has technical background). In the recent 5 years eight of the studied SFF have introduced over 530 new products, services and processes. Observed innovation activity of the SFF is dynamic, with successors taking more active role in development activities of SFF.

3.4.2 Entrepreneurialism

Working outside the family firm gives the successors "a more detached perspective over how to run and how to introduce changes and innovation in the business" (Chirico, 2008, p. 447) and usually occurs before the successor enters a family business for full time. Having previous working experience successor can integrate the knowledge transferred by the predecessor with the knowledge acquired during training process to assess and manage the firm's familiness as well as to invest in replenishing, increasing and upgrading these knowledge bases as valuable resources (e.g., Cabrera-Suárez et al., 2001). Findings of our research reveal that only two of the successors have previous working experience from the other firm in a different industry, and one has worked before in two other firms, in a different and same industry. All others report no previous working experience in other firms. Two successors also report internships in other firms in a different industry. Nowadays lack of working experience in other, but family firms, is strongly connected with economic situation and lack of job opportunities in Slovenia. According to seven successors' communications skills, attitude toward negotiation and marketing knowledge and competence are the most affected by working experiences outside the SFF. Attitude toward problem solving is highly ranked but given less importance in comparison with the previously mentioned factors. The least importance is given to administrative knowledge and competences and attitude toward risk, while all other factors, from attitude toward entrepreneurship to motivation skills are evaluated as having moderate impact on development of entrepreneurial competences of successors. A right mix of out- and inside training experience is fundamental to acquire technical and managerial knowledge of the business and leadership abilities (Cabrera-Suárez et al., 2001). It plays a key role in creativity and innovation process (Litz & Kleysen, 2001).

The following proposition is derived upon above described findings:

Proposition 1 Previous working experiences outside a SFF are positively related to formation of entrepreneurial competences such as communication skills, attitude toward negotiation, marketing knowledge and competences, attitude toward problem solving and are negatively related with attitude toward risk; and consequently entrepreneurial competences are positively related to innovativeness of successors in SFF.

In family business research there is overwhelming support for the significant influence on successor's performance played by educational level of successor (Cabrera-Suárez et al., 2001; Steier, 2001). Successor's educational level should meet requirements needed to be an entrepreneur in a knowledge-based economy. It is no longer enough just to know how to perform a specific activity and/or function. Being competitive requires being able to create new knowledge. Successors in our study are all well educated: one of successors has a technical university degree, one in economics, others graduated or (three) still study entrepreneurship. In the eyes of successors, the most important significance is given to formal education's impact on development of technical knowledge and competences, followed by marketing, administrative knowledge and competences and attitude toward team working. The least impact is given to working commitment and motivating skills. Formal education is basis for formation of human capital. In teaching the accent should be given to skills like critical thinking, creativity, communication, user orientation and team work, using domain specific and language knowledge. Entrepreneurship studies cover all these. The research has revealed that formal education in the eyes of successors affects development of creativity, but not to the same extent as e.g., technical or marketing knowledge and competences.

On the basis of above discussion we develope the following proposition:

Proposition 2 Formal education is positively contributing to formation of entrepreneurial competences such as technical and marketing and administrative knowledge and competences and is negatively related to attitude toward risk; entrepreneurial competences are positiviley related to innovativeness of successors in SFF.

The familiness can be understood as a mixture of cultural values, entrepreneurial attitudes and behaviors. According to Cabrera-Suárez et al. (2001) there is great influence of a predecessor and a family on a successor in terms of cultural values, entrepreneurial attitudes and behaviors. Familiness is according to different authors (e.g., Sirmon & Hitt, 2003) a resource that is unique to family firms. Habbershon, Williams, and MacMillan (2003) define familiness as the set of resources controlled by a firm resulting from a continuous overlap of a family system with the business system in a firm. Since familiness results from interactions among individuals, a family, and a firm over time (Chrisman, Chua, & Steier, 2003) which are the key variable of innovativeness of family firms, resulting in joint innovative results (Litz & Kleysen, 2001), it is an intangible, unique resource. As a distinctive bundle of intangible assets, Matz Carnes and Ireland (2013) believe that familiness has the potential to affect a family firm's efforts to innovate. On the other side, familiness assumes a too strong involvement of founders into operative decision making and family issues, thus reducing their readiness for risk taking (Sethi, Smith, & Park, 2001). Our research revealed that in the eyes of successors (eight) familiness has a very strong impact on development of working commitment and attitude toward entrepreneurship (seven), followed by a strong impact on technical knowledge and competence (five), social relationships and attitude toward risk. Less but still important impact is assigned to motivating skills, marketing knowledge and competences, and attitude toward negotiation.

Most of successors (six) assign a very strong impact of entrepreneurial competences on their innovativeness, and agree (eight) that working experience outside the SFF and familiness has a strong impact on their innovativeness, while formal education has only moderate impact (seven) on their innovativeness.

From discussion above, the following proposition can be derived:

Proposition 3 *Familiness relates positively to formation of most of entrepreneurial competencies and consequently most of entrepreneurial competences relate positively to innovativeness of the next generation in a SFF.*

3.4.3 Knowledge Transfer and Creation

Firms need to transfer and acquire new knowledge as they seek to innovate and enhance performance (e.g., Nonaka et al., 2000; Nonaka & von Krogh, 2009). In SFF it is very important how and in which way predecessors transfer their tacit knowledge to successors thus enabling successor to get "hands-on" knowledge about the SFF and the industry. For this reason we explored different methods of tacit knowledge transfer (experiential and routine knowledge) from founders to successors of SFF. Many authors (e.g., Cabrera-Suárez et al., 2001; Gersick et al., 1997) suggest that early exposure to a family business through summer and lower category jobs are valuable experiences for successors since they acquire in this way tacit knowledge, which is usually linked to a founder and therefore of particular importance during the transfer from the founding to the second generation (e.g., Cabrera-Suárez et al., 2001). The successor can also absorb tacit knowledge about the business at home since "conveying the psychological legacy of the firm is an important part of child rearing from the beginning" (Gersick et al., 1997, p. 71). Especially, maintaining creative environments in families during childhood are prerequisite for creativity and innovation in businesses (e.g., Zenko & Mulej, 2011). The findings of our research show that most (seven) successors found early exposure and involvement into SFF as an important way of acquiring founder's tacit knowledge. Most of them (nine) were exposed early, already as small children, to the family business environment.

Another important way of enhancing successor's knowledge found in the literature (e.g. (Cabrera-Suárez et al., 2001; Chirico, 2008) is by mentoring and supervising relationships with family business leaders since they believe that the close interactions between them and their successor is a superior form of experience supporting development of tacit knowledge by successors. Mentoring is an effective way of transferring critical skills (i.e., technical and managerial), knowledge on managerial systems (especially of informal managerial systems), norms of behavior and firm's values (Swap, Leonard, Shields, & Abrams, 2001). There is no common agreement on whether the parents are the most suitable mentors (e.g. Gersick et al., 1997), as well as diverse opinions on the role of formal in informal mentoring exist (e.g., Boyd et al., 1999). Our analysis revealed that all ten successors found mentoring as an important way of assimilating critical knowledge and skills (technical and managerial), mostly informal knowledge about management, norms of behavior, and SFF values. Nine successors were informally mentored by their parent, while seven were formally mentored by a non-family member.

Tacit knowledge can also be passed between family generations in the form of apprenticeship (Chirico, 2008), which is found to be an excellent training especially in traditional industries that do not operate in environments of rapid change. The findings of our research reveal that most (eight) of successors went through the apprenticeship in their SFF and four of them stressed that apprenticeship with observing, imitating and practising represents an excellent method of transferring founder's tacit knowledge and their training.

In family businesses successors have the opportunity to learn directly from the preceding generation in a "learning-by-doing process" how to run the family firm, and "..., specially, all the 'tricks of trade' related to the business" (Chirico, 2008, p. 441). The findings showed that learning-by-doing, according to all ten successors' high agreement, enables them indirect access to founder's knowledge about managing the family business and business tricks. Seven of successors could learn about their family business directly from their parents.

Successor's active participation in decision-making is found to be of crucial importance since both generations have the opportunity to offer suggestions for managing and improving processes and at the same time being able to learn from the other by transferring knowledge (e.g., Kellermanns & Eddelston, 2004). Mazzola et al. (2008) explored the role of strategic planning in the strategic decision-making process and revealed that the involvement of the next generation family members in the planning process, especially in the strategic planning, benefits their developmental process. This involvement enables the development of shared vision, provides the next generation with crucial tacit business knowledge and skills, deep industry and business knowledge, contributes to building credibility and legitimacy for the next generation as well as improves the relationships of successors with internal and external stakeholders. Namely, involvement of successor's in meetings and communication with internal and external stakeholders (Mazzola et al., 2008) enables the assimiliation of the tacit knowledge of customers and suppliers and incorporation of that knowledge into new concepts, technologies, products or systems (Nonaka, von Krogh, & Voelpel, 2006). Case analysis revealed that most (seven) successors highly agree, while nine of them were also included, that involvement in the planning processes, especially strategic planning, enables them to assimilate critical tacit (business) knowledge and skills, insight into industry development, improves successor's relationships within SFF and with partners out of the SFF thus contributing to their innovativeness. Nine successors have been involved into meetings even before they formally enetered the family firm.

Team work is found to be an important way of knowledge creation since "... through dialogue, their mental models and skills are probed, analyzed and converted into common terms and concepts" (Nonaka et al., 2006, p. 1185). Team knowledge is viewed as an important source of innovation since the combination of team member's knowledge leads to new knowledge (Delgado-Verde, Martín-de Castro, & Navas-López, 2011). Team work, especially on the same project or as a part of processes of strategic planning and decision-making, is considered compulsory for the development of successor's managerial carrier (e.g., Ganzaroli et al., 2006). Since it facilitates the creative interactions of both generations, is essential for a family firm to be creative and innovative entity (e.g., Litz & Kleysen, 2001). Family members' specialized knowledge and its recombination enables the adaptation of the family firm to changes in environmental conditions (Chirico & Salvato, 2008). Majority of successors (eight) agree on the importance of the team work for knowledge transfer and creation of new knowledge as a source of innovations. Eight successors reported on working in teams as part of their training.

In the light of the above discussion the following propositions have been developed:

Proposition 4 Early exposure to a family firm, mentoring, apprenticeship, learning-by-doing, active successor's participation in decision-making, (strategic) planning and team work are effective ways of knowledge transfer and creation, and are positively related to innovativeness of the next generation in SFF.

According to Szulanski (1996) there might be some obstacles that hinder knowledge transfer to the next generation in SFF, and that are: random ambiguity and unproven correctness, founder not interested to transfer knowledge, successor not motivated to accept knowledge, factors of circumstances, like limitations in organizations and bad relationship between predecessor and successor. Asking successors a question about the importance of founders' interest for transferring knowledge to the successor, importance of successor's motivation for accepting knowledge from the founder and importance of a good relationship between the founder and successor, we were not surprised, that all successors strongly agreed that these criteria are a pre-condition for successful transfer of knowledge. In all studied cases the pre-conditions for successful succession were at place which is confirmed by characteristics of the studied sample: regarding succession, in two SFF succession has been already fully done (management and ownership), in one case the founder is actively present in the firm while being retired, in the other case the founder is working for his SFF as a single entrepreneur. In two SFF management has been transferred to the successors, transfer of ownership is in procedure, both founders are retired, but active in the firms. In one SFF management is transferred, but not ownership, although founder is retired, but active. Three other SFF are in the midst of transfering ownership and management, one is in transfer of ownership only, the founder being still employed, but co-founder died, so transfer of ownership is more a process of regulating heritage. Only in two SFF there are only plans for succession and founders do not know or say when.

Proposition 5 Interest of the founder, successor's motivation and good relationship between the predecessor and successor are positively related to successful knowledge transfer and consequently innovativeness of the next generation in SFF.

3.4.4 Social Capital

In our study we examined structural and relational dimension of internal social capital, while Burt's (1992) perspective of social capital, primarily focusing on external linkages and what benefits arise from structural holes found within the network of relationships (Adler & Kwon, 2002), was omitted.

Structural dimension of internal social capital, which involves the pattern of relationships between network actors (Nahapiet & Ghoshal, 1998), and can be studied through openness and quality of communication channels between the family members and between family and non-family members in SFF, is according to findings of our research very strongly present in SFF. The majority of successors (seven) highly agrees that honest communication between the family members as well as between family and non-family members in SFF is very important and contributes to creation of special and valuable ability to maintain long-term competitiveness and eases transfer of knowledge. As well they say that in their firms honest communication is taking place. Six successors say that it is very important not to have hidden agendas in front of other family members, and in their cases they omit such practice. Willingly sharing information with one another is being assessed as highly important by seven successors and flow of information does not represent an obstacle. The research shows the pattern of relationships which are based upon honest communication and information sharing between the family members, which enhances knowledge mobility and sharing between persons. This factor contributes to enhance innovation (Ganzaroli et al., 2006).

The relational dimension of internal social capital refers to the nature of the relationships themselves and the assets that are rooted in them (Tsai & Ghoshal, 1998). It manifests itself in strength of relations and trust. Strength reflects the closeness of a relationship between actors, and increases with frequency of communication and interaction (Hansen, 1999). Strong ties lead to greater knowledge transfer (Reagans & McEvily, 2003). Although some studies indicate that a high level of trust may also create collective blindness and inhibit the exchange and combination of knowledge (e.g., Lane, Salk, & Lyles, 2001), previous research has generally argued that trust increases organizational knowledge transfer. Trust enables the transfer of organizational knowledge since it increases partners' willingness to commit to helping partners understand new external knowledge (Szulanski, Cappetta, & Jensen, 2004). The findings of our research reveal that all ten successors highly agree about importance of confidence in one another and a great deal of integrity with each other. Trust is strongly built into the relationships between the family members. All successors confirm that confidence strengthens the ties they have developed, increases open communication and knowledge sharing between the family members (e.g., Reagans & McEvily, 2003), thus contributing to their commitment to the SFF (e.g., Szulanski et al., 2004). We were not surprised by the finding that seven successors said that family members, meaning mostly founders, are not thoughtful regarding feelings of each other. According to Ganzaroli et al. (2006), founders have difficulties with succession, as decision for "stepping out of power" is not an easy one. There are many reasons, like fear for the future of the firm, for his/her own self-respect and identity, potential loss of respect—in family and in the community, and the lack of trust in successor's skills, that help explain, why they might not be thoughtful regarding feelings of successors. They had to work hard for their success, they worked long hours, took responsibility and risk, so they expect from successors to show the highest level of commitment to the firm.

The above discussion leads us to the following proposition:

Proposition 6 Internal social capital facilitates transfer of knowledge through structural (i.e. number of relations and centrality) and relational capital (i.e. tie strength and trust) and its sharing between generations in SFF and consequently it is positively related to innovativeness of the next generation in SFF.

4 Conclusion with Limitations and Future Research Directions

In our study we investigated the factors influencing innovativeness of successors in SFF in transition economies on the case of Slovenia. We identified three constructs that help us to explain innovativeness of successors in SFF: entrepreneurial competences, knowledge transfer and creation, and social capital. Specifically we examined the impact of the following factors: previous working experience outside the SFF, formal education (in entrepreneurship) and familiness on development of entrepeneurial competences of the successor in SFF; different methods of knowledge transfer and creation: early exposure to the business, mentoring, apprenticeship, involvement in decision making, strategic planning, learning by doing, team working; structural and relational dimension of internal social capital and its impact on knowledge transfer and consequently on innovativeness of the successor in SFF. We developed a research model and introduced six propositions supported by data from ten cases thereby integrating them in the context of the succession and successor's innovativeness in SFF in transition economies.

Propositions provide the basis for developing empirical testing, where the combination of qualitative and quantitative research methods should be applied in the future research. These propositions also have implications for practice as they provide useful cognitions for stakeholders involved in the succession process (i.e., especially family members) as well as professionals dealing with family businesses' succession issues and innovativeness.

Our study provides a starting point for further, detailed research on family business and innovation management in SFF in transition economies, especially of factors enhancing/hindering innovativeness of founders, successors, SFF and innovative performance of SFF.

References

Adler, P. S., & Kwon, S. (2002). Social capital: Prospects for a new concept. *Academy of Mangement Review, 27*, 17–40.

Bekö, J., & Jagrič, T. (2011). *Demand models for direct mail and periodicals delivery services: Results for a transition economy* (Applied economics). London: Chapman and Hall.

Boyd, J., Upton, N., & Wircenski, M. (1999). Mentoring in family firms: A reflective analysis of senior executives' perception. *Family Business Review, 12*(4), 299–309.

Burt, R. S. (1992). *Structural holes: The social structure of competition.* Cambridge, MA: Harvard University Press.

Cabrera-Suárez, K., De Saa-Pérez, P., & García-Almeida, D. (2001). The succession process from a resource and knowledge-based view of the family firm. *Family Business Review, 14*(1), 37–46.

Chirico, F. (2008). Knowledge accumulation in family firms: Evidence from four case studies. *International Small Business Journal, 26*(4), 433–462.

Chirico, F., & Salvato, C. (2008). Knowledge integration and dynamic organizational adaptation in family firms. *Family Business Review, 21*(2), 169–181.

Chrisman, J. J., Chua, J. H., & Sharma, P. (2003). *Current trends and future directions in family business management studies: Toward a theory of the family firm.* Article written for the 2003 Coleman White Paper series.

Chrisman, J. J., Chua, J. H., & Steier, L. P. (2003). An introduction to theories of family business. *Journal of Business Venturing, 18*(4), 441–448.

Coleman, J. S. (1990). *Foundations of social theory.* Cambridge, MA: Harvard University Press.

Dana, L. P., & Dana, T. (2003). Management and enterprise development in post-communist economies. *International Journal of Management and Enterprise Development, 1*(1), 45–54.

Delgado-Verde, M., Martín-de Castro, G., & Navas-López, J. E. (2011). Organizational knowledge assets and innovation capability: Evidence from Spanish manufacturing firms. *Journal of Intellectual Capital, 12*(1), 5–19.

Donckels, R., & Fröhlich, E. (1991). Sind Familienbetriebe wirklich anders? Europäische STRATOS-Erfahrungen. *Internationales Gewerbearchiv, 4*, 219–235.

Duh, M. (2008). *Overview of family business relevant issues,* Country fiche Slovenia. Institute for Entrepreneurship and Small Business Management, Faculty of Economics and Business, University of Maribor.

Duh, M., & Tominc, P. (2005). Pomen, značilnosti in prihodnost družinskih podjetij (Importance, characteristics and future of family enterprises). In M. Rebernik, P. Tominc, M. Duh, T. Krošlin, & G. Radonjič (Eds.), *Slovenski podjetniški observatorij 2004, 2. del (Slovenian entrepreneurship observatory 2004, 2. part)* (pp. 19–31). Institute for Entrepreneurship and Small Business Management, Faculty of Economics and of Maribor.

Dyck, B., Mauws, M., Starke, F. A., & Mischke, G. A. (2002). Passing the baton. The importance of sequence, timing, technique and communication in executive succession. *Journal of Business Venturing, 17*(2), 143–162.

Eisenhardt, K. (1989). Building theories from the case study research. *Academy of Management Review, 14*(4), 532–550.

Ganzaroli, A., Fiscato, G., & Pilotti, L. (2006). *Does business succession enhance firm's innovation capacity? Results from an exploratory analysis in Italian SMEs.* Working paper [n. 2006–29], 2nd Workshop on family firm management research, Nice, Italy. Available at: http://ideas.repec.org/p/mil/wpdepa/2006.29.html (Accessed 5 February 2014).

García-Álvarez, E., López-Sintas, J., & Gonzalvo, P. S. (2002). Socialization patterns of successors in first- to second-generation family businesses. *Family Business Review, 15*(3), 189–203.

Gersick, K. E., Davis, J. A., McCollom Hampton, M., & Lansberg, I. (1997). *Generation to generation. Life cycles of the family business.* Boston: Harvard Business School Press.

Glas, M., Herle, J., Lovšin Kozina, F., & Vadnjal, J. (2006). The state of family firm management in Slovenia. In *Proceedings of 2nd workshop on family firm management research,* EIASM, Nice, Italy.

Habbershon, T. G., Williams, M. L., & MacMillan, I. C. (2003). A united systems perspective of family firm performance. *Journal of Business Venturing, 18*(4), 451–465.

Hansen, M. T. (1999). The search transfer problem: The role of weak ties in sharing knowledge across organizational subunits. *Administration Science Quarterly, 44*, 82–111.

Inkpen, A. C., & Tsang, E. W. K. (2005). Social capital, networks and knowledge transfer. *Academy of Management Review, 30*(1), 146–165.

Kellermanns, F. W., & Eddelston, K. A. (2004). Feuding families: When conflict does a family firm good. *Entrepreneurship Theory and Practice, 28*(3), 209–228.

Lane, P. J., Salk, J. E., & Lyles, A. (2001). IJV learning experience. *Strategic Management Journal, 22*, 1139–1161.

Le Breton-Miller, I., Miller, D., & Steier, L. P. (2004). Toward an integrative model of effective FOB succession. *Entrepreneurship Theory and Practice, 28*(3), 305–328.

Light, I., & Dana, L.-P. (2013). Bounaries of social capital in entrepreneurship. *Entrepreneurship Theory and Practice, 37*(3), 603–624.

Litz, R. A., & Kleysen, R. F. (2001). Your old men shall dream dreams, your young men shall see visions: Toward a theory of family firm innovation with help from the Brubeck family. *Family Business Review, 14*(4), 335–352.

Lumpkin, G. T., & Dess, G. G. (1996). Clarifying the entrepreneurial orientation construct and linking it to performance. *Academy of Management Review, 21*(1), 135–172.

Mandl, I. (2008). *Overview of family business relevant issues*. Final report, Austrian Institute for SME Research, Vienna. Available at: http://ec.europa.eu/enterprise/entrepreneurship/craft/family_business/family_business_en.Htm (Accessed 31 July 2009).

Matz Carnes, C., & Ireland, D. (2013). Familiness and innovation: Resource bundling as the missing link. *Entrepreneurship Theory and Practice, 37*(6), 1399–1419.

Mazzola, P., Marchision, G., & Astrachan, J. (2008). Strategic planning in family business: A powerful developmental tool for the next generation. *Family Business Review, 21*(3), 239–258.

Močnik, D. (2012). Temeljne značilnosti slovenskega podjetništva v primerjavi z evropskim (Basic characteristics of Slovenian entrepreneurship in comparison with the European). In K. Širec & M. Rebernik (Eds.), *Razvojni potenciali slovenskega podjetništva: Slovenski podjetniški observatorij 2011/12 (Developmental potentials of Slovenian entrepreneurship: Slovenian entreprenurship observatory 2011/12)* (pp. 15–28). Maribor: Faculty of Economics and Business.

Morris, M. H., Williams, R. O., Allen, J. A., & Avila, R. A. (1997). Correlates of success in family business transitions. *Journal of Business Venturing, 12*(5), 385–401.

Mrak, M., Rojec, M., & Silva-Jáuregui, C. (Eds.). (2004). *Slovenia: From Yugoslavia to the European Union*. Washington, DC: World Bank.

Nahapiet, J., & Ghoshal, S. (1998). Koper: Social capital, intellectual capital, and the organizational advantage Koper. *Academy of Management Review, 23*(2), 242–266.

Nonaka, I., Toyama, R., & Konno, N. (2000). SECI, Ba and leadership: A unified model of dynamic knowledge creation. *Long Range Planning, 33*(1), 5–34.

Nonaka, I., & von Krogh, G. (2009). Tacit knowledge and knowledge conversion: Controversy and advancement in organizational knowledge creation theory. *Organization Science, 20*(3), 635–652.

Nonaka, I., von Krogh, G., & Voelpel, S. (2006). Organizational knowledge creating theory: Evolutionary paths and future advances. *Organization Studies, 27*(8), 1179–1208.

Nordqvist, M., Habbershon, T. G., & Melin, L. (2008). Transgenerational entrepreneurship: Exploring EO in family firms. In H. Landström, H. Crijns, & E. Laveren (Eds.), *Entrepreneurship, sustainable growth and performance: Frontiers in European entrepreneurship research* (pp. 93–116). Cheltenham: Edward Elgar.

Pearson, A. W., Carr, J. C., & Shaw, J. C. (2008). Toward a theory of familiness: A social capital perspective. *Entrepreneurship Theory and Practice, 32*(2), 949–969.

Ramadani, V., & Dana, L.-P. (2013). The state of entrepreneurship in the Balkans: Evidence from selected countries. In R. C. Schneider & V. Ramadani (Eds.), *Entrepreneurship in the Balkans* (pp. 217–250). Berlin: Springer.

Reagans, R., & McEvily, B. (2003). Network structure and knowledge transfer: The effects of cohesion and range. *Administrative Science Quarterly, 48*(2), 240–267.

Rebernik, M., Tominc, P., Crnogaj, K., Širec, K., Bradač Hojnik, B., & Rus, M. (2014). *Spregledan podjetniški potencial mladih: GEM Slovenija 2013 (Overlooked entrepreneurial potential of young people: GEM Slovenia 2013)*. Maribor: University of Maribor, Faculty of Economics and Business Maribor.

Sethi, R., Smith, D. C., & Park, C. W. (2001). Cross-functional temas, creativity, and the innovativeness of new consumer products. *Journal of Marketing Research, 38*(1), 73–86.

Sharma, P., Chrisman, J. J., & Chua, J. H. (2003). Succession planning as planned behavior: Some empirical results. *Family Business Review, 16*(1), 1–14.

Širec, K. (2012). Razvojni potenciali slovenskega podjetništva (Developmental potentials of Slovenian entrepreneurship). In K. Širec & M. Rebernik (Eds.), *Razvojni potenciali slovenskega podjetništva: Slovenski podjetniški observatorij 2011/12 (Developmental potentials of Slovenian entrepreneurship: Slovenian entrepreneurship observatory 2011/12)* (pp. 7–13). Maribor: Faculty of Economics and Business.

Sirmon, D. G., & Hitt, M. A. (2003). Managing resources: Linking unique resources, management and wealth creation in family firms. *Entrepreneurship Theory and Practice, 27*(4), 339–358.

Steier, L. (2001). Next generation entrepreneurs and succession: An exploratory study of modes and means of managing social capital. *Family Business Review, 14*(3), 259–276.

Swap, W., Leonard, D., Shields, M., & Abrams, L. (2001). Using mentoring and storytelling to transfer knowledge in the workplace. *Journal of Management Information Systems, 18*(1), 95–114.

Szulanski, G. (1996). Exploring internal stickiness. Impediments to the transfer of best practice within the firm. *Strategic Management Journal, 17*(Special Winter Issue), 27–43.

Szulanski, G., Cappetta, R., & Jensen, R. J. (2004). When and how trustworthiness matters: Knowledge transfer and the moderating affect of causal ambiguity. *Organization Science, 15* (5), 600–613.

Tsai, W., & Ghoshal, S. (1998). Social capital and value creation: The role of intrafirm networks. *Academy of Management Journal, 41*(4), 464–476.

Uzzi, B. (1997). Social structure and competition in interfirm networks: The paradox of embeddedness. *Administrative Science Quarterly, 42*, 35–67.

Vadnjal, J. (2006). Innovativeness and inter-generational entrepreneurship in family businesses. In *Cooperation between the economic, academic and governmental spheres—Mechanisms and levers*. Proceedings of the 26th conference on entrepreneurship and innovation, Maribor.

Ward, J. L. (1997). Growing the family business: Special challenges and best practice. *Family Business Review, 10*(3), 323–337.

Yin, K. R. (2003). *Case study research, design and methods* (3rd ed.). Thousand Oaks, CA: Sage.

Zahra, S. A., & Sharma, P. (2004). Family business research: A strategic reflection. *Family Business Review, 17*(4), 331–346.

Zenko, Z., & Mulej, M. (2011). Diffusion of innovative behavior with social responsibility. *Kybernetes, 40*(9), 1258–1272.

Family Business Succession Risks: The Croatian Context

Iva Senegović, Valerija Bublić, and Gordana Ćorić

Abstract Family business represents the most common form of the company ownership and management organization. According to the most recent research of the International Family Enterprise Research Academy, between 80 and 95 % of all private companies worldwide belong to the family businesses and generate more than 75 % of GDP while employing more than 85 % of the total number of employees. The average life span of family business is 24 years which clearly demonstrates the generation change issue in the family businesses, and consequently—growth and sustainability issues. Beside the ownership function, the family business entrepreneur also carries out management functions by leading and directing the family business. The performance of this function is reflected in the vital decision making on the work processes and results towards achieving sustainable growth. The function is regularly performed by the owner but in recent times it has been partly or completely transferred to the professional managers. Accordingly, the two entrepreneurial functions bear distinctly recognized risks associated with their performance. During the transfer of ownership and leadership in the family businesses, the crucial entrepreneurial and managerial risk is by its nature non-transferable and internally conditioned. Being inevitable in such a situation, additionally burdened with growth, sustainability and innovation imperatives, the risk requires an expert analytical and critical approach by use of all available research methods and techniques for its best estimate. The biggest entrepreneurial and managerial risk lies in the resistance to changes or, in this case, the postponement of ownership and leadership transfer decision-making. Such an approach will only increase the problems unique to family businesses such as the problem of the successor legitimacy and authenticity, rigidity, non-transparent communication related to the transfer planning, etc. On the other side, a well-led transfer with adequate approach to the associated risks can result in the company transformation into a growing or dynamic venture.

Keywords Family businesses • Risk • Risk management • Life span • Croatia

I. Senegović • V. Bublić (✉) • G. Ćorić
Entrepreneurship and Management Department, University of Applied Sciences VERN', Trg bana Josipa Jelačića 3, 10000 Zagreb, Croatia
e-mail: iva.senegovic@vern.hr; valerija.bublic@vern.hr; gordana.coric@gmail.com

© Springer International Publishing Switzerland 2015
L.-P. Dana, V. Ramadani (eds.), *Family Businesses in Transition Economies*,
DOI 10.1007/978-3-319-14209-8_9

1 Introduction

Family business represents the most common form of the company ownership and management organization. According to the most recent research of the International Family Enterprise Research Academy, between 80 and 95 % of all private companies worldwide belong to the family businesses and generate more than 75 % of GDP while employing more than 85 % of the total number of employees (Kružić, 2004). There are different reasons for starting a family business: family members can recognize a business opportunity and make a common decision to start the business, one or more family members acquire the knowledge that will enable and facilitate the entrepreneurial startup, a family member losing permanent job can look for a new start in the family business, one or more family members develop an original entrepreneurial idea, one or more family members inherit a real property, offices, land, already established stable business or a considerable amount of money, newcomer from another family business joining the family through marriage, etc. (Federal Ministry of Development, Entrepreneurship and Craft, Federation of Bosnia and Herzegovina, 2009). Regardless of which of the above motives trigger entering into entrepreneurship, each of them includes a mixture of family interest and the business to be taken care of. Namely, there is no family business without an active role of the family in it (through the ownership and leadership); neither can the family business exist without integrating business interests. Also, the source of financing the entrepreneurial startup by family entrepreneurs is very often found among the family members and own savings and (un)successful business can jeopardize the existence of the whole family.

Family entrepreneurship can be understood as the family upgrade in the same manner as the family endows the business with a more human sense of collectiveness, care for others and confidence, which characteristic do not pertain to non-family businesses. Every transfer of ownership and leadership will be profitable to both family and business: every new owner and/or leader will introduce some novelties and refresh the business while the family will grow with every successful transfer of ownership and family business expansion in every sense. Such a positive mixture of family and business, if properly lead and managed, can build a sustainable system to exist successfully for centuries. In the contrary case, the lack of consciousness, denial, lack of recognition and timely and adequate reaction to the entrepreneurial and managerial risks accompanying every transfer of ownership and leadership in the family businesses, most frequently end up with the business liquidation (Dana & Dana, 2003).

In order to increase the awareness of the issues of transfer of ownership and leadership in the family businesses as well as the accompanying entrepreneurial and managerial risks we have identified two basic goals of research:

1. Understand the main features of the family business population facing the issues of the transfer of ownership and leadership, recognize the main problems they come across, get their opinion and see if there is a real need to use an intermediary when facing the above problems.

2. Identification of the need to create a specific program focused on the transfer of ownership and leadership in family businesses in Croatia, aiming to reduce associated entrepreneurial and managerial risks.

2 Literature Review

This chapter represents an overview of the existing literature and research concerning the family business ownership and leadership transfer and associated risk management.

2.1 Theoretical Hypotheses of the Family Entrepreneurship

The importance of theory is best illustrated by Leonardo da Vinci quote: "He who loves practice without theory is like the sailor who boards ship without a rudder and compass and never knows where he may cast."

Theory is indispensable for the explanation of the phenomenon or the problem being the subject of the research. Although of a universal character, theory has its drawbacks due to the fact that it is a result of a limited number of researches. The goal is to continuously test, amend and create new theories (Mejovšek, 2003).

When dealing with theoretical hypotheses of the family entrepreneurship, the research is getting more complicated since as of today there has been formulated no unique definition which would enable a simple monitoring of this special type of entrepreneurship within a country, not to mention the comparison among the family businesses in Europe or around the world. The lack of the genuine definition of the family entrepreneurship has also been recognized by the European Commission. In order to facilitate the creation of valid policies and other initiatives aiming to use the full potentials of family businesses, it took a number of measures. Among others, the Commission accepted the proposal of the Finnish Expert Group to adopt a European definition of a family business. A firm, of any size, is a family business, if:

(a) The majority of decision-making rights is in the possession of the natural person(s) who established the firm, or in the possession of the natural person (s) who has/have acquired the share capital of the firm, or in the possession of their spouses, parents, child or children's direct heirs;
(b) The majority of decision-making rights are indirect or direct;
(c) At least one representative of the family or kin is formally involved in the governance of the firm;
(d) Listed companies meet the definition of family enterprise if the person who established or acquired the firm (share capital) or their families or descendants possess 25 % of the decision-making rights mandated by their share capital.

The definition also covers family businesses which have not yet gone through the first generational transfer, sole proprietors and the self-employed, providing there is a legal entity which can be transferred to the next generation (European Commission, 2009).

There is a common agreement that the participation of the family in the ownership structure and the governance make essential difference between the family entrepreneurship and other types of entrepreneurship and the research will continue based on this premise. It is also important for the family business to increase the participation of the family members and strengthen their control function in the family business. Family businesses do not operate in the same manner due to the family systems unique for every family business. According to the leading authority in the family business research Ph.D. Ivan Lansberg, beside the family system another two systems make every family business—business and ownership systems and their overlapping makes an integral part of family entrepreneurship issues (Dussault, 2008).

2.2 Ownership Transfer in a Family Business

Family business is often described by the expression: looking back with pride, moving forward with hope. Although each and every business is susceptible to failures regardless of their ownership structure, family businesses are particularly susceptible in the phase of succession planning, getting listed on a stock exchange, when introducing non family members into the management board or other executive functions and while making efforts to maintain the relevance of the products and services they have been offering through generations. Difficulties such as family everyday quarrels, lack of competent successors, and tensions among family and non-family managers can shake up even the most successful firms.

The challenges of transfer of ownership and leadership within the family businesses can be best illustrated by worldwide relevant statistics. According to the Family Firm Institute only about 30 % of family and businesses survive into the second generation, 10 % are still viable into the third generation, and only about 3 % of all family businesses operate into the fourth generation (Family Firm Institute 2013). Research results have shown that one third of the family firms possess ownership and leadership succession plans while the vast majority is informal and poorly communicated by the owner/founder. There is an additional problem of partial retirement when the founder formally withdraws from the position of owner and leader but still makes key decisions related to the family business (Bruc & Picard, 2005). It also brings the issue of how to create supportive, innovation-embracing environment for sustainable entrepreneurial growth (Ćorić, Meter, & Bublić, 2012), and thus achieve sustainability in spite of transition of leadership in family businesses.

Family members have a strong urge to supervise the firm management and increase its efficiency to the maximum level. They also perceive the firm operation, employees, business partners and other key stakeholders in a long-term perspective which makes the business more efficient. Besides, the family members are more aware of their family business performance since it directly affects the family reputation and position in the society. They also possess a broad knowledge and vast experience in the family business operation having been familiar with its operation since early childhood. These circumstances provide plenty of opportunities to provide conditions for controlled and sustainable growth.

Major problems are caused by the lack of well-defined roles and responsibilities of the family members working for the family business so that authority is vested in family owners rather than the family operators. Family stakeholders, particularly those belonging to older generations, are reluctant to employ external professional managers capable of responding to all the new technological challenges, changes in the business environment and professionalize family business. This can create obstacles to the business development and decrease the firm efficiency in the long term. In support of the above statement a broad research has been led by "Financial Times" and it encompassed successful family businesses some of them being older than 200 years. The research aimed at providing response to the question: "What has been crucial for your firm growth over the years and its survival through generations?". The following answers have been obtained: exceptional quality of product or services; profit reinvestment; readiness to exclude incompetent family members from business, and desire and readiness to employ non-family managers possessing unique skills and set of values. Non-family managers had priority over the family managers possessing sufficient qualifications (Medić, 2009).

Family business succession is not an event but a time-consuming process. It encompasses the transfer of ownership and leadership. Succession is not completed until both ownership and leadership rights have been transferred onto the next generation. It is important to emphasize that in very rare cases the transfer of ownership and leadership occur simultaneously. Older generations tend to hang on to ownership until death or even beyond if ownership is vested in family trusts (Brett Davies Lawyers, 2009; Kamei & Dana, 2012). Parents by their own free will decide to hand over the burden of leadership to the next generation much earlier than they give up the privilege of the family business control. This would mean the loss of power, status and even identity. Simultaneous transfer of ownership and leadership would occur should the owner decide to sell the business or completely withdraw from the business (The Economist, 2004).

During his active participation in the family business, the founder should select, train and nominate his successor. However, very often this is not the case and after the founder's death the business is left to the family member who is not ready to continue running it. The resistance to succession planning is due to many reasons some of them being the following: it reminds the founder of getting old and dying and the fact of inevitable loss of power. Besides, when stepping down, the founder closes a very important phase of his life which has most probably defined him as a person and is now forced to compare his achievements in the business and private life in his life balance sheet. Such introspection can be frightening for the founder who was completely preoccupied with business issues from day to day up to that moment of decision. There is also a likelihood of lack of trust in the potential successors.

Family members can also reluctantly accept the process of change as it can cause radical changes in their lives. Internal family relationships will be put to the test. Employees and other family business stakeholders will be afraid of changes and potential losses of their positions since they had their business relations established with the founder. Having in mind the previously described reasons, one of the key factors contributing to the successful ownership and leadership succession is a timely communication with the clients, suppliers, employees and other people to be affected by the change. Discussion with high-level management should be led at least 6 months earlier so that when the time comes, everybody is ready for changes without negative connotations (The Business Development Bank of Canada, 2008). The transfer of ownership and leadership must be a win-win situation for all the participants in the process.

The most successful transfers of ownership and leadership occur when there is a good cooperation between the founder and the next generation successors. It is recommended that the succession plan be developed in writing in order to minimize conflicts and disagreements and it should include the gradual stepping down of the founder and adequate training of the successor. The founder is a key person in the planning of ownership and leadership transfer. It is also desirable to involve other family members in the planning in order to define their roles in the process. The hiring of external family business consultants is also recommended with the aim to professionally and objectively lead the process and especially in the cases when there are either more candidates for the successor position or there is none.

From the founder's perspective, traditionally the founder's son (or daughter) is almost universally considered the most desirable candidate for the successor position regardless of the country in which the transfer occurs. However, this option should not be insisted on especially when children have no interest in a business career. The research of respected business school London School of Economics has shown that family businesses run by an outside professional C.E.O. performed on average 12 % better than the average family business while the companies run by the eldest son, as the most desirable logical successor in the family business, underperformed the average by 10 %. Analysts maintain that one reason for this disparity is that oldest sons know that they will eventually inherit the company and do not work as hard as someone else who is competing for the post (Bray, n. d).

Other families consider that all the descendants should be equal in the succession rights and find solution in changing the potential family successors in the leading positions until the best candidate is recognized or two or more persons can be selected to share the leading position having precisely defined their areas of activity. In the absence of a natural successor to the family business, some founders employ non-family professional manager to perform leadership function for a while or they decide to sell the company. Whatever decision they make, the founders must be aware of all the options the transfer of ownership and leadership offers at the time when they make decision to step down from the family business and from that time on they should initiate necessary changes accordingly. Insisting on the traditional patterns in the family business succession can be disastrous for both the family and business. Delay in the decision making is by far the worst option for both the business and family.

3 Family Businesses in Croatia

The concept of family business in Croatia is not officially defined. The existing legislative framework regulating business subjects does not contain a definition of a family business. Current statistical monitoring of economic activities does not enable the differentiation of family businesses from the other legal forms. It is therefore difficult to identify, to trace the development and to assess the impact of family businesses on the national economy. The issue of family businesses is not the focus of national policies and programs focused on the economic development, except in the area of specific policies that are aimed at family businesses as the main beneficiaries of incentive measures in the area of agriculture, tourism or crafts. It is assumed that 50 % of all employees in Croatia are employed by family owned companies. Family businesses are most micro and small enterprises, owned by the first-generation entrepreneur who is also the manager. There are examples of large companies that operate as family businesses—both in terms of ownership structure, and in terms of business process management, as well as in terms of the family involvement in the strategic decision making process. On the other hand, there are companies owned by one person, so called registered crafts, have no characteristics of family businesses, but only constitute a legal form of an economic activity (Crnković, 2008; Ramadani & Dana, 2013).

The issue of the succession and management in family businesses is a topic about which a little is discussed. There are a few local examples of the good practice of the succession. The practices of the succession in family business in the transition economies in the region are not well known, and there is a lack of educational programs and experts who could facilitate the process. The complexity of the succession process is enhanced by the fact that most owners of family businesses in Croatia do not have their personal experience of the succession of a business from the previous generation (Alpeza & Peura, 2012).

4 Business Risk, Succession Risk and Risk Management in Family Businesses

Risk is defined as a situation involving exposure to danger (Oxford University Press, 2013); as a possibility of loss or injury including the degree of probability of such loss (Merriam-Webster Incorporated, 2013); as a probability or threat of damage, injury, liability, loss, or any other negative occurrence that is caused by external or internal vulnerabilities, and that may be avoided through preemptive action (Web Finance Inc., 2013a). Organizations of all types and sizes face internal and external factors that make it uncertain whether and when they will achieve their objectives. The effect this uncertainty has on an organization's objectives is risk. An effect is a positive or negative deviation from what is expected (International Organization for Standardization, 2009, p. v).

Business risk is defined as the probability of loss inherent in an organization's operations and environment that may impair its ability to provide returns on investment (Web Finance Inc., 2013b); the possibility that a company will have lower than anticipated profits (Investopedia, 2013), or that it will experience a loss rather than a profit; as the effect of uncertainty on objectives, whether positive or negative (Standards Australia/Standards New Zealand Standard Committee, 2009).

Risk management is the identification, assessment, and prioritization of risks followed by coordinated and economic application of resources to minimize, monitor, and control the probability and/or impact of unfortunate events or to maximize the realization of opportunities (Hubbard, 2009). In practice, the process of assessing the overall risk can be difficult, as well as balancing resources used to mitigate between risks with a high probability of occurrence and lower loss versus risks with lower probability of occurrence and high loss. A complete risk management aims to protect the value already created by the organization, as well as its future opportunities, favoring secure growth. Managing risk effectively helps organizations to perform well and keep sustainable growth in an environment full of uncertainty (Bublić, Hunjak, & Varlandy-Supek, 2013, p. 61). Managerial risk taking propensities vary across individuals and across contexts. Managers recognize both the necessity and the excitement of risk taking in management, but they report that risk taking in organizations is sustained more by personal than by organizational incentives (March & Shapira, 1987).

Risk taking is an important dimension of entrepreneurial orientation and has big impact on the family businesses. Agency theory stresses that the extent of involvement in risky activities is likely to be influenced by the ownership and governance of the business. Family businesses share certain characteristics that render them unique in terms of patterns of ownership, governance, and succession. Owner-families share the desire for ownership control and the continuity of family involvement in the business. To fully appreciate these special characteristics, it is crucial to focus on family businesses where the family is likely to have considerable impact on entrepreneurial activities. In family businesses there is one family group which controls the company through a clear majority of the ordinary voting shares, the family is represented in the management team, and the leading representative of the family perceives the business to be a family business. In family businesses the processes and practices related to entrepreneurial activities involve an element of risk taking. Family businesses are likely to handle risk differently than other types of organizations, partly because management and ownership are not clearly separated. Managers-owners of family businesses take risk to a lesser extent than managers of non-family firms do (Naldi et al., 2007).

Succession risk management refers to strategic implementation of activities and processes designed to decrease the likelihood of lengthy vacancies in critical roles, and limit the impact of vacancies in critical roles when they do occur. It involves regular and structured discussions among the leaders of an organization, division or work unit about: the significant work that needs to be done to achieve the organization's primary outcomes; the types of roles critical to this work and the nature of these roles; the potential for current staff to undertake different types of critical role; the potential for the external labour market to provide candidates for certain types of critical roles; the extent to which the need to fill critical roles and the capacity of the workforce to undertake these roles may not be aligned; the potential most likely misalignments that may have the greatest impacts; risk mitigation strategies: what can be done with available resources to reduce the likelihood or potential impact of long-term vacancies in the critical roles (Victoria State Services Authority, 2008).

Succession planning is a process of developing talent to meet the needs of the organization in future. Organizations that do not take steps to plan for future talent needs at all levels will face certain disruption, an even disasters, when key employees leave (Rothwell, 2010). One of the major risks family business owners do face is how to manage an orderly and affordable transfer of the business to the next generation and/or key employees. There are three main challenges of a business succession plan: management, ownership and transfer taxes. It is important to recognize that management and ownership are not the same thing. Day-to-day management of a business may be led by one family member, while ownership of the business is split among all family members. It is also possible that management may be vested in the hands of key employees rather than family members. The second challenge of a business succession plan is ownership. Business owners may prefer to leave their businesses to those family members that are active in the business, but would still like to treat all of their family members fairly, therefore business owners must assess the most effective means of transferring ownership and the most appropriate time for the transfer to occur. The transfer tax challenge of business succession planning involves strategies to transfer ownership of the business while minimizing gift and estate taxes (Grassi & Giarmarco, 2008).

Succession planning is one of the main areas of inactivity when it comes to governance of family businesses. Gaps in governance and a lack of succession planning can impact long-term success. Succession planning can be an uncomfortable topic for owners, especially founders. By creating a stronger governance and succession strategy, a family-owned business is much more likely to preserve the founder's long-term vision for generations to come. Quite a few owners-managers of family businesses review succession plans only when a change in management requires and many non-executive family members are unfamiliar with succession plans (McGee & Rosone, 2013). The transfer from founders to other leaders entails serious risks, the most significant of which is overlooking entrepreneurial activities. This risk could be minimized by grooming successors and nurturing their ability to innovate. A key challenge facing family businesses lies in the complexity of entrepreneurial risk taking. It is important to involve different family members in the company as a means of preparing them to lead the firm. Capitalizing on the talents, skills, and connections of different family members can spur innovation and support companies' growth (Zahra, 2005).

5 Methodoloy and Data

For the analysis needs, a scientific methodology will be applied in the problem research and the results of scientific research presented. The methodology enables the acquiring of reliable, systematic, structured and authentic information on the research problem (Zelenika, 1998).

5.1 Questionnaire Method

The goal of the research is to collect primary data related to the transfer of ownership and leadership issues in the family businesses in Croatia. Questionnaire method will be applied. The purpose of the questionnaire is to identify burning issues, needs and readiness of family entrepreneurs to face the challenges of ownership and leadership transfer. Since the research is focused on the current problems and needs of family entrepreneurs in the process of ownership and leadership transfer, one research organization will be sufficient to reach the goal. The authors of this paper bear the responsibility for the questionnaire procedure.

The target population in this research involves all the family members to be taken into account when drawing conclusions based on the research results. Specifically, in this case, the focus is on the adult population of family entrepreneurs and members tied to the family business. The target group of family members consists of the existing users of services provided by the University of Applied Sciences VERN', a higher education institution from which the authors of this paper come, and the majority of VERN' students come from entrepreneurial families. From all the population selected for research, a sample should be chosen for the survey. The sample methodology has to be defined beforehand. The best one and the only scientific methodology is the one based on a random sampling of population. However, in the absence of relevant statistical data on the population under survey in Croatia, the non-random sampling method comes out as a logical option.

Family entrepreneurs are not prone to openly discuss their private problems which affect their family business. Written questionnaire will guarantee anonymity and facilitate discussion on sensitive topics. Questionnaires will be directly distributed among the students and they will give them to their parents—owners of family firms. Since some of the family entrepreneurs do not live nearby, questionnaires will be sent to the e-mail addresses the students write on the registration forms at the beginning of their studies and for the needs of Entrepreneurship Department.

Given the set goals of the questionnaire, its contents will include the family, business and ownership systems of the family business. The success or failure of the family firm in the transfer of ownership and leadership will strongly depend on the appropriateness of its governance of the three systems. The last section of the questionnaire will be devoted to the support of family business consulting institutions and to the inclination of family entrepreneurs to ask for their assistance.

The most complicated part of the survey preparation is setting up questionnaire questions. Most of the questions are closed-ended and limit the respondents' answers to the options provided. Usually three choices are offered with the option to add some wording in writing when none of the choices completely reflects their opinion. Closed-ended questions have been selected in order to eliminate misunderstanding or misinterpretation of certain questions. Had the decision been made to acquire data orally and not in writing, such difficulties would be less likely to occur since there would always be a possibility to additionally explain the question. However, the questioning process would take much longer and get more complicated since the respondents live in different locations.

With the aim of obtaining an all-encompassing picture of the family business situation, it is highly recommendable that the questions be answered by both the owners and family members relevant for the family business. Therefore, the questionnaire is divided in two parts: the first part is filled in by the family business owner while the second part is filled in by the family members tied to the family business. The questionnaire has been prepared in the manner that both the owner and family members respond to the same set of questions in order to get the information on the difference in their perception of the family business ownership and leadership transfer issues.

Demographic data are given in the introductory part of the questionnaire. This part contains the information on the family business and its owner. It helps us in obtaining crucial information on the time of the owner's decision to step down from ownership and leadership positions.

When setting up the questionnaire, all the three systems have been considered: family, business and ownership systems. Their interdependence has been recognized in the family business and therefore, it is important to observe their relationship during every serious ownership and leadership transfer planning.

The first part of the questionnaire is focused on the issues related to the family business family system. The most challenging part of this section is the level of objectivity in the answers of the family business owners so that other business-related family members answering the same questions will become corrective factors. The target of this set of questions is to get better knowledge of family member's communication and the relationships they cherish. Most of the questions are provided with answer choices and there is a possibility that the respondent selects few of them. The choice of answers has been very carefully selected as they have proven to affect positively or negatively the communication and relationships in the family. Some answers allow for additional explanations since every family is specific and it is important to grant the possibility of emphasizing such specifics through the individual answers of the respondents.

The second part of the questionnaire deals with the questions related to the family business system. The objectivity of the family business owner's answers will be the biggest challenge again and the participation of other family members is, therefore, very important. The target of this set of questions is to get better insight into the quality of communication between the owner and other interest groups of the family business, get better information on the existence of formal operating procedures for certain tasks, and individual performance indicators measurements and planning of future for senior and junior successors.

The third part of the questionnaire deals with the questions related to the family business ownership system. It is important to involve the family members who are potential family business successors. This is due to the fact that family business owners can be apt to impose the decisions on the family succession even in the cases when particular members have no interest to participate in the family business. The intention is also to get the information if the family business owner tends to list on the stock exchange and opens the business to non-family influences.

The last set of questions focuses exclusively on the family business owners. The goal is to get direct feedback as to their inclination to hire professional consultants in the process of ownership and leadership transfer. Besides, critical points during the transfer of ownership and leadership of Croatian entrepreneurs are also expected to be identified. Namely, the relevant literature mostly deals with the problems of foreign entrepreneurs. Although their problems may be identical for the most part, the premise is that there are certain specifics inherent to the Croatian entrepreneurs when compared to others. The closing part of the questionnaire is meant to determine the potential difference or similarity among them.

During the first year of their studies of the Entrepreneurship Economics, the students of VERN' fill in their registration forms. Among others, the students provide information if they come from the family business. Out of 1,349 students who filled in the forms, 408 (or 30.24 %) answered positively. Therefore, the questionnaire for the family entrepreneurs has been sent to 408 e-mail addresses. The students still attending the university studies at VERN' have been given the questionnaires in person with the intention to increase their motivation to fill them in. In total, 40 questionnaires have been returned (in percentage—9.8 %). Three have been excluded from further statistical processing because of being partly or wrongly filled in.

The data analysis has been performed by use of the computer program Microsoft Access. The selection of the program was made due to very good visibility of data written in the tables. In this manner graphical and table presentation of the research results in Microsoft Excel will be facilitated. Besides, Microsoft Access enables the application of more up-to-date statistical analysis methods such as correlation, which is very important for the questionnaire processing and making of relevant conclusions.

5.2 Research Results

When answering the questions related to the family business family system, the owners and family members had a very high percentage of same answers (89.2–97.3 %). Obviously there is a very good flow of information among the family members so that they mostly share the same positions as to the functioning of the family system. This set of questions refers to the employment of family members, communication, values, development of younger generation, appraisal system and payment of family members as well as the common leisure time sharing.

To the question: "What are you proud of and what requires improvements on the family level?", the respondents provided the following answers: the vast majority of 68.9 % emphasized that in particular they are proud of mutual respect and support among the family members. They reached the maximum agreement in answering that question (76.9 %). They also share the same position as to the need to work on the improvement of communication (68.9 %). They reached the maximum agreement in answering that question as well (76 %). When answering the above two questions, the respondents had a possibility to provide their own answers by selecting the option "Others". With relation to the first question on family pride they also emphasized closeness among the family members, while within the area for improvement a need to spend more time together has been clearly emphasized although currently unfeasible due to numerous business obligations.

Based on the answers to the questions related to the family entrepreneurship business system, and when comparing the answers provided by both family business owners and member(s), we come to the first important conclusion elaborated below. The question is:

Is there any development or succession plan for the introduction of the new generation of successors to the family business?   YES   NO   DON'T KNOW

Only 59.5 % of the family business owners and members provided the same answer to the question. Obviously, there is a big discrepancy in the answers provided. It can be concluded that the entrepreneurs have a plan of their own (with a very low probability that the plan is written or systematized in any formal shape), and have not forwarded it to other family members tied to the family business. Less than a half of entrepreneurs have any development or succession plan whatsoever (only 48.6 %). Out of this group of entrepreneurs, 94.4 % of them believe that they sufficiently invest in the development of the new generation, which is an expected answer, as the investments are most probably a part of development and succession plan for the introduction of the new generation in the family business.

The second important conclusion drawn from the research results, and concurrent with the literature on unsuccessful ownership and leadership transfers, is that the planning of retirement of the senior family members has low priority. Only

46 % of the family business owners provided positive answers on the existence of financial plans for financing of senior generation retirement days.

As to the question related to the existence of a written business development plan, only 35.1 % of the owners provided positive answers. They also verified their business capabilities to meet those plans (84.6 % of them). Out of the above 35.1 %, 76.9 % owners transmitted the plan to the family members, employees and consultants, meaning that only 27 % of the entrepreneurs under survey professionally and completely perform their business development planning and information dissemination among the family members who have to be informed thereof. Moreover, only 7.7 % of them have included in the written business development plan the section covering ownership transfer plan for the next generation!

Then, 86.5 % of the family business owners and family members gave identical answers to the question related to the existence of formal job description and specification for each job in the family firm. 43.8 % of the respondents provided negative answers, which lead us to the conclusion that almost one half of the family businesses has no clear job description based on which the employee would be acquainted with the desired outputs of his work and thus has no clue where his duties begin or end. Out of 56.2 % of the respondents providing positive answers, only 37.8 % of them have developed some form of performance indicator measurements for their employees in line with their job description and specification. As a conclusion, only 21.3 % of the analyzed family businesses have formal job description and specification and a developed system of the employees' performance measurement! Such informalities in the human resource management can be very dangerous for a family business due to a very small probability that the best employee would really be given adequate position due to nepotism, misunderstanding of the employee (what is expected from him, how he will be rewarded for good performance and what the criteria are for a well performed job).

Based on the answers to the questions related to the family entrepreneurship ownership system, the first conclusion to be drawn based on the answer to following question is:

Has family business successor(s) been selected?	YES	NO	DON'T KNOW

Out of 83.8 % of the respondents providing identical answers to the question (including both the owner and family member), 54.8 % of them have already selected the family business successor. 42.1 % of entrepreneurs between the age of 45 and 55 have selected the successor, while the entrepreneurs older than 55 have done that in a higher percentage rising to 71.5 %. The above two age groups of entrepreneurs have been selected with a purpose. Since the ownership transfer programs in the countries with the developed system of family entrepreneurship support take between 3 and 5 years, it is high time that the entrepreneurs belonging to the oldest age group should select the successor. The younger group is also interesting since the majority of them have children at the age when professional orientation should have already occurred. If the agreement on the successor has already been reached, there is higher probability that the child will be professionally oriented towards the needs of the family business.

In 62.2 % cases it has been agreed that the business ownership will remain in the family, while in 10.8 % cases only consensus has been reached that non-family members may enter the ownership structure. The family firms that decided to open to the non-family ownership influences are mostly small limited liability companies.

The questions related to the strengths and weaknesses of the family business ownership, were answered by the respondents in the following manner: the devotion and commitment to the family business have been highly recognized as strength of the family business (66.2 %) as well as reliability viewed from the customer and supplier perspective (55.4 %). The maximum percentage (47.3 %) of the respondents have recognized lack of discipline and formal operating procedures as a weakness of the family-owned business. Additional problem of insufficient planning, mixing of personal and business life, and inability to find a high performing manager have also been identified as weaknesses.

Non-family managers are often engaged to prevent that the family rules prevail and govern the business as they are exclusively led by the management principles. Another added value of non-family managers is the family business professionalization and exit from so called "bird cage management" in which the members of the same family are reasoning in the similar or same manner concerning certain problems and have very often limited skills and knowledge. On the other hand, it is not an easy task to find an available highly qualified person possessing knowledge, skills and experience in the intended field of employment who nourishes the same set of values as those cherished by the family-owned business. Besides, there is no institution whatsoever offering "good non-family managers", that would, based on the above criteria, connect such managers and family-owned firms. It goes for a long-term cooperation having inevitable impact on the business and family so that a wrong selection might have far-reaching repercussions.

The rest of the questionnaire analysis will refer to the questions given to the family business owners only as they make decisions on the family business successors and engagement of professional consulting institutions in the field of ownership and leadership transfer. 56.6 % of all respondents have already selected the successor, motivated by different reasons such as a recognized need for gradual introduction of the successor to the business (61.9 %), soon retirement (47.6 %), or desire to reduce tensions and conflicts among potential successors (4.8 %). 43.2 % of all the respondents have not selected the successor, and 62.5 % of them are between 45 and 55, while 18.8 % are older than 55. They have not selected the successor as they believe that the time for the decision has not yet come (75 %). Three respondents have selected the option "Others" and commented that firstly, the desired successor has no ambition to take over the family business, secondly, they do not see any future of business in Croatia and have serious thoughts on liquidating the business and thirdly, after retirement, they plan to close the business. Both the respondents who do not see any future of business in Croatia and plan to close the business work in the construction industry. This is not a surprise since the construction industry and the related businesses felt the hardest impact by the economic crisis.

One of the key goals of the questionnaire was to get answers to two questions:

(a) How useful would the engagement of professional consulting institutions be related to the ownership and leadership transfer in your family business?
(b) Provide your estimate if you would use the services of professional consulting institutions when planning the transfer of ownership and leadership in your family business?

Most respondents (59.5 %) consider that the benefit of engaging professional consulting institutions in the planning of ownership and leadership transfer in their case is "exceptionally small" or "small". One fifth (or 21.6 %) of them believe that the benefit of such engagement would be "neither small, nor big", 5.4 % of respondents see a "big" or "exceptionally big" benefit, while 13.5 % of them cannot estimate how useful it would be to engage professional consulting institutions when planning the transfer of ownership and leadership in their businesses (Fig. 1).

Then, 37.5 % of respondents who have not yet selected the successor to the family business consider that the benefit of engaging professional consulting institutions when planning the transfer of ownership and leadership in their business would be "small" or "exceptionally small". None of them considers that the benefit would be "big" or "exceptionally big". 56.3 % of them "cannot estimate" or consider the benefit of such engagement to be "neither small nor big". This information is indicative and coincides with the thesis that a number of family entrepreneurs actually do not know what to expect from such institutions and generally, have bad experience with the institutions specialized in the field of entrepreneurial consulting. Their comments provided together with the answers speak for themselves:

"In need of suggestions how to perform the ownership transfer, I am not sure that such an institution would be of much help."
"I am not familiar with such institutions and their effects."
"I do not know that such institutions exist."
"I have no confidence in such institutions."

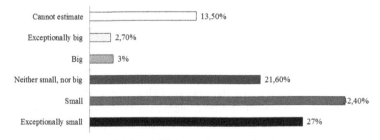

Fig. 1 The benefit of engaging professional consulting institutions in the planning of ownership and leadership transfer (source: Authors)

Others are inclined to support the second thesis also related to the family entrepreneurs—they consider that they can do all by themselves and need no help whatsoever. Their comments supporting their positions are mostly the following:

> *"No need!"*
> *"Do not consider it necessary!"*
> *"Owner is experienced enough to perform the task without consultation."*
> *"I believe that we will be able to resolve alone all potential problems including ownership transfer."*

On the other hand, the selection of the best successor among the family members has been recognized as the most critical point in the ownership and leadership transfer by 37.5 % of respondents and 25 % of them emphasized as the most critical one the ignorance of good practices in the ownership and leadership transfer. They are obviously aware of their lack of knowledge on good practices in the performance of such a transfer but still they do not open the door to the engagement of external consultants. One of the reasons for their reluctance can be found in the comment of a respondent who nicely presents the specifics of the family business related to the external consulting. It also points to the worries of family entrepreneurs and they have to be taken particular care of when developing the ownership and leadership transfer program.

> *"I think that I have the best knowledge of all the factors affecting the future successful operation of my family business. A consultant might objectively suggest the best successor but I want my choice to have subjective elements as well ..."*

71.4 % of respondents who have already decided on the family business successor consider there would be "small" or "exceptionally small" benefits of engagement of a professional consulting institution for ownership and leadership transfer. 9.5 % of them responded that the benefit would be "big" or "exceptionally big". 19 % "cannot estimate" or believe that the benefit of such an arrangement would be "neither small nor big". Such a feedback is expected given the fact that the family successor has been decided and there are no reasons to discuss the issue with the supporting institutions. Unfortunately, not many entrepreneurs are aware of the fact that with the selection of the successor they have not resolved the issue of ownership and leadership transfer. This is only the beginning of a complex, sensitive and long process which requires special attention, professional knowledge and experienced management.

From their own example, the entrepreneurs have recognized as the most critical points in the ownership and leadership transfer process—ignorance of good practices in the ownership and leadership transfer (42.9 %) and the issues related to the clear defining of the family business founder's/owner's role after his stepping-down from the lead position (28.6 %). Even the entrepreneurs who have already selected the successors are aware of their ignorance of ownership transfer best practices but still they do not see any need to engage supporting professional institutions. Clear defining of the founder's role in the family business after his withdrawal from the leadership position is crucial and can considerably contribute to the success of ownership and leadership transfer to the next generation. Namely, due to this unresolved issue, the entrepreneurs mostly select the successor but in practice keep on postponing the transfer owing to the fact that their role in the family business after withdrawal has not been defined. As they see their family business as an essential part of their lives, they are not ready to easily pass reins to their successors.

Based on their comments, conclusions can be drawn on the decision-making criteria related to the ownership and leadership transfer process:

"Since we are a small family-business, there is only one potential successor."

"My daughter being the only family successor is my only choice for the potential leadership position in our family business."

"Potential successors are not yet actively involved in the business and due to this I still do not think of the ownership transfer."

"As our firm is involved in technical business, which is overwhelmingly male business, I consider leaving the business to my son who alone showed some interest."

Recognized key factors in the decision-making process on the selection of the family business successor are: size of business, importance of having as a successor a family-member in the leadership position, active operative involvement in the business, interest of potential successors to get involved in the business and the division of labor in relation to gender-based stereotypes like "male" and "female" occupations.

At the conclusion, the respondents have been asked if they would consult professional institutions when planning the ownership and leadership transfer in their family business.

Most of respondents (51.4 %) answered negatively, 37.8 % could not decide, while only 10.8 % of respondents would consult such institutions (Fig. 2). People in charge of such programs should make the family entrepreneurs aware of positive effects the consulting institutions have in reducing the number of closing family businesses during the vital process of ownership and leadership transfer. The fact that there is a number of indecisive respondents is in favour of this

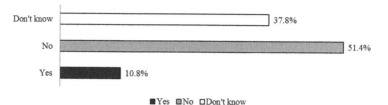

Fig. 2 Would you consult professional institutions when planning the ownership and leadership transfer in your family business? (source: Authors)

recommendation. Besides, among the respondents providing negative answers to the question, 21 % of them are not able to evaluate or cannot decide on the benefits such consulting institutions might provide. There is obviously some room for the attitude change towards such consulting institutions and services they offer.

6 Discussion

While preparing the questionnaire, the search for respondents and then their inclusion in the research was very time-consuming (including also search for and studying of relevant literature dealing with questionnaires, defining the question-naire purpose and main goals, search for relevant documentation, making contacts with the population selected for the research, examining of colleagues' willingness to distribute and then collect questionnaires, selecting of professionals who will according to their field of specialization make a critical overview of the question-naire and assist in tailoring questions to the target group, etc.) There are no available data on the number of family businesses in Croatia. Moreover, there is no widely accepted definition of the family business that would represent a relevant framework for further research. Therefore, it has been a real challenge to define the sampled population.

At the beginning of the questionnaire distribution, some respondents insisted on filling in printed versions of the questionnaires while others had no problem in filling them out on-line (as originally envisaged). Regardless of very detailed instructions how the questionnaire should be filled in, a small percentage of respondents have got the questionnaires returned for completion as they forgot to answer some questions. The questionnaire has also been filled out in different manners (despite exact instructions) so that the data processing took longer than anticipated.

It was interesting to observe how eager some respondents were to fill in the questionnaire while others had to be reminded several times. Some were not motivated enough and they never returned the questionnaire. It has also been observed that the percentage of filled in questionnaires was higher among those respondents who already had some contacts with the authors of the survey or had positive experience with the distributors of the questionnaires. It can be concluded that personal contact has been decisive for their participation. Such a reaction is not surprising given the fact that a portion of the questionnaire is necessarily personal. Once the decision has been made to conceptualize and start the program for family businesses, it is highly important that professional, skillful and experienced people be engaged to represent the institution of confidence and possess subtle feelings for people.

A more intensified recent focusing on the issues of the family business in Croatia will make the repeating of the questionnaire in few years very interesting. The results of the repeated questionnaire will reflect trends and potential changes in views as well as the impact of Croatia's accession to the EU on the SME segment. Beside the inevitable internationalization of the family business operation, "border opening" will enable easier approach to the specialized institutional support to all the Croatian family businesses.

7 Conclusion

Today's business world has been constantly changing. Organizations of all types and sizes face internal and external factors that make it uncertain whether or when they will achieve their objectives. The effect this uncertainty has on organization's objective is risk. Organizations manage risk by identifying it, analyzing it and then evaluating whether the risk should be modified by risk treatment in order to satisfy their risk criteria. A complete risk management aims to protect the value already created by the organization, as well as its future opportunities, favouring secure growth. Risk taking is an important dimension of entrepreneurial orientation and its impact on the family businesses. The transfer from founders to other leaders entails serious risks, the most significant one being overlooking entrepreneurial activities. This risk could be minimized by grooming successors and nurturing their ability to innovate.

The questionnaire results have identified the need for creating a family business ownership and leadership transfer program. The supporting fact is that a number of related issues and needs of the respondent family entrepreneurs have been recognized and the respondents alone do not recognize them and are not capable of resolving them without assistance. However, there is a noticeable resistance of entrepreneurs towards the entrepreneurial supporting institutions primarily due to the past bad experience and skepticism as to the usefulness of such institutions in the process of ownership and leadership transfer. They consider themselves capable and experienced enough to perform the transfer on their own.

It will take some time to make the family entrepreneurs aware of the importance of the professionally led transfer. This can be done through the dissemination of best practices of foreign institutions specialized in the family entrepreneurship as well as by use of world statistics on the increased small business death rate during the ownership and leadership transfer. It is highly important to regain entrepreneurs' confidence in the supporting entrepreneurial institutions.

Every business is unique. Since family businesses contain an additional (family) system, which makes them particular, special attention has to be paid to the subjective elements when making decision on ownership and leadership succession. The only way to perform it properly is by active participation of the entrepreneur in the planning and implementation of ownership and leadership transfer.

We believe that the future will bring about interesting turnabouts in the ways of thinking and working with the family businesses. There is a decline in the traditional family businesses, such as traditional handicrafts and peasant farms. Changing dynamics of the family as an institution is accompanied by the changes in society. Traditional family concept based on the family relationships is fading out and gradually puts forward the family as a social and economic community of people not necessarily tied by blood. Due to these changes it is very likely that we shall come to understand and recognize the ways how to approach family businesses but such knowledge will be of no use any more.

References

Alpeza, M., & Peura, K. (2012). *Razvoj i održivost obiteljskih poduzeća u Hrvatskoj*. Zagreb: Centar za politiku razvoja malih i srednjih poduzeća CEPOR.

Bray, S. (n.d). Family business: Planning for a successful transfer to the next generation. Available from http://thefamilybusinessschool.com/node/68 [23 May 2010].

Brett Davies Lawyers. (2009). Family trusts. Available from http://www.taxlawyers.com.au/manuals/familytrusts.htm [6 January 2009].

Bruc, D., & Picard, D. (2005). Succession can breed success, Canadian Federation of Independent Business. Available from http://www.newsaskcfdc.ca/pdf/Succession%20Can%20Breed%20Success.pdf [20 July 2013].

Bublić, V., Hunjak, T., & Varlandy-Supek, M. (2013). Risk management in SMEs: The Croatian experiences. In V. Ramadani & R. Schneider (Eds.), *Entrepreneurship in the Balkans: Diversity, support and prospects* (pp. 57–76). Berlin: Springer.

Ćorić, G., Meter, J., & Bublić, V. (2012). Evidence from the Project Croatian Gazelles—Promotion of sustainable growth. Revija Mednarodno inovativno poslovanje, Letnik 4 (2012), #2.

Crnković P. S. (2008). Overview of family business relevant issues: Country Fiche—Croatia. Available from http://ec.europa.eu/enterprise/policies/sme/files/craft/family_business/doc/familybusines_country_fiche_croatia_en.pdf [15 May 2014].

Dana, L.-P., & Dana, T. (2003). Management and enterprise development in post-communist economies. *International Journal of Management and Enterprise Development, 1*(1), 45–54.

Dussault, M. R. (2008). What is a family business? *Cygnus Business Media*, Fort Atkinson.

European Commission. (2009). Final report of the European Commission Expert Group overview of family-business-relevant issues: Research, networks, policy measures, and existing studies. European Commission, Directorate-General for Enterprise and Industry. Available from http://ec.europa.eu/enterprise/policies/sme/promoting-entrepreneurship/family-business/index_en.htm#h2-expert-group-on-family-business [5 November 2009].

Family Firm Institute. (2013). Available from http://www.ffi.org/?page=History [15 May 2013].

Federal Ministry of Development, Entrepreneurship and Craft, Federation of Bosnia and Herzegovina. (2009). Available from http://www.fmrpo.gov.ba/UserFiles/File/Web-obiteljsko_poduzetnistvo.pdf [5 January 2009].

Grassi, V. J., Jr., & Giarmarco, J. H. (2008). Practical succession planning for the family-owned business. *CCH Journal of Practical Estate Planning.* February-March 2008, Wolters Klower, p. 39–49. Available from http://www.disinherit-irs.com/articles/Practical_Succession_Plan ning_for_the_Family-Owned_Business.pdf [10 June 2013].

Hubbard, D. (2009). *The failure of risk management: Why it's broken and how to fix it.* Hoboken, NJ: Wiley.

International Organization for Standardization. (2009). ISO/FDIS 31000:2009(E) Risk management—Principle and guidelines, Final Draft, International Organization for Standardization, Geneva

Investopedia. (2013). Available from http://www.investopedia.com/terms/b/businessrisk.asp [20 May 2013].

Kamei, K., & Dana, L.-P. (2012). Examining the impact of new policy facilitating SME succession in Japan: From a viewpoint of risk management in family business. *International Journal of Entrepreneurship and Small Business, 16*(1), 60–70.

Kružić, D. (2004). *Obiteljski biznis.* Zagreb: RRIF Plus d.o.o.

March, J. G., & Shapira, Z. (1987). Managerial perspectives on risk and risk taking. *Management Science, 33*(11), 1404–1418. Available from http://faculty.babson.edu/krollag/org_site/org_theory/march_articles/marshap_mgrrisk.html [15 June 2010].

McGee, T., & Rosone, B. (2013). Perspectives on family-owned businesses governance and succession planning, Deloitte Development LLC, New York, NY. Available from http://www.corpgov.deloitte.com/binary/com.epicentric.contentmanagement.servlet. ContentDeliveryServlet/USEng/Documents/Board%20Governance/Private%20and%20Not-for-Profit%20Organizations/Perspectives%20on%20Family%20Owned%20Businesses_Deloitte_June%202013.pdf [20 July 2013].

Medić, M. (2009). Lecture notes distributed in Family Business Management Course at The University of Osijek, Faculty of Economics.

Mejovšek, M. (2003). *Uvod u metode znanstvenog istraživanja u društvenim i humanističkim znanostima.* Zagreb: Slap.

Merriam Webster Inc. (2013). Merriam-Webster Dictionary. Available from http://www.merriam-webster.com/dictionary/risk [5 May 2013].

Naldi, L., Nordqvist, M., Sjöberg, K., & Wiklund, J. (2007). Entrepreneurial orientation, risk taking, and performance in family firms. *Family Business Review, 20*(1), 33–47.

Oxford University Press. (2013). Oxford Dictionaries. Available from http://oxforddictionaries. com/definition/english/risk [5 May 2013].

Ramadani, V., & Dana, L.-P. (2013). The state of entrepreneurship in the Balkans: Evidence from selected countries. In V. Ramadani & R. C. Schneider (Eds.), *Entrepreneurship in the Balkans.* Berlin: Springer.

Rothwell, W. J. (2010). *Effective succession planning: Ensuring leadership continuity and building talent from within* (4th ed.). New York: AMACOM.

Standards Australia/Standards New Zealand Standard Committee. (2009). AS/NZS ISO 31000:2009 Risk management—Principles and guideline, Standards Australia/Standards New Zealand Standard Committee, Sidney.

The Business Development Bank of Canada. (2008). Success story: Family succession know-how. Available from http://www.businessdictionary.com/definition/risk.html [20 May 2013].

The Economist. (2004). Special report, "Family Businesses Passing on the crown", 7 November. Available from http://www.economist.com/node/3352686 [5 January 2013].

Victoria State Services Authority. (2008). Succession risk management: Basic principles. Author Victoria State Services Authority, Melbourne. Available from http://www.ssa.vic.gov.au/prod ucts/view-products/succession-risk-management-toolkit.html [20 July 2013].

Web Finance Inc. (2013a). Business Dictionary, Web Finance Inc. Available from http://www. businessdictionary.com/definition/risk.html [20 May 2013].

Web Finance Inc. (2013b). Business Dictionary, Web Finance Inc. Available from http://www. businessdictionary.com/definition/business-risk.html [20 May 2013].

Zahra, A. S. (2005). Entrepreneurial risk taking in family firms. *Family Business Review, 18*(23), 1–19.

Zelenika, R. (1998). *Metodologija i tehnologija izrade znanstvenog i stručnog djela.* Rijeka: University of Rijeka, Faculty of Economics.

The Succession Issues in Family Firms: Insights from Macedonia

Veland Ramadani, Alain Fayolle, Shqipe Gërguri-Rashiti, and Egzona Aliu

Abstract The purpose of this book chapter is to share findings related to succession of family businesses in Republic of Macedonia. In order to gain a better picture of the current situation, problems and perspectives that stand in front of families with respect to succession issue it was conducted a survey. The questionnaire was distributed to the owners of several businesses as well as through e-mail. The questionnaire was distributed to 140 businesses, depending on the size of cities.

Keywords Family firms • Succession • Problems • Perspectives • Macedonia

1 Introduction

The purpose of this book chapter is to share our findings related to succession of family businesses in Republic of Macedonia. In order to gain a better picture of the current situation, problems and perspectives that stand in front of families with respect to succession issue it was conducted a survey. The questionnaire was distributed to the owners of several businesses as well as through e-mail. The questionnaire was distributed to 140 businesses, depending on the size of cities. The questionnaire consisted of 20 questions. We asked business owners to send us

V. Ramadani (✉)
Faculty of Business and Economics, South-East European University, Ilinden 335, 1200 Tetovo, The Republic of Macedonia
e-mail: v.ramadani@seeu.edu.mk

A. Fayolle
EM Lyon Business School, 23 Avenue Guy de Collongue, Ecully Cedex, 69134 Lyon, France
e-mail: fayolle@em-lyon.com

S. Gërguri-Rashiti
College of Business Administration, American University of Middle East, Kuwait City, Kuwait
e-mail: shqipe.gerguri-rashiti@aum.edu.kw

E. Aliu
Euroactiva, Skopje, The Republic of Macedonia

LEORON Professional Development Institute, Dubai, United Arab Emirates
e-mail: gonaaliu@hotmail.com

© Springer International Publishing Switzerland 2015
L.-P. Dana, V. Ramadani (eds.), *Family Businesses in Transition Economies*,
DOI 10.1007/978-3-319-14209-8_10

the completed questionnaire within 2–3 weeks. Of these 140 businesses, 112 responded positively to our questionnaire and thanked us for the commitment to the study of these businesses, ways of their functioning and our advice from our research report that can help exploit the issue of succession. The number of businesses that have not answered is 16 and 12 businesses have stated that they do not consider their business as a family business. The largest number of businesses that responded to us was located in Skopje, where 32 % of surveyed businesses expressed a desire to meet us; 18 % of family businesses that answered our questionnaire operate in Tetovo; the number of surveyed businesses from Kićevo, Struga and Kumanovo was 10 % each; 14 % of the family businesses surveyed were from Gostivar, and 6 % from Ohrid. Businesses were identified as family businesses if the manager or owner confirmed to us that their business was a family business. The book chapter will end with a case study, where we analyzed the succession process issues.

2 Literature Review

The succession issue of family firms has been addressed comprehensively in the literature (Cabrera-Suarez, Saa-Perez, & Garcia-Almeida, 2001; Dyck, Mauws, Starke, & Mischke, 2002; Fattoum & Fayolle, 2009; Gimeno, Gemma, & Coma-Cros, 2010; Handler, 1990, 1994; Ip & Jacobs, 2006; Steier, 2001; Wang, Watkins, Harris, & Spicer, 2004). This process, as presented in Fig. 1, includes three elements: *processes* (management and ownership succession), *activities* (intended to integrate family members into the management and ownership succession processes and to feel comfortable with both succession processes and outcomes) and *desired outcomes* (integrated family members, informed decision making, etc.).

In general, succession process in family firms is analyzed as a transfer of the management and ownership of the business. Ownership succession focuses on who will own the business, and when and how this process will occur. Management

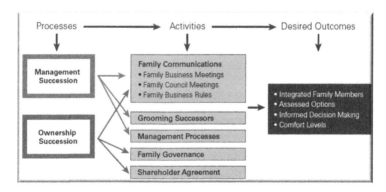

Fig. 1 Elements of succession in family firms (source: Walsh, 2011, p. 15)

succession focuses on who will lead the business, what changes will occur, when they will be accountable for the results and when these results will be achieved (Fig. 1).

Effective integration and management of the family component will have a decisive effect on the success of the succession process (Walsh, 2011). As a definition, succession is the replacement of the founder and management tasks by the successor. According to Handler (1990) the continuity process is described as a joint arrangement of the role between members of the current and succeeding generations. In order to become a successful leader, the successor must be fully engaged in the process of continuity. The process of continuity in family businesses is intended to provide competent leadership in all generations. This process involves changes at a managerial level that includes CEO and top management and ownership level (Giudice, Peruta, & Elias, 2011).

Succession is the biggest challenge facing family businesses in the long term. The desire of the owners to plan for succession in ownership and management is often the main factor that determines survival or failure of their business (IFC, 2008). The generation change process is difficult and continuity is required as the last and most difficult test for family businesses. Succession is not a single event that occurs when the old leader retires and passes the torch to the new leader, but is a process driven by development that begins very early in the life of some families and continues through maturation and aging generations. Succession is a process of preparation and forecasting, which helps in better way to surrender the keys of leadership, regulation and business adjustment in cases of illness or sudden death. This process in family businesses, presents a unique opportunity for strategic re-orientation based on the shared values of the family (Gersick, Davis, Hampton, & Lansberg, 1997; Kamei & Dana, 2012; Shi & Dana, 2013).

The faces of every business change. If there is no a succession plan, the sudden death of the founder can throw everything and everyone in a real chaos. Who should lead the business now? Will it be able to operate effectively? Can business survive under new leadership? Shall I have a job? What will I do after retirement? When there is no a succession plan such questions may be submitted to an organization and can reduce the morale, productivity, and can overthrow the gains of the company. With aim that everyone in an organization can breathe easily and be more relaxed, it is required that change in leadership be planned, since so they will feel more confident about the future and their future business. The purpose of succession planning is to achieve the transfer of control and responsibility in the family business in the best way possible to the next generation (Kaneff, 2011).

One of the most difficult obstacles to the stability and growth of the family business is the issue of succession. For a business to remain a family business, each generation must be followed by another, which often is the final challenge of management. The generation that is in power should be removed and the next generation should be involved. Succession imposes a variety of significant changes in the ownership structure and management of the family business at the same time (Venter, 2002).

For the majority of family businesses, succession can be a minefield as it is a very complicated process. Problems that family businesses face at the time of succession can break family relationships and can cause conflicts that could cause the destruction of the business (Family Business Experts, 2012).

The importance of succession for family businesses is such that one of the authors has studied the most the phenomenon of family business defines these businesses in terms of their potential for succession. His defining for family business is: "The family business is a business that will pass to the next generation of the family to manage and control" (Ward, 1987 p. 252).

The founder should commit to transfer his knowledge and intellectual capital to the next generation, so that his family business can survive and continue on to the next generation. It is important that the founder convey to his children a sense of pride for the family business and at the same time sincerely discuss the risks and problems that they may face. In order to become a successful succession, planning is required as is mentoring the next generation, because the succession is a process that takes time to develop and requires management if we want to be the successful (Lipman, 2010). An academic study divides this knowledge into three categories (Lipman, 2010, pp. 8–9):

- Competencies related to the industry (more specifically unique knowledge for industry);
- Business competencies (e.g., methods of business operation, products and services, calculating risks, problem solving and conflicts);
- Competencies of ownership (e.g., governance, maintaining a fair balance between the different actors, and the addition to the business of the economic value).

Succession planning should be the most important task of the leader of the family business and should be initiated at an early stage of the life cycle of the business. Succession includes two movements: the successor that moves and takes office and the leader who retire. This motion is very important for the process of succession as it should be done with the selection of the right successor. Succession planning is like insurance, as it protects the family from the destruction of financial value (Hess, 2006).

Continuity planning in family businesses is the critical issue. Succession may be the crowning achievement for a family business owner, as that is the time when he could share the success with his son or daughter. More than 30 % of all family businesses survive the second generation, and after that the numbers begin to fall, where only 12 % of family businesses are able to move on to the third generation, and only 3 % can continue in the fourth generation (Strategic Designs for Learning, 2012).

Good succession planning takes time and is successful when it results from the creation of good relations with the next generation and is based on responsibility, commitment and mutual respect. This planning should begin as soon as it is established if the company's target is keeping the business within the family, as it is necessary that strong leadership guide the business through the transition process.

Both generations have to look at succession as a process and not as an event (IFC, 2008).

For the transfer of control and responsibility of the family business to take place in the best way possible it is necessary that the next generation become the main purpose of succession planning that has to be achieved. Preparation for the transfer of ownership is to say to one's son/daughter that the transfer of the business will be made to him/her. Change of leadership should be planned carefully and should avoid making hasty decisions based on events that may occur as: diseases, marriages, separations or deaths.

Kaneff (2011) proposes that the preparations for the transition be made in a way similar to preparations made for a family trip, where preparations are made much earlier. Preparations must be made for contingencies that may occur and the needs and concerns of all those involved should be taken into consideration. So as to enhance possibilities for a memorable and hassle-free transition, the prepared itinerary should answer the following three questions (Kaneff, 2011):

1. *What are your destinations?* For transition journey three main areas should be addressed: leadership selection, transfer of ownership and estate planning. When providing information and making decisions, or when circumstances change, one should check out these three areas as these have an impact on each other. For example, if in the end, the chosen successor does not want to work in the family business, it makes it necessary to return to the process of selecting a successor. One needs to make the adjustment of property planning documents, in order to reflect the change and then has to create a new strategy for the transfer of ownership to a another successor. This three-part journey should be broad in scope and should go beyond the appointment of the new leader. The current leader and all other stakeholders need to address the many issues of personal concern, in the form of special points to be written out for the purpose of record keeping.
2. *What is your schedule?* Once a succession plan is decided, a detailed schedule must be created, in order to move on the journey together. When arranging the trip, one must also plan for emergencies, because different crises can arise. For example, a major customer could slip to a competitor, one of the main members of the family in the business may die suddenly or may divorce, or any natural issue can result in a lawsuit. These unforeseen events are another reason to start the journey as soon as possible.
3. *Who is the leader?* Usually the leader who will lead the process of succession is the current chief executive, who should possess strong leadership skills, the ability to make others listen and who must demonstrate sensitivity to all members of the family. The leader should guide the planning, but it must do so in a patient and persistent manner.

The formula for success in transition journey that Kaneff (2011) presents is:

$$Path + Time + Leader = Successful\ Transition\ Journey$$

The purpose of the succession is to make the business successful in the future, and at the same time be independent from the outgoing chief executive. The family business should be left to the successor in the best possible condition so that he/she can easily integrate into the business and continue successfully. The business should be left for the successor in the same way it should be presented for sales, with the highest value possible.

3 Succession Models

A succession model presents a frame of phases related to each-other. In the literature about family businesses are presented different models from different authors.

Authors, Rubenson and Gupta (1996), developed a contingency model for initial succession. This is a situation when the founder/owner takes a decision to depart from the business. This model is presented in Fig. 2.

The authors have identified three perspectives of succession: (a) *Succession as an inconsequential event*: This perspective is related to larger companies which are characterized with bureaucratic structure and the departure of founder will have

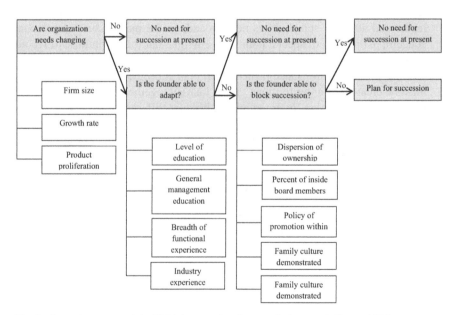

Fig. 2 A contingency model of initial succession (source: Rubenson & Gupta, 1996)

little impact on the company; (b) *Succession as a disruptive event*: This perspective is related to small entrepreneurial companies and the departure of founder will have relevant impact on the company performance; (c) *Succession as a rational organizational adaptation*: The eventual departure of the founder is seen as a catalyst that causes the company to concentrate proactively on ways it can increase the possibility of an adaptive succession.

Churchill and Hatten (1987) have developed a life cycle approach in order to explain the process of succession between father and son in a firm. They separate this process into four phases: (a) management by the owner, (b) training and development, (c) the stage of partnership between father and son, and (d) power transfer.

The first phase, management by the owner, is the stage where the owner is the only family member directly involved in the business, and the successor is not directly involved in the business. At this stage, the founder has complete business direction and is using his/her skills trying to create organizational culture which on the one hand it is necessary to run the daily affairs of the business and in the long term is beneficial for successful succession. During this stage the founder learns to delegate.

The second phase is known as training and development phase and is the phase where the successor becomes familiar with the business. At this stage the successor has entered into organization and has begun to participate in the daily chores. The descendant learns and develops his/her skills to run the business and also develops the ability to delegate.

The third phase is the stage where the partnership develops between ancestors and descendants. Here more authority is given to the descendants and a strong relationship between the two is developed.

The fourth phase is the last stage where the current power is transferred under the responsibility of the descendants business. At this stage the ancestors seek new opportunities for his/her life which really simplifies the process of succession.

The model presented by Scarborough (2012) consists of five stages. This model is presented in Table 1.

Another model of the succession process model is the model known as "six stairs to transfer the family business" (Fig. 3). This model is presented by Lambrecht (2005) and is based on empirical research where different family businesses were taken into consideration.

In this model, the *first stair* is entrepreneurship, where during this degree the transfer of professional knowledge, values, management, leadership characteristics and the soul of the organization are transferred to the next generation. The parent distinguishes three stages of the child's life that affect the transfer of professional knowledge. Potential offspring can learn the secrets of product and sales through these three stages. Family business is like a playground for children. In the second stage, successors are given the easiest tasks in the family business and in the third phase are asked to perform more serious tasks in the family business.

The *second stair* for the successful transfer of family business consists of studies. Most of the successors are encouraged before entering fully into family business to

Table 1 The succession process in family businesses

Stage I	Stage II	Stage III	Stage IV	Stage V
Early involvement with the business in routine tasks (while very young and in high school	Rotation among various assignments on summer/holiday vacation time (while in college)	Entry-level position with planned job rotations, regular performance evaluations and mentoring by both insiders and outsiders	Greater responsibility	General manager
			Department or functional manager; service on advisory board	Transition phase; membership on the board
			Decision-making responsibility	

Source: Scarborough (2012, p. 675)

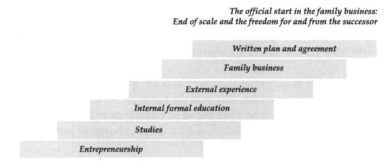

Fig. 3 Six-stairs model for family business transfer (source: Adapted from Lambrecht, 2005)

take an advanced degree, where in most cases the studies are oriented towards a family business sector. In other cases, the potential successors are free to choose which discipline they wish to study.

The *third stair* consists of internal formal education. During this phase, the successor learns about great business contacts and is provided with the business contacts, after meetings in order to achieve a proper understanding of the business. At this stage the potential successor skills are judged by the predecessor.

In the *fourth stair* the successor gain experience through working in other companies. This experience provides the potential successor with a knowledge and wisdom that helps him/her to cultivate self-confidence.

The *fifth stair* is the official beginning of the successor in the business. Before the successor takes a management position, it usually passes through the various departments in the business. In this way, the successor becomes self-proven and tries to win the trust of employees, and reveals business sectors and consumers. Freedom for the successor means taking responsibility, respecting previous generations, seeking advice from the transferor, and realize that the past is the basis which leads to the future.

The *sixth stair* is associated with planning and writing arrangements. Here consideration is given to the needs that may arise in the bad days of business that may come as a result of the death or resignation of a member of the family. Written plans should be well planned because poor planning can be very costly for the family and for business.

4 Business Climate for Family Businesses in Macedonia

Republic of Macedonia is small country located in South-East Europe, i.e. Central Balkan Peninsula, and is one of the successor states of the former Yugoslavia. Republic of Macedonia declared its independence in September 8, 1991, while member of the United Nations became in April, 8, 1993. As a result of a dispute with the southern neighbour, Greece, regarding the name issue, it was admitted under the provisional reference of the Former Yugoslav Republic of Macedonia, abbreviated as FYROM (United Nations, 1993). It covers 25,713 km^2 (9,928 square miles), bordering Albania, Kosovo, Serbia, Bulgaria and Greece. The capital is Skopje, the largest city of the Republic of Macedonia, inhabited by 30 % of the total population. According to State Statistical Office of Republic of Macedonia (2005), based on the data from the last Census of Population, Households and Dwellings in 2002, the Republic of Macedonia had 2,022,547 inhabitants, which is 3.9 % more compared with the Census in 1994 and 43 % more compared with the Census in 1948. Population of Republic of Macedonia according to ethnic group, based on Census 2002, consists of: Macedonians, 1,297,981 (64.2 %); Albanians, 509,083 (25.2 %); Turks, 77,959 (3.9 %); Romani, 53,879 (2.7 %); Serbs, 35,939 (1.8 %); Bosnians/Muslims, 19,571 (0.9 %) and others, 30,688 (1.4 %). The gross domestic product (GDP) in 2011 was 461,730 million denars (the currency of the RM) and in comparison with 2010 it increased by 6.4 % in nominal terms. The real GDP growth rate in comparison with 2010 was 2.8 % (State Statistical Office of Republic of Macedonia, 2012).

As a country where EU integration is among the top priorities, Republic of Macedonia significantly improved the overall business environment in recent years, as Doing Business in its 2013 Report ranked it 23rd out of 185 countries (IBRD/ World Bank, 2013). This was as a result of great efforts which were made in this segment by the government. However, in certain segments that make up the overall business environment, major changes are needed. Useful recommendations are given in Dana (1997). As for the political environment Macedonia is ranked in 62nd place, regulatory environment in 55th place, human capital and research in 72nd place, infrastructure in 72nd place, market sophistication in 62nd place, business sophistication in 95th place, scientific outputs in 52nd place and creative outputs in 84th place (Dutta, 2011). If we compare Macedonia only in one segment, for example, business environment, even with a country such is Sweden, it can be seen that Macedonia is in a very similar position, but the problem is that comparing in other segments Republic of Macedonia is not "in a good position". In order to have a better result in entrepreneurial process, it is necessary to put additional efforts in all areas on a continuous base.

Regarding the key segments that make up the environment for family businesses, the situation in Republic of Macedonia is as follows:

(a) *Ownership rights*. Good protection of property rights, effective execution of contracts and the law is directly related to fostering and development of the entrepreneurial activities. The protection of property rights remains to be a real challenge for Republic of Macedonia. According to International Property Rights Index 2011, from 129 analyzed countries, Republic of Macedonia is on 87th place, a position which shows that in our country property rights are not strongly protected (Jackson, 2011). But despite the progress, the judicial system is still inefficient and subject to political influence.

(b) *Corruption*. According to a report of the EBRD (2005), although in Republic of Macedonia (and transition countries in general) there was a certain reduction of corruption in its three basic forms of existence: *bribe tax*, as a percentage of total sales of enterprises, *kickback tax*, as a percentage of the value of contracts in the form of additional and unofficial payments to ensure receipt of contracts and *bribery frequency*, as percentage of respondents who said they accepted to pay bribes in customs, tax administration etc., it still presents a problem. A comparison between Republic of Macedonia and the countries in region is shown in Table 2. According to The 2009 Global Corruption Barometer Report of Transparency International, on the question "which sectors/institutions are most affected by corruption", the answers were as follow: 50 % of respondents said that it is the judiciary, 23 % said it is the public administration and 11 % pointed at the political parties (Riaño, Hodess, & Evans, 2009). Therefore, it is necessary for state institutions to undertake more concrete and stringent measures in this direction, that would result in cutting lengthy court procedures, simplifying complicated procedures for obtaining various permits, facilitating the introduction and transfer of new technologies, consistently protecting intellectual property etc. This can increase the rate of entry of new small and medium enterprises and enterprises with high growth potential, as well as the interest of potential investors to invest money, expertise and time.

Table 2 Corruption widespread in Republic of Macedonia and the region

Type of corruption	Bribe tax		Kickback tax		Bribery frequency	
Country/year	2002	2005	2002	2005	2002	2005
Macedonia	0.79	0.62	2.91	1.83	22.70	25.28
Bulgaria	1.95	1.58	2.51	3.32	32.79	15.70
Croatia	0.64	0.76	0.89	0.69	12.86	11.27
Albania	3.31	1.80	6.00	6.15	36.37	46.11
Bosnia and Herzegovina	0.95	0.39	1.19	0.51	22.42	9.63
Romania	2.57	0.81	2.11	0.67	36.74	22.56
Serbia and Montenegro	1.52	0.67	1.84	1.36	15.88	33.20

Source: EBRD (2005, p. 13)

(c) *Administrative and bureaucratic obstacles.* Long administrative and bureaucratic procedures represent a serious obstacle of doing business. Many studies
noted high correlation between the administrative and bureaucratic procedures
(expressed by the number of necessary procedures and required days for
starting a new business) and corruption—the more procedures, the more
opportunities for corruption. Regarding this issue, Republic of Macedonia
marks a significant improvement. The introduction of the so-called one-stop
system in 2006 contributed significantly to shortening the procedures and
times to start a new business. In the first months of 2006 were registered
5,400 new businesses (EBRD, 2006). The time needed for registration of new
enterprises was cut from 48 to 2 days, while the number of procedures has
been shortened to only 2. These improvements contributed as the Doing
Business Report 2013 ranked Republic of Macedonia in the fifth place out
of 183 analyzed countries in terms of this issue. But, when it comes to the
question of closing a business, Macedonia is ranked 116th place, because this
activity takes 2 years (IBRD/World Bank, 2013).

(d) *Tax policy.* The government of Macedonia introduced the flat tax in 2007,
which reduced the tax burden on enterprises. Income tax paid by businesses
firstly decreased from 15 to 12 %, while in the beginning of 2008 it decreased
to 10 %. The existing three marginal tax rates for personal income tax (15, 18
and 24 %) were replaced with one rate—10 %. But, there is no special relief
for start-up companies or for women entrepreneurs.

(e) *State regulation.* Considering this issue, it is necessary to strengthen the
independence of regulatory bodies, thus ensuring fair and predictable regulation of the domains of market failure (public goods, asymmetric information,
externalities, the existence of monopolies, unequal distribution of income,
etc.) and deregulation, removal of numerous administrative and bureaucratic
obstacles that impede faster growth of businesses respectively. According to
Schwab and Sala-i-Martin (2009), Republic of Macedonia is in the 83rd place,
out of 133 analyzed countries with a score of 3.7 (1–7, where 1 is the worst,
while 7 is the best rating).

(f) *Infrastructure.* Infrastructure as a general input of economic activity has a
significant impact on costs for business. This applies to large-scale infrastructure such as roads, railways, airports, energy, telecommunications, etc.
According to the Report of the World Economic Forum, Republic of Macedonia is in the 88th place (out of 133 countries analyzed) in terms of quality of
infrastructure. Separately, in terms of the quality of roads, it is in the 87th
place, quality of rail in the 71st place, quality of electricity supply in the 79th
place, the quality of telecommunications in the 58th place. The worst position
is related to airports, as Republic of Macedonia takes the 123rd place (Schwab
& Sala-i-Martin, 2009).

5 Succession in Macedonian Family Businesses

The issue of succession is one of the main and more critical problems and challenges for every family business. The larger number of family businesses fails to pass in the third generation. According to some researches, only 10 % of these businesses manage to enter into the third generation (Beckhard & Dyer, 1983; Efendioglu & Muscat, 2009; Gashi & Ramadani, 2013; Le Breton-Miller, Miller, & Steier, 2004; Mazzarol, 2006). In family business, succession is the transfer of business from one generation to the next. It is very important to prepare continuity of these family businesses in order to continue the family goals. Typical problems that arise at this stage involve business founders' resistance to retire, missing of planning for succession process, difficulties in determining the CEO, difficulties between founders and successors, and some different approaches to management (Cabrera-Suarez et al., 2001; Dyck et al., 2002; Gimeno et al., 2010; Handler, 1990, 1994; Ip & Jacobs, 2006; Steier, 2001; Wang et al., 2004). Many business owners in Macedonia fear that if they leave their business, then their jobs inherited by their successors may fail. They find it difficult to accept the fact that someone can replace them and can do the job with great success and maybe even do it better. For any family business entrepreneur it is their dream that 1 day they will pass on the business to the successor. In order that the successor succeeds, he should not only see his family business as a liability which must be met, but he must see it as a challenge and a special honor to be at the top of the business, which he inherited from his family. The advantage of a family business is that the children of the business owner usually gets involved at an early age in the business, and expends a lot of energy to train their successors, as a means to help one get acquainted with the procedures and challenges of the business. They must be aware of everything that happens in the business, and should be an example for other workers by being the first to arrive at work and the last to leave.

As it was mentioned before, in order to gain a better picture of the current situation, problems and perspectives that stand in front of families with respect to succession issue it was conducted a survey which covers 112 family businesses. The following report provides summarized results of the survey conducted in the period of March–July 2012 and was related to conditions, problems and challenges of the succession process.

The summary of responses collected by the questionnaire and the respondents are arranged in tables and graphics, and are presented in the order of the questions on the survey. After each section the results are discussed.

(a) *Business sector.* Macedonian family businesses operate in various sectors such as trade, services, construction, manufacturing and other sectors. According to the research data, 71 % of respondents operate in the trade sector, 8 % of family businesses provide various services, 11 % are in the construction sector, 8 % are in the manufacturing sector and 2 % stated that they operate in other sectors.

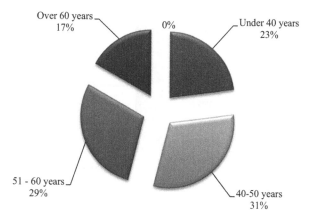

Fig. 4 Age of the founders of the business (source: Authors' field research)

(b) *Gender of the founder.* Regarding the gender of the founder of the family business, 96 % of businesses stated that they were men and only 4 % are women. This, at best, demonstrates the difficulties that still exist for a female to establish a business. Women need to have greater support to establish their businesses.

(c) *Age of the business founder.* In Fig. 4 the age of the business founder is illustrated. According to the statistics that we extracted, it was learned that 23 % of the founders of the business are under the age of 40 years, while 31 % are between 40 and 50 years. According to this survey, 29 % of the respondents were between 51 and 60 years and 17 % were over 60 years.

(d) *Age of the business.* Regarding the age of the business (number of years in business), most of the respondents stated that their business was in a very young age, which means that it is still in the first or second generation and none of the respondents stated that their business was in the third generation, which is quite disturbing. For a family business it is a very difficult transition to the third generation.

From the data presented in the Fig. 5, it can be seen that 33 % of businesses are under the age of 10 years, which means that they are still in the early stages of the business. Of the family businesses, 29 % were between the ages of 10 and 15 years. In the 15–20 years age range were 25 % of the family businesses. Only 13 % of businesses were over 20 years of age.

(e) *The level of education of the founders.* Regarding the issue of the level of education of the founders of the business, our data showed that 14 % are with primary school, 48 % of these founders are with secondary school, and 35 % are with faculty. Only 3 % of business founders are with masters or PhD (Fig. 6).

(f) *Number of the employees.* We have been interested to derive information about how many employees are employed in family enterprises in order to better appreciate their contribution to the economy and society at large. From the survey data (Table 3) it can be concluded that 27 % of family businesses

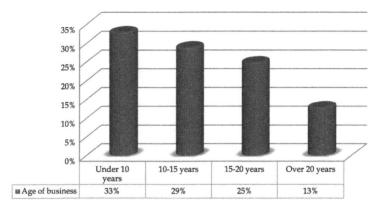

Fig. 5 Age of business (source: Authors' field research)

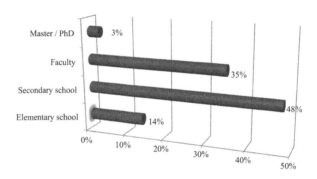

Fig. 6 Level of founder's education (source: Authors' field research)

Table 3 Number of employees in family businesses surveyed

Number of employees	Less than 10 employees	From 10 to 15 employees	From 50 to 250 employees	Over 250 employees
Percentage of businesses	27 %	42 %	26 %	5 %

Source: Authors' field research

are employing less than ten employees. Family businesses that employ 10–50 workers constitute 42 %. Family businesses that employ 50–250 workers account for 26 %, while those employing more than 250 workers make up 5 %.

It is important to know the number of family members employed in these enterprises. These data are shown in Table 4.

(g) *The gender of the first child.* Another interest of the study was to learn whether the first child of the founder was male or female. Also a goal was to learn of the founder's intention of transferring the business over to a female even if she was the oldest. The data showed that, from the family businesses surveyed, 61 % of the founder's first child was a boy and in 39 % of the cases,

Table 4 Number of employees who are members of the family

Number of employees that are family members	75–100 % are members of family	50–75 % are members of family	30–50 % are members of family	Under 30 % are members of family
Percentage of businesses	36 %	29 %	21 %	14 %

Source: Authors' field research

    a girl. Discussion takes place later, relative to the transfer of the business in terms of the first child, other children, and sons or daughters as heirs.

(h) *The level of education of the founder's children.* Education of children is very important to the founder if he wants his child 1 day take over the leadership of the business. The more prepared their child, the more successful will be the leadership of the business. Statistics from our data showed that in 32 % of the businesses, the founders' children are still in school and are not engaged in business. There are 12 % of businesses where the founders' children are not in school and are not engaged in business. In 31 % of businesses, the owners' children are at school or studies, but also are engaged in the business part-time in order to become more familiar with their family business and be ready when the time comes to make business decisions. There are 25 % of businesses, where the children of the founders have completed their studies and are engaged together with their parents in everyday tasks of full-time businesses.

(i) *Planning of the succession issue.* According to respondents, 29 % of family businesses do not have a plan regarding the issue of succession. Many of these have no knowledge about the issue of succession, as some even asked what it means. Our society has learned to leave the business to the son or daughter when it comes time to retire or when the founder cans no longer work. Not all businesses are taught that everything in life should be planned, and succession should be in place so as to be prepared for the unexpected. Founders who have planned succession constitute 23 % of the businesses. Those who think about the issue of succession constitute 21 % of businesses. Of the businesses, 22 % of the founders responded that for a time they are not planning anything. These data are of concern to family businesses, since each founder should plan his retirement and needs to arrange the preparation of the seed which will deal with the business in the future.

(j) *The child that will inherit the business.* The data from Fig. 7 are showing that the majority of family business founders or 41 % shall transfer business leadership to their first child, because they thought that the oldest child can better lead the business and is more experienced for business leadership. Those who have declared that they will transfer their business leadership to the second child make up 22 % of businesses; however, most of those indicated that the gender of the first child was "female". It seems that founders of businesses still do not have the courage to transfer the business leadership

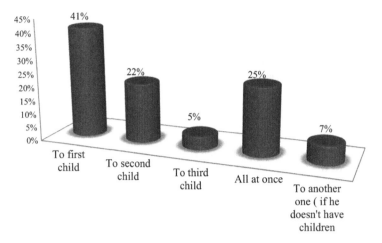

Fig. 7 The child that will inherit the business (source: Authors' field research)

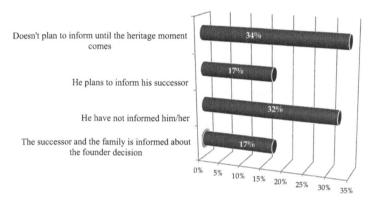

Fig. 8 Founder and informing the heir for leadership post (source: Authors' field research)

to their girls. The founders that claim that they will transfer the business leadership to their third child constitute 5 % of businesses. A large number of founders wish to transfer business leadership to all the children at once, and they make up 25 % of the businesses, since they do not want to make distinctions among their family to have conflicts. Of the businesses 7 % of the founders stated that their business leadership could be transferred to someone else because they do not have children.

(k) *Naming and informing the successor for it.* In order to avoid family conflicts the business founder often does not announce who they prefer to have as heir to the leadership of the business. In Fig. 8 data from the survey is presented pertaining to the founder and whether he has identified and informed his successor of such. Of the family business founders, 17 % informed their successors of their role as a successor. Those who have not yet informed their successor constitute 32 % of family businesses. Some founders (17 %) are planning in the near future to notify their successors. Many founders of businesses (34 %) do not want to inform their successor about the decision until the time comes to transfer the leadership because as was stated, they wish not to bring about jealousy between their children.

(l) *The age of founder's children.* Children of the founders of family businesses vary in age. The survey results revealed that the chosen successor of the founder who is under the age of 20 constitutes 18 % of family businesses. Chosen successors in the age range 20–25 constitute 21 % of family businesses. Most founders declared that their chosen heir for business leadership is between the ages of 26–30 and they constitute 39 % of businesses, while those founders who constituted 22 % of family businesses declared that their chosen successor is over the age of 30 years.

(m) *The ideal age for the founder to transfer the business management.* What is the ideal age for the founder to transfer the business management to his successor? This is a very difficult question for business founders, because for many, a retreat from the family business presents a real challenge for them, because there is often a fear of retirement and what they will do after leaving the business. This is best shown by the responses of the founders with only 9 % stating that the ideal age to inherit business management to successor is under the age of 50. A slightly larger number of them (31 %) think that the ideal age to transfer the management of the business is between 50 and 55 years of age. The largest number (46 %) of founders of businesses, think that it is best to transfer the business management to the successor when they are between 55 and 60 years of age. According to them, this is the best time for retirement and for a more comfortable senility. But those who think that the ideal age to transfer the management of businesses to a successor after 60 years of age constitute 14 % of the businesses surveyed.

(n) *Heir of the family business and management experience.* Before successors take over the management of the family business, he should be familiar with the business and the industry in which it operates the family business. Also he must understand how the business is operating if he wants to continue to successfully conduct businesses which his parents have led for many years. From Fig. 9 it can be seen that the family business successor that is expected to be in their family business management and has no management experience makes up 18 % of the businesses surveyed. Those who have at least 5 years management experience make up about 25 % of the businesses surveyed. More family business successors are expected to manage the business with 5–10 years of experience in management, and they constitute 36 % of the businesses surveyed. Those who have over 10 years of experience in management positions constitute 21 % of family businesses.

(o) *Length of "owner-successor" joint management.* For the successor it is important that in the early years as a business manager that he work along with and take business decision leadership advice from his parents who previously led the business in order to better learn about the business. The

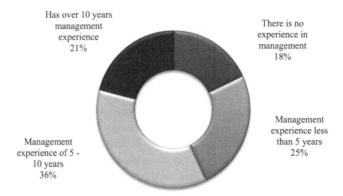

Fig. 9 Heir of the family business and management experience (source: Authors' field research)

successor should also be taught how to avoid conflicts among family members, which can arise and can cause many problems. According to data from
the field, 31 % of the founders stated that after inheriting the management of
the business, the successor should work together with the founder to manage
the business for at least 2 years. This shows the commitment of the founder to
the family business and their desire to prepare the successor for leadership, to
help prevent failure during the transition. Founders at the rate of 25 %
believed that they should manage the first 5 years together with the successor.
There are also those who think to manage the business along with successor to
death, and they make up 18 % of the respondents. But there are also founders
who think they will leave immediately after they transfer their business to the
heir. They probably want to relax from daily chores, because business leadership requires an energy and high potential.

(p) *The willingness of the children to manage the business in the future.* There are
children who do not wish to continue the business of their parents but wish to
pursue their dreams. Maybe they do not want to be entrepreneurs but they
want to be actors, singers or another profession that is not related to the
entrepreneur. For a business founder and for business in general, it is more
important that the successor be dedicated when taking over the torch of
leadership in his hands. The successor must also be eager to take over the
business because they really want to be entrepreneurs or maybe just because it
is naturally expected. Thoughts of the founders of the business are different.
From the survey, the data showed that 41 % of the business founders think
their heir wants to manage the businesses surveyed. Those thinking that their
heir does not want to manage the business but that there was no other choice
accounted for 10 % of the respondents. Taking over a business because there
is no other choice can be dangerous and can lead to business failure. Often it is
better that the heir goes to work somewhere else, and then return to the family
business. He would benefit from experience outside the family business and
will be informed of the strategies used by other businesses that in the future

would be competing for his family business. Some respondents (31 %) felt that their successor will work elsewhere and then return to the family business along with the experience it has gained which will contribute to the success of the enterprise. Those who do not have information on what their descendants prefer to do in terms of taking over the family business make up 18 % of the respondents.

(q) *Succession process and conflicts.* During the succession process often conflicts arise. Perhaps each of the children wants to be in charge of the family business in the future, which can cause family problems. Business founders (29 %) felt that the process of succession in family business will pass without dispute. Small disagreements can often occur, and it is the opinion shared by 34 % of respondents that the process of succession in their business will pass with petty disputes. But jealousy and expectations of children can lead to major disputes according to the opinion of 23 % of the founders of family businesses. Founders at a rate of 14 % think and expect that the process of succession in their business will pass with very large odds.

Every successful founder of the family business has a plan for the succession process. Conflicts and disagreements can happen, but is there a plan to resolve them? The founders did indicate that they have a plan for conflict management related to succession. On the basis of statistical data it is clear that 31 % of respondents have a plan to solve possible disputes over the succession process, while 35 % of respondents are developing a plan. Those who do not have plans about the resolution of conflict for the moment constituted 31 % of the respondents. For some entrepreneurs, the development of a plan for the succession process included a dispute resolution but it was not always of primary importance. According to 3 % of the respondents, they can resolve their differences without such a plan.

6 Case Study

In order to connect the literature provided with an everyday successful operations we have chosen to study the company, called Euro-Aktiva, which operates in Macedonia and Kosovo as well. Euro-Aktiva has started its business in the year of 1996 in Kosovo, being as an exclusive distributor of Sidenor which is a successful company based in Greece, which manufactures mainly steel but sells as well other building materials. Euro-Aktiva has started its roots 15 years ago, mainly selling building materials in Kosovo, then after 5 years the same business started operating in Skopje as well.

Indeed, Euro-Aktiva started expansion by becoming a distributor for many other companies which contributed in achieving of becoming a leader in the building business, by covering 70 % of the Macedonian market and 80 % of the Kosovo market. Since then it has continually expanded its market in many other branches such as opening a petrol station, restaurant, service for cars, it has its own security agency, construction and building and gathering scrap metal. Moreover, we believe that the founder who has also been the owner for 15 years has entrepreneurial soul who is always looking for new opportunities in the market that are more likely to add more value to the name Euro-Aktiva and make it even more stronger. If we present the business plan of Euro-Aktiva you are about to see how completed and related every branch and aspect of this business family is.

The owner together with his two brothers has stick together in the worst and best times of this company by putting the needs of the company first and then dividends were distributed after the storms would leave. This company still is led in a traditional way, there is no board in charge but the owner is willing to start changing the day to day operations. The founder is still the owner and the CEO where one of the brothers is the vice president and finance consulate and the other one is in charge of supplies. The three main and strongest positions are led by them since they still feel the need to be in charge of everything. The owner thinks that the best time to transfer the business management is between 55 and 60 where he himself is slowly approaching that age. Therefore, he believes that the next 5 years managing together with the offspring's will help the next leaders gain higher experience and he will be more positive that the family business will run more years to come successfully.

As we mentioned above, this is a family run business where the owner has always emphasized the long term continuity of this company mainly because most of the employees hired are family.

Around 50 % of the employees are family members, starting from the lowest position to the highest. Nevertheless, communication and trust between family and business is high which has helped maintain control and effectiveness over the business for all these years.

The founder and the brothers have prioritized and encouraged their children to study and get well educated by sending them outside the country for a better education. Moreover, the second generation has started working at a young age whether as a salesperson in one of the markets they have or working at one of their warehouses for building materials. Nevertheless, they have been part of the family business while they were in high schools which has appointed and prepared them from that age that 1 day they are going to have to be part of this business. Furthermore, there was no room for other "dreams" or whatsoever; the decision has already been made. In their defense, the next generation had everything they needed ready to show more success and grow even more.

Moving on, as the offspring grew, responsibilities grew for them. The daughter of the owner and the son of one of the brothers had finished their master studies so now the company was starting to adapt to the family structure and have divisions accordingly to them so each of them can be included. The owner has always encouraged their heirs to be part of other projects as well occurring in this country whether in non-governmental or foreign organizations in order to gain more experience. He says "I need to have you fully prepared for our market, so people, companies will have to pay you for your opinion". Moreover, what his point has always been that no matter what happens in the future with this company you are still going to be able to survive by finding good jobs if you have the needed background. Nevertheless, the responsibilities did not finish here, the heirs had to enrich their social networks and grow each day more.

The founder continues to be the CEO till his retirement but he is looking into joining venture before he leaves. One of the businesses of Euro-Aktiva has already created partnership with a Turkish company but he is looking forward to have the entire company partnered with the same Turkish company in order to move the company into a higher and more perspective level. Basically he has been following the succession model proposed by Churchill and Hatten (1987) which is based on the life cycle and maturity of this family business.

7 Suggestions for Further Research

In this research, efforts have been made to raise the awareness of the founders of family businesses in regards to the importance of succession planning and dealing with problems arising from this transformation. The findings of this research provide an overview of family businesses in Macedonia and succession issues in these businesses, viewed from the perspective of business founders. Therefore, we suggest that in the future, similar research be conducted from children/heirs perspective and to see what attitudes they have about the issues of succession and management of family businesses.

8 Conclusion

Succession can be defined as the process by which the transfer of leadership takes place from the outgoing generation to the next generation, which may include family members or non-family members. The founders of businesses should start planning the succession process in the early time of starting their business, so that any sudden necessity for change does not find them unprepared. When children should get involved in the business, when to identify the successor and begin his training, and when the founder must retire and transfer business leadership to the successor are critical questions that must be answered by the founder of the business.

It is important for the successor to be equipped with the knowledge and experience before he begins running the business. The founder should probably play the role of mentor by transferring his knowledge and experience in order to learn about business concepts. It is good that sometimes he gives the opportunity to the successor to take control of the business decisions.

Expansion of the family can be good for businesses but it can also create problems. Women or men of the founders' children, and grandchildren of the founder, may want to join the family business even though there may not be room for everyone. Therefore it is necessary to create a transparent process and to establish some criteria for those who want to get involved in the family business, especially those serving in managerial positions.

Family businesses need to understand the business environment and must be flexible to adapt to changes that come from it. They should create a respectful position in the market and should be creative innovations in order to have longevity and success.

References

Beckhard, R., & Dyer, W. G. (1983). Managing continuity in the family-owned business. *Organizational Dynamics, 12*(1), 4–12.

Cabrera-Suarez, K., Saa-Perez, P., & Garcia-Almeida, D. (2001). The succession process from a resource and knowledge-based view of the family firm. *Family Business Review, 14*(1), 37–48.

Churchill, N. C., & Hatten, K. J. (1987). Non-market-based transfers of wealth and power: A research framework for family businesses. *American Journal of Small Business, 12*(2), 53–66.

Dana, L.-P. (1997). Waiting for direction in the former Yugoslav Republic of Macedonia (FYROM). *Journal of Small Business Management, 36*(2), 62–67.

Dutta, S. (2011). *The Global Innovation Index 2011: Accelerating growth and development.* Fontainebleau: INSEAD/The Business School for the World.

Dyck, B., Mauws, M., Starke, F. A., & Mischke, G. A. (2002). Passing the Baton: The importance of sequence, timing, technique, and communication in executive succession. *Journal of Business Venturing, 17*(2), 143–162.

EBRD. (2005). *Transition report.* London: European Bank for Reconstruction and Development.

EBRD. (2006). *Transition report-finance in transition.* London: European Bank for Reconstruction and Development.

Efendioglu, M. A., & Muscat, E. (2009). Internal disruptions in family business succession: Death, divorce, and disability. *Journal of Industrial Relations and Human Resources, 11*(1), 17–31.

Family Business Experts. (2012). *Want to fix or avoid problems in your family business?* Retrieved November 7, 2012, from www.family-business-experts.com

Fattoum, S., & Fayolle, A. (2009). Generational succession: Examples from Tunisian family firms. *Journal of Enterprising Culture, 17*(2), 127–145.

Gashi, G., & Ramadani, V. (2013). Family businesses in Republic of Kosovo: Some general issues. In V. Ramadani & R. Schneider (Eds.), *Entrepreneurship in the Balkans: Diversity, support and prospects.* New York: Springer.

Gersick, K. E., Davis, J. A., Hampton, M. M., & Lansberg, I. (1997). *Generations to generations: Life cycles of the family business.* Boston: Harvard Business School Press.

Gimeno, A., Gemma, B., & Coma-Cros, J. (2010). *Family business models.* New York: MacMillan.

Giudice, M. D., Peruta, D. M. R., & Elias, G. C. (2011). *Knowledge and the family business: The governance and management of family firms in the new knowledge economy.* New York: Springer.

Handler, W. C. (1990). Succession in family firms: A mutual role adjustment between entrepreneur and next-generation family members. *Entrepreneurship Theory and Practice, 15*(1), 37–51.

Handler, W. C. (1994). Succession in family businesses: A review of the research. *Family Business Review, 7*(2), 133–157.

Hess, E. D. (2006). *The successful family business: A proactive plan for managing the family and the business.* Westport: Praeger.

IBRD/World Bank. (2013). *Doing business 2013* (10th ed.). Washington, DC: International Bank for Reconstruction and Development/World Bank.

IFC. (2008). *Family business governance handbook*. Washington, DC: International Finance Corporation.

Ip, B., & Jacobs, G. (2006). Business succession planning: A review of the evidence. *Journal of Small Business and Enterprise Development, 13*(3), 326–350.

Jackson, A. K. (2011). *International Property Rights Index: 2011 report*. Washington, DC: Americans for Tax Reform Foundation/Property Rights Alliance.

Kamei, K., & Dana, L.-P. (2012). Examining the impact of new policy facilitating SME succession in Japan: From a viewpoint of risk management in family business. *International Journal of Entrepreneurship and Small Business, 16*(1), 60–70.

Kaneff, M. (2011). *Taking over: Insider tips from a third-generation CEO*. New York: Teen Eagles Press.

Lambrecht, J. (2005). Multigenerational transition in family business: A new explanatory model. *Family Business Review, 18*(4), 267–282.

Le Breton-Miller, I., Miller, D., & Steier, L. P. (2004). Towards an integrative model of effective FOB succession. *Entrepreneurship Theory and Practice, 28*(4), 305–328.

Lipman, F. D. (2010). *The family business guide, everything you need to know to manage your business from legal planning to business strategies*. New York: Macmillan.

Mazzarol, T. (2006). *Small business management*. Prahan: Tilde University Press.

Riaño, J., Hodess, R., & Evans, A. (2009). *The 2009 global corruption barometer report*. Berlin: Transparency International.

Rubenson, G., & Gupta, A. (1996). The initial succession: A contingency model of founder tenure. *Entrepreneurship: Theory and Practice, 21*(2), 21–35.

Scarborough, N. (2012). *Effective small business management* (10th ed.). Harlow: Prentice Hall.

Schwab, K., & Sala-i-Martin, X. (2009). *The global competitiveness report 2009–2010*. Geneva: World Economic Forum.

Shi, H. X., & Dana, L.-P. (2013). Market orientation and entrepreneurship in Chinese family business: A socialisation view. *International Journal of Entrepreneurship and Small Business, 20*(1), 1–16.

State Statistical Office of Republic of Macedonia. (2005). *Census of population, households and dwellings in the Republic of Macedonia, 2002*, Book XIII. Skopje: Government of Republic of Macedonia.

State Statistical Office of Republic of Macedonia. (2012). *Macedonia in figures*. Skopje: Government of Republic of Macedonia.

Steier, L. (2001). Next-generation entrepreneurs and succession: An exploratory study of modes and means of managing social capital. *Family Business Review, 14*(3), 259–276.

Strategic Designs for Learning. (2012). *The use of assessments for succession planning in family owned businesses*. Retrieved November 10, 2012, from http://www.strategicdesigns.net/SDL_SuccessionPlanning_FamilyBusiness.pdf

United Nations. (1993). *Admission of the state whose application is contained in document A/47/876-S/25147 to membership in the United Nations*. Retrieved November 22, 2012, from http://www.un.org/documents/ga/res/47/a47r225.htm

Venter, E. (2002). *The succession process in small and medium-sized family businesses in South Africa*. Unpublished Ph.D. Thesis, University of Port Elizabeth.

Walsh, G. (2011). *Family business succession, managing the all-important, family component*. Ottawa, ON: KPMG Enterprise.

Wang, Y., Watkins, D., Harris, N., & Spicer, K. (2004). The relationship between succession issues and business performance: Evidence from UK family SMEs. *International Journal of Entrepreneurial Behaviour and Research, 10*(1/2), 59–84.

Ward, J. L. (1987). *Keeping the family business healthy: How to plan for continuing growth, profitability and family leadership*. San Francisco: Jossey-Bass.

Attributes of Financial Management of Family Companies in the Czech Republic and Slovakia

Jaroslav Belás, Přemysl Bartoš, Roman Hlawiczka, and Mária Hudáková

Abstract The aim of the research is to define and compare important attributes of financial management of family small and medium-sized companies (SMEs) in selected regions of the Czech Republic and Slovakia. The majority of SMEs in the Czech Republic and Slovakia has a character of family companies. These companies have been established on the basis of family capital. Preferable family member worked in them and these companies are managed also preferable by them. In this context, SMEs sector in the Czech Republic and Slovakia may be perceived as the sector of family companies. As the part of this focus, the dependence of financial risks' perception, relationships with commercial banks, the ability to manage financial risks and the level of entrepreneurial optimism depending on company' age, owner's education and company's size have been examined. Research of entrepreneurs' opinions in Zlin Region (Czech Republic) and Zilina Region (Slovakia) has been examined in 2013. These regions have similar economic parameters and are distant from each other only few kilometers. Results of our research proved that it cannot be definitely confirmed but neither rejected that financial risk's perception in Czech and Slovak enterprises is different within a defined groups, i.e. depending on company's age, owner's education and company's size.

Keywords Family companies • Small and medium-sized enterprises • Financial risk • Financial management • Entrepreneurial optimism

J. Belás (✉) • P. Bartoš • R. Hlawiczka
Department of Enterprise Economics, Faculty of Management and Economics, Tomas Bata University in Zlín, Mostni 5139, 76001 Zlín, Czech Republic
e-mail: belas111@gmail.com; bartos@fame.utb.cz; hlawiczka@fame.utb.cz

M. Hudáková
Faculty of Special Engineering, University of Žilina, Ul. 1. mája 32, 01026 Žilina, Slovakia
e-mail: Maria.Hudakova@fsi.uniza.sk

© Springer International Publishing Switzerland 2015   223
L.-P. Dana, V. Ramadani (eds.), *Family Businesses in Transition Economies*,
DOI 10.1007/978-3-319-14209-8_11

1 Introduction

The quality of a business environment represents an integral part of every developed market economy and is a determinant for long-term development of business activities, sustainable increase of economic performance and living standard of the population. Experiences from previous years showed that systematic introduction of positive changes in the business environment can substantially accelerate the economic development in the medium horizon.

Business environments in the Czech Republic and Slovakia have to be seen in a historical context. In 1990, the transformation system started which has been targeted for the transition from a socialist production system to a market economy (Dana, 2000).

In this period, many dramatic economic changes have been detected where a privatization of state assets was the significant one which took place in several stages and which caused a formation of business class without any proper experience in Slovakia. Dana and Dana (2003), personalities of corporate management in post-communist countries have been defined.

Since that time more than 20 years which brought a historically unique experience in the economic field has been passed. At the same time, it was a relatively short time to form a standard business environment and SMEs which have a unequivocally character of family companies that suffer from many problems and where the most important issue is presented by a high intensity of a financial risk in the business environment.

The financial crisis and the gradual recovery of economies in the European Economic Area brought the deterioration of the business environment. It can be assumed that financial risks have increased due to turbulence in the economic system. Small and medium-sized companies operate in more challenging economic environment respectively many of them are struggling for survival. It is evident that all these risks are transformed in a financial management of companies.

The financial crisis did not have to necessarily cause problems in the corporate finance but definitely revealed several weaknesses in the business policy, in business processes and in key financial strategies. For example, one of the major errors was the fact that many enterprises as a result of past development planned only the growth of their activities without any consideration about the possibility of decline. They failed during a regular verification of the real market situation. Financial department in companies did not manage in time to catch the warning signs of upcoming problems. The most frequently reported failures during the crisis may be mentioned incorrect management of cash flows, incorrect management of financial risks, i.e. lack of early warnings from financial manager (insufficient planning and forecasting). Another mistake was that companies insufficiently examined their processes to see if they could not manage their financial needs from internal sources. Companies were not able to manage negotiations with banks about more favorable lending conditions.

National Agency for Development of Small and Medium-Sized Enterprises (2013a) evaluated in its report that the quality of the business environment has not been improved in Slovakia nor even in 2012. Slovakia has problem with a growth of energy cost and particularly with the electricity prices, tax increases, a growing number of administrative barriers and a lack of rapid infrastructure development. Also problem in SMEs financing approach continues to deepen which due to effect of the global economic crisis and the adjustment of the banking sector to Basel III criteria has deteriorated in recent years.

In this chapter, current trends in the area of financial risk of small and medium-sized family companies in selected regions of the Czech Republic and Slovakia have been examined. Within this focus, also the dependence of financial risk perception, relationships with commercial banks, the ability to manage financial risk and the level of entrepreneurial optimism depending on the age of company, the education of owner and the size of the company have been investigated.

2 Theoretical Aspects of Family Companies Business in SME Segment

Economic sphere perceived family companies as companies which are managed by one or several families whose members are also involved in the management or at least in the position determining the company strategy (Di Giuli, Caselli, & Gatti, 2011; Stewart & Hitt, 2012). In this context it is obvious that family companies can have various sizes but in term of Czech and Slovak economies it can be assumed that SMEs have dominant character of family enterprises. It relies on the historical experiences of the transformation process where result of which was a situation that the largest companies in Slovakia are owned by foreign capital and SMEs have gained an unambiguous character of family companies.

SMEs have become an increasingly important component of economic development representing a substantial proportion of the national economies all around the world (Karpak & Topcu, 2010). In this context, Henderson and Weiler (2010) state that SMEs can be characterized as a major engine of economic growth.

SMEs have an important task also in economic system of the Czech Republic and Slovakia. For example, the share of SME in total number of active enterprises in the Czech Republic in 2012 was 99.86 %. Share of added value in 2012 was 53.81 %. Share of SME's employees in total employment in business sector in the Czech Republic in 2012 was 59.43 %. (www.mpo.cz) In the Slovakia, share of SME in total number of active enterprises was 99.2 %, in total employment was 72.2 %. Share of added value was 55.6 % and share of SME in profit before taxes was 51.6 %. (Národná agentúra pre rozvoj malého a stredného podnikania, 2013a).

Entrepreneurial orientation has a very important task for SMEs. Soininen, Martikainen, Puumalainen, and Kyläheiko (2012) consider innovativeness, risk-taking and proactivity as the basic characteristics of entrepreneurial orientation.

According to Eggers, Kraus, Hughes, Laraway, and Snycerski (2013) to drive firm growth, the firm will need to deploy a strategy centered on entrepreneurial orientation or else risk stagnation. Avlonitis and Salavou (2007) indicate that active entrepreneurs unlike passive entrepreneurs adopt a more aggressive orientation characterized by willingness to undertake action of high risk and before that of competition. According to Keh, Nguyen, and Ng (2007) entrepreneurial orientation plays an important role in enhancing firm performance.

Authors examine different aspects of SMEs business. For example, Anderson and Eshima (2013) indicated the influence of firm age and intangible resources on the relationship between entrepreneurial orientation and firm growth. Lasagni (2012) investigate the role of external relationships as key drivers of small business innovation. Kraus, Rigtering, Hudges, and Hosman (2012) state that innovative SMEs do perform better in turbulent environment. In this context, Ramadani, Gerguri, Rexhepi, and Abduli (2013) argue that innovation is essential for sustainable growth and development, and it is one of the key European Union (EU) strategies.

SMEs are exposed to many risks. It can agree with Ramadani and Gerguri (2011), which argue that companies are trying to achieve competitive advantage in order to help them obtain a better and a stable position in the marketplace which operate in SMEs environment with extreme intensity.

According to Fetisovová, Vlachynský, and Sirotka (2004), between essential business risks of SMEs in the Czech Republic and Slovakia it can be included limited approach to loans, small capital strength, increased competition, high tax and levy burden, lower level of managerial skills, low level of business diversification, administrative complexity, high risk of failure, connection of professional and private life.

Ministry of Industry and Trade of the Czech Republic (2011) in its SWOT analysis indicated these weaknesses of Czech SMEs as follows: insufficient capital facility; weak emphasis on marketing due to a limited finances; limited funds for technical equipment of companies; insufficient; protection of intellectual property rights; preponderance of production with low value-added; insufficient emphasis on human resource development (another professional education); lack of cooperation between SMEs.

National Agency for Development of Small and Medium Business (2013b) on its website state that main disadvantages and risk of the business in SMEs segment are as follows: the risk of failure; increasing competition; administrative difficulty; high tax and levy burden; badly prepared business plan and connection of professional and private life. It is obvious that the perception of SMEs business environment is very similar in both countries.

The approach of Slovak companies to a risk management is less systematic compared with developed countries. Level of business risk in Slovak conditions is perceived with different intensity although all entrepreneurs realize a presence of the business risk, which is confirmed also our research. Solutions are often limited to an informal assessment of the risks. In business practice, effective tools for business risks management are missing.

An important feature of SMEs management in Czech and Slovak business environment is the fact that the management of family companies has to spend a lot of time to perform unproductive activities which are for example disproportionate administrative and legislative burden. It is assumed that this time demands of these activities are binding the managerial capacity of the owner of small company at least of 20 %. It would be better to invest this time to productive activities of the company that are related with a subject of the company business and which are able to generate a higher profitability. As a result of objective factors of business of small company, it can be assumed that these activities and many others are cumulated on a small amount of employees.

Small and medium-sized companies face a number of disadvantages that have in relation to large companies (Belás, 2013). Disadvantages within the area of Czech and Slovak SMEs financing mainly flow from small possibilities of finance availabilities for individual entrepreneurs. The main source of SMEs financing is a self-financing. In this context Májková-Sobeková (2011) states that use of the equity (savings, membership contributions, etc.) is the most common way how to start-up the business within all size categories. The intensity of use of this type of financing is slightly but systematically decreased with an increase of size category of the company. Equity has been used in the establishment of 96 % of micro-enterprises, 94 % of small enterprises, 92 % of medium-sized enterprises and 84 % of large companies in Slovakia.

Moro and Fink (2013) indicate that banks play an essential role in financing firms, especially SMEs since they have more difficulty accessing equity capital markets. The process used by banks to decide whether and how much to lend relies on different lending technologies and banks usually tend to use more than one technology at a time.

According to Májková-Sobeková (2011), high risk of SMEs in Slovakia lies in the fact that it is characterized by a high level of indebtedness and limited ability of guarantee. Due to this fact, it is very difficult to obtain banks' loans for such companies.

Di Giuli et al. (2011) argue that for small and medium enterprises is credit availability a very important element for their development.

Dierkes, Erner, Langer, and Norden (2013) state that SMEs are smaller, more informationally opaque, riskier and more dependent on trade credit and bank loans. According to Canales and Nanda (2012) small businesses, and particularly young small businesses, have little internal cash flow to finance their operations and are also associated with significant asymmetric information.

Nueberger and Räthke (2009) argue that small companies are characterized by higher information asymmetry and credit risk. This opinion was confirmed by Kirschenmann and Norden (2012).

Our previous researches showed that the assessment of company's creditworthiness represents very important area for the credit risk management of commercial bank which has a significant impact on the financial performance of commercial banks (Belás & Cipovová, 2013; Belás, Cipovová, Novák, & Polách, 2012). It was also found that the accuracy of used banking models for credit assessment of the client is in a certain way questionable what worsened the SMEs approach to loan financing. (Belás & Cipovová, 2013).

The vast majority of SMEs in the Czech Republic and Slovakia have a character of family businesses. These companies have been established on the basis of family capital, was managed by family members and preferably family members are working there also. In this context, sector of SMEs in the Czech Republic and Slovakia can be perceived as the sector of family companies.

In this chapter, significant attributes of financial management of small and medium-sized companies in selected regions of the Czech Republic and Slovakia have been examined.

3 Objective and Methodology of the Research

The aim of our research was to define and compare important attributes of a financial management of family small and medium-sized companies in selected regions of the Czech Republic and Slovakia. Within this objective, dependence of the financial risks' perception, the relationship with commercial banks, the ability to manage financial risk and the level of entrepreneurial optimism has been examined.

The research of fundamental determinants of the SMEs financial stability has been conducted in 2013 in selected regions of the Czech Republic and Slovakia through a questionnaire survey. In Zlin region, data about 180 SMEs and in Zilina region, 164 SMEs was obtained. Data about companies was provided by their owners.

Zlin region has an area of 3.964 km^2, has about 600,000 inhabitants, GDP per capita is about 11.720 EUR, the unemployment rate in 2012 was about 8 %.

Zilina region has an area of 6,800 km^2. Total population is up to 700,000 and the population density is 102 inhabitants per km^2. Unemployment in 2011 was raised to 11.91 %. GDP per capita was in Zilina region 10.794 EUR in the year 2011.

In our research in Zlin region, the largest share was consisted of SMEs that operate in trade activities (35 %), followed by manufacturing companies (29 %), construction firms (12 %), transport companies (4 %), agricultural enterprises (3 %). The remaining share was formed of companies that operate in other sectors. In Zilina region, the structure of companies was as follows: in the manufacture sector operate (17 %) of companies, in a trade sector (21 %), in construction companies (17 %), in transport sector (6 %), agricultural sector (1 %). The largest portion of companies operates in other sectors (38 %).

From the total number of 180 surveyed firms in the Zlín region, 70 % of them were doing business more than 10 years, 21 % of them between 10 and 5 years, 9 % of them between 1 and 5 years. Therefore it can be stated that we have quite experienced entrepreneurs. Age structure of companies was as follow: 58 % were micro-enterprises, 31 % were small enterprises and 11 % were medium-sized companies. From the total number of 164 surveyed firms in the Zilina region,

38 % of them were doing business more than 10 years, 32 % of them between 10 and 5 years, 30 % of them between 1 and 5 years. Therefore it can be stated that companies were equally distributed regarding with the length of doing business. Age structure of companies was as follow: 66 % were micro-enterprises, 20 % were small enterprises and 14 % were medium-sized companies.

In this research, five scientific hypotheses though estimation techniques have been set:

H1. Companies which are doing business more than 10 years perceived a financial risks as a key business risk less often than other companies; entrepreneurs with university education than others and medium-sized companies than other companies

H2. Companies which are doing business more than 10 years know lending criteria better of banks than other companies; entrepreneurs with university education than others and medium-sized companies than other companies

H3. Companies which are doing business more than 10 years evaluated bank's approach to SMEs financing better than other companies; entrepreneurs with university education than others and medium-sized companies than other companies

H4. Companies which are doing business more than 10 years indicated in more responses that they can better manage financial risks in their companies (line 1) than other companies; entrepreneurs with university education than others and medium-sized companies than other companies

H5. Companies which are doing business more than 10 years believe that their company will survive in next 5 years more than other companies; entrepreneurs with university education than others and medium-sized companies than other companies

Associations in contingency tables were analyzed by Pearson statistics for count data. P-value is being compared with standard 5 % confidence level. P-value lowers than confidence level leads to rejection of the null hypothesis. The null claims there is no association between variables. Calculations have been performed in statistical packages XLStatistics and R. Instruments of descriptive statistics such as percentages, averages and indexes have been used.

4 Results

Entrepreneurs in the Czech Republic and Slovakia perceived following risks as the most important one: market, financial and personnel risks. Intense influence of the market risk was reflected in a significant decrease of performances and profitability of companies. The average decrease of performances represents 15.80 % in the Czech Republic (weighted average of upper values of individual intervals). The average decrease of performances was 18.78 % in Slovakia. The average decrease of the profitability was higher than 10 % in both countries.

Table 1 The perception of a financial risk in the Czech Republic and Slovakia

Financial risk	CR(ZL) in %	SR(ZA) in %	p-value
Total	57.22	58.54	0.8910
Average value[a]	34.00	32.95	1.032[b]
A1–5	62.16	48.98	0.3187
A6–10	75.00	64.15	0.6141
A10 and more	53.54	62.90	0.2879
p-value	0.0830	0.7255	–
BSE-M	54.17	71.43	0.4801
BSE+M	61.33	58.21	0.8355
BUE	54.32	57.83	0.7676
p-value	0.2877	0.4255	–
GMICRO	55.77	61.61	0.4638
GSMALL	62.50	46.88	0.2302
GMEDIUM	50.00	65.00	0.5224
p-value	0.3507	0.7447	–

Source: Created by authors

[a]Average of values which were stated by entrepreneurs

[b]I_{ch}—share of the indicator in CR/SR; A1–5—period of doing business from 1 to 5 years; A6–10—period of doing business more than 10 years; BSE-M—secondary education without GCSE exam; BSE+M—secondary education plus GCSE exam; BUE—entrepreneur has university education; GMICRO—microenterprise; GSMALL—small-sized enterprise; GMEDIUM—medium-sized enterprise

Up to 57.22 % of entrepreneurs in the Czech Republic and 58.54 % in Slovakia identified the financial risk as the key risk. According to the perception, statistically important differences between regions have not been found. The average value of the financial risk which was stated by entrepreneurs in the Czech Republic was 34.00 % and 32.95 % for Slovakia.

Table 1 show obtained data about the fact how the financial risk has been received by companies in the Czech Republic and Slovakia depending on the age of the company, education of an owner of the company and the size of the company. Percentage share in Table 1 refer to the share of companies in the given class which was stated that the financial risk is currently the key business risk.

In order to verify the hypothesis no. 1, merging of categories has been transferred as follows: old companies versus companies with a history of 1–10 years; medium-sized companies versus small-sized and micro companies and management with a university education versus graduation education. In addition, proportion test has been used within each state. This approach has been applied in all tables.

Our data shows that there were not found any differences in the perception of financial risk within individual separated criteria in the Czech Republic and Slovakia (period of doing business; education of company' owner; size of the company). Similarly, there has not been found any differences comparing results

Table 2 Knowledge of lending criteria by entrepreneurs

Do you know the criteria that banks use in lending process?	CR(ZL) in % A1–5/A6–10/A10 and more BSE-M/BSE+M/ BUE GMICRO/ GSMALL/ GMEDIUM	SR(ZA) in % A1–5/A6–10/A10 and more BSE-M/BSE+M/ BUE GMICRO/ GSMALL/ GMEDIUM	p-value ZL/ZA A1–5/A6–10/A10 and more BSE-M/BSE+M/ BUE GMICRO/ GSMALL/ GMEDIUM
1. Yes	43.89 45.95/43.75/43.31	33.54 18.37/22.64/56.45	0.0634 0.0120/0.1810/ 0.1230
p-value**	0.5314 33.33/45.33/45.68	<0.01 21.43/37.31/33.73	– –/0.4250/0.1600
p-value**	0.3871 44.23/41.07/50.00 0.3650	0.5000 29.46/43.75/45.00 0.2002	– 0.0350/0.9840/ 1.0000 –
2. No	14.44 5.41/18.75/16.54 20.83/16.00/11.11 14.42/16.07/10.00	17.68 26.53/15.09/12.90 28.57/19.40/14.46 17.86/12.50/25.00	0.5020 –/–/0.6630 0.8840/0.7560/ 0.6840 0.6170/0.8870/–
3. I have some idea about it	41.67 48.65/37.50/40.16 45.83/38.67/43.21 41.35/42.86/40.00	48.78 55.10/62.26/30.65 50.00/43.28/51.81 52.68/43.75/30.00	0.2240 0.7070/0.1430/ 0.2670 1.0000/0.6980/ 0.3440 0.1260/1.0000/ 0.740

Note: Data cannot be correctly calculated
Source: Created by authors

in the Czech Republic and Slovakia. Indication of us assumed trend was discovered in the Czech Republic when older companies were compared (companies which were doing business more than 10 years) with companies which were doing business from 0 to 10 years (p-value = 0.0830) (Table 2).

Obtained results confirmed that a structure of answers of all Czech and Slovak entrepreneurs has not been statistically significantly different although it has been found that the differential value between both countries in the response in line 1 was close to the value of the criterion-referenced test (p-value = 0.0634).

Significant differences were found only in comparison of young Czech and Slovak companies that operate on the market up to 5 years where p-value = 0.0120, in comparison of Czech and Slovak microenterprises where p-value = 0.0350. The share of small and medium-sized companies and microenterprises which knew lending criteria of banks was significantly lower than the share of Czech young companies.

The share of old companies (10+) in Slovakia which thought that they know lending criteria is better than the share of companies which were doing business up to 10 years (p-value = <0.01). In the case of other classifications in the Czech Republic and also in Slovakia, any significant differences have not been detected (Table 3).

Table 3 Banks' approach to SMEs financing

How do you evaluate the banks' approach to SMEs financing?	CR(ZL) in % A1–5/A6–10/ A10 and more BSE-M/BSE+M/ BUE GMICRO/ GSMALL/ GMEDIUM	SR(ZA) in % A1–5/A6–10/ A10 and more BSE-M/BSE+M/ BUE GMICRO/ GSMALL/ GMEDIUM	p-value ZL/ZA A1–5/A6–10/ A10 and more BSE-M/BSE+M/ BUE GMICRO/ GSMALL/ GMEDIUM
1. Banks fully accept our needs and have good relationship with us	4.44 0.00/0.00/6.30 4.17/5.33/3.70 1.92/5.36/15.00	3.05 2.04/1.89/4.84 0.00/2.99/3.61 1.79/6.25/5.00	0.6930 –/–/– –/–/– –/–/–
2. Banks behave appropriately p-value (lines 1 + line 2)	38.89 40.54/31.25/ 39.37 25.00/40.00/ 41.98 29.81/50.00/ 55.00	20.12 12.24/28.30/ 19.35 21.43/22.39/ 18.07 17.86/21.88/ 30.00	<0.01 0.0060/1.0000/ 0.0100 1.0000/0.0380/ 0.0020 1.0000/0.0380/ 0.0020
p-value (line 1 + line 2)	0.2078 0.3360 0.0104	0.4796 0.6068 0.1456	– – –
3. Banks behave to us shortly	8.89 16.22/18.75/ 5.51 % 4.17/9.33/9.88 11.54/7.14/0.00	14.02 12.24/15.09/ 14.52 7.14/11.94/16.87 14.29/12.50/ 15.00	0.1830 0.8320/1.0000/ 0.0700 –/0.8170/0.2780 1.0000/0.8170/–
4. Banks use too harsh criteria in providing loans	26.11 18.92/31.25/ 27.56 41.67/22.67/ 24.69 32.69/14.29/ 25.00	37.20 36.73/35.85/ 37.10 35.71/37.31/ 36.14 36.61/40.63/ 30.00	0.0360 0.1180/0.9690/ 0.2430 0.9860/0.0850/ 0.1550 0.9860/0.0850/ 0.1550
5. I cannot evaluate	21.67 24.32/18.75/ 21.26 25.00/22.67/ 19.75 24.04/23.21/5.00	25.61 36.73/18.87/ 24.19 35.71/25.37/ 25.30 29.46/18.75/ 20.00	0.4630 0.3210/1.0000/ 0.7880 0.7400/0.8570/ 0.5070 0.7400/0.8570/–

Note: Data cannot be correctly calculated
Source: Created by authors

In comparison with Slovak companies, Czech companies evaluated banks' approach to financing their needs better because of significant differences when responses about the fact that bank behave appropriately were marked. This fact was stated by Czech young companies which were doing business up to 5 years, Czech companies which were doing business more than 10 years, owners of Czech companies with a higher education and Czech small and medium-sized companies. Compared to Czech companies, Slovak enterprises significantly more indicated that banks use too harsh criteria for lending.

Within H3 hypothesis, evidence about the argument that the share of medium-sized Czech companies which answered positively to line 1 and line 2 is significantly higher than in the case of Czech small and micro enterprises has been found. This argument does not apply to Slovakia where the share of small-sized companies which were satisfied with the bank (line 1 + line2) is 21.52 %. The proportion of satisfied medium-sized companies is 35 % but due to the low number of observations, this difference is not demonstrable (p-val = 0.1456).

The ability to manage financial risks has been verified through following question. Results are shown in Table 4.

Czech enterprises more often indicated clear answer that they are able to manage financial risks properly. Statistically significant differences in answers of owners of Czech companies with a secondary education and Czech microenterprises that indicated to certain extend an answer no. 1 than comparable companies in Slovakia have been found.

In the Czech Republic and also in Slovakia, significant differences answering a response no. 1 have not been found, if companies that were doing business more than 10 years compared with other enterprises and the education of entrepreneurs and the size of enterprises have been compared.

The indication of the trend that higher education leads to a clear answer to a given question has been found in Slovak business environment (p-value = 0.0571).

The level of business optimism has been examined through a following question. Results are shown in Table 5.

Within entrepreneurial optimism evaluation, any significant differences between Czech and Slovak entrepreneurs have not found. Slightly larger optimism has been observed in Czech enterprises that were doing business from 1 to 5 years compared to young Slovak companies (p-value = 0.0800).

In Slovakia, it has been found that medium-sized companies more significantly indicated that they unequivocally believe that their company will survive the next 5 years.

Table 4 The ability to manage financial risks in the company

Do you think that you are able to manage financial risks in your company?	CR(ZL) in % A1–5/A6–10/A10 and more BSE-M/BSE+M/ BUE GMICRO/ GSMALL/ GMEDIUM	SR(ZA) in % A1–5/A6–10/A10 and more BSE-M/BSE+M/ BUE GMICRO/ GSMALL/ GMEDIUM	p-value ZL/ZA A1–5/A6–10/A10 and more BSE-M/BSE+M/ BUE GMICRO/ GSMALL/ GMEDIUM
1. Yes	41.11 45.95/31.25/40.94 37.50/45.33/38.27 47.12/33.93/30.00	23.17 24.49/15.09/29.03 14.29/17.91/28.92 24.11/15.63/30.00	<0.01 0.0640/0.2790/ 0.1520 –/0.0010/0.2700 0.0010/0.1080/ 1.0000
p-value (line 1)	0.5000 0.7082 0.7968	0.1158 0.0571 0.3122	– – –
2. To a certain way	55.00 48.65/68.75/55.12 58.33/53.33/55.56 49.04/62.50/65.00	67.68 59.18/75.47/66.13 78.57/76.12/57.83 66.07/84.38/45.00	0.0210 0.4520/0.8320/ 0.1980 0.3610/0.0080/ 0.8910 0.0170/0.0550/ 0.3400
3. No	0.56 0.00/0.00/0.79 4.17/0.00/0.00 0.96/0.00/0.00	1.83 4.08/3.77/1.61 0.00/1.49/4.82 1.79/0.00/15.00	– –/–/– –/–/– –/–/–
4. I cannot judge	3.33 5.41/0.00/3.15 0.00/1.33/6.17 2.88/3.57/5.00	7.32 12.24/5.66/3.23 7.14/4.48/8.43 8.04/0.00/10.00	– –/–/– –/–/0.7980 –/–/–

Note: Data cannot be correctly calculated
Source: Created by authors

Table 5 The level of entrepreneurial optimism

Do you believe that you company will survive in next five years?	CR(ZL) in % A1–5/A6–10/ A10 and more BSE-M/BSE+M/ BUE GMICRO/ GSMALL/ GMEDIUM	CZA) in % A1–5/A6–10/ A10 and more BSE-M/BSE+M/ BUE GMICRO/ GSMALL/ GMEDIUM	p-value ZL/ZA A1–5/A6–10/ A10 and more BSE-M/BSE+M/ BUE GMICRO/ GSMALL/ GMEDIUM
1. Definitely	49.44 54.05/37.50/ 49.61 37.50/50.67/ 51.85 42.31/60.71/ 55.00	40.85 32.65/39.62/ 48.39 28.57/43.28/ 40.96 36.61/40.63/ 65.00	0.1360 0.0800/1.0000/ 1.0000 0.8400/0.4800/ 0.2100 0.4700/0.1100/ 0.7500
p-value	0.5000 0.3320 0.3859	0.0859 0.5000 0.0178	– – –
2. No	0.56 0.00/0.00/0.79 4.17/0.00/0.00 0.96/0.00/0.00	2.44 0.00/5.66/1.61 0.00/2.99/2.41 2.68/3.13/0.00	0.3140 –/–/– –/–/– –/–/–
3. With some concerns	45.56 43.24/56.25/ 44.88 50.00/42.67/ 46.91 50.96/35.71/ 45.00	49.39 59.18/54.72/ 40.32 57.14/46.27/ 53.01 54.46/50.00/ 30.00	0.5430 0.2100/1.0000/ 0.6600 0.9300/0.7900/ 0.5300 0.7000/0.2800/ 0.5100
4. With serious concerns	4.44 2.70/6.25/4.72 8.33/6.67/1.23 5.77/3.57/0.00	7.32 8.16/0.00/9.68 14.29/7.46/3.61 6.25/6.25/5.00	– –/–/0.3200 –/1.0000/– 1.0000/–/–

Source: Created by authors

5   Conclusion

Aim of our research was to verify the validity of established hypotheses. According to H1 it has been assumed that companies that doing business 10 and more years (called "older companies") perceive a financial risk less intense then other companies; entrepreneurs with university education perceive a financial risks less intense than other companies and medium-sized enterprises perceive a financial risk less intense then other companies. The validity of this hypothesis has not been confirmed. Indication of this trend has been found in older Czech companies which perceive a financial risk less intense than younger companies.

Within H2 hypothesis, it has been assumed that older companies have better knowledge about loans criteria of commercial banks than other companies;

entrepreneurs with university education are more familiar to loans criteria of banks than entrepreneurs with different education structure and medium-sized companies know better loans criteria of banks than other companies. The validity of this hypothesis has been rejected. It was examined that medium-sized companies in Slovakia declared that they know better loans conditions than small-sized companies.

In H3 it has been supposed that older companies evaluated a banks' approach to SMEs financing better than other companies; entrepreneurs with university education assessed a banks' approach to SMEs financing better than others and medium-sized companies evaluated a banks' approach to SMEs financing better than other companies. The validity of this hypothesis has not been confirmed. However it has been found that Czech medium-sized companies compared to smaller enterprises evaluated a banks' approach to financing better.

According to H4, older enterprises are able to manage financial risks in their companies better than younger companies; entrepreneurs with university education are able to manage financial risks in their companies better than others and medium-sized enterprises are able to manage financial risks in their companies better than other companies. The validity of this hypothesis was not confirmed. In Slovakia it was discovered that entrepreneurs with a university education believed that they can manage own financial risks then other entrepreneurs.

H5 assumed that older companies are more confident that their company will survive in next 5 years than younger firms; entrepreneurs with university education believed more that their company will survive in next 5 years than others and medium-sized enterprises believed that their company will survive in next 5 years than other companies. The validity of this hypothesis was rejected. It was found out that medium-sized companies in Slovakia are bigger optimists than smaller firms.

Acknowledgments This chapter was supported by Project No. FaME/2013/MSPRISK: Current trends in the area of business risks of small and medium-sized enterprises in selected regions of the Czech Republic and Slovakia.

This chapter was created at the Tomas Bata University in Zlin and was supported by Project No. IGA/FaME/2013/010: Satisfaction mirror effect and bank financial performance.

This chapter was created at the Tomas Bata University in Zlin and was supported by Project No. IGA/FaME/2014/06: Optimalizácia parametrov finančnej výkonnosti komerčnej banky.

References

Anderson, B. S., & Eshima, Y. (2013). The influence of firm age and intangible resources on the relationship between entrepreneurial orientation and firm growth among Japanese SMEs. *Journal of Business Venturing, 28*, 413–429.

Avlonitis, G. J., & Salavou, H. E. (2007). Entrepreneurial orientation of SMEs, product innovativeness, and performance. *Journal of Business Research, 60*, 566–575.

Belás, J. (2013). *Credit risk management of SMEs.* Žilina: Georg.

Belás, J., & Cipovová, E. (2013). The quality and accuracy of bank internal rating model. A case study from Czech Republic. *International Journal of Mathematics and Computers in Simulation, 7*(1), 206–214. http://www.naun.org/multimedia/NAUN/mcs/2002-114.pdf

Belás, J., Cipovová, E., Novák, P., & Polách, J. (2012). Impacts of the foundation internal ratings based approach usage on financial performance of commercial bank. *E+M Ekonomie a Management, 15*(3), 25–38.

Canales, R., & Nanda, R. (2012). A darker side to decentralized banks: Market power and credit rationing in SME lending. *Journal of Financial Economics, 105*, 353–366.

Dana, L. P. (2000). The hare and the tortoise of former Czechoslovakia: Reform and enterprise in the Czech and Slovak Republics. *European Business Review, 12*(6), 337–344.

Dana, L. P., & Dana, T. (2003). Management and enterprise development in post-communist economies. *International Journal of Management and Enterprise Development, 1*(1), 45–54.

Di Giuli, A., Caselli, S., & Gatti, S. (2011). Are small family firms financially sophisticated? *Journal of Banking & Finance, 35*(2011), 2931–2944.

Dierkes, M., Erner, C., Langer, T., & Norden, L. (2013). Business credit information sharing and default risk of private firms. *Journal of Banking & Finance, 37*(2013), 2867–2878.

Eggers, F., Kraus, S., Hughes, M., Laraway, E., & Snycerski, S. (2013). Implications of customer and entrepreneurial orientations for SME growth. *Management Decision, 51*(3), 524–546.

Fetisovová, E., Vlachynský, K., & Sirotka, V. (2004). *Financie malých a stredných podnikov.* Bratislava: Ekonómia.

Henderson, J., & Weiler, S. (2010). Entrepreneurs and job growth: Probing the boundaries of time and space. *Economic Development Quarterly, 24*(1), 23–32.

Karpak, B., & Topcu, I. (2010). Small medium manufacturing enterprises in Turkey: An analytic network process framework for prioritizing factors affecting success. *International Journal of Production Economics, 125*, 60–70.

Keh, H. T., Nguyen, T. T. M., & Ng, H. P. (2007). The effect of entrepreneurial orientation and marketing information on the performance of SMEs. *Journal of Business Venturing, 22*, 592–611.

Kirschenmann, K., & Norden, L. (2012). The relationship between borrower risk and loan maturity in small business lending. *Journal of Business Finance & Accounting, 39*(5–6), 730–757.

Kraus, S., Rigtering, J. P. C., Hudges, M., & Hosman, V. (2012). Entrepreneurial orientation and the business performance of SMEs: A quantitative study from the Netherlands. *Review of Managerial Science, 6*, 161–182.

Lasagni, A. (2012). How can external relationships enhance innovation in SMEs? New evidence for Europe. *Journal of Small Business Management, 50*, 310–339. doi:10.1111/j.1540-627X. 2012.00355.x. ISSN 1540-627X.

Májková-Sobeková, M. (2011). Analýza bariér a faktorov financovania malých a stredných podnikov v SR. *Ekonomický časopis, 59*(10), 1033–1046.

Ministerstvo priemyslu a obchodu České republiky. (2011). *Zpráva o vývoji malého a středního podnikání a jeho podpoře v roce 2010.* Praha: MPO ČR. http://download.mpo.cz/get/44606/50107/581082/priloha001.doc

Moro, A., & Fink, M. (2013). Loan managers' trust and credit access for SMEs. *Journal of Banking & Finance, 37*(2013), 927–936.

Národná agentúra pre rozvoj malého a stredného podnikania. (2013a). *Správa o stave malého a stredného podnikania v Slovenskej republike v roku 2012.* Bratislava: NARMSP.

Národná agentúra pre rozvoj malého a stredného podnikania. (2013b). *Hlavné nevýhody a riziká podnikania.* Bratislava: NARMSP.

Nueberger, D., & Räthke, S. (2009). Microenterprises and multiple relationships: The case of professionals. *Small Business Economics, 32*, 207–229.

Ramadani, V., & Gerguri, S. (2011). Theoretical framework of innovation and competitiveness and innovation program in Macedonia. *European Journal of Social Science, 23*(2), 268–276.

Ramadani, V., Gerguri, S., Rexhepi, G., & Abduli, S. (2013). Innovation and economic develop-
ment: The case of FYR of Macedonia. *Journal of Balkan and Near Eastern Studies, 15*(3),
324–345.
Soininen, J., Martikainen, M., Puumalainen, K., & Kyläheiko, K. (2012). Entrepreneurial orien-
tation: Growth and profitability of Finnisch small- and medium-sized enterprises. *International
Journal of Production Economics, 140*, 614–621.
Stewart, A., & Hitt, M. A. (2012). Why can't a family business be more like a non family business?
Modes of professionalization in family firms. *Family Business Review, 25*(1), 58–86.

Ownership Structure, Cash Constraints and Investment Behaviour in Russian Family Firms

Tullio Buccellato, Gian Fazio, Yulia Rodionova, and Natalia Vershinina

Abstract In this chapter, using a large representative panel dataset of 8,637 large firms in the European part of Russia and their balance sheet information over the period 2000–2004, we investigate the extent to which Russian firms and in particular a smaller sample of family firms are liquidity constrained in their investment behaviour and how ownership structure changes the relationship between internal funds and the investment decisions of these firms. Family firms differ from nonfamily firms due to the unique influence of family members in ownership, strategic control and succession and play a critical role in most economies throughout the world. We estimate a structural financial accelerator model of investment and first test the hypothesis that Russian firms overall and family firms in particular are cash constrained by conducting random-effects estimation. Our results confirm that firms are liquidity constrained when the ownership structure is not included in the econometric specifications. With regards to the ownership structure and the degree of ownership concentration, we find that companies owned by private

We are grateful to the participants in the AFE 2011 conference on Samos Island, Greece, the 10th EACES Conference in Moscow, the CICM 2009 conference at London Metropolitan University, BAFA 2012 conference in Brighton, the departmental research seminar as well as the 1st CROG conference at Leicester Business School at DMU, and to Ismail Adelopo, Phil Almond, Panagiotis Andrikopoulos, Ashley Carreras, Anthony Ferner, Tomila Lankina, Fred Mear, Tomek Mickiewisz, Alexander Muravyev, and especially to Pasquale Scaramozzino for helpful comments and suggestions on the previous versions. The usual caveat applies.

T. Buccellato
Ernst and Young, Paris, France
e-mail: tullio.buccellato@fr.ey.com

G. Fazio
School of Slavonic and East European Studies, University College, London, UK

Y. Rodionova
Department of Accounting and Finance, Leicester Business School, De Montfort University, Leicester, UK
e-mail: yulia.rodionova@dmu.ac.uk

N. Vershinina (✉)
Department of Strategic Management and Marketing, Leicester Business School, De Montfort University, Leicester, UK
e-mail: nvershinina@dmu.ac.uk

© Springer International Publishing Switzerland 2015
L.-P. Dana, V. Ramadani (eds.), *Family Businesses in Transition Economies*, DOI 10.1007/978-3-319-14209-8_12

239

individuals and families are less cash constrained, which is in agreement with previous literature. We also find that state-owned companies are less cash constrained, independently of whether their ownership structure is concentrated. No significant impact is found for banks and institutions.

Keywords Ownership • Investment • Cash constrains • Russia

1 Introduction

The importance of family control as a particular type of ownership structure has motivated a number of theoretical and empirical papers, which attempt to identify the key features associated with this organisational form. Researchers have also suggested several advantages and disadvantages attached to family control (Anderson & Reeb, 2003; Lee, 2006). Furthermore, recent studies have compared family control to other corporate ownership structures in an effort to disentangle whether control by a family is an efficient organisational structure, which however with mixed results. While some papers find that family firms generally outperform other types of organisations (Anderson & Reeb, 2003; Barontini & Caprio, 2006; Lee, 2006; Maury, 2006; Villalonga & Amit, 2006), others reach the opposite conclusion (Barth, Gulbrandsen, & Schone, 2005; Cronqvist & Nilsson, 2003; Miller, Le Breton-Miller, Lester, & Cannella, 2007).

In this scenario, in which family control is so prevalent all over the world and market imperfections give rise to distortions in firms' investment decisions, this paper aims to empirically investigate whether being a family firm contributes either to mitigate or to exacerbate the sensitivity of investment to internal funds. Consequently, in this study we combine two different but equally interesting issues that have aroused the interest of scholars in the finance and management literature for decades, namely corporate investment and family control of corporations. Additionally, family firms' literature has found evidence of lower investment–cash flow sensitivities to internal funds in a number of European and Asian countries, and this paper examines this question in the context of Russian economy. This papers contribution lies not only in this examination, but also in comparisons of investment–cash flow sensitivities for other types of firms operating in Russia, including state-owned, private industrial companies, banks, and others.

According to neoclassical theory, the investment behaviour of a firm is independent of its financial structure. Under the assumption of perfect capital markets, internal and external funds can be considered perfect substitutes and, hence, intertemporal optimization can be solved regardless of financial factors. In this setting, the only factor affecting a firm's investment decision is the benefit received from an additional unit of capital relative to its replacement cost, i.e. Tobin's Q. However, empirical evidence suggests an excess reaction of investments to cash flow. One possible explanation for this stylized fact has been found in the presence of asymmetric information, which makes internal funds less costly relative to new debt or equity finance (Fazzari, Hubbard, Petersen, Blinder, & Poterba, 1988). In this paper, we investigate whether this is the case for Russian firms and assess the extent to which these are cash-constrained in their investment decisions, differentiating between several ownership structures. This emphasis on ownership structures and their importance for firms' financing and investment is currently all the more important an issue for Russia, where the corporate governance regime has been constantly changing since the break-up of the Soviet Union in 1992 (Buck, 2003; Buck, Filatochev, & Wright, 1998; Estrin & Wright, 1999; Judge, Naoumova, & Koutzevol, 2003; McCarthy & Puffer, 2003; Meyer, 2003). The initial attempt by reformers to create an Anglo-American shareholder type of corporate governance system failed. Various hybrid forms of the stakeholder type of corporate governance bearing similarities to the German-Japanese system emerged instead, but these also gave rise to the principal-principal problem of the abuse of minority shareholders by large shareholders and stakeholders (see also Mickiewicz, 2006). Such changes in corporate governance mechanisms could not leave unaffected the various opportunities that firms have had for financing their investment projects.

In our analysis, we employ a financial accelerator approach introduced in Gilchrist and Himmelberg (1998), which, in addition to measuring the non-financial indicators such as the expected marginal return to capital captured in Tobin's Q model, adds financial frictions as one of the state variables in the investment decision of the firm. The common proxies used for such financials are cash flow and cash stock. In a similar spirit, Love (2003) uses the financial accelerator approach to conduct a cross-country study of the relationship between the depth of a country's financial market and its level of financial development. According to the predictions of both models, if the firm is being financially constrained, then it will use its own internal funds to finance investment as they are a cheaper or the only available alternative. In such a case, the authors predict a positive relationship between investment as a share of capital stock and the amount of internal funds. We extend this framework by hypothesising that this relationship will vary greatly with the type of ownership (e.g., state versus private ownership by a bank, investment fund or insiders). The discussion presented in Sect. 2 justifies our hypothesis as the changes of ownership during the transition years have been thought of as a major driving force behind companies' performance, of which the investment decision is an important characteristic. Our findings confirm the generally accepted prior findings that firms in Russia are liquidity constrained, but that certain types of ownership make them more or less so. In our estimations we rely on panel data random- and fixed-effects procedures.

Empirical studies of the effect of ownership on firms' liquidity constraints in Russia usually go beyond merely confirming the existence of such constraints to focus mostly on the analysis of the impact of firms' participation in their financial-industrial groups (FIGs). This is the case because the ownership structure prevailing in Russian industry in the time period considered was oriented towards financial-industrial groups.

However, diversified conglomerates (financial-industrial groups) may perform differently according to the economy in question. Perotti and Gelfer (2001) argue that while in developed economies this ownership arrangement tends to underperform,[1] they often prosper in developing countries. This is mainly because, in a more volatile and less transparent environment, a FIG may offer useful governance functions and may create an internal capital market which ensures management decisions are monitored. Moreover, these kinds of conglomerates may be well-positioned to capture scarcity rents through—for instance—political connections and obtain political favours such as advantageous terms (credit or licensing) and favourable regulations.

The factors that specifically determine diversified conglomerates' performance in Russia are the oligopolistic structure of industry, the underdeveloped capital market, the poor flow of information (and investors-firm asymmetries), an undeveloped legal system and unreliable enforcement procedures. In this environment, banks have increased their ownership of industry through loans-for-shares deals and insider-dominated privatization sales.

Still, according to some authors (Johnson 1997), FIGs lead to the lack of access to external funds due to bad governance and the limits it imposes on the scope for dispersed ownership. On the contrary, Volchkova (2000), using the financial accelerator framework to assess the effect of the firm's participation in the financial-industrial group on its liquidity constraint using a sample of 115 firms from Goskomstat in 1997–1998, finds a positive relationship between participation of a firm in the FIG and investment as a share of capital. She explains this outcome as a result of reduced moral hazard on the part of managers who do not siphon off as much cash for their personal benefit when their performance is being controlled by a partnering financial institution. Perotti and Gelfer (2001) estimate Tobin's Q model to test the importance of the firm's participation in the financial-industrial group for the dependence of its investment decisions on the internal funds on a sample of 76 Russian public companies in 1995 and 1996. They find that investment is sensitive to internal funds for the group of firms not participating in the FIG. They also find that "while investment is not significantly correlated with cash flow in industry-led group firms (unlike in independent firms), there is a negative significant correlation for bank-led firms, suggesting a more extensive financial reallocation and the use of profitable firms as cash-cows".

Our chapter contributes to the existing literature in a number of ways. First, we perform estimations on a large and representative sample of 8,637 firms in the European part of Russia so that it allows us to draw conclusions about the full extent of the liquidity constraint issue facing Russian firms. Second, we extend this analysis to identify the effects of various ownership types and the degree of ownership concentration on credit constraints for all the firms surveyed, in particular the situation with family firms in Russia.

---

[1] In terms of the group trading at a discounted value relative to a control group; lower Tobin's Q; suboptimal allocation of resources across divisions.

The chapter is organised as follows. Section 2 reviews some of the literature building on three main strands of studies: literature on family firms, and further studies specific to the Russian experience while others consider the relationship between ownership and firms' performance more generally. In Sect. 3 we present the structural financial accelerator model of investment. Section 4 details our empirical analysis based on over 8,000 firms, including a description of the dataset, the model and our results. Finally, Sect. 5 concludes.

2   Literature Review

2.1   Family Firms

Family firms differ from nonfamily firms due to the unique influence of family members in ownership and management (Chrisman et al., 2005), strategic control and succession as well as business goals (Collins & O'Regan, 2010). Family firms have played a critical role in most economies throughout the world as well as contributing to employment and economic output (Borheim, 2000).

Most research to date on family firm performance has been in the realm of comparing the family firm to the non-family firm. The research has examined the relationship between firm performance and family influence as well as strategic planning and firm performance. The results have been mixed. Several studies have found that family businesses are more profitable than non-family businesses. Monsen, Chiu, and Cooley (1968) found that owner-controlled firms experienced greater profits than management controlled firms. Anderson and Reeb (2003) found that large quoted firms with founding family presence outperform those with more dispersed ownership structures. In contrast, other similar studies have found that family ownership and management can have little or even a negative effect on firm performance. For example, Cucculelli and Micucci (2008) found that quoted family firms that continue to be managed within the family has a negative impact on post-succession firm performance. Perez-Gonzalez (2006) found that when control is inherited by a family member the company experiences large declines on asset values that are not experienced by firms that promote CEOs not related to the controlling family. It is evident that no conclusion can be made as to the extent that family control or family management has a positive or negative impact on firm performance.

Most studies into family firm performance focus on large quoted family businesses. This is understandable as financial data is more readily available for quoted companies than unquoted companies. However, considering that less than 1 % of all business structures in Canada, USA and the UK are quoted companies, these studies should not be generalized and applied to the family business organization in other geographical locations. Thus, to advance in the field of family firm performance

(Astrachan & Zellweger, 2008) it is appropriate for family business researchers to shift the focus toward family firms in other regions and privately owned firms.

There are few studies on the performance of private family firms. This is due in most part to methodological issues as, access to private family firm data has not been readily accessible. Additionally, the reliability of private family firm data is limited as owners have a bias toward tax minimization (profit minimization) in the preparation of the company accounts. Nonetheless, many researchers have explored the performance of private family firms (Castillo & Wakefield, 2007; Randoy & Goel, 2003; Schulze, Lubatkin, & Dino, 2003; Smith & Amoako-Adu, 1999; Steijvers, Voordeckers, & Vanderloof, 2010; Ward, 1997). For instance, Westhead and Cowling (1998) examined data of UK privately held family firms and found that these family firms did not report superior performance along the traditional accounting measures of performance. However, the most interesting aspect of the study was that it suggested that private family firms have a definite focus on specific non-financial objectives (i.e. family agendas). Some "family agenda" objectives tested in the study included independent firm ownership, employment for family members and accumulation of family wealth. In comparing family firms that simultaneously manage the family system and the business system to family firms that only manage the business system Basco and Rodriguez (2009) used a multidimensional scale to measure performance. The authors measured performance using economic variables as well as Sorenson's (1999) scale of non-economic variables. These studies are extremely valuable as they are moving the field of performance research in unquoted family firms in a direction that considers non-economic performance dimensions. To further the field of family firm performance, researchers must gain a deeper understanding of the performance dimensions of the family system.

Further studies linking financial investment with family firms have investigated for instance the consequences of managerial successions for the financial policies of Italian family firms (Amore, Minichilli, & Corbetta, 2011), where it has been found that the appointment of non-family professional CEOs leads to a significant increase in the use of debt, primarily driven by short-term maturities with substantial heterogeneity in the impact of professional successions on debt financing: the increase in debt is particularly pronounced for young firms, firms with a high level of investment, and firms in which the controlling family maintains a dominant representation on the board of directors. Similarly, Pindado, Requejo, and de la Torre (2011) considered the ownership structure of family firms to determine whether family control alleviates or exacerbates investment–cash flow sensitivity in the Euro zone and found that family-controlled corporations have lower investment–cash flow sensitivities and this reduced sensitivity is mainly attributable to family firms with no deviations between cash flow and voting rights and to family firms in which family members hold managerial positions.

Although there is now plethora of literature on family firms, but with respect to the particular case of family-controlled corporations, only few studies provide insight regarding whether this type of organizational form either attenuates or exacerbates the dependence of firms on internally generated funds when undertaking new investments. Of the studies that are available, a paper by Wei and Zhang (2008) concludes that ownership concentration reduces the investment–cash flow sensitivity in East Asia, where family control is widespread.

Finally, what remains unclear is whether family influence provides an advantage in transitioning economies (Banalieva, Eddleston, & Zellweger, 2014). While some studies portray family firms as virtuously filling institutional voids for the benefit of stakeholders (Gedajlovic & Carney, 2010; Miller, Le Breton-Miller, & Lester, 2010), others characterize these firms as villains that expropriate wealth from minority shareholders and as ill-equipped to deal with dynamic environments (Bertrand, Mehta, & Mullainathan, 2002; Claessens, Djankov, & Lang, 2000). The next section of the paper will explore Russian context within which the study is undertaken.

2.2 Historic Background, Transparency and the Insiders' Advantage

As already stated in the introduction, we expect the relationship between the firm's share of investment to capital and its financials (such as cash flow) to be affected by the type of ownership. This section sheds light on the importance of different ownership types in the business environment and firms' decisions in Russia. While changes in ownership in transition economies have been associated with improvements in firms' performance (Megginson & Netter, 2001), whether these changes materialise will also depend on the business climate of the country in question. In the case of Russia, Estrin (2002) points out that both the regulatory environment and institutional development might not have reached a level which would allow certain types of ownership to enhance performance. In particular, privatization itself did not result in beneficial changes in those sectors in which an appropriate competition policy had been implemented. In addition, financial reporting practices in Russia still lag behind the leading international accounting practices. An S&P report [quoted in Kochetygova, Popivshchy, and Vitalieva (2004)] notes that of the 42 largest firms, only 40 % of these disclose, in full, their ownership details. The present opaqueness of ownership structures is, in large part, attributable to historical reasons. The first mass privatization occurred during the Yeltsin era and, at this time, insiders could dispose of privileged information concerning the strategic standpoint of many former public firms. After having acquired an advantageous position, managers developed a strong opposition and reluctance to any reform aimed at enhancing the level of transparency.

More precisely, the main changes in ownership realized since the beginning of the transition in Russia have always moved along with the process of liberalization, which can be schematically divided into three phases. First, the early mass waves of privatisations (1992–1995) were characterised by the so called "corporate wars" in which firms often utilised dubious manoeuvres such as false bankruptcies and improper notifications of official meetings to achieve their objectives (Kochetygova et al. 2004). It is during this period that many firms decided to allocate the majority (usually 51 %) of their shares to employees and managers giving a considerable advantage to insiders.

The second stage of privatization, realized in December 1995, was the so called Loans-for-Shares Privatization scheme.[2] This latter allowed banks to acquire a large number of shares in the largest corporations and gave rise to a general lack of transparency in the bidding process, which also brought about the emergence of industrial lobbies headed by the so-called oligarchs. Finally, it has been observed that in this context management ownership appears to be limited partly because managers may hide their ownership stakes. The situation is exacerbated by the fact that managers tend to divert cash flows from the payment of dividends to hide assets and reduce the probability of takeover bids or intervention from the government (Rozinskii, 2002; Shama, 2001; Yakovlev, 2001).

Thirdly, the already precarious situation, which developed towards the end of the 1990s, was compounded by the Russian economic crisis of 1998 which had two main effects: firstly, some of the largest banks collapsed forcing some of the firms they owned into liquidation; secondly, a considerable number of foreign investors left the country. This turbulent business climate may also explain the comparatively low levels of FDI in the late 1990s, less than 1 % of GDP compared with 5–10 % for other Central and Eastern European economies [see e.g., Estrin and Wright (1999)].

Overall, privatization in Russia has resulted in the emergence of a relatively small number of very large investors. Guriev, Lazareva, Rachinsky, and Tsukhlo (2003) estimate that the 23 largest firms in the country control at least 36 % of output and employment. Interestingly, while these firms are not too dissimilar in terms of sales growth and labour productivity, they find these firms to have invested significantly more than other firms controlled by other Russian owners. This is likely to be a result of larger firms having a lower cost of capital and having a general advantage in raising funds for investment. Controlling for depreciation and balance sheet adjustments, the authors estimate growth in fixed assets (as a proxy for investment) and find the largest private firms, together with foreign owned firms, to be investing considerably more than the rest (25 % or 30 % more) of remaining Russian firms. Additionally, Sprenger (2011) find that firms in financial distress show a higher incidence of insiders selecting the option of privatization leading to high insider ownership.

Ultimately, however, insider-owned firms, in contrast to financial-industrial groups, possessed neither the managerial nor the financial resources needed to restructure their enterprises. Moreover, even when outsiders provided some external capital (in return for ownership) anecdotal evidence [in Perotti (2000)] suggests

---

[2] "This scheme envisaged that banks would acquire the state-owned shares in 21 bluechip public companies as collateral for granting credits to the federal government. Twelve auctions were implemented under this scheme, bringing total revenue of 5.1 trillion roubles to the federal government (Radygin et al. 2003)."

that one result has been fierce power struggles for control. Mickiewicz, Bishop, and Varblane (2004) find, using a panel of Estonian firms, that domestically owned firms are more financially constrained than foreign-owned entities and that size also plays a role, with larger firms being less constrained. Perotti and Gelfer (2001) note that the majority of the literature in this area advocates that firms with a dispersed ownership structure and/or insider control tend to be more inertial and face higher agency costs when raising finance. However, family owned firms with concentrated degree of ownership and strong insider control are currently gaining prominence in Russia. In relation to this the central question of this paper is to explore whether financial constraints exist and, if so, how they vary for different owners, such as family firms and various degrees of ownership concentration.

More recently, during the Putin era, Russia has seen the re-emergence of the state as an active player in the corporate arena. According to KPMG (2013), "the state-owned enterprise (SOE) sector accounts for about 50 % of GDP as some of the largest public companies are controlled by the state". The state has indeed acquired control of important firms in strategic sectors as, for example, in hydrocarbon production. This kind of state capture process brought about a new set of organizational features, leaving unchanged the underlying mechanism. In actual fact, the energy sector is witnessing the emergence of a renewed state monopoly, implying a shift from a system of oligarchic control to a system of *bureaugarchic* control of hydrocarbon revenues (Buccellato & Mickiewicz, 2007). Gugler and Peev (2010) find evidence of soft budget constraints for state-owned enterprises in transitional economies.

3 A Model of Investment

The model of investment used in our estimations is based on Gilchrist and Himmelberg's (1998) financial accelerator model in the basic setup and on the setting in Love (2003) in that we assume of no external bond financing. In the model, the firm maximizes the present discounted value of the cash flows, so that the dynamic maximization problem is given by:

$$V_t(K_t, \xi_t) = \max_{\{I_{t+s}\}_0^\infty} D_t + E_t \left(\sum_{s=1}^\infty \beta^{t+s-1} D_{t+s} \right) \tag{1}$$

$$D_t = \Pi(K_t, \xi_t) - C(I_t, K_t) - I_t \tag{2}$$

$$K_{t+1} = (1 - \delta)K_t + I_t \tag{3}$$

$$D_t \geq 0 \tag{4}$$

Where, D_t are the dividends paid to shareholders at time t; the first constraint represents the budget constraint on the cash flow; β denotes the discount factor; K_t is the capital stock at the beginning of period t; I_t is period t's investment; and δ is the rate of depreciation.

$\Pi(K_t, \xi_t)$ represents the maximized value (with respect to variable costs) of the profits, with the usual assumptions on the profit function, where ξ_t is a productivity shock.

$C(I_t, K_t)$ denotes the adjustment costs of investment. The Lagrange multiplier (henceforth denoted λ_t) on the non-negativity of the dividends constraint represents the shadow price of paying negative dividends (i.e., of issuing equity), or the shadow cost of internally generated funds. This shadow price will later be used for the estimation of the financing constraint.

The Euler equation resulting from this optimization problem is given by:

$$1 + \left(\frac{\partial C}{\partial I}\right)_t = \beta_t E_t \left[\theta_t \left\{ \left(\frac{\partial \Pi}{\partial K}\right)_{t+1} + (1-\delta)\left(1 + \left(\frac{\partial C}{\partial I}\right)_{t+1}\right) \right\} \right] \quad (5)$$

Where, $\partial C/\partial I$ is the marginal adjustment cost of investment, $\partial \Pi/\partial K$ is the marginal profit of capital (MPK), and $\theta_t = \frac{1+\lambda_{t+1}}{1+\lambda_t}$ is the relative shadow price of external funds in periods t and $t+1$.

This equation describes the inter-temporal investment decision, since the marginal cost of today's investment (on the left-hand side, given by the cost of investment goods plus the marginal adjustment cost) has to be equal to the discounted marginal cost of investing tomorrow (the sum of today's marginal benefit forgone, adjustment cost and the price of investment tomorrow) (Love, 2003).

As Love (2003) points out, "the firm's inter-temporal allocation of investment depends on its effective discount factor, which is given by the product of its internal discount factor β, and θ, the discount factor associated with the external finance premium". If a firm is constrained, which in the model is equivalent to the inability to pay negative dividends (i.e., to issue new equity), the shadow value of these funds rises today relative to tomorrow (i.e., $\lambda_t > \lambda_{t+1}$,). Because of the negative dependence of θ_t on this shadow value, the effective discount rate of the firm drops and the firm postpones investment to the next period.

Financing constraints in the model are given by the parameter $\theta_t = \frac{1+\lambda_{t+1}}{1+\lambda_t}$.

In perfect capital markets,[3] $\lambda_t = \lambda_{t+1} = 0$, and $\theta_t = 1$. If the capital markets are imperfect, θ_t will depend on a number of state variables, including some observable firm characteristics. Although the model does not provide an explicit formula for this factor, the relevant literature relies on an ad hoc parameterization of this parameter using indicators of the firm's financial health. Love (2003) parameterizes θ_t as a linear function of the stock of a firm's liquid assets, the stock of cash and marketable securities. We use a similar approach, while in the estimations, we scale the variable by the value of the previous period's fixed assets.

---

[3] $\theta_t = 1$ could also reflect stationarity in the cash constraint. However, it does not change the implications for the main hypothesis of this paper.

If $\lambda_t > \lambda_{t+1}$, then $\theta_t = \frac{1+\lambda_{t+1}}{1+\lambda_t} < 1$ and it serves as an additional discount factor, in the sense that the current period's funds are more expensive to use than the next period's funds, so the firm is financially constrained and θ_t indicates the degree of this financial constraint.

We use Cash Flow[4] as a measure of internal funds available to the firm (or of the firm's financials). If external financing is costly, then it will imply a positive relationship between investment and cash stock.

Cash Flow serves in the model as a proxy for future growth opportunities in the absence of external financing because if the firm foresees high investment in the future, it will choose to accumulate liquid assets today (which is costly) (Love 2003). Therefore, we could parameterize the financing constraint as a linear relationship:

$$\theta_{it} = a_{01} + aCash_{it-1}, \tag{6}$$

Where, a_{01} represents a firm—specific level of financing constraints (which enters into the fixed effects) and a is the sensitivity of investment to the amount of internal funds available to the firm at time $t - 1$. In this linear representation, the cash flow affects the rate of inter-temporal substitution between today's and tomorrow's investment. If the firm is not liquidity constrained, $\theta_t = 1$, the effective discount factor is therefore given by β and the impact of cash flow on the inter-temporal allocation of investment is zero. The larger the extent of the firm being liquidity constrained, the bigger the impact of the cash flow on the firm's discount factor. Alternatively, an increase in the cash flow increases the effective discount factor and lowers the shadow cost of capital, thus making investment today more attractive than investment tomorrow.[5]

Under perfect capital market conditions where firms can borrow and lend freely and will not therefore be financially constrained, we will have $\theta_{it} = 1$, implying that $a = 0$ and $a_{01} = 1$ (i.e., investment is not related to internal funds).

The main argument of this paper is that different types of ownership may change the sensitivity of investment to internal funds (e.g., ownership by a bank or by a financial company may give higher access to external financing acquired through banks or financial intermediaries because of the reduced asymmetric information problem). Thus, θ_{it} may also be parameterized as depending on the type of ownership:

$$\theta_{it} = a_{01} + (a_1 + a_2 OT_i) * Cash_{it-1}, \tag{7}$$

Where, the coefficient a_2 is expected to be positive or negative for various

---

[4] A discussion of the relative merits of Cash Stock (Cash Flow + Marketable Securities + Inventories) versus Cash Flow variables can be found in Love (2003). Cash Stock is less correlated with the "fundamentals" in the model, i.e. with the marginal profitability of capital.

[5] Love (2003).

ownership types. For a subset of firms, instead of the ownership type variable, we also consider ownership concentration (OC) and its effect on the degree of the firm's liquidity constraint.

4 Empirical Analysis

4.1 The Data

This study uses a 2006 version of the Amadeus Database compiled by Bureau van Dijk which covers all European countries and contains firm-level information on financial performance and ownership for the 2000–2004 period. Amadeus is compiled from various sources but the bulk of the information available has been derived from the official accounts presented by firms at the end of their financial reporting year.[6] The amount of information available in Amadeus varies depending on the size of the enterprise we are observing. Smaller firms are likely to present less data while selecting larger companies will guarantee almost no missing values. Only two restrictions have been applied in selecting firms for the analysis: firms had to have at least 250 employees (this is in line with other studies on the subject) and firms had to be financially active. Applying these restrictions leaves a working sample of 8,637 firms (the number might change in some model specifications according to the different variables characterizing the ownership structure considered) over the 5 year period 2000–2004 (see Tables 1 and 2 for a detailed classification of the firms according to their size). This time period in Russia was chosen as the economic recovery from the liberalisation of early 1990s as well as the default of 1998 has started. As discussed in the paper the 1990s a tremendous decline of production in Russia, which was greater than the Great Depression in the USA, and a prevalence of barter based transactions and major adjustment of economic links between enterprises after the collapse of the Soviet Union. Thus

Table 1 Summary statistics on firm size (author's own calculations)

Employees 2004	No. firms
250–500	2,842
501–1,000	1,887
1,001–5,000	1,239
5,001–25,000	160
over 25,000	12
Missing	2,497
Total	8,637

[6] It is worth noting that the regulations regarding financial reporting can vary across the countries covered by Amadeus and hence a degree of error is unavoidable.

Table 2 Summary statistics of the main variables (author's own calculations)

Statistics	Investment$_{(t)}$/K$_{(t-1)}$	Cash$_{(t)}$/K$_{(t-1)}$	Profits$_{(t)}$/K$_{(t-1)}$
Mean	0.102	0.186	0.892
Median	0.037	0.028	0.323
Std dev.	0.372	0.499	21.487
Min	−1.000	0.000	−2,266.600
Max	1.992	4.951	34.958

the majority of enterprises found themselves in difficult financial situation. However, the chosen period for this study of 2000–2004 is characterised by increasing rates of economic growth in Russia, and in general improvement of the economic activity.

The dataset includes firms based in so called European Russia, that is geographically located west of the Ural mountains. We hence excluded from our analysis all firms located in West Siberia and further East because of a limitation of the standard Amadeus dataset for Europe. However, excluding regions which are heavily dependent on oil (such as the Tyumensk Region and its autonomous part) renders our analysis immune to biases deriving from anomalous behaviours present in the hydrocarbon sector. However, for those firms which are legally registered in the financial centres such as Moscow, we can still control for the sector-specific fixed effects by including an industry variable (as NACE classification is provided in Amadeus[7]).

A central feature of the Amadeus dataset is that it contains four firm ownership variables. Two variables characterizing the type of shareholders present in the company, the Ultimate Owner Controlling Type (UOCT) and the Shareholder Type (ST), are available. UOCT indicates whether the dominant shareholder of the company is also its ultimate owner. A shareholder is considered an ultimate owner when it owns more than 24.9 % of the company with no other single shareholder owning a larger percentage. If such a shareholder is itself a company, for it to be classified as the Ultimate Owner (UO), it must be itself independent.[8] ST is defined as UOCT irrespective of the percentage of shares owned as long as the holding represents a relative majority of shares but less than 24.9 %. Overall, there are 11 ownership types.

Furthermore, the data provided by Amadeus allows us to differentiate according to the degree of ownership concentration and independence of the company through the Ultimate Owner Controlling Qualification (UOCQ) and Independence Indicator (II) variables respectively. The minimum qualification level is reached when the

---

[7] Although, for taxation purposes, some firms may have reported profits realized in the hydrocarbons sector as profits derived from other commercial activities not directly related to the hydrocarbons sector (World Bank 2004). In this case results obtained while controlling for NACE codes might still be biased.

[8] The classification of ownership can be very complex for larger organisations and for multinational corporations. A more detailed description of how Amadeus classifies ownership variables is available from www.bvdep.com.

ultimate owner does not directly control the company and possesses less than 25 %
of its total shares. UOCQ further qualifies UOs according to their relationship with
each of their subsidiaries. The ultimate owner qualification maximum value is when
the UO has a percentage of the shares greater or equal to 98 % (this case is labelled
as "CR+") having full control of the company. A shareholder is qualified as a
Controlling Company ("CR") when it complies with the same qualifications as an
UO but its independence indicator is U (i.e. a company with no recorded shareholders or with all shareholders recorded with a "n.a." percentage of ownership).
The II indicates the degree of independence of a company with regard to its
shareholders (this ranges from "A", meaning that the firm in question is attached
to a company not owning more than 24.9 % of its shares and with 4–5 identified
shareholders, whose ownership percentage is known, to "C" where 98 % of the
company's shares are controlled by an individual firm).

Table 3 details the various cases for each of these ownership variables, lists the
qualifying criteria for the classifications used by Amadeus and also shows how
many observations are present for each subcategory.

4.2 Empirical Specification

The model presented in the previous section lends itself to being tested empirically.
The main aim of our analysis is to test whether different types of ownership can
affect the sensitivity of the firm's investment to internal funds. Throughout, we use
the following base equation obtained as an optimal solution of our investment
model:

$$\left(\frac{I_{i,t}}{K_{i,t-1}}\right) = \beta_0 + \beta_2(\pi_{i,t-1}) + \beta_3(Cash_{i,t-1}) + \beta_4(Cash_{i,t-1})*OT_i + \varepsilon_{it}, \quad (8)$$

where, our dependent variable capturing the rate of investment, $(I_{i,t}/K_{i,t-1})$, is the
change in fixed assets over the fixed assets in the previous year, $(\pi_{i,t-1})$ is the profits
at t − 1 and allows us to control for the size of firms, $(Cash_{i,t-1})$ is the cash and cash
equivalents at t − 1 and $(Cash_{i,t-1})*OT$ is also the cash and cash equivalents at
t − 1 but interacted with the ownership type variables (namely UOCT, ST, UOCQ
and II) presented in the previous subsection. In order to correct for size effects we
also standardize all the variables by fixed assets. The estimation procedure adopted
in this paper uses cash flow as a proxy for financial constraints taking a stance
within the ongoing debate on what researchers should use as valid measures of
financial constraints. In particular, we follow certain previous studies (Fazzari et al.,
1988, 2000, Fazzari, Hubbard, & Petersens, 2000), which have argued that investment to cash-flow sensitivities are higher for firms facing a larger gap between
internal and external costs of funding, thereby demonstrating that they are financially constrained. On the other hand, Kaplan and Zingales (1997, 2000) have

Table 3 Types of owner and control structure of the companies surveyed, including the number of firms in each category (author's own calculations)

UOCT Ultimate owner controlling type—when an UO owns > 24.9 % of the company with no other single shareholder owning a larger percentage	No. firms	ST Shareholder type	No. firms	UOCQ Ultimate owner controlling qualification	Definition	No. firms	II Independence indicator—signifies the degree of independence of a company with regard to its shareholders	Definition	No. firms
Bank	4	Bank	6	CR	Controlling company with ≤ 50 % of shares or 1 % between 50.01 % and 97.99 %	198	A	Attached to company not having more than 24.9 % of shares AND with 4–5 identified shareholders, whose ownership percentage is known	113
Employees/ managers	1	Employees/ managers	1	CR+	Controlling company with ≥ 98 % of shares	253	A+	As above with ≥ 6 identified shareholders	3,449
Financial company	11	Financial company	15	CR−	Controlling company with ≤ 25 % of shares or 1 % between 25.01 % and 49.99 %	318	A−	As above with 1–3 identified shareholders	567

(continued)

Table 3 (continued)

UOCT Ultimate owner controlling type—when an UO owns > 24.9 % of the company with no other single shareholder owning a larger percentage	No. firms	ST Shareholder type	No. firms	UOCQ Ultimate owner controlling qualification	Definition	No. firms Independence indicator—signifies the degree of independence of a company with regard to its shareholders	II	Definition	No. firms
Foundation	2	Individual (s) or family (ies)	143	JO	Jointly owned = 50 %	96	B	Attached to company having >24.9 % but <49.9 % of shares AND with 4–5 identified shareholders, whose ownership percentage is known	2
Individual(s) or family(ies)	70	Industrial company	2,168	LI	listed	46	B+	as above with ≥ 6 identified shareholders	480
Industrial company	1,822	Mutual and pension fund/trust/ nominee	8	UO	Ultimate Owner ≤ 50.00 % or at least 1 % between 50.01 % and 97.99 %	128	B−	as above with 1–3 identified shareholders	130
Mutual and pension fund/trust/nominee	3	Other unnamed shareholders	11	UO+	Ultimate owner ≥ 98.00 %	728	C	Attached to company having >49.9 %	14

	State, public authority	UO–	Ultimate Owner ≤ 25.00 % or at least 1 % between 25.01 % and 49.99 %	C+	Attached to company having ≥ 98 %	6
State, public authority	141	53	287			
Unnamed private shareholders		3,899		D		1,453
				U	Companies that are not in A, B or C hence unknown degree of independence	2,423
Total	2,054	total		total		
	total	6,304	2,054	total		8637

questioned whether investment-cash flow sensitivities can actually be used as a meaningful measure of financial constraints since these sensitivities are not necessarily monotonic. Their concerns regarding the Fazzari et al. methodology were later addressed by these authors themselves. This debate has more recently been continued by Almeida et al. (2004), who introduce a new methodology for identifying financially constrained firms, and by Baum et al. (2011), who apply their methodology to a sample of 80,000 firms from around the globe. We do not, however, elaborate further on this issue.

Given the model presented in the previous section of the paper, we expect the coefficient associated with cash and cash equivalents to capture the extent to which a firm is liquidity constrained in planning its investment strategy. A positive coefficient would support the thesis that liquidity constraints are present in the investment decision, while a coefficient of zero (or a negative coefficient) would contradict the theoretical findings. Finally, we expand our baseline model by allowing for the presence of different ownership control variables by interacting them with the cash and cash equivalents owned by the firm. This allows us to assess directly how the type of ownership structure of the company affects its level of liquidity constraint in its investment strategy.

Some variables in the estimation equations may be jointly endogenously determined. For example, firm value and investment may be jointly determined by unobserved productivity or technology shocks. While higher firm value may cause higher investment, it may equally be possible that higher investment increases firm value. Ideally, to account for this problem, one would use the forward-mean differencing (FMD) technique introduced by Holtz-Eakin et al (1988), Arellano and Bond (1991) and Arellano and Bover (1995).[9] This procedure estimates first-differences for each of the variables, gets rid of firm-specific effects and also uses all possible lags of all the explanatory variables as instruments. The use of a system GMM would be even more appropriate in this context as it is more robust than the Arellano-Bond differenced GMM procedure for cases when the time span of the data is limited (and so is the number of available lagged instruments).

However, given that our dataset has only 3 years of usable data (and hence would not allow for the adoption of the GMM approach), we use panel estimation including both fixed and random effects.

4.3 Results

We start our empirical analysis by testing whether the firms are cash constrained as predicted by the theoretical model. First we implement a random effect specification, the results of which are displayed in Table 4. More specifically, Table 4 reports

---

[9] We assume away the possibility of corner solutions to the Euler equation. Aguirregabiria (1997) provides a comprehensive discussion of potential biases induced by the discrete choice problem.

Table 4 Cash and cash equivalent interacted with the type, qualification and concentration of ownership and their effect on investment. Random effects, controlling for regional and sector effects (author's own calculations)

Term	Baseline model	Ultimate owner controlling type		Shareholder type		Ultimate owner controlling qualification		Independence	
Cash	0.086 (0.01)[a]		0.108 (0.021)[a]		0.082 (0.016)[a]		0.124 (0.053)[b]		0.093 (0.089)[b]
Profit	0.001 (0.0002)[a]		0.002 (0.0006)[a]		0.001 (0.000)[a]		0.002 (0.001)[a]		0.001 (0.000)[a]
		Bank	10.269 (9.27)	Bank	0.745 (0.155)[a]	CR	0.092 (0.089)	A	−0.075 (0.09)
		Employees/managers	8.749 (5.89)	Employees/managers	8.76 (5.876)	CR+	0.013 (0.088)	A−	−0.068 (0.094)
		Financial company	−0.166[c] (0.1)	Financial company	−0.267 (0.462)	CR	0.064 (0.094)	B	−0.686 (0.408)
		Foundation	4.923[c] (2.553)	Individual(s) or family(-ies)	−0.112 (0.054)[b]	JO	−0.093 (0.082)	B+	−0.05 (0.1)
		Individual(s) or family(ies)	−0.147 (0.071)[b]	Unnamed private shar., agg.	0.019 (0.024)	LI	0.028 (0.262)	B−	−0.102 (0.139)
		Mutual & Pension fund/Trust/ Nominee	−2.274 (0.891)[b]	Mutual & pension fund/trust/ nominee	−0.009 (1.131)	UO	0.061 (0.089)	C	1.8 (1.9)
		State, Public authority	−0.06 (0.036)[c]	Other unnamed shar., agg.	0.2 (0.241)	UO−	−0.016 (0.058)	C+	0.8 (1.9)
				State, Public authority	−0.05 (0.035)			D	−0.055 (0.1)
								U	−0.145 (0.09)[c]

(continued)

Table 4 (continued)

	Baseline model		Ultimate owner controlling type		Shareholder type		Ultimate owner controlling qualification		Independence	
Constant	0.072		0.043		0.05		−0.007		0.046	
	$(0.016)^a$		(0.032)		$(0.02)^a$		(0.036)		(0.028)	
Observations	16297		4269		12243		5502		21945	
Number of id	6884		1671		4798		1677		6975	
R-squared	0.022		0.037		0.024		0.042		0.038	

Heteroskedasticity-robust standard errors in parentheses

[a]Significant at 1 %

[b]Significant at 5 %

[c]Significant at 10 %

results of the heteroskedasticity-corrected random effects estimation, which includes control variables for the sector and region specific effects, proxied by two digit NACE codes and regional dummies respectively. The predictions obtained in the specifications without the regional dummies and industry dummies (results available upon request from the authors) are found to be robust to the inclusion of such controls.

The first column refers to the baseline model without ownership control variables and confirms the model's hypothesis that firms tend to be cash constrained in their investment decisions. This is consistent with other studies on Russia [see e.g., Aukutsionek and Batyaeva (2000)].

The coefficient attached to the cash flow variable is indeed positive and highly significant at a 99 % confidence level. This finding is very robust in both sign and magnitude across all specifications considered. A 10 % increase in the share of cash flow to capital is associated with an around 2 % increase in investment as a share of capital (evaluated at means). For profits, a 10 % increase in profits (as a share of capital) brings about a 0.2 % increase in the investment-to-capital ratio (again, evaluated at means). The second column introduces a control variable for the Ultimate Owner (UO) interacted with the cash flow variable. It should be emphasized that the cash flow variable remains positive and significant, confirming, once again, the hypothesis of cash constraints for firms. Again it is worth noting that the cash flow coefficient is robust in both sign and magnitude in this specification. Regarding the UO variable, our results suggest that individuals/family-owned and state-owned companies and financial companies and mutual funds[10] tend to be less cash constrained than industrial companies at the 95 and 90 % levels of significance respectively. In fact, for individually-owned and family-owned companies, liquidity constraints completely disappear. Banks do not appear to be significantly less cash constrained than firms owned by other types of shareholders. The results for family firms are consistent with those presented for European Union (Pindado et al., 2011) and East Asia (Wei and Zhang, 2008).

When, on the other hand, we add shareholder type (column 3), the results are again confirmed in sign, magnitude and significance. This seems to suggest that state-owned companies (marginally significant in the equation in column 3) and private individuals/families are less cash constrained and not only when their ownership structure is at the same time more concentrated. This is consistent with the findings by Mickiewicz (2006) that "... corporate control by individuals emerges as a typical outcome of post-privatisation evolution in Russia." Interestingly, the results displayed in the fourth column of Table 4, which relate to the degree of concentration proxied by the UOCR variable, indicate that ownership concentration does not play a significant role in explaining the degree of liquidity constraint (Audretsch and Elston (2002) obtain the same result for the insignificance of ownership concentration when testing liquidity constraints on German

---

[10] However, for the latter two, we interpret this result with caution due to the small number of such companies in the sample.

firms). Similar results are obtained in terms of the independence indicator as provided by Amadeus. Indeed, results displayed in the fifth column suggest that firms classified as U are less cash constrained. However, it must be remarked that the U classification groups together a variety of cases including the case of omitted information concerning the degree of independence of the company.

Finally, we should note that we also estimated a fixed effect specification. A Hausman test comparing these results with both the specifications (with and without sector and region dummies) suggests that fixed effects are preferred. However, this test does not take into account the reduced time span of the data which only covers three years. Such a narrow time span can strongly bias the process of demeaning over time, which underlies the fixed effect procedure. In other words, results can experience pronounced changes due to the inclusion of additional years to the analysis since these would directly affect the value of the mean as computed over time. In addition, Baltagi (2008) emphasizes the importance of having a long panel for the usage of the fixed effects. We therefore present the random effects results.

5 Conclusion

In Russia firms operate in a context characterised by high capital market imperfections and, as a consequence, the wedge between the cost of internal and external sources of funds is increased. Using sensitivity of investment to cash flow as a proxy for the wedge, we find that in general Russian firms are financially constrained. Our main result, which is robust to many different specifications estimated in this paper, confirms the presence of liquidity constraints in Russia as expressed by the significant sensitivity of their investments to cash flow. This finding is in line with a number of empirical analyses that point to the presence of liquidity constraints in many sectors of the Russian economy [e.g., Perotti and Gelfer (2001) and Volchkova (2000)].

Our results on the impact of ownership on the tightness of liquidity constraints are mixed. In particular, we find that individual and family owned and state-owned companies are less cash constrained relative to other ownership structures. The fact that state-owned firms appear to be less cash constrained can be partially explained through the intricate modes of presence of the public sector in hydrocarbons management during the period considered. More surprising is the fact that we do not find evidence of lower cash constraints for banks (in the equation for the UO, bank-owned firms are even found to be more liquidity constrained, which could be reflective of the aftermath of the 1998 crisis in Russia). However, for family firms, the investment cash flow sensitivity is low, and hence the investment decisions are less dependent upon its cash flow. This finding extends our understanding on family firms financial investments behaviour and hence contributes to the literature on family firms. In comparison with other privately owned firms, family firms appear to have more resources, and further research on the more recent data can explore the particular aspects of why family firms appear to be in such position.

We consider at least three possible ways of going forward with our research. First, while at the moment we use a panel data random- and fixed-effects estimation technique, our next step is to increase the time length of the sample to be able to exploit all the benefits of the GMM estimator. This would allow us to include the lagged I/K term [following Love (2003)] in order to account for any possible strong persistence in investment-to-capital ratios over time. Second, following the work of Kaplan and Zingales (1997, 2000) which strongly criticizes the use of cash flow as a proxy for financial constraints, one could select other variables to interact with the property structure. Finally, provided that our evidence concerning the ownership structure is mixed, one could also consider the possibility of splitting the sample according to average investment-capital ratio and average dividend payments (as for example in Scaramozzino (1997)) to check whether there is a group of mature companies with well-known prospects which does not suffer any cash constraints and undertakes its investment decisions purely according to the neo-classical criterion of Tobin's Q.

References

Aguirregabiria, V. (1997). Estimation of dynamic programming models with censored dependent variables. *Investigaciones Economicas, XXI*(2), 167–208.

Almeida, H., Campello, M., & Weisbach, M. (2004). The cash flow sensitivity of cash. *Journal of Finance, 59*(4), 1777–1804.

Amore, M. D., Minichilli, A., & Corbetta, G. (2011). How do managerial successions shape corporate financial policies in family firms? *Journal of Corporate Finance, 17*(4), 1016–1027.

Anderson, R. C., & Reeb, D. M. (2003). Founding family ownership and firm performance: Evidence from the S&P 500. *Journal of Finance, 58*(3), 1308–1328.

Arellano, M., & Bond, S. (1991). Some tests of specification for panel data: Monte Carlo evidence and an application to employment equations. *The Review of Economic Studies, 58*(2), 277–297.

Arellano, M., & Bover, O. (1995). Another look at the instrumental variable estimation of error-components models. *Journal of Econometrics, 68*(1), 29–51.

Astrachan, J. H., & Zellweger, T. (2008). Performance of family firms: A literature review and guidance for future research. *Zeitschrift fur KMU und Entrepreneurship, 56*(1/2), 1–22.

Audretsch, D. B., & Elston, J. A. (2002). Does firm size matter? Evidence on the impact of liquidity constraints on firm investment behavior in Germany. *International Journal of Industrial Organization, 20*, 1–17.

Aukutsionek, S., & Batyaeva, A. (2000). Investment and non-investment in the Russian industry. *Journal of East-West Business, 6*(4), 5–22.

Baltagi, H. B. (2008). *Econometric analysis of panel data* (4th ed.). Chichester: Wiley.

Banalieva, E. R., Eddleston, K. A., & Zellweger, T. M. (2014). When do family firms have an advantage in transitioning economies? Toward a dynamic institution-based view. Strategic Management Journal. doi:10.1002/smj.2288.

Barontini, R., & Caprio, L. (2006). The effect of family control on firm value and performance: Evidence from continental Europe. *European Financial Management, 12*, 689–723.

Barth, E., Gulbrandsen, T., & Schone, P. (2005). Family ownership and productivity: The role of owner-management. *Journal of Corporate Finance, 11*, 107–127.

Basco, R., & Rodriguez, M. J. P. (2009). Studying the family enterprise holistically: Evidence for integrated family and business systems. *Family Business Review, 22*(1), 82–95.

Baum, C. F., Schafer, D., & Talavera, O. (2011). The impact of financial structure on firms' financial constraints: A cross-country analysis. *Journal of International Money and Finance, 30*, 678–691.

Bertrand, M., Mehta, P., & Mullainathan, S. (2002). Ferreting out tunneling: An application to Indian business groups. *Quarterly Journal of Economics, 117*, 121–148.

Borheim, S. (2000). *The organizational form of family business.* Massachusetts: Kluwer.

Buccellato, T., & Mickiewicz, T. (2007). Oil and gas: A blessing for few hydrocarbons and within-region inequality in Russia", *Economics Working Paper No. 80*, UCL SSEES, September.

Buck, T. (2003). Modern russian corporate governance: Convergent forces or product of Russia's history? *Journal of World Business, 38*, 299–313.

Buck, T., Filatochev, I., & Wright, M. (1998). Agents, stakeholders and corporate Russian firms. *Journal of Management Studies, 35*, 81–104.

Castillo, J., & Wakefield, M. (2007). An exploration of firm performance factors in family businesses: Do families value only the bottom line? *Journal of Small Business Strategy, 17* (2), 37–51.

Chrisman, J. J., Chua, J. H., & Sharma, P. (2005). Trends and directions in the development of a strategic management theory of the family firm. *Entrepreneurship Theory and Practice, 29*(5), 555–575.

Claessens, S., Djankov, S., & Lang, L. (2000). The separation of ownership and control in East Asian Corporations. *Journal of Financial Economics, 58*, 81–112.

Collins, L., & O'Regan, N. (2010). The evolving field of family business. *Journal of Family Business Management, 1*(1), 5–13.

Cronqvist, H., & Nilsson, M. (2003). Agency costs of controlling minority shareholders. *Journal of Financial and Quantitative Analysis, 38*, 695–719.

Cucculelli, M., & Micucci, G. (2008). Family succession and firm performance: Evidence from Italian family firms. *Journal of Corporate Finance, 14*(1), 17–31.

Estrin, S. (2002). Competition and corporate governance in transition. *Journal of Economic Literature, 16*(1), 101–124.

Estrin, S., & Wright, M. (1999). Corporate governance in the former Soviet Union: An overview. *Journal of Comparative Economics, 27*(3), 398–421.

Fazzari, S. M., Hubbard, R. G., Petersen, B. C., Blinder, A. S., & Poterba, J. M. (1988). Financing constraints and corporate investment. *Brooking Papers on Economic Activity, 1*, 141–206.

Fazzari, S. M., Hubbard, R. G., & Petersens, B. C. (2000). Financing constraints and corporate investment: Response to Kaplan and Zingales. *Quarterly Journal of Economics, 115*(2), 695–705.

Gedajlovic, E., & Carney, M. (2010). Markets, hierarchies, and families: Toward a transaction cost theory of the family firm. *Entrepreneurship: Theory and Practice, 34*(6), 1145–1172.

Gilchrist, S., & Himmelberg, C. (1998) Investment, fundamentals, and finance. *NBER Macroeconomics Annual 1998*, MIT Press, Cambridge, MA.

Gugler, K., & Peev, E. (2010). Institutional determinants of investment-cash flow sensitivities in transition economies. *Comparative Economic Studies, 52*(1), 62–81.

Guriev, S., Lazareva, O., Rachinsky, A., & Tsukhlo, S. (2003) Corporate governance in Russian industry, *Working Paper Centre for Economic and Financial Research*, Moscow.

Holtz-Eakin, D., Newey, W., & Rosen, H. (1988). Estimating vector autoregressions with panel data. *Econometrica, 56*(6), 1371–1395.

Johnson, J. (1997). Understanding Russia's emerging financial–industrial groups. *Post-Soviet Affairs, 13*(4), 333–365.

Judge, W., Naoumova, I., & Koutzevol, N. (2003). Corporate governance and firm performance in Russia: An empirical study. *Journal of World Business, 38*(4), 385–396.

Kaplan, S. N., & Zingales, L. (1997). Do investment-cash flow sensitivities provide useful measures of financing constraints? *The Quarterly Journal of Economics, 112*(1), 169–215.

Kaplan, S., & Zingales, L. (2000). Investment-cash flow sensitivities are not valid measures of financing constraints. *The Quarterly Journal of Economics, 115*, 707–712.

Kochetygova, J., Popivshchy, N., & Vitalieva, V. (2004). Corporate governance in Russia analytical report. *Corporate Ownership and Control, 1*(2), 156–166.

KPMG. (2013). The world of corporate governance: Russia. *Audit Committee News.* Edition 43, Q4/2013.

Lee, J. (2006). Family firm performance: Further evidence. *Family Business Review, 19,* 103–114.

Love, I. (2003). Financial development and financing constraints: International evidence from the structural investment model. *The Review of Financial Studies, 16*(3, Fall), 765–791.

Maury, B. (2006). Family ownership and firm performance: Empirical evidence from Western European corporations. *Journal of Corporate Finance, 12,* 321–341.

McCarthy, D. J., & Puffer, S. M. (2003). Corporate governance in Russia: A framework for analysis. *Journal of World Business, 38,* 397–415.

Megginson, W., & Netter, J. (2001). From state to market: A survey of empirical studies on privatization. *Journal of Economic Literature, 39*(2), 321–389.

Meyer, K. (2003). Privatisation and corporate governance in Eastern Europe: The emergence of stakeholder capitalism. Keynote address, Chemnitz East Forum, 19–22 March 2003. Working Paper. http://www.klausmeyer.co.uk/publications/2003_meyer_chemnitz.pdf

Mickiewicz, T. (2006). Corporate governance in Russia and Poland in comparative perspective: An introduction. In T. Mickiewicz (Ed.), *Corporate governance and finance in Poland and Russia* (pp. 3–22). Basingstoke: PalgraveMacmillan.

Mickiewicz, T., Bishop, K., & Varblane, U. (2004). Financial constraints in investment. Panel data results from Estonia, 1995–1999. *Acta Oeconomica, 54*(4), 425–449.

Miller, D., Le Breton-Miller, I., Lester, R. H., & Cannella, A. A. (2007). Are family firms really superior performers? *Journal of Corporate Finance, 13,* 829–858.

Miller, D., Le Breton-Miller, I., & Lester, R. (2010). Family ownership and acquisition behavior in publicly traded companies. *Strategic Management Journal, 31,* 201–223.

Monsen, R. J., Chiu, J., & Cooley, D. E. (1968). The effect of separation of ownership and control on the performance of the large firm. *Quarterly Journal of Economics, LXXXVII,* 435–451.

Perez-Gonzalez, F. (2006). Inherited control and firm performance. *The American Economic Review, 96*(5), 1559–1588.

Perotti, E. (2000). *The 1998 Russian Meltdown: Microfoundations of a systemic collapse.* Amsterdam: Mimeo, University of Amsterdam.

Perotti, E., & Gelfer, S. (2001). Red barons or robber barons? Governance and investment in Russian financial-industrial groups. *European Economic Review, 45,* 1601–1617.

Pindado, J., Requejo, I., & de la Torre, C. (2011). Family control and investment-cash flow sensitivity: Empirical evidence from the Euro zone. *Journal of Corporate Finance, 17*(4), 1389–1409.

Radygin, A., Entov, R., & Shmeleva, N. (2003). Problems of mergers and takeovers in the Russian corporate sector. *Problems of Economic Transition, 46*(7), 5–64.

Randoy, T., & Goel, S. (2003). Ownership structure, founder leadership, and firm performance in Norwegian SME's: Implications for financing entrepreneurial opportunities. *Journal of Business Venturing, 18*(5), 619–637.

Rozinskii, I. (2002) Mekhanizmy polucheniya dokhodov i korporativnoe upravlenie v rossiiskoi ekonomike. In *Predpriyatiya Rossii: Korporativnoe Upravlenie i Rynochnye Sdelki: Institutsionalinye Problemy Rossiiskoi Ekonomiki,* Tom 1 (pp. 168–182). Moscow: Gosudarstvennyi Universitet – Vysshaya Shkola Ekonomiki (in Russian).

Scaramozzino, P. (1997). Investment irreversibility and finance constraints. *Oxford Bulletin of Economics and Statistics, 59*(1), 0305–9049.

Schulze, W. S., Lubatkin, M. H., & Dino, R. N. (2003). Exploring the agency consequences of ownership dispersion among the directors of private family firms. *Academy of Management Journal, 46*(2), 174–194.

Shama, A. (2001). Private sector management: The case of Russia. *Journal of Small Business Management, 39*(2), 183–192.

Smith, B. F., & Amoako-Adu, B. (1999). Management succession and financial performance of family controlled firms. *Journal of Corporate Finance, 5*(4), 341–368.

Sorenson, R. L. (1999). Conflict strategies used by successful family businesses. *Family Business Review, 12*(4), 325–339.

Sprenger, C. (2011). The choice of ownership structure: Evidence from Russian mass privatization. *Journal of Comparative Economics, 39*(2), 260–277.

Steijvers, T., Voordeckers, W., & Vanderloof, K. (2010). Collateral, relationship lending and family firms. *Small Business Economics, 34*, 243–259.

Villalonga, B., & Amit, R. (2006). How do family ownership, control and management affect firm value? *Journal of Financial Economics, 80*, 385–418.

Volchkova, N. (2000) Does financial-industrial group membership affect fixed investment: Evidence from Russia, *EERC Working Paper No. 01/02.*

Ward, J. (1997). Growing the family business: Special challenges and best practices. *Family Business Review, 10*(4), 323–337.

Wei, K. C. J., & Zhang, Y. (2008). Ownership structure, cash flow and capital investment: Evidence from East Asian economies before the financial crisis. *Journal of Corporate Finance, 14*, 118–132.

Westhead, P., & Cowling, M. (1998). Family firm research: The need for a methodological rethink. *Entrepreneurship: Theory and Practice, 23*(1), 31–56.

World Bank. (2004). Russian Economic Report. Retrieved March, 12, 2015, from http://docu ments.worldbank.org/curated/en/2004/11/6690582/russian-economic-report

Yakovlev, A. (2001). 'Black cash' tax evasion in Russia: Its forms, incentives, and consequences at firm level. *Europe-Asia Studies, 53*(1), 33–55.

Part III
Internationalisation and Other Issues

Family Businesses Motives for Internationalisation: Evidence from Serbia

Radmila Grozdanić and Mirjana Radović-Marković

Abstract This book chapter contributes to understanding of family firms in Serbia by examining the importance for national economy, business ambient for work and sustained businesses, as well as institutional infrastructure support, educational, innovation and financial support. This chapter seeks to explain resource-seeking internationalization among Serbian family firms, which belong mostly to SMEs, by investigating, based on based on resource dependency theory and the model of entrepreneurial internationalization, whether resource-seeking internationalization can be linked to a family businesses' resource deficiencies. It researches whether perceived resource constraints in terms of labor, finance and new technology increase the likelihood of family firms to use internationalization as a means to access or acquire the lacking resources, relative to not internationalizing. By binomial logistic regression analysis method used for the testing in the chapter are elaborated the findings which indicate that perceived lack of skilled labor drives family firms to pursue internationalization as a means for accessing labor and that perceived constraints regarding access to finance are an important determinant for family firms to pursue foreign markets as a means to access capital. These results suggest that perceived constraints in terms of skilled labor and finance are pushing firms to overcome internal resource deficiencies through internationalization, as well as that, these firms which are already internationally active to use their international activity as a means to access or acquire these resources. The contribution of the chapter could be seen also in the suggestion that resource-constrained family firms can be considered as entrepreneurial firms that proactively exploit internationalization as a strategy for addressing current resource needs. The findings of the research also support the awareness of the mangers/owners of the family firms of the possibility to use internationalization as a means for overcoming resource constraints, as well as policy makers awareness increase to improve general doing business parameters in the country giving that internationalization could become easier and resources could become more easily transferable across borders.

R. Grozdanić • M. Radović-Marković (✉)
Faculty of Business Economics and Entrepreneurship, Belgrade, Serbia
e-mail: sme_rada@hotmail.com; mradovic@gmail.com

© Springer International Publishing Switzerland 2015
L.-P. Dana, V. Ramadani (eds.), *Family Businesses in Transition Economies*,
DOI 10.1007/978-3-319-14209-8_13

Keywords Family firms • SMEs • Perspectives • Entrepreneurial • Business •
Theoretical • Behavior

1 Introduction

Family businesses make up between 65 and 80 % of all European companies,
accounting for on average more than 40–50 % of all jobs. Family businesses
constitute a substantial part of existing European companies and have a significant
role to play in the strength and dynamism of the real economy. Family firms are
important, not only because they make an essential contribution to the economy,
but also because of the long-term stability they bring, the specific commitment they
show to local communities, the responsibility they feel as owners and the values
they stand for.

Family businesses are an important part of the national economies of many
countries (Mandl, 2008), including Serbia (Grozdanic, Radovic-Markovic, &
Vucic, 2009). This is not a new phenomenon in Serbia it has happened many
times before but there is a major element of economic life which endures and
often prospers through difficult events, Family Business.

Families in business have a self, some say a more enlightened, interest in the
enterprise they own and infuse it with a controlling set of values. By their nature
they think longer term and act and invest accordingly.

The contribution and stability that family businesses bring to the society is now
being adequately recognized and there is a positive curiosity about the features
which make it a successful form of organization. It is Serbian Family Business's
mission to convince Government and policy makers to maintain a healthy environment in which family businesses can thrive by removing discriminatory measures
against it promoting its best practices (Radović-Marković, Nelson-Porter, &
Grozdanic, 2013)

Family companies are by many features particular types of business. Most
family businesses are small and medium-sized companies, but the public usually
does not know that there are also many large family-owned companies.

In developing economies, it is common for family ties and relationships to be
more overt in business activities. Developing economies are characterized by
institutional voids, market imperfections, unreliable information flows, and fragile
legal and financial frameworks.

In today's global economy resources have become more mobile and it has
become easier to transfer resources between different countries (Autio, 2005;
Sapienza, Autio, George, & Zahra, 2006) and it may be a common or even
necessary strategy for organizations, including resource-constrained SMEs, to use
internationalization as a means to obtain resources from external sources and fulfill
a perceived research need. The idea that scarcity may enhance resource-seeking
internationalization also builds on an emerging area of research that focuses on the
enabling features of resource scarcity (Katila & Mang, 2003). One of the central

tenets of economics, especially those in the transition as Serbia is, is that scarcity in terms of limited availability of goods, services or factors of production (such as labor or capital) drives the economic behavior of individual economic agents. Resource dependency theory builds on this economic rationale. According to this theory resource scarcities provide a need for firms to acquire or gain access to resources from external sources (Barringer & Harrison, 2000). The model of entrepreneurial internationalization as proposed by Oviatt and McDougall (1994) acknowledges that for resource-constrained ventures internationalization may be a necessary strategy to access value-creating resources (Kuemmerle, 2002; Oviatt & McDougall, 1994). Based on resource dependency theory and the model of entrepreneurial internationalization it is argued in this paper that family firms, facing particular resource scarcities may enter international markets to fill a perceived resource need.

The chapter is structured as follows. After introduction, the second chapter addresses the literature overview on most famous theories of family businesses and resource theory and internationalization. Next chapter provides an overview of SMEs sector and family businesses in Serbia with family good practices presented with most internationalized businesses. An overview of doing business indicators concerning domestic conditions for family firms business is given with institutional, innovation, education and financial support infrastructure and services for internationalization. The results of the survey of the luck of access to skilled labour, finance and new technology as motives for family firms internationalization are given in fifth part of the paper. The paper concludes with a discussion of the applicability of theoretical approaches and proposals for future activities of the managers/owners of family firms and Serbian authorities in improving the legal and macro ambient for family firms internationalization development, and awareness of the motives for export and import.

2 Literature Overview

The family business is often said to be a special kind of firm. It is special in the way family members involved combine family life and work. Therefore, it is difficult to view the business, the management and the ownership separately. Different "borrowed" paradigmas are in use: *Agency theory* (Schulze and Gedajevic, 2010), *Resource-based* view of the firm (Habbershon & Williams, 1999; Habbershon, Williams, & MacMillan, 2003), *Stewardship theory* (Miller & Le Breton-Miller, 2006a, 2006b). Many authors, like Chrisman, Chua, and Litz (2003) found that family and non-family firms had similar economic performance as measured by short-term sales growth; similarly Grozdanic (2005) found no significant differences in performance (measured by economic efficiency and value added per employee) between Serbian family and non-family enterprises.

Entrepreneurial energy exists, but where properly channeled it can result in activities that are undesirable for the state and its society. Forms of entrepreneurship to thrive were informal economic activity, internal economic activity with no transaction, and activity economic activity (Dana & Dana, 2003; Ramadani & Dana, 2013). Whether or not transition is taking place gradually or rapidly, alongside political reform or in its absence, the mindset of people often holds onto perceptions of former times. Consequently, in order to gain an understanding of the behaviour of entrepreneurs and of the nature of their enterprise, one must first become familiar with a variety of explanatory variables, including culture, historical experience, and government policy. Transition is a function of all of these a causal variables (Dana, 2010; Ramadani & Dana, 2013)

Macroeconomic background and the SME sector in the Balkan countries as typical case of transition, EU pre-accession economies could provide background information on the structure and recent economic trends of the economies covered by the paper, draw a profile of the SME sector in each of the observed transition economies and present the internationalization approach. Create an environment in which entrepreneurs and family businesses can thrive and entrepreneurship is rewarded share two common features: they are all engaged in the EU pre-accession process, although at different stages, and they have adopted the EU Small Business Act as their main SME policy framework, as part of the policy convergence towards the EU. Croatia and Serbia are the two largest economies in the Western Balkans, accounting for 12 % of the combined GDP, but with significantly different income levels. Croatia has the highest *per capita* income level in the Western Balkans, while Serbia has the third highest *per capita* income level after Montenegro. Both highly open economies, Croatia and Serbia share a high level of economic integration with the EU, accounting for over 61.1%1 and 63.6%2 of their trade flows respectively and 92.2%3 and 85%4 of their FDI inflow respectively, and a significant level of regional trade integration with their CEFTA partners. Both countries are specialized in low and medium technological products, with a strong presence of sectors such as agri-business, metal working, chemical products, pharmaceutical product, mechanical components, automotive components and transport equipment. The remaining economies in the Western Balkans (Albania, Bosnia and Herzegovina, the Former Yugoslav Republic of Macedonia, and Montenegro) are relative small open economies with an advanced level of trade integration with the EU and the CEFTA area with an income *per capita* ranging from middle to middle low income level. Their traditional specialization is in highly labor intensive industries (garments, textiles and leather) and commodity transformation sectors (smelting, metal working and agribusiness). Tourism and construction account for a significant share of GDP in Montenegro while remittances play an important role in supporting domestic demand and small-scale investment in Albania, Bosnia and Herzegovina (Table 1).

The global financial crisis of 2009 had a significant impact on the Western Balkans region although less so in Turkey. With the exception of Albania, which appeared to weather the crisis relatively well, most economies in the region went through a prolonged period of recession in 2009 and early 2010. The contraction was most severe in Croatia and Montenegro where the decline in external demand was compounded by a significant domestic credit crunch. Economic activity in the

Table 1 Structural and macroeconomic indicators, Balkan countries, 2012

	Albania	Bosnia and Herzegovina	Croatia	Macedonia	Montenegro	Serbia
Population in millions	3.2	3.8	4.4.	2.1	0.6	7.3
GDP growth % year-on-year	3.1	1.8	0.1	3.0	2.7	1.6
Inflation (% average)	3.5	3.6	2.1	3.9	2.9	11.2
Government balance % of GDP	−3.5	−3.1	−5.5	−2.6	−6.5	−4.0
Current account balance % of GDP	−13.2	−8.3	0.9	−2.8	−19.4	−9.1
Net FDI in EUR millions	695.7	317.3	1,023.7	307.2	389.2	1,823.0
Gross reserves in % of GDP	20.7	18.8	24.4	22.9	9.6	34.0
Nominal GDP in EUR millions	9.3	12.9	45.9	7.4	3.3	32.4

The figure is estimated as the weighted average of the 2012 GDP growth projections for the economies in the region, including Albania, Bosnia and Herzegovina, Croatia, the Former Yugoslav Republic of Macedonia, Montenegro and Serbia. The figure is based on EBRD forecasts from January 2012

Source: EBRD data, World Bank, National Statistical Agencies and Central Banks, 2011

Western Balkans economies began to pick up again in the latter part of 2010 and in the first half of 2011, mainly on the back of a strong recovery in exports. In this period, GDP growth figures became positive again in all economies except for Croatia, which experienced one of the most severe and most protracted recessions in the region. Montenegro has been experiencing the most prolonged credit crunch—credit to the private sector has been falling continuously since the start of the crisis as the enormous pre-crisis credit boom continues to be unwound. Inflation has exhibited a strong downward trend in most economies in the region. In Serbia, inflation fell from a peak of 14.8 % year on year (y-o-y) in April 2011 to 3.2 % y-o-y in March 2012. In response to the downward trend in inflation and overall economic conditions, central banks in most of the region have been loosening monetary policy. The banking sectors in the region have remained sound and liquid, though the level of non-performing loans (NPLs) is high and still increasing in some economies. The large proportion of foreign banks (75 % or more of the total banking asset share in most of the economies) makes the region particularly vulnerable to developments in the euro zone that may affect the parent banks. So far, there has been little evidence of a major impact on Greek or Italian-owned banks in the region, but the risks remain high.

The outlook for the region, or group of transition countries, in the coming year remains relatively gloomy. The persistent and potentially worsening crisis in the euro zone is bound to be felt throughout the Western Balkan region, because of the close trade, investment and financial linkages. Some mitigating factors are present:

most economies have been fiscally prudent throughout the crisis, banking sectors are well-capitalized and several economies are benefiting from IMF programmes. Nevertheless, the prospects for a rebound in growth this year are relatively low. Under the current forecasts, the region will grow on average 1.1 % in 2012. The downside risks, however, are high and further downward revisions of the forecasts are not unlikely.

2.1 The SME Sector in the Balkan Countries as, EU Pre-accession Economies

There are no comprehensive and comparable SME data for the whole pre-accession region, based on the EU definition of an SME. The level of statistical information varies considerable within the region: Croatia and Serbia provide extensive and updated sets of business statistics; Albania, the Former Yugoslav Republic of Macedonia and Montenegro provide structural SME data, while there are no official SME statistics available for Bosnia and Herzegovina comparable with the other economies. The only information available there is from the company register or independent company surveys.

The structure of the SME sector in the EU pre-accession economies for which comparable data are available mirrors that of the European Union. Micro-enterprises (fewer than ten employees, including sole entrepreneurs) account for an extremely large share of the registered enterprises (ranging from 88.9 % in Montenegro to 95.9 % in Serbia) but their contribution in terms of employment and particularly value added is significantly lower, reflecting a much lower productivity per employee than that of small and medium enterprises. Many of those micro-enterprises are operated by necessity driven entrepreneurs. Unsurprisingly, the economic crisis of 2009 caused deterioration in the business climate and worsened the economic performance of SMEs in the Western Balkan region. The lack of data from the individual economies makes it difficult to quantitatively assess the impact of the crisis on the SME sector specifically however certain trends emerge when comparing data from Croatia, Serbia In Serbia, for example, the number of SMEs in 2009 increased by 9,337, 45 % less than in 2008. Moreover, this slowdown in the emergence of new SMEs was coupled with a considerable increase in the number of firms that were forced to close. In Croatia SME turnover fell by 5 % between 2009 and 2010. While the total number of SMEs continued to grow by 7 % between 2009 and 2010, a rate similar to pre-crisis levels, the number of employees in the SME sector was significantly affected by the economic downturn. Between 2008 and 2010, the total number of employees in the SME sector decreased by 7 %. Recent data from Croatia allows for a more complex analysis of post-crisis levels of employment based on firm size. Between 2008 and 2010, the total number of employees in small enterprises fell by 33,483 while medium enterprises experienced a loss of 12,891. In Tables 2, 3, and 4 are given statistics of the SME sector in transition countries, evidence from Balkan countries, 2011.

Table 2 Number of the enterprises in Balkan countries, 2011

	Albania		Croatia		Macedonia		Montenegro		Serbia	
	Number	%	Number	%	Number	%	Number	%	Number	%
Micro	66166	95.8	130066	90.4	65841	92.8	20820	88.9	274021	95.9
Small	2386	3.5	1132	7.9	3706	5.2	2 083	8.9	6065	2.1
Medium	432	0.6	2048	1.4	1159	1.6	428	1.8	282259	0.8
SMEs	68984	99.9	143434	99.7	70 506	99.7	23332	99.6	484	98.8
Large	54	0.1	484	0.3	204	0.3	95	0.4	285641	0.2
Total	69038	100	143918	100	70710	100	23710	100		100

Source: SBA factsheets, 2011

Table 3 Value added in Million Euro, realized in SMEs of Balkan Countries, 2011

	Albania		Croatia		Serbia	
	Number	%	Number	%	Number	%
Micro	0.55	24.7 %	4	16.6 %	3	22.3 %
Small	0.41	18.4 %	5	20.2 %	2	15.7 %
Medium	0.31	13.9 %	5	20.3 %	3	18.3 %
SMEs	1.27	57 %	13	57.1 %	8	36.3 %
Large	0.96	43 %	10	42.9 %	6	43.7 %
Total	2.23	100 %	23	100 %	14	100 %

Source: SBA factsheets, 2011

Table 4 Employment realized in enterprises in Balkan Countries, 2011

	Albania		Croatia		Montenegro		Serbia	
	Number	%	Number	%	Number	%	Number	%
Micro	109894	45.9 %	305218	45.9 %	40078	20 %	377599	31.6 %
Small	45720	19.1 %	221155	19.1 %	40348	20.1 %	181814	15.2 %
Medium	40393	16,9 %	210785	16,9 %	43314	21.6 %	228071	19.1 %
SMEs	196007	81.8 %	737158	81.8 %	123738	61.6 %	787584	65.9 %
Large	43538	18.2 %	360391	18.2 %	76996	38.4 %	406845	34.1 %
Total	239545	100 %	1097549	100 %	200734	100 %	1194429	100 %

Source: SBA factsheets, 2011

Although a drastic loss of jobs in the wake of an economic crisis is to be expected, comparing this data with the number of emerging small and medium-sized firms during this same period reveals an interesting trend. While 7,197 new small enterprises were established between 2008 and 2010 in Croatia, the number of medium sized enterprises fell by 17 firms. Therefore, while the total number of employees working in small firms dramatically decreased, the number of new firms remained virtually unaffected by the crisis. This development could possibly be explained by the rise of necessity-driven entrepreneurs, possibly individuals who had lost their job as a result of the crisis, forming micro-enterprises. Apart from the emergence of a possible new group of necessity-driven entrepreneurs, the most significant impact of the crisis on the SME sector concerns the shrinking availability of financing for these companies. Banks tightened lending standards during the financial crisis while governments simultaneously increased their borrowing to cover deficits, resulting in a crowding out of financing for SMEs. In Serbia, even though financial support for SMEs increased in 2009, it was still insufficient to prevent a recession. As previous research has shown, financial constraints affect the smallest firms most adversely, and thus with the possible emergence of an even greater amount of these micro and small enterprises, as seen in Croatia, the difficulty in accessing finance will continue to be a major deterrent to the recovery of this important sector.

Table 5 Weighted score for Internationalisation of SMEs in Balkan countries as EU pre-accession economy and regional average

	Albania	Bosnia and Herzegovina	Croatia	Macedonia	Montenegro	Serbia	WBT average
Weighted average	3.25	2.25	4.00	3.75	3.25	4.25	3.50

Source: SBA assessment 2012

Internationalisation of SMEs in Balkan countries focused on government support towards promoting export-oriented SMEs and helping them access international markets is shown in Table 5.

In general, all of the economies have an export promotion policy and measures in place. However, the level of implementation of the strategies and financial allocation to export promotion activities vary throughout the pre-accession region. The most advanced economies are Croatia, Serbia, which provide a wide range of well-financed export promotion services. The governments of the Former Yugoslav Republic of Macedonia and Montenegro score slightly lower in this dimension, allocating less financial support and often relying on external donor funding. The export base in Bosnia and Herzegovina is still limited. Export promotion agencies in the Western Balkans should pay more attention to assisting SMEs to access foreign markets and become more internationally competitive. This could be done by enhancing their access to trade finance and export insurance and helping them obtain creditworthiness. Further support measures include providing international market information, finding international partners for research and development and implementing international quality standards. In addition, governments need to better co-ordinate and systematically monitor their export promotion activities to increase their efficiency.

3 Family Business in Serbia

The family businesses do have a great importance in contemporary market Serbian economy and this significance will be even higher in time.

Family business is a very old type of business activity in Serbia, especially in certain parts of the country with long tradition and entrepreneurial spirit, which is historically related to farmers, guilds, craftsmen, local traders, textile and shoes production, legal, medical, pharmaceutical, repairing professional services, etc. The level of connection between families and work is shown in the fact that before the industrial age families lived in the same space (buildings, farms, etc.) where they performed economic activity, and only with the industrialization and the increased number of paid workers who were not family members the family and work are separated.

Table 6 Number of family firms in total enterprises in 2012

Enterprise type	SMEs No.	Large No.	Total No.	SMEs structure (%)	FF out of enterprises structure (%)
Enterprise	91.030	506	91.536	28.8	20.0
Entrepreneur/solo trader	226.132	0	226.132	71.2	60.0
Total	317.162	506	317.668	100.0	100.0
Structure (%)	99.8	0.2	100.0		

Source: Serbian Business Registers Agency (Authors' calculation)

SMEs sector in Serbia in 2012 has got 317.162 enterprises, making 99.8 % of all enterprises in the country, 317. 668. 95.0 % are micro enterprises and solo traders, 62 % private owned. There is no official data on family businesses and firms in Serbia, but according to the sporadic analysis it can be projected that they make around 60–70 % of SMEs sector, mostly in professional businesses and services as solo traders or properties. Traditional family sectors are in processing industry, bred, drinks, fruit, and vegetables, milk production, than in textile and furniture production, chemical, pharmaceutics. The importance of the SMEs sector can be seen in the facts that they make 60 % of GDP, 70 % of employment, 65 % of GVA and 52 % of Serbian export (Table 6).

Family businesses most often start their business in further sectors: *Trade* (27.0 %), *Processing industry* (13.7 %), *Accommodation and food services* (12.1 %). In the sector of processing industry dominate low technology level family companies, with the share of 50 % with low profit margins and those in high technology sector are less than 9.5 % (Table 7).

In 2012, 10.672 SMEs of Processing industry and 10.096 from trade have realized 788.1 billion RSD in export, making 45.9 % of total export of non-financial sector and 89.8 % of the total SMEs export. Then:

- 29.5 % of all start-ups are initiated by existing family firms.
- 16.9 % of new firms are related to existing family firms.
- 17.8 % of established entrepreneurial firms are related to another family firm.
- 29.5 % of start-ups expect family ownership.

3.1 The Impact of Motives on the Internationalization of the Selected Family Firms from Serbia

In this part of the chapter are presented some of successful family businesses exporters from Serbia, mostly basing their success on traditionally high entrepreneurial index of the cities they come from, modern management style, innovation and high quality standards implementation.

Table 7 Indicators of family firms (SMEs) in processing industry (%)

Industry	No. of SMEs	FF out of SMEs structure (%)	No. of employees	Trade	GVA	Export	Import
SMEs in Processing industry	100.0	20.0	100.0	100.0	100.0	100.0	100.0
Low technology Food, drinks, tobacco, textile, furniture, paper production	62.8	80.0	58.5	54.4	51.4	49.6	37.2
Medium technology sectors	27.8	10.0	25.2	25.4	26.8	28.7	29.6
Medium-high technology sectors Chemic, electro, motor, travel equipment and products production	6.5	6.0	12.7	14.3	16.7	18.6	21.8
High technology sectors Pharmacy, optics, computers and electro products production	2.9	4.0	3.5	5.9	5.1	3.2	11.5

Source: Authors' calculation based on Serbian Business Registers Agency data, 2012

CINI Cacak

CINI Cacak is a privately owned company, 100 % family business, established in 1977 in Cacak, Serbia. Cacak used to be one of the leading cities with the highest entrepreneurial index, and great tradition in family business. At the very beginning CINI defined business orientation as development through wide range of products and appropriate growth of production, which has been approved and maintained during the 30 years of firm existence. CINI today represents an example of successful Serbian manufacturing metal company with a range of its own products, mainly in the field of thermo techniques. CINI employs 90 workers, out of which 40 % have higher education (engineers of different profiles, economists, lawyers). Thanks to them, as well as to a lot of different types of qualified workers, business organization covers all phases of product realization through its own development, purchasing, manufacture, marketing, sales and post-purchase service department. The concept that CINI strives to:

- Application of patents;
- Innovations;
- New technologies implementation.

The company has always been supported of young, creative and successful people. In top management are the members of the founder family Spasovic, managing the company in the change and modern management style, respecting long tradition and skills, which enable them to run business efficiently, and at the same time make CINI a suitable partner for business collaboration in different areas and levels. All aspects of business are based on high quality standard set by ISO 9000-2000, which assures quality of products through documented procedures and work processes as well as their strict application. Special attention is paid to professional business communication, advertising, active participations on domestic and foreign fairs, but also to direct presentations to potential customer groups. Most of the products have export potential, and some of them have already secured a good position on the markets in Russia, Ukraine, Poland, Bulgaria, BIH, Croatia and Macedonia, but also on developed markets of Sweden, Denmark, Germany and Spain. According to resources and abilities of CINI, following ways of collaboration are developed:

- Placement of finished products in both direction;
- Joint development and efficient conquest of new products;
- Manufacturing of certain parts and components;
- Complete mounting and final analysis of products in CINI;
- Post-purchase service in guarantee and after-guarantee period;
- Transfer of commonly manufactured products to the markets of ex east European block, where CINI is already present;
- Setting up and coordination of collaboration and conduct of cooperation with other Serbian enterprises, on requested level.

The internationalization of the business has been motivated by luck of finance.

"Extremeintimo" Company
Extremeintimo was founded in 1992, as family business, in Arilje, Serbia. Arilje is a branded small city for biggest group of private textile family firms. The Company is medium-size company. It is textile industry production. Endeavours creation business of modern items, from underwear, nightwear and swimming costumes, with good design very popular at the market. Export retail network covers several countries, Montenegro, Bosnia-Herzegovina, Croatia, Slovenia, Macedonia, Russia, Czech Republic and South Africa. Most important motive for internationalisation of the business of this family firm is luck of new technology.

Ivancic & Sons Company
Ivancic & Sons company has been founded in 1991 in Belgrade, Serbia, as a company that manufactures and markets pharmaceutical products. That same year the first Ivancic & Sons pharmacy was open for business, followed by the second in 2000, the third in 2004, and the fourth in 2007. Company has 128 employees on long term contracts: 65 in production, 34 in management, 15 pharmacists and 14 pharmaceutical technicians. The company's pharmacies are reputable health institutions, with tradition, and HACCP system implemented. The manufacturing facilities are located in Stari Banovci, while the management, including marketing, sales and purchasing department, rests in a stylish location in Belgrade.

High quality of 22 products, medicine and dietary supplements (both in capsule and powder forms), created using the latest in medical technology and contemporary packaging design, and made the firm very recognised at the market.

Modern technology based management style promotes teamwork, strong work dynamics, modern organization and, above all, expertise. To that effect, more than third of the employees are highly qualified, primarily in the fields of medicine, pharmacy and pharmaceutical technologies. Continuous professional education is one of the tasks presented before all employees in the company. Following the global trends in the fields of medicine, pharmacy and pharmaceutical technologies, as well as implementing new ideas, is a priority in the company's development plans, marketing, packaging designs of new products, as well as recognizable advertisements, which convey a clear message to the consumers. Placing a new product on the market is based on original ideas, years of experience, as well as application of the latest expert findings. Marketing activities are aimed toward expert public and toward the ultimate consumers alike. Export retail network covers huge number of foreign countries. Most important motive for internationalisation of the business of this family firm is luck of new technology.

"Nektar" Company

The Company has been established in 1990 as a small family venture in fruit processing industry. In 2013 the Company became the biggest fruit juice maker in the region and the fruit processor in the South East Europe with a production capacity of 120.000 tons per a season, and the biggest exporter. Nektar has the most important international quality certificates, most modern technology and a complete production process- from growing, through fruit processing to the product. It is well known as organic producer with the Organic Control System and the German BCS Eco Guarantee, in tune production tuned with the requirements of the Organic certification. Apart from keeping up with current global trends, Nektar is a leader in creating new market tendencies, mainly based on innovations and technology management style, where beside the family are engaged a number of high qualified manages, experts and specialists. Most important motives for internationalisation of the business of this family firm are luck of new technology and finance.

4 The Business Environment for the Family Firms Internationalization in Serbia

The Macroeconomic ambient for Family businesses in Serbia is further characterized by set of indicators of doing business and competitiveness, what is illustrated in Tables 8 and 9.

General rank of comparable working ambient for family firms is ease of doing business is 93, out of 189 economies.

Table 8 Some elements of easy of doing business for family firms (SME) in Serbia, 2013

	Rank	Procedures (number)	Time (days)	Cost To export (US$ per container)	Cost To import (US$ per container)	Time To import (days)	Documents To import (number)
Trading across borders	98	6	12	1,455	1,760	15	7

Source. Doing Business, World Bank 2013

Table 9 Some indicators of Global Competitiveness Index (GCI) for Serbia, 2013–2014 (of importance for family businesses internationalization motives)

GCI 2013–2014	Rank	Score
Efficiency enhancers (50.0 %)	92	3.8
Higher education and training	83	4.0
Labor market efficiency	119	3.9
Financial market development	115	3.5
Technology readiness	60	3.9
Goods market efficiency	132	3.6
Market size	69	3.7

Source: The Global Competitiveness Report 2013–2014, World Economic Forum

According the Competitiveness Index, Serbia has been at 101th position in 2013- out of 145 countries (OECD, 2012).

The most problematic factors for Family firms (FF) according to field research realized in 2013 by Employers Association are: very high corruption in the country (13.8), inefficient government bureaucracy (13.1), access to financing (11.1), government instability coups (10.9), inadequate supply of infrastructure (7.3), poor work ethic in national labor force (3.3), inadequate educated workforce (3.1).

4.1   The Family Business Support Infrastructure

Through business support infrastructure is often mentioned in specialized literature and the official documents of different levels of authorities, there is no unique definition of this term. The term "business support infrastructure" includes a network of institutions and organizations providing services to potential entrepreneurs, entrepreneurs or small- and medium-sized enterprises for the development of their business capacity (human, organizational, marketing, etc.) or providing physical facilities for business operations. In terms of capacity, structure and purpose, business support infrastructure should be in accordance with local and regional development potential, as well as market demands. The primary goal of business support infrastructure development is the overall economic development at local, regional and national level, with a special emphasis on polycentric development.

Business support infrastructure operations are often geographically limited, mostly to municipalities and cities, but sometimes also to broader geographical units, such as districts and regions. Business support infrastructure rarely provides services across the whole territory of a country, which is also the case in the Republic of Serbia.

The business support infrastructure mostly includes business incubators, clusters, industrial zones and technology parks, active on different territorial levels and spread throughout the Republic Development of business support infrastructure in Serbia is in line with the processes of economic transformation towards a market-oriented economy. The pioneering steps in business support infrastructure development were initiated through the project interventions of numerous international organizations, and later on continued through the activities of the line ministry, the National Agency for Regional Development and many development agencies and associations active at a national, provincial/regional or local level. In many cases business infrastructure was developed without receiving support from the public institutions, based on the initiative of private agencies, nongovernmental organizations, or as individual initiatives by people who wanted to put their personal effort into the promotion of economic development in their communities.

Strengthening of business infrastructure is part of many strategic and programme documents of the Government of the Republic of Serbia, the Government of the Autonomous Province of Vojvodina, and local governments. Business infrastructure development has mostly been recognized through its contribution to the competitiveness of small and medium-sized enterprises and entrepreneurship, and family businesses inside of it, and is consequently mentioned in official documents and programmes in that context. However, it should be emphasized that there is no unique document focused only on business infrastructure development, and this field is divided between several strategic documents and programmes. One of the first documents dealing with business support infrastructure development is the National Economic Development Strategy of the Republic of Serbia for the period 2006–2012, as the first development document consistently and comprehensively defining the basic development priorities of the country and the ways to achieve them in the following years.

The Ministry of Economy, Serbian Agency for the Development of Small and Medium-sized Enterprises and Entrepreneurship and the Norwegian organisation SINTEF prepared the Programme for Development of Business Incubators and Clusters 2007–2010, which included recommendations for the establishment of at least 15 business incubators and the national umbrella association of business incubators, the establishment of at least one technology park and ten clusters. This document is linked to the implementation of the SME and Entrepreneurship Development Strategy 2003–2008, National Economic Development Strategy 2006–2012, as well as the Serbian Government's Plan for Promotion of Small and Medium-sized Enterprises and Entrepreneurship 2005–2007. National Agency for Regional Development established in 2009 is a legal successor of the Serbian Agency for the Development of Small and Medium-sized Enterprises and Entrepreneurship.

The Strategy for Development of Competitive and Innovative Small and Medium-sized Enterprises for the period 2008–2013 also supports the implementation of programmes for the development of business incubators and clusters and emphasizes the necessity to improve institutional support for the development of entrepreneurship and small- and medium-sized enterprises. The Regional Development Strategy of the Republic of Serbia for the period 2007–2012 is the first strategic development document focused on regional development in Serbia, with the goal to improve polycentric regional development of Serbia through entrepreneurship and SME development policies in Serbia, in order to reduce differences in regional development through better economic links among regions (cluster associations and connections between enterprises, establishment of business and technology incubators in local municipalities and science and technology parks in university centres. The recently adopted Strategy of Industrial Development of the Republic of Serbia 2011–2020 also considers the necessity to develop business support infrastructure in its section focusing on regional development. According to this Strategy, the term "business support infrastructure" includes mapping, constructing and equipping industrial zones, industrial parks, business incubators, clusters, logistic and business centres and tourist infrastructure. It is important to underline that this Strategy provides the first map of business support infrastructure in the Republic of Serbia. The need for business support infrastructure development is also recognized by those EU institutions that have, in different ways, supported numerous project initiatives throughout the Republic of Serbia. In addition to that, business support infrastructure is recognized as one of the measures for the development of competitiveness within the Economic Development Operational Programme 2012–2013 of IPA component III. Business support infrastructure development has been significantly contributed to by many bilateral organizations, funded by the Government of the Kingdom of Norway, that initiated the development of business incubators and clusters in Serbia, as well USAID who have been active in this field for several years through several projects, the Government of the Kingdom of Denmark through the LEDIB programme, implemented in the territory of Nišava District, and finally the Austrian Development Agency, active in business incubator development in Vojvodina. Development of business support infrastructure was also supported by several other donor programmes, EU projects including SECEP, RSEDP 2 and MISP, GIZ Private Sector Development Projects WBF (later ACCESS), LEDIB project funded by the Danish Government, BBI project funded by the Austrian Government and the USAID project "Competitiveness".

In order to increase competitiveness of SMEs and family businesses as their part, it is necessary to target specific regions, and through development and transformation of business infrastructure and by establishing industrial and technology parks and industrial zones, to identify independent, private companies, specialized in a certain field, and linked through joint technology and knowledge. The concentration of similar and/or complementary business activities in an area, with mutual synergy effects and joint strategic approaches, enables a dynamic development of those activities, through competitive products. When selecting the basic direction of economic development, an advantage is given to those activities where available resources, market conditions and technical advancements provide for a faster development. This analysis identified 23 business incubators, 85 cluster initiatives, 92 industrial zones, 2 existing and 4 planned industrial and technology parks, 4 existing and 4 planned free zones and 66 brown-field locations in Serbia.

4.1.1 Financial Support

Entrepreneurs mostly rely on their own sources of finance. Around 70 % of SMEs are financed from their own sources, both in case of working capital (73 %), or investments (69 %). It could be indicated a decreasing trend of entrepreneurs taking loans to implement investment plans. External sources of finance are used by 26 % of SMEs which is 18 % less than in 2013, or 10 % less than in 2010.

Medium-sized (39 %) and small enterprises (33 %) use external sources more to finance investments, as well as working capital. On the regional level, entrepreneurs from South and East Serbia take least loans both for working capital and for investments.

Of external sources of revenues, commercial banks' loans are used the most (48 %), followed by, but significantly less, loans from state funds (14 %) and foreign loans (10 %). Loans from banks are followed by loans from relatives and friends (8 %). Loans from commercial banks are mostly used by medium-sized (64 %) and small enterprises (58 %), whereas sole traders mostly rely on relatives and family (Fig. 1). More than half of SMEs do not have loans, of which the least debtors are among micro enterprises and sole traders (58 %) and in Belgrade Region (56 %). Small and medium-sized enterprises with loans mostly successfully pay it off, and medium-sized enterprises have more delays in annuity payments. Loan payment periods, and short deadlines to fulfill obligations still present some of

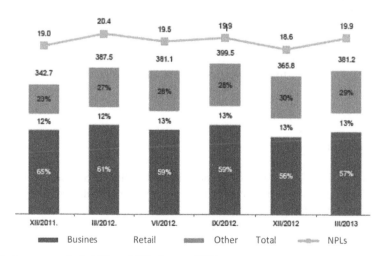

Fig. 1 Loans growth (in billions RSD). Source: NBS

Table 10 Financial incentives by type of company, by purpose in Serbia, in RSD, 2013

Type of financial incentive	2013	Type of beneficiary	2013	Purpose	
Total regional development incentives	173,661,103	Large companies	52,609,547	Employment	4,101,315
Loan	136,717,134	SMEs	22,696,597	Export	5,361,510
Non-returnable subsidy	12,789,463	Entrepreneur (solo trader)	361,501	Manufacture	11,273,268
For attracting investments	1,052,198	Agricultural holdings	3,682,339	Agriculture	4,697,158
Non-returnable resources	263,059	Business incubator/cluster	9,888	R&D	7,833,035
				Education, science, sport infrastructure	3,454,514

Source: Serbian Business Registers Agency, 2013

the most frequent financial problems in business operations, especially for smaller business entities. More than a half (53 %) of entrepreneurs fulfill their obligations towards suppliers within less than 30 days, and only 32 % manage to collect their payments in the same period of time.

According to the field research of the Serbian Business Registers Agency, *2013*S, SMEs are interested in state support programs (58.6 %), primarily those of financial nature (54.5 %). Details are shown in Table 10. The biggest interest for support is in medium-sized enterprises, and the smallest in micro enterprises and sole traders. Small enterprises show more interest in consulting and training compared to other types of surveyed business entities. Subsidies for improved business operations are the most favorable state support programs for two thirds of entrepreneurs, and mostly in West Serbia and Sumadija (72 %). They are followed by subsidies for job creation, which have the most interest from small enterprises (42 %).

4.1.2 Advisory Services

According to the field research of Employers Association of Serbia (2013), SMEs, among them family firms have ranked their business aspects like: advisory services have so far been used by 39 % of respondents; free services were mostly used in the field of business start-up consulting (33.5 %), marketing/promotion and sales trainings, then business planning, legal services and training for computer skills. On the other hand, entrepreneurs most often paid for services in accounting (64 %), legal services (59.5 %) marketing/promotion and sales (35.6 %), work safety and protection (31.1 %) and information technologies (23.5 %). Ranking the different aspects of their business, SMEs are most successful by the quality of their products/ services, qualifications of their employees and relations with business partners. Most problems they have are related to payment collection and financial aspects (financial stability) and competitiveness in the market. According to the opinion of half of respondents, in order to have a more successful business, payment collection should be improved first (48 %) and the financial aspect of company's business operations (47 %). Market demand (40 %) is ranked third, and market competi- tiveness (33 %) fourth among priorities for improvement.

4.1.3 Human Resources and Technology Aspects

An innovation is the implementation of new or significantly improved product, service or process, a new marketing method, or a new organizational method in business practices, workplace organization or external relations (OECD, 2005). A business entity can have several types of innovative activities in the defined period. Some field research results on innovation of SMEs in 2013 are shown in Table 11.

There are 65 accredited higher schools of professional studies (state and private) in Serbia with 378 study programs, /more than 50 % study programs are in the field of technical and technological sciences with a very different distribution. In the state schools TTS programs are dominant, with 61 %, private schools realize predominantly study programs in social sciences and humanities (66 %). According to the Scientific field in the period of 2008–2012, there were in HSS 21.384 students, in TTS 26.343, and in medical scientific field (MS) 2.262 students. By

Table 11 Business entities (technological innovators) that reported high importance of the source of innovation information

Sources		Total	Small	Medium
Internal	With the business entity or group it belongs to	32.25	31.06	35.88
Market	Suppliers	16.86	15.53	20.89
	Clients or customers	24.60	22.99	29.50
	Competitors or other business entities in the industry	10.07	8.58	14.60
	Consultants, business research agencies/IR	6.28	5.84	7.64
Institutional	Universities/higher education institutions	4.58	3.60	7.54
	State or Public Scientific Institutes	2.59	2.17	6.58
Other	Conferences, trade fairs, exhibitions	14.75	14.64	15.09
	Scientific magazines and technical publications	9.86	9.76	10.15
	Professional and industry associations	5.49	4.86	7.93

Source: NARD, 2013

Law, all education providers (including VET) have to establish an internal *Quality Assurance and Evaluation Commission.*

5 Access to Skilled Labour, Finance and New Technology as Motives for Family Firms Internationalization

In this part of the paper are presented some of main results of testing family firms motives for internationalization like: luck of access to finance, skilled labour and new technology as situation which move family firms to internationalize their business. Internationalization is defined as being involved in exports, imports and/or foreign direct investments (including joint ventures abroad).

5.1 Methodology and Data

The hypotheses are tested by means of binomial logistic regression analysis. The analyses are based on a sample of 98 family firms from Serbia. Information was obtained from the family SMEs owner/managers through field research survey held in 2013, for the period 2010–2013, as activity and results of the firm. The survey used a disproportionate stratified sample by, sector and size class and therefore does not (directly) reflect the structure of the Serbian SME sector. However, this does not bias the regression estimates since control variables are included sector and size class, i.e. the stratification dimensions.

Dependent variables. Dependent variables are constructed for internationalization for the following motives: *access to new knowledge and technology, access to labor and access to finance.* With the motive to access the specific resource abroad:

- *Perceived lack of skilled labor*, (Coded 1 when an owner/manager of the family firm indicates that lack of skilled labor has been a main constraint on the firm's performance over the past 2 years and otherwise coded 0.
- *Perceived lack of access to /finance*, (Coded 1 when an owner/manager of the family firm indicates that lack of access to finance has been a main constraint on the firm's performance over the past 2 years and otherwise coded 0);
- *Perceived lack of new technology/know now*, (Coded 1 when an owner/manager of the family firm indicates that lack of new technology/know how has been a main constraint on the firm's performance over the past 2 years and otherwise coded 0.)

In the survey the owners/managers were asked to indicate how important each of these motives was for the internationalization of their family business. Indicating the motive as "very important" or "important" this family firm was classified into the category "internationalization with the motive to access the specific resource".

For each of the three internationalization motives two dummy variables are constructed, one with "no internationalization" as the reference category, and one with "internationalization without the motive to access the specific resource" as the reference category.

The following control variables are included in the analysis: *Log firm size*—This variable is expressed in terms of (natural log of) number of employees; *Industry dummies*—Industry dummies are constructed for the following industries: manufacturing, wholesale, business and personal services.

5.2 Findings

The regression results are reported in Tables 12 and 13. The tables present log odds ratios and odds ratios. When the coefficient of the odds ratio is above unity (which corresponds to a log odds ratio above zero) this implies that the corresponding variable increases the odds of belonging to the category in question relative to the reference category.

Figures 2 and 3 display results for internationalization with the motive "access to labor" as the dependent variable and perceived lack of labor as the explanatory variable; Figs. 4 and 5 display results for internationalization with the motive "access to finance" as the dependent variable and perceived lack of access to finance as the explanatory variable, and Figs. 6 and 7 display results for internationalization with the motive "access to new technology and know-how" as the dependent variable and perceived lack of new technology as the explanatory variable.

The results indicate that perceived lack of labor, finance and new technology increases the odds for a family SME to be internationally active with the motive to access labor, finance and new technology (relative, both to not internationalizing and to internationalizing without the motive to access labor, finance and new technology).

Table 12 Basic parameters of key variables and perceived family business constrains

Variable	Mean	Standard deviation	O.R.	Log O.R.
Motives for internationalization				
Access to skilled labour	0.313	0.464	0.4556	−0.7861
Access to finance	0.563	0.496	1.2883	0.2533
Access to new technology/know how	0.569	0.495	1.3202	0.2778
Perceived family business constrains				
Luck of skilled labour	0.342	0.474	0.5198	−0.6544
Luck of access to finance	0.628	0.483	1.6882	0.5236
Luck of new technology/know how	0.392	0.488	0.6447	−0.4389

Source: Survey results, author's calculations, 2014

Table 13 Binomial logistic regression results for internationalization with three motives

Variables	Access to skilled labor		Access to finance		Access to new technology	
	O.R.	Log O.R.	O.R.	Log O.R.	O.R.	Log O.R.
Dependent variable : Internationalization with access to: (Reference category: no internationalization)						
1. Luck of skilled labour	1.141	0.132	0.403	−0.908	0.394	−0.932
2. Luck of finance	3.705	1.310	1.310	0.270	1.279	0.246
3. Luck of new technology/ know how	1.415	0.347	0.500	−0.692	0.488	−0.717
Controls						
Industry-manufacturing	1.463	0.381	5.268	1.662	18.965	2.943
Wholesale	0.732	−0.312	2.634	0.968	9.482	2.249
Business services	1.182	0.167	4.255	1.448	15.318	2.729
Firm size (log)	3.292	1.192	11.85	2.473	42.670	3.754
Regression constant	0.775	−0.254	2.193	0.785	2.247	0.810

Source: Survey results, author's calculations, 2014

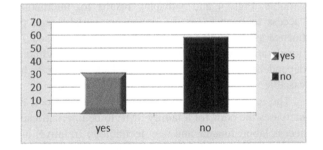

Fig. 2 FF Internationalization with the motive "access to labor". Source: Survey results, author's calculations, 2014

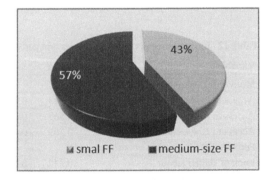

Fig. 3 FF Internationalization with the motive "access to labor", by SME size. Source: Survey results, author's calculations, 2014

Fig. 4 FF Internationalization with the motive "access to finance". Source: Survey results, author's calculations, 2014

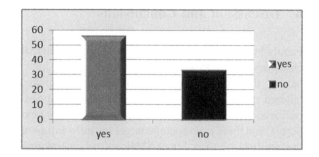

Fig. 5 FF Internationalization with the motive "access to finance", by SME size. Source: Survey results, author's calculations, 2014

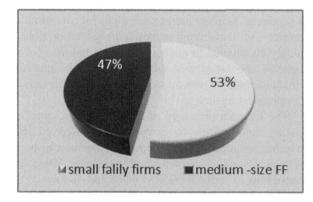

Fig. 6 FF Internationalization with the motive "access to new technology". Source: Survey results, author's calculations, 2014

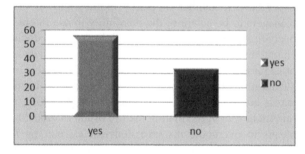

Fig. 7 FF Internationalization with the motive "access to new technology", by SME size. Source: Survey results, author's calculations, 2014

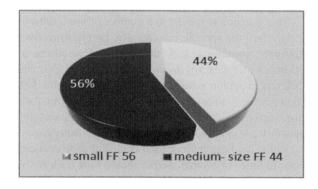

6 Discussion and Conclusions

Family businesses are the backbone of the Serbian real economy and incubators for entrepreneurship. Productivity, competitiveness, job creation and sustainability are part of their success and development, as well as of institutional support and tailored qualitative services. There is an unbalanced geographical distribution of business, innovative, financial and educational support infrastructure elements in Serbia, and there is no specific target business infrastructure which supports exactly the family businesses, but as SMEs sector general approach. It is more significantly distributed in five large cities in Serbia: Belgrade, Novi Sad, Niš, Subotica and Kragujevac. Some of numerous reasons for concentration in these cities include the presence of donor programmes and regional or SME development agencies that jointly contributed to raising awareness and the idea about the need for development of business support infrastructure. In the analysis of business support infrastructure could be seen an weak link between clusters, incubators, universities and development agencies.

The research presented in this paper on resource-seeking internationalization among family firms by investigating, based on resource dependency theory, whether resource-seeking internationalization can be linked to a SME's resource deficiencies, has confirmed given hypothesis. These results suggest that perceived constraints in terms of skilled labor and finance are pushing firms to overcome internal resource deficiencies through internationalization. The findings of this paper have a number of policy implications. It is important for SME owner/ managers to be aware of the possibility to use internationalization as a means for overcoming resource constraints. Policy makers could help to increase awareness among resource-constrained firms that internationalization as a means for accessing or acquiring resources has become a (more) feasible option, given that internationalization has become easier and resources have become more easily transferable across borders (Autio, 2005; Sapienza et al., 2006); policy makers could play an important role in facilitating the use of international activities by family firms as a means to overcome resource deficiencies, e.g. by facilitating the formation of alliances with foreign partners for the use of foreign resources (for instance through matchmaking) or by removing constraining regulation, such as restrictions on the free movement of labor.

This research is subject to a number of limitations too: not being able to provide insight into the specific reasons why family firms owner/managers are perceiving resource constraints; how the stocks of resources available in home and host countries affect family firms' involvement in internationalization, not looking at differences within industries, (Westhead, Wright, & Ucbasaran 2001) found that resource constraints are significantly more relevant for manufacturing firms than for firms active in the construction and services sector), etc. Future research could benefit from undertaking industry-specific analyses.

Serbia has been built on their contribution to economic and social prosperity, and now, in times of trouble, Serbia should look back to its roots, valuing and fostering the necessary role of family businesses as a reliable and committed driving force for recovery and new employment creation through pushing qualitative doing business ambient for internationalization.

References

Autio, E. (2005). Report on high expected entrepreneurship, global entrepreneurship monitor.

Barringer, B. R., & Harrison, J. S. (2000). Walking a tightrope: Creating value through interorganizational relationships. *Journal of Management, 26*(3), 367–403.

Chrisman, J. J., Chua, H., & Litz, R. A. (2003). A unified systems perspective of family firm performance: An extension and integration. *Journal of Business Venturing, 18*(5), 467–472.

Dana, L. P. (2010). *When economies change hands: A survey of entrepreneurship in the emerging markets of Europe from the Balkans to the Baltic states.* New York and Oxford: Routledge.

Dana, L. P., & Dana, T. (2003). Management and enterprise development in post-communist economies. *International Journal of Management and Enterprise Development, 1*(1), 45–54.

Grozdanic, R. (2005). Efekti preduzetničkog sektora malih i srednjih preduzeća u Srbiji sredinom 2005. godine. *Ekonomski vidici 10*(3): 237–246.

Grozdanic, R., Radovic-Markovic, M., Vucic, M. (2009). Entrepreneurship in Serbia: Women as entrepreneurs, Chapter 16. The new economy: Challenges, opportunities and choices. http://www.iabooks.com/servlet/iaGetBiblio?bno=38433o. Accessed 28 Nov 2014.

Habbershon, T. G., & Williams, M. L. (1999). A resource-based framework for assessing the strategic advantages of family firms. *Family Business Review, 12*(1), 1–21.

Habbershon, T. G., Williams, M. L., & MacMillan, I. C. (2003). A unified systems perspective of family firm performance. *Journal of Business Venturing, 18*(4), 451–465.

Katila, R., & Mang, P. (2003). Exploiting technological opportunities: The timing of collaborations. *Research Policy, 32*, 317–332.

Kuemmerle, W. (2002). Home base and knowledge management in international new ventures. *Journal of Business Venturing, 17*(2), 99–122.

Mandl, I. (2008). Overview of family business relevant issues, Vienna.

Miller, D., & Le Breton-Miller, I. (2006a). Family governance and firm performance: Agency, stewardship, and capabilities. *Family Business Review, 21*(1), 73–87.

Miller, D., & Le Breton-Miller, I. (2006b). Priorities, practices, and strategies in successful and failing family business: An elaboration and test of the configuration perspective. *Strategic Organization, 4*(4), 379–407.

OECD. (2005). *Oslo manual: Guidelines for collecting and interpreting innovation data* (3rd ed.). Paris: OECD.

OECD. (2012). SME policy index: Western Balkans and Turkey 2012: Progress in the implementation of the small business act for Europe, OECD Publishing. 10.1787/9789264178861-en.

Oviatt, B. M., & McDougall, P. P. (1994). Toward a theory of international new ventures. *Journal of International Business Studies, 24*, 45–64.

Radović-Marković, M. Nelson-Porter, B., Grozdanic, R. (2013) Rural women innovation and entrepreneurship in transition countries, International Conference *Contemporary. Research on Organization Management and Administration* 2013, No. 1 ISSN (online) 2335-7959, pp. 86–97.

Ramadani, V., & Dana, L.-P. (2013). The state of entrepreneurship in the Balkans: Evidence from selected countries. In V. Ramadani & R. C. Schneider (Eds.), *Entrepreneurship in the Balkans* (pp. 217–250). Berlin: Springer.

Sapienza, H. J., Autio, E., George, G., & Zahra, S. A. (2006). A capabilities perspective on the effects of early internationalization on firm survival and growth. *Academy of Management Review, 31*(4), 914–933.

Schulze, W., & Gedajlovic, E. (2010, March).Whither family business? *Journal of Management Studies, 47*, 2.

Westhead, P., Wright, M., & Ucbasaran, D. (2001). The internationalization of new and small firms. A resource-based view. *Journal of Business Venturing, 16*(4), 333–358.

Entering New Markets: Strategies for Internationalization of Family Businesses

Gadaf Rexhepi

Abstract Having in consideration that almost all family businesses face with the problem of their growth after e period of time especially when they reach its maturity phase they need to enter new markets in order to continue its growth. These and lots of other reason influence family businesses to become part of globalization and follow the trend of most of the successful family businesses in the world who have internationalize their activities. This chapter focuses on the possible strategies that enterprises can use in order to perform in the international markets. The objectives of the study are to examine how to enter in new markets by using the best appropriate strategies in order to achieve competitive advantage in international markets. Expect theoretical analysis and suggestion on strategies for internationalization an empirical research has been done in 75 family businesses in Albania. The final results showed that as the best strategy for the Albanian family businesses for entering in international markets is export strategy, mainly because of the current economic situation in Albania (cheap working force, very qualified working force, etc.) this strategy can produce competitive advantage for Albanian family businesses in entering new markets.

Keywords Internationalization strategy • Export strategy • Multistate strategy • Licensing strategy • Franchising strategy • Global strategy • Albania

1 Introduction

Before entering into the field of finding the best strategies for enterprises entering in international markets, I will try to briefly describe the Albanian economy. This because even though that we are discussing about strategies for internationalization of family businesses in general, operating this businesses in developed country is different than operating it in a under-developed country or post-communist country such is Albania.

G. Rexhepi (✉)
Faculty of Business and Economics, South-East European University, Tetovo, Macedonia
e-mail: g.rexhepi@seeu.edu.mk

© Springer International Publishing Switzerland 2015   293
L.-P. Dana, V. Ramadani (eds.), *Family Businesses in Transition Economies*,
DOI 10.1007/978-3-319-14209-8_14

Albania has a population of approximately 3.2 million inhabitants' but a lot of Albanians migrate mainly in Greece, Italy and all around the world. Located in the Balkan Peninsula, in southeastern Europe, Albania is one of the oldest nations in the region. It inherited many natural resources and an authentic culture and tradition. Historic and political events left this small country on the Adriatic coast for 500 years under the Ottoman Empire, which did not stimulate development and prosperity. After the Second World War it joined the European communist bloc, followed by 45 years of autocratic rule and extremely self-isolated policy. Albania entered the fight to create a democratic society and a market economy in the beginning of 1990 (Muço, 1999). Albania even though it exist as a state from the year 1912 its first pluralistic election were held on 1991, but since then the country had face a very turbulent political climate which had influence on the economic condition. In this first pluralistic election the democratic anti communistic party won, and immediately they started with some changes that in the beginning seemed that Albania will be very soon prospering.

Albania has been a communist country from 1945 till 1991 and almost all of this period it has been under the dictatorship. During the 45 years of communist rule Albania had become a very rigorously centralized economy. Central planning had virtually replaced all forms of market mechanisms. Within the context of 5-year plans, all economic decisions on production, pricing, wage setting, investment and external trade were centralized, while changes between the plans were generally minimal. A four-tier, decision-making hierarchy was instituted starting with the Council of Ministers and followed by Branch Ministries, Executive Committees and state enterprises. All economic information was strictly reported vertically, and the decision making center was the central authorities (Muço, 1999). Albania was under soviet domination but only until Enver Hoxha become a president who alien Albania to China. During the Hoxha's presidentship he banned some products such as bananas, beards, bright colors, foreign journals, most imports and religion (Dana, 1996). Only after the death of the dictator Hoxha in 1985 when the president of Albania become Ramiz Alia for the first time some very small scope for small businesses and introduced some liberal reforms including the multiparty political system (Dana, 1996; Ramadani & Dana, 2013).

Even though that Albania started to improve it institution still its GDP is one of the poorest in the region. Albania's GDP purchasing Power Parity is estimated to be only 25 % of EU countries. Another problem with Albanian economy is the Gini coefficient who showed that economic inequality had continue to increase (from 20 had jump to 34), also there are significant disparities between urban and rural areas (Muço, 1999). Albania also had a very high rate of informal economy which in 2012 was estimated from 35 to 40 % (Muço, 1999). Albanian economic system is a very open and this was the reason that the economic crises influence the Albanian economy also, especially the economic crises that captured Greece as neighboring country where about 700.000 Albanians migrate (Muço, 1999). Adding to the confusion is the fact that under strict Communism, all forms of entrepreneurship were deemed immoral and illegal. Now, entrepreneurship has been authorized, and the immoral aspect has been lifted. Regrettably, a serious problem has developed in this new interpretation where a prostitute is still a profitable export (Dana & Dana, 2003).

The last decade is considered as one of the most successful decade in the contest of consolidation of macro-economic indicators (Sicignano & Capurso, 2011). Today Albania has made much progress in its transition into a political democratic regime and a market economy and in re-establishing relations with the world after many years of isolation (Yujnovsky & Mece, 2006). Emerging in modern times from 50 years of the most isolationist totalitarian regime was a decisive factor why the new political leadership supported a neo-classical or neo-liberal economic perspective on development. This approach, which dramatically shrinks the role of the state and liberalizes the participation of private sector, played an important role in terms of future institutional reforms in Albania (Konda, 2003). In 1992 the unemployment rate has been 50 % but just after 2 years it went down to 30 % (Dana, 1996) and today this percentage is under 20 %. The most positive achievement for Albania was its inclusion as NATO member state and visa liberalization from 2009 respectively 2010 which came after a very hard process.

2 Reasons for Internationalization

According to the KPMG report in 2009 the GDP growth was 5–10 % not only in China, India and Brazil, but also in Turkey, Indonesia, Mexico, parts of Eastern Europe and the Middle East which continues still to grove in most of these countries. The basic economic logic says that companies should always use an opportunity and this is a great opportunity for businesses to start and expand their business into new markets. Identifying the less developed economic regions and harnessing their potential could be a winning strategy (KPMG, 2011).

Even though that internationalization of family isn't the first thing that will come up in mind when you think on how to grow family businesses still internationalization of family business can play a crucial role on its growth and creation of competitive advantage. This is mainly because family businesses have been percept as domestic businesses. Family business needs to be seen as separate businesses entity in selecting strategies for internationalization and that's why it is important to identify their specific features in the context of internationalization (Kontinen & Ojala, 2010).

It is very important to ask the question will going outside current state borders influence the current economic performance of SMEs. Several studies have indicated that internationalization is often accompanied by improved firm performance, growth and competitiveness. In addition, the subsequent larger sales volumes enable firms to achieve economies of scale and increase labour productivity and management efficiency. There is convincing evidence from researcher that efficient firms become exporters: exporters are larger, more productive and have higher employment growth before their first exporting activities (Onkelinx & Sleuwaegen, 2010).

There are several reasons why family businesses enter in the international market, among which as most important are (Thompson et al., 2007, p.163):

- *Securing access to new customers*—this is most commonly used incentives from enterprises that are in the maturity stage and where the opportunities for expanding in the domestic market are limited. Companies like Cisco Systems, Dell, Sony, Nokia, Avon and Toyota are constantly trying to penetrate every corner of the global market.
- *Achieving lower costs and enhance of competitiveness of enterprises*—usually small markets are the reason for not using the productive potential of enterprises. This cause's higher production cost, i.e. higher prices which makes the products of those companies uncompetitive in the market.
- *Capitalization of its core activity*—the company can exploit its competitive advantage which it has in the domestic market, using the benefits of their own competencies and capabilities. Wall-Mart used his expertise in the retail discounts and successfully expanded into China, Latin America and parts of Europe.
- *Risk diversification*—the company's expansion in different regions affects the reduction of risk of failure comparing with the case when enterprises act only in domestic market.

These are just some of the most important reasons that motivate family businesses to perform in the international market although the number of reasons is much greater.

The first decision that family businesses need to make when they perform in international market is to decide whether the new created companies to operate autonomously or their management will be controlled by central organization. Selecting the first or the second option would reflect the final choice of strategies for these family businesses. Other important aspects that family businesses should have in mind in terms of strategies for internationalization are (Thompson et al., 2007):

- Evaluation of differences between countries in terms of culture, demographic and market conditions,
- Costs associated with the location,
- The effect of differences in exchange rate,
- The policy of domestic government.

Any family businesses that wants to succeed on the international market, it is necessary to bear in mind all of previous aspects. When formulating successful strategies for performance on the international market, it appears as necessity to incorporate these aspects in the strategy. Usually in the decision on internationalisation of the business influence entrepreneurial vision and the initial resource endowment this is particularly true for knowledge-intensive industries (Kiran, Majumdar, & Kishore, 2013).

3   Types of Strategies for Performing in International Markets

SMEs need to carefully consider the entry mode, timing, scope and pace at which they deploy their international activities. Several behavioural process models have been developed in this regard. The best known model is the so-called "Uppsala model" which sees firms growing internationally in a staged approach first entering and committing resources in psychically close markets before moving on very gradually to more distant markets (Onkelinx & Sleuwaegen, 2010).

Different authors recommend different strategies that family businesses can use to perform in the international market. The most important strategies that can be used are (Thompson et al., 2007):

- *Export strategy*—this strategy is used when companies use their existing production facilities and then offer their products on the international market. Positive characteristic in this strategy is that it can be used with very low additional cost. Export strategy can be executed in an *indirect* way by using intermediaries of their own country who will be in charge for the export, *direct export/distributors*, which don't use brokers or agents from the domestic country (distributors) and branch/subsidiary where exports depend on the operational business units of the company's in the targeted country (Root, 1994). This strategy is commonly used by businesses in China and Korea where enterprises use existing capacities in domestic market for designing and producing the products which will be sold in the foreign market. Very often, this strategy proved to be very successful especially because it helped to achieve cost reduction with the economy of scale and experience curve. This strategy isn't recommended in case (1) when production costs in the home country are higher than in the countries where we export, (2) the cost of distribution in these countries are high, and (3) there are big exchange rate differences.
- *Licensing strategy*—this strategy is used in the case when the company owns a valuable technical know—how or unique patent, and the company lack the needed amount of money or the company don't have the ability alone to enter in the international market. In this way the risk for the success of the license and resources is in the side of the user of the licensee. The negative side of this strategy is that it transfers important knowledge and technology to the other companies which may influence loss of control over these valuable resources. It is most commonly used by the software and pharmaceutical companies.
- *Franchising*—this strategy is usually used by retailers who aim to expand globally. McDonalds, Pizza Hut, KFC, Hilton Hotels are just some few examples of enterprises that use franchising. Franchise has almost the same characteristics as the licensing except that in franchising the franchisee is obliged to take the costs associated with training, support, provision of resources and monitoring the establishment of the company. The biggest problem related with franchising is quality control; in some countries usually they don't pay

attention to a control at all. Sometimes there is another problem which is related with the need to modify products in order to meet the demands of local consumers.

- *Multistate strategy*—this strategy requires that enterprises by themselves enter in the international market. This approach requires from the enterprises to adjust to market demands and consumers preferences. Multistate strategy involves modifying the design of products and marketing strategies to suit the specific requirements of each individual country separately (Daft, 2010). Usually it is used in situations where large differences occur in consumer preferences, buying habits of products, distribution channels and marketing methods. With this strategy most if not all production and acquisition value is located in the home country. The products or services that are provided in international market are adapted according to requirements of local consumers. Such strategies are used by General Motors who through its subsidy OPEL achieved to produce cars adapted to European market needs (Johnson et al., 2008).
- *Global strategy*—This strategy sees the world as a global market. The global strategy is a strategy in which companies have almost equal access in all countries in which they perform. This strategy can help companies improve efficiency by standardizing the design of products, production, use of common suppliers, easier presentation of products around the world, coordination of prices and elimination of duplication of facilities (Daft, 2010). We sell the same products using the same brand, use similar distribution channels and compete on the same marketing approaches wherever they perform (Gerry, Kevan, & Whittington, 2006). The global strategy is recommended in case (Cathy, 2010, p. 405):

  - When there is a global segmentation of products or services,
  - When there is economic efficiency that is associated with a global strategy,
  - When there are no external obstacles for implementing the global strategy,
  - When there are no internal barriers.

This strategy is mostly used by manufacturing companies when products are produced in certain locations and further distributed globally.

- *Alliances and joint ventures*—are strategies which have also been successfully used by companies to enter in the international market. Most frequently used to join the low developed countries. Many researchers had pointed out that there today businesses need to cooperate among themselves in order to be globally competitive, strategic alliances are an excellent way for enterprises to commercialize their products internationally and to make up for a certain rarity of resources (Su & Poisson, 2000). Many companies in the U.S. and Japan in order to enter their markets, they join with companies from China, India, Malaysia, Thailand and other Asian countries. The research study also concludes that networking affected internationalization of the business; that networking is very important in the improvement of operational efficiency of international

<u>Strategic possibilities</u>   Ways of dealing with inter-state variation

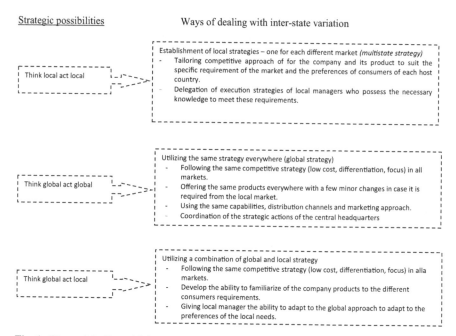

Fig. 1 Ways of dealing with inter-state variations. Source: Thompson et al. (2007, p. 170)

business. It also confirms that network relationship enhances sharing of resources, knowledge, skills and experience (Oseh, 2013).

Analysing the strategies presented earlier it can be noticed that some tend to enter foreign markets directly and others indirectly mainly by signing a contract. For family businesses that use a strategy "directly enter the foreign markets" in Fig. 1 we present the following strategic options for dealing with inter-state variations in consumer preferences and market conditions.

These are just some of the most important and recommended strategies that family businesses should use, in order to successfully compete in the international market. Family businesses who decide to enter the international market should consider that the time horizon for these strategies to succeed in the international market is 3–5 years. It is very important to realize the importance of having a clear strategy when enterprises decide to enter in international market. Very often family businesses even though they lack a clear strategy they chose to enter the international market. For such family businesses we say that they have "sales" approach in the international market but not a strategy.

One of very frequent asked question from family businesses is whether they should *expand their business in the international market or to remain to operate in the existing market?* Before taking such a decision, the family businesses should answer the following few questions (Thompson et al., 2007, p. 163):

- Whether the domestic market will allow the company for further increase of their profits and enterprise growth, or is it necessary to expand in the international market?
- Does the expansion into international market provide advantages related with location that are related with the production costs, distribution of products and services to consumers?
- Will the company be able effectively to transform the advantages of its resources and competitive capabilities of the home country to another country, in order to achieve competitive advantage?
- Will the risk associated with business reduce or increase, by choosing a strategy for entering in international market?
- Is it best to use the same competitive strategy as in the home country, or it should be modified for each country separately?
- Whether the company can independently create a competitive advantage in international markets, or to seek help from some ally from the home country where they perform?

These are some important questions that family businesses need to answer in qualitative way if they want to succeed in their objective to enter on the international market. Previous explanations concerning strategies can offer tremendous help in answering these questions. We should have in mind that some markets may be the same or similar to the domestic market but some others may be very different from that of the domestic market. Strategies may be best modified depending on the requirements of the country that are playing as well depending on the product or service offered. Another aspect from which it depend the selection of internationalization strategy is the reputation of the family businesses into the market that they intend to enter. If the family businesses that performs in foreign markets where they have good reputation will have fewer difficulties (Mercedes, IBM, Milka, etc.) in operating in these markets, compared to those family businesses that don't have good reputation. One of the main problems in internationalizations of the family businesses is differentiations in culture. Studies have shown that among the managers in France and UK there are different views on all of these dimensions. This indicates the importance of the factors in determining the management style and thus the choice of strategies of family businesses (Groeschl & Borrows, 2003). Family businesses can achieve competitive advantage in the international market only if they achieved to offer greater value to consumers than their competitors (Spulber, 2007).

Family businesses also can choose for a so called sprinkler strategy, targeting multiple countries at once. Another option is a waterfall strategy, slowly cascading from one country to the next (Onkelinx & Sleuwaegen, 2010, p. 6).

4 Research Result: Strategies for Performance in International Market of Albanian Family Businesses

During the research we used questionnaires which were formulated after a lengthy review of the literature in strategies for entering international markets. We sent in total 150 questioners, from which 75 were returned (50 %), 0 were returned by e-mail, 2 by post and 73 were personally collected. The respondents came from Senior Management and Middle Management level.

Subject of analysis in this research were the strategies that these family businesses use when they enter in the international market. From the results presented in Fig. 2 it can be seen that as most common strategy for entering in the international market that family businesses use in Albania is the *export strategy*. The results showed that 60 % of Albanian family businesses act alone in the international market, 25 % of these analysed enterprises cooperate with an international partner who is not from the country in which they operate, while 14 % of these enterprises cooperate with local partners who are from the country in which they perform.

The survey also showed that 58 % of family businesses participating in the international market offer the same products in these markets as in the domestic market, while 39 % of family businesses use different products for different countries and for international market, and the rest 3 % use different products for all international market, presented in Fig. 3.

Regarding the origin of products that participate in the international market, 65 % of family businesses produce their products in the domestic market, while 29 % of family businesses produce part of their products in domestic and part of them in the international market, and only 6 % of family businesses produce all of their products in the international market (Fig. 4).

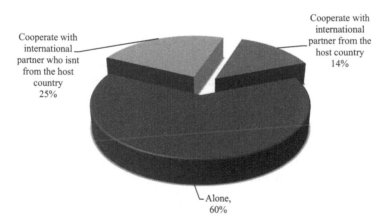

Fig. 2 The way how Albanian family businesses perform in international market (Source: Author's survey)

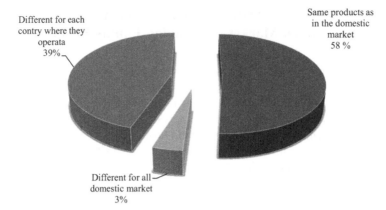

Fig. 3 Differences of the products in domestic and international market (Source: Author's survey)

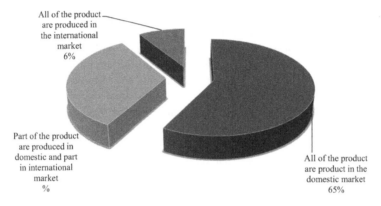

Fig. 4 Origin of the products (Source: Author's survey)

5 Conclusion

During the theoretical analysis of the possible strategies for internationalization of family businesses we can conclude that as the best strategy that family business in transition economy and economies that still aren't developed enough and have cheap working force is *export strategy*. Albania and most of the countries in the Balkans are characterized with not well developed economy and that's why we proposed for family businesses to use the export strategy, which according to the research result this was the case. Selecting this way to approach in the international market (using the export strategy and producing their product in the domestic market) of Albanian family businesses is mainly because of the cheap working force, cheap transportation, qualified working force and small exchange rates difference allows great competitive advantage in using of this strategy. Research result that we found in Albania was very similar to those that we found in Macedonia.

References

Cathy, E. A. (2010). *Hospitality strategic management: Concepts and cases* (2nd ed.). New Jersey: Wiley.

Daft, R. L. (2010). *Management* (9th ed.). Mason: South Western Cengage Learning Publisher.

Dana, L.-P. (1996). Albania in the twilight zone: The *perseritje* model and its impact on small business. *Journal of Small Business Management, 34*(1), 64–70.

Dana, L. P., & Dana, T. (2003). Management and enterprise development in post-communist economies. *International Journal of Management and Enterprise Development, 1*(1), 45–54.

Gerry, J., Kevan, S., & Whittington, R. (2006). *Exploring corporate strategy* (7th ed.). Harlow: Pearson Education Limited.

Groeschl, S., & Borrows, W. C. (2003). A cross cultural comparison of French and British managers: An examination of the influence of higher education on management style. *Tourism and Hospitality Research, 4*(3), 228–246.

Johnson, G., Scholes, K., & Whittington, R. (2008). *Exploring corporate strategy: Text and cases* (8th ed.). Harlow: Prentice Hall.

Kiran, V., Majumdar, M., & Kishore, K. (2013). Internationalization of SMEs: Finding a way ahead. *American International Journal of Research in Humanities, Arts and Social Sciences, 2* (1), 18–23.

Konda, G. (2003). *Institutional reform in Albania*. Washington, DC: IFC.

Kontinen, T., & Ojala, A. (2010). The internationalization of family businesses: A review of extant research. *Journal of Family Business Strategy, 1*(2), 97–107.

KPMG. (2011). *Succeeding in a changing world, International Strategy future markets, future growth*. Europe: KPMG LLP.

Muço, M. (1999). *Economic transition in Albania: Political constraints and mentality barriers*. Tirana: University of Tirana.

Onkelinx, J., & Sleuwaegen, L. (2010). *Internationalization strategy and performance of small and medium sized enterprises*. Brussels: National Bank of Belgium.

Oseh, C. K. (2013). Factors associated with internationalization of small and medium enterprises in Thika town, Kenya. *European Journal of Management Sciences and Economics, 1*(3), 128–136.

Ramadani, V., & Dana, L. P. (2013). The state of entrepreneurship in the Balkans: Evidence from selected countries. In V. Ramadani & R. C. Schneider (Eds.), *Entrepreneurship in the Balkans*. Berlin: Springer.

Root, F. R. (1994). *Entry strategies for international markets*. San Francisco: Jossey-Bass.

Sicignano, A., & Capurso, F. (2011). *Enhancing SMEs development in Albania: A study on macro-financial soundness indicators*. Tirana: Ministry of Economy and Trade.

Spulber, D. F. (2007). *Global competitive strategy* (1st ed.). New York: Cambridge University Press.

Su, Z. M., & Poisson, R. (2000). Utilisation of strategic alliances in the processes of internationalisation: an empirical study of small and medium sized high-tech enterprises, *Proceedings of the 9th International Conference on Management of Technology*, Université Laval, Québec.

Thompson, A. A., Strickland, A. J., III, & Gamble, J. E. (2007). *Crafting and executing strategy: The quest for competitive advantage—concepts and cases* (15th ed.). Irvine, CA: McGraw Hill.

Yujnovsky, O., & Mece, M. (2006). Evaluation of national human development report system, Case Study Albania, UNDP.

Family Business in Sport Organizations: Western Experiences as Lessons for Transitional Economies

Vanessa Ratten

Abstract This chapter examines family businesses in the sport industry. The reasons why family owned, managed and operated businesses exist in the sport arena are examined within the theoretical framework of family business. The changing definition of family is discussed in the chapter that leads to an analysis of how the community including family businesses help encourage sport-related activity. The role of sport clubs acting as family businesses is highlighted that includes the importance of family's in promoting the cohesiveness and community that sport as a service and product entails. The analysis reveals important business and lifestyle considerations of family owned sport businesses. These considerations include the importance of family businesses properly managing sport franchises and sport-related business ventures. This chapter focuses on the reasons why family's manage sport organizations in terms of community and location preferences in the context of family business evolution. The role of conflict, generational issues and succession plans related to family business in the sport context are also examined. The chapter concludes by stating research and management implications of family owners of sport organizations.

Keywords Family business • Sport • Community development • Public-private partnerships

1 Introduction

Family businesses are important drivers of economic development as they encourage the connectivity between individual involvement and business development (Kuratko & Hodgetts, 2004). Family businesses encourage workforce engagement by focusing on the importance of future planning to enable its survival in difficult economic times (Liang, Wang, & Cui, 2014). They do this by being dynamic organizational structures that develop and change depending on changing

V. Ratten (✉)
School of Management, La Trobe Business School, La Trobe University, Melbourne, VIC, Australia
e-mail: v.ratten@latrobe.edu.au

© Springer International Publishing Switzerland 2015
L.-P. Dana, V. Ramadani (eds.), *Family Businesses in Transition Economies*,
DOI 10.1007/978-3-319-14209-8_15

environmental conditions. Family businesses often link multiple family groups and can be a factor in international expansion and entering into different economic activities, which can include sport-related activities (Moss, Payne, & Moore, 2014). Family businesses are better than non-family businesses at enjoying the private benefits of control including extracting value and using company assets for personal gain (Westhead & Cowling, 1997). Some of these discretionary benefits have seen family's investing in professional sport franchises due to the link sport has with the community (Agyemang, 2014).

Family businesses vary in the amount of equity held in the business, which influences the level of family involvement in development activities (Steward & Hitt, 2012). The definition of 'family' in the workplace has changed with society and technological advances. This has lead to changes in society meaning that the traditional concept of family is altering but the concept of sport has remained important to most families regardless of their size or wealth. Family now more commonly refers to social and economic communities of individuals coming together for a similar purpose. Family businesses incorporate multiple definitions of family including intermarriage, kinship and apprenticeship exchanges (Kuper, 2009).

There are a variety of different definitions of family business with most focusing on the ownership, structure and governance roles that distinguish them from other types of business (Chua, Chrisman, & Sharma, 1999). The term 'family' has different definitions but most commonly it refers to blood relations between individuals (Pukall & Calabrò, 2014). However, the concept of 'family' is changing due to shifting social understandings of the term and it can include people related by marriage, partnership or shared interest. Poza, Hanlon, and Kishida (2004) defines a family business as having ownership control by two or more members of a family that strategically influences business decisions. A broad definition of a family business adopted in this chapter is when an economic entity has the majority of ownership or control from members of a family (Brockhaus, 2004). The majority of businesses around the world are family businesses and much large multinationals start as family businesses. In transition economies, family businesses dominate with a large proportion of overall enterprises being family owned.

This chapter investigates the development of family businesses in the sport sector by examining their evolution and importance in the global economy. The role of family business in sport start-up, growth and community renewal are discussed. The unique role of family business in the sport sector is explored. There is limited research in the sport sector concerning family business despite well known families owning famous sport clubs and organizations. As the topic of family business and sport organizations is limited, the research in this chapter draws on the broader literature of family firms as well as sport management to understand sport based family businesses.

This chapter proceeds as follows. First, the literature on family business is reviewed that suggest the advantages and disadvantages of family businesses contributing to community development. Next, the role of family businesses in sport clubs is discussed. This includes a summary of the arguments for family businesses investing in sport clubs due to geographic, historical and economic reasons. As a result of this discussion the chapter concludes with reasons why the sport industry, private foundations and government authorities might encourage further involvement of family businesses in the local community. The chapter concludes with suggestions and directions for future research. The next section will provide an analysis of how family businesses in the sport context can operate more efficiently.

2 Literature Review

2.1 Role of Family Business

Family businesses have the overall motive of using the business for the advancement of the family (Chua et al., 1999). The goals of a family business involve more than the usual profit maximization objective of other firms that often stem from their connection to the community. Family business can be distinguished between those that develop as a means of livelihood compared to the more interested orientated family businesses that are centered around family activities (Singer & Donahu, 1992). As family businesses adapt to changing conditions different types of organizations are derived from the new market dynamics including those balancing both family and business needs compared to businesses focusing primarily on family concerns.

Family businesses have many different goals including both financial and non-financial depending on the owners willingness to accept lower returns on investments. The financial goals can include job security, income return and tax benefits whilst non-financial goals incorporate quality of work, personal growth and autonomy (Andersson, Carlsen, & Getz, 2002). Some family businesses are established to provide employment for family members that ensure financial and economic independence (Andersson et al., 2002). However, non-financial reasons including working in a happy atmosphere with other family members can encourage family businesses to accept longer paybacks on financial investments. In addition, being the owner manager of a family business can give individuals a sense of social advancement that enables innovation to develop. Often family businesses are continued for lifestyle reasons rather than solely financial reasons thereby in the process accepting lower profit revenues that could otherwise be obtained (Westhead, 1997).

Family businesses evolve in three development stages: early, middle and late that depends on the business environment and motivation of the owner (Ward, 1991). The early stage involves examining the success of the family business, the middle stage involves incorporating children into the family businesses development and the late stage involves family harmony and unity (Andersson et al., 2002).

As a family business evolves it incorporates into traditions of greater involvement of more family members thereby ensuring a legacy for future generations.

A number of forces influence the disposition of family businesses including the characteristics, nature and climate of the organization, extent of family dominance and rationale of the owner-manager (Andersson et al., 2002). Often owner managers of new businesses evolve into family enterprises in which the founder sees the business as a family asset rather than solely a business activity (Andersson et al., 2002). The excitement of starting a business impacts the development of future family orientated activities when opportunities are seized upon. Running a family business can put financial and non-financial strain on families depending on the hours and nature of the business. For these financial and non-financial reasons there are strong incentives for the establishment of family businesses in transition economies due to capital restrictions that encourage involvement of community members to a regions development.

Family businesses are often founded in order to pursue a dream that can include meeting a lifelong goal, getting rich or desire to be independent (Andersson et al., 2002). Often individuals are involved with family businesses due to their link with a specific location that they might have strong ties. As example of this is the Rooney family's association with the Pittsburgh region and their ownership of the Pittsburgh Steelers football franchise, There are also advantages to having a family business associated with a sports team in a particular region that include lifestyle and personal goals but there are also disadvantages including debt and decreased leisure time.

2.2   *Family Business and Sport Clubs*

Many sport clubs act as family businesses due to the involvement of generational interchange of family members (Ratten, 2014). There are different reasons for starting or continuing a family business in the sport context. Many large sports organizations including the Pittsburgh Steelers owned by the Rooney family have focused on the generational ownership of a professional sports team that is a key part of the community in Western Pennsylvania. The Rooney family has mixed family interest in owning a National Football League team with their interest in integrating community participation in a sports team. Part of the Rooney family's connection to the Pittsburgh Steelers flows from the sense of collectivism and community engagement associated with owning a sports team. This is due to sports teams by their nature being like a family due to the fan and city's connection to the football team (Anagnostopoulos, Byers, & Shilbury, 2014).

The participation of the family in a sports club is important in order to strengthen the control of the family in business decisions. Sport clubs that are owned by families often focus on key community stakeholders including the local council and government authorities to make their organizations more efficient (Billings & Hardin, 2014). A sports club who wins a premiership title further positively affects the family's reputation and position in society. For many families there is the advantage of generational ownership as they learn about the business since childhood thereby increasing their knowledge and experience about the sports club. An example of this is the two families who own the New York Giants football team. The Mara and Tisch family share ownership of the New York Giants and within both families there are a large number of family members involved in the sports business operations.

Some family businesses are founded for corporate social responsibility or public relations reasons to give families a better image in their local and international community. The Kansas City Chiefs a baseball team is owned by the Hunt families who have been prominent in Kansas City businesses over the past decades. Often families have ties to a special location that creates a desire of family members to continue the business and fulfill legacy goals. The family character of a business impacts the employees, stakeholders and members of the family. Stakeholders including suppliers and clients are impacted by the inclusion of a family business in a community.

Family business managers often focus on bonding with the community due to the set of values they have about balancing profit and non-profit activities (Godfrey, 1995). Some family business owners feel a closer bond to the community due to being in close proximity that encourages more philanthropic activities (Castro, 1997). Family businesses act as a member of the local community by promoting the cohesiveness of the region (Robbins, 1998). For many families sports clubs are a key part of community and social life (Janin, 1998). Sports clubs are social stakeholder groups that have a relationship with family business owners (Janin, 1998). Some family businesses donate time or money to sport teams as a way of helping the local community. The spirit of a community can be boosted when sports clubs win trophies and promote the business of family organizations. This is due to family businesses often having special relationships with sport clubs linked to the family aspect of the business. This can be due to direct family connections with the sports club being supported which may be hereditary since previous generations were also active members of the sports club.

Due to many family businesses having the family surname as the business name then there is reputational considerations from partnering with sports clubs. When sport clubs perform well then the family's business sponsorship is considered a good business decision and this has happened over the past decade with the Buss's family's ownership of the LA Lakers and the clubs multiple premiership wins. Some family businesses due to their close links with the community view sports clubs as a source of extended family. This is due to sports clubs feeling directly responsible for the community due to close ties with stakeholders in the business community. Sports clubs act as social stakeholders due to the constant activity of sporting events that are tied to business and family activities. The Chicago Cubs owners the Ricketts family are a good example of this as their ownership of the iconic baseball team is tied to the cities historical development. The community involvement of family businesses with sports clubs helps to explain the nature of relationships within a community. Family businesses usually behave in a social responsibility manner that conforms to societal expectations about community involvement with sports clubs.

2.3 Management of Family Businesses

Family businesses are managed by following the vision of key family members about future direction. Family businesses focus on the potential sustainability of the management structure in order that the business continues to develop and grow for future generations of a family (Alderson, 2011). Sometimes it is difficult to manage a sport-related family business due to the balancing required of family needs and business opportunity. In a study of Argentine family owned food processors, Hatum, Pettigrew, and Michelini (2010) found that more adaptive family firms focus on internal promotion in conjunction with external recruitment of individuals that have a cultural fit with the family's existing management structure. This means that depending on the desires of family members there may be an imbalance between the control of who makes key decisions for the business and remuneration of family members for work performed. This can lead to criticisms of family businesses by family members who want to reinvest profits for the future development of the sport business and other family members who derive most of their income from the family business. Recently the LA Dodgers baseball team was sold by Frank McCourt and his ex-wife Jamie McCourt who had a long association with the management of the team tried unsuccessfully to stop the sale of the sport team.

Family businesses are considered to have a management style more emotional and intuitive rather than the analytical style of nonfamily enterprises, which may be the reason many family's are involved in sport-related activities. The stereotypes of family businesses are not universally applied due to differences in education, decision making and management styles (Steward & Hitt, 2012). Some family businesses recognize the role merit based performance plays in the success of the business and tie this to the overall performance of their sponsored sports team. However, increasing numbers of family firms are educating succeeding generations in business schools in order to have a more broader and global perspective of business (Tsui-Auch, 2004).

Institutional factors including stock exchange requirements affect the composition of family businesses due to the legal requirements affecting governance mechanisms (Oxfeld, 1993). These institutional factors can encourage family business participation in the sport context particularly in professional sport leagues in the United States where there is limited corporate ownership of teams. These institutional factors influence the social networks used by family members in management structures (Arregle, Hitt, Simon, & Very, 2007). Cromie, Stephenson, and Monteith (1995) in a study of small family businesses in Britain found that formalized and rational management systems exit. In addition, Chrisman, Chua, and Litz (2004) found that there are advantages for private family firms of using family members as owners, agents and managers due to the decreased cost in finding the appropriate and knowledgeable people.

2.4 Conflict and Family Business Structures

Family businesses are different from other businesses due to the presence of family in the management and ownership of the business. Often there is conflict in family businesses due to the different roles and requirements of family members participating in the day to day management activities. Research by Poza et al. (2004) found that leaders of family businesses had a higher evaluation of their management that may bias the overall performance. However, another study by Tsui-Auch (2004) in a study of Chinese family firms found no significant difference between educational levels of family members and overall performance of the family business. This means that there is difficulty with some family businesses in that the founder's desires may not be inherited by heirs and lead to investments in sporting clubs either being divested or sold to third parties. This may also result in confusion in the family business about management expectations and the merging of work/life balance. Stress can increase in family businesses when there is a long seasonal work hours that may be made worse by gender roles expected despite society changes.

Some problems exist in defining roles and responsibilities of family members of a family business due to differing opinions. Particularly older members of family businesses may be reluctant to make structural changes to the family business despite technological changes influencing the professionalization of family businesses. However, some family owned sport teams including the Glazer family who owns Manchester United in the English Premier league have adopted the use of technology and worldwide viewing audiences to increase the profits of the sport franchise. The readiness to employ non-family members with specific skills helps in the business development. Family businesses handle risk differently as there are less external restrictions around controls on their business activities. Naldi, Nordqvist, Sjoberg, and Wiklund (2007) found that owner managers of family businesses view risk as less important than overall business performance and may be more willing to take greater chances because of their ownership control and desire for continual family involvement in the business.

Family members can influence the business by financial ownership, being a shareholder or serving in an advisory role. Family businesses blend the social unit of a family with economic objectives and desire to achieve social prestige from owning a sports team. This is due to family business owners tending to have more personal relationships with employees and customers (Donckels, 1998). The most direct contact family businesses have with customers often enables more community cohesiveness and encourages their linkage with sport. Compared to non-family businesses there is a different and more personal commitment to employee's wellbeing in family businesses. This sometimes leads to more forward thinking planning that considers strategically the impact of decisions for employees (Castro, 1997).

Family firms include informal social ties that enhance knowledge sharing internal to the firm. This coordination of information flows facilitates change based on external market conditions. Johannisson (2002) in a study of family firms over a 15 year time period found that the interplay between the family as a social institution and having passion for change drives the success of family businesses. The secrecy and trust embedded in many family firms is useful in transition economies that place value on low key business relationships. The discretion of family firms is useful for clandestine agreements with governments in transition economies that is mutually beneficial. This means that the interface between family and business offers entrepreneurial opportunities for family businesses. In a study of United States family firms, Haynes, Onochie, and Muske (2007) found that increased financial performance does not influence the family's success. Instead, family businesses that use both family and business interests to retain a sense of tradition and purpose perform better over the long term (Steier, 2003)

3   Generational and Succession Issues for Sport-Related Family Businesses

The key concern for most family businesses is the continuity of the business across generations based on a common interest. Family businesses can include first generational families that have started or bought a business that has a legally recognized structure. Many family businesses do not survive multiple generational ownership due to the difficulty of incorporating non family members, tensions amongst family members and lack of proper planning. The Family Firm Institute (2013) states that only 10 % of third generation family businesses survive and this decreases to 3 % in the fourth generation. For some family businesses there are difficulties when the key leader and visionary retires or withdraws but still participates in decisions (Bruc & Picardg, 2005). Tax reasons including inheritance and estate taxes are an important issue of succession planning for family businesses (Grassi & Giarmarco, 2008). The nurturing of younger generations is a key aspect of succession planning for members of family businesses. By grooming potential successors this will help family business move into the next generation.

Family businesses can suffer from challenges derived from succession planning and loss of leadership when the business is listed on the stock exchange or enters into a new product or service segment. An example of this is the death in 2014 of Malcolm Grazer the head of the family who owns the Tampa Bay Buccaneers in the American Football League and Manchester United in the English Premier League died and the ownership transferred equally to all his children. Many family businesses lack formal succession plans due to poor communication by the founder of the business about leadership and ownership direction. This is made more difficult when there are family quarrels amongst different children and their families in family firms. In order to achieve sustainable entrepreneurial growth it is important for firms to create a supportive and innovative environment that derives its success from change (Coric, Meter, & Bublic, 2013).

Succession issues of family businesses are a concern particularly if incompetent family members have the desire to take over the leadership of the business. Sometimes the older leader or founder of a family firm can make succession issues harder when there is no heir apparent or if ownerships of the business is held in a family trust. The resistance to succession planning for leaders of family businesses may result from the business being the founder's key sense of power (Ramadani, Fayolle, Gerguri, & Aliu, 2013). This may lead to successors being unprepared to take over as they have not been trained in family business matters. The convergence of business and private lives for many leaders of family businesses can further confuse the succession issue resulting in a lack of trust from other family members in proper planning. There are also potential gender biases in succession planning with many family businesses assuming the eldest son is the logical successor despite other family members being just as knowledgeable or more capable. Some family businesses take the approach that all descendants regardless of gender or age should be equal in succession talks and the best candidate should be chosen to lead the family firm.

Family business usually has concentrated kinship based ownership that can be governed by secrecy due to the linkage between cash flow and ownership rights (Steward & Hitt, 2012). Family businesses compared to nonfamily businesses have more private benefits for family that can include a nepotism based reward system (Steward & Hitt, 2012). The embedded kinship networks in family businesses include entrenched long tenured leadership roles for family members (Oswald, Muse, & Rutherford, 2009). As leadership succession is usually drawn from the kinship pool there can be an autocratic instead of rational management style of family business.

Family businesses join groups of associated kinship connected firms to gain access to nonmarket inputs to create jointly operated entities (Steward & Hitt, 2012). These family business groups are common in transition economies when information about commercial activities is less freely available (Gilson, 2007). Hsieh, Yeh, and Chen (2010) in a study of Taiwanese electronics firms found those associated with a business group outperform others. Family business groups are common in medium to large scale enterprises due to the informal social ties that encourage collaboration (Steward & Hitt, 2012). These family business groups enable knowledge sharing and interfirm trust to develop amongst firms. Kinship networks enable businesses to provide linkages and pool resources to pursue a single goal. Small family businesses utilize kinship to integrate diverse interests and provide multiple sources of income (Creed, 2000). This is useful when uncertain economic conditions exist that help small family business has fallback positions in case one business is not going too well. Kinship enables internal incentives rather than financial reasons to dominant business decisions of family firms. This can be made difficult when cross-generational unity is harmed by individuals entering a family business (Steward & Hitt, 2012). Some noble or well recognized families enter into marriage exchanges with wealthy families for financial opportunities (McDonogh, 1986). In a similar vein, some newly wealthy families trade capital for sporting prestige. Some family businesses seek relationships with sports clubs as a way of reuniting scattered kin for a common interest.

4   Family Business and Sport Culture

Culture is an important part of family business due to the expectation of redistributing money amongst kin (Watson, 1985). The failure to recognize kinship and family relationships can lead to interpersonal conflicts in family businesses. Sometimes it is hard in family businesses to recognize merit based performance rather than viewing an individual's own children instead of the extended family as more capable (Tsui-Auch, 2004). The problem of favoring certain family members is seen as endemic in family businesses due to the competing interests of different members (Steward & Hitt, 2012). This happened recently in the English Premier League with the Oyston family who owns Blackpool suffering considerable negative press in the media because of their payments to themselves and related family companies that were considered inappropriate by fans.

Family businesses have idiosyncratic cultures existing in the workplace that might impede regular social skills and communication mechanisms that are apparent of non-family businesses (Helin, 2011). Socioeconomic wealth rather than pure financial wealth is important to family business wanting to maintain the prestigiousness of owning a family operated and established business (Berghoff, 2006). Socioeconomic wealth can include providing sponsorship of sports clubs or providing employment for athletes. Van Essen, Carney, Gedajlovic, Heugens, and Van Oosterhout (2010) found that successive generations of family firms are more risk averse due to their focus on preserving wealth rather than creating wealth. This risk aversion is due to founders already establishing the business with an ongoing profit stream.

Greenhalgh (1994) in a study of Taiwanese family firms found that kinship traditions enabled the development of family talents and loyalties. The unique access to family resources allows family businesses access to privileged control such as strategic decisions. Intrafamily conflicts are common in family businesses that can potentially lead to decreased financial resources available for future development (Watson, 1985). Family members who are younger or from lesser known branches of a family often find it hard to obtain opportunities to collaborate with lesser known sports clubs. The lack of openness and disclosure of financial capabilities of family businesses makes it hard for some owners of sports clubs to further develop their teams.

5 Conclusion

The future will bring interesting developments about the role family businesses have in both professional and amateur sports organizations. Whilst there may be a decline in the traditional sense of what a family business is this will lead to new opportunities for sports entities to enter into and maintain relationships with family businesses. This chapter provides practical assistance to policy makers and foundations interested in encouraging greater support by family businesses in the sport context. More philanthropic support by family businesses is needed to support various stakeholders of sports clubs beyond the basic level required to maintain the sports club operations. As family businesses represent the majority of companies in most transition economies, the findings of this chapter can be drawn upon to help sports clubs. Family businesses support the general economic conditions of a community by contributing jobs and commerce. Family businesses usually support sports clubs close to their geographic location. In this chapter it is argued that a better understanding of the role of family businesses to sport clubs is needed.

References

Agyemang, K. J. (2014). Toward a framework of "athlete citizenship" in professional sport through authentic community stakeholder engagement. *Sport, Business and Management: An International Journal, 4*(1), 26–37.

Alderson, J. K. (2011). *Understanding the family business.* New York: Business Expert Press.

Anagnostopoulos, C., Byers, T., & Shilbury, D. (2014). Corporate social responsibility in professional team sport organisations: Towards a theory of decision-making. *European Sport Management Quarterly, 1*(1), 1–23.

Andersson, T., Carlsen, J., & Getz, D. (2002). Family business goals in the tourism and hospitality sector: Case studies and cross-case analysis from Australia, Canada and Sweden. *Family Business Review, 15*, 89–104.

Arregle, J. L., Hitt, M. A., Simon, D. G., & Very, P. (2007). The development of organizational social capital: Attributes of family firms. *Journal of Management Studies, 44*, 73–95.

Berghoff, H. (2006). The end of family business? The Mittelstand and German capitalism in transition, 1949-2000. *Business History Review, 80*, 263–296.

Billings, A. C., & Hardin, M. (2014). *Routledge handbook of sport and new media.* London: Routledge.

Brockhaus, R. H. (2004). Family business succession: Suggestions for future research. *Family Business Review, 17*(2), 165–177.

Bruc, D., Picard, D. (2005) *Succession can breed success,* Canadian Federation of Independent Business, www.newsaskcfdc.ca, last visited 1 August 2014.

Castro, B. (1997). Manufacturing jobs, local ownership and the social health of cities—a research note. *The Responsive Community,* Winter: 63–66.

Chrisman, J. J., Chua, J. H., & Litz, R. A. (2004). Comparing the agency costs of family and non-family firms: Conceptual issues and exploratory evidence. *Entrepreneurship: Theory and Practice, 28*, 335–354.

Chua, J. H., Chrisman, J. J., & Sharma, P. (1999). Defining the family business by behavior. *Entrepreneurship: Theory and Practice, 23*(4), 19–39.

Coric, G., Meter, J., & Bublic, V. (2013). Evidence from the project Croatian Gazelles—Promotion of sustainable growth. *Revja Mednarodno Inovativno Poslovanje, Letnik, 4*, 2.

Creed, G. W. (2000). Family values and domestic economies. *Annual Review of Anthropology, 29*, 329–355.

Cromie, S., Stephenson, B., & Monteith, D. (1995). The management of family firms: An empirical investigation. *International Small Business Journal, 13*(4), 11–34.

Donckels, R. (1998). Ondernemen in het familiebedrijf. In D. P. Scherjon & A. R. Thurik (Eds.), *Handboek Ondernemers en Adviseurs in het Midden-en Kleinbedrijf*. Devanter: Kluwer BedrijfsInformatie.

Family Firm Institute. (2013). www.ffi.org, last visited 1 August 2014.

Gilson, R. J. (2007). Controlling family shareholders in developing countries: Anchoring relational exchange. *Stanford Law Review, 69*, 633–655.

Godfrey, J. (1995). What's good for women is good for the country. *Vital Speeches of the Day, 61*(173), 538–541.

Grassi, V. J., & Giarmarco, J. H. (2008). Practical succession planning for the family-owned business. *CCH Journal of Practical Estate Planning*, February–March: 39–49.

Greenhalgh, S. (1994). Deorientalizing the Chinese family firm. *American Ethnologist, 21*, 746–775.

Hatum, A., Pettigrew, A., & Michelini, J. (2010). Building organizational capabilities to adapt under turmoil. *Journal of Change Management, 10*, 257–274.

Haynes, G. W., Onochie, J. I., & Muske, G. (2007). Is what's good for the business, good for the family? A financial assessment. *Journal of Family and Economic Issues, 28*, 395–409.

Helin, J. (2011) *Living moments in family meetings: A process study in the family business context*, Unpublished doctoral dissertation, Jonkoping International Business School, Jonkoping, Sweden.

Hsieh, T. J., Yeh, R. S., & Chen, Y. J. (2010). Business group characteristics and affiliated firm innovation: The case of Taiwan. *Industrial Marketing Management, 39*, 560–570.

Janin, H. (1998). *Culture Shock! A guide to customs and etiquette- Netherlands*. Portland: Graphic Arts Center.

Johannisson, B. (2002). Energising entrepreneurship: Ideological tensions in the medium sized family business. In D. Fletcher (Ed.), *Understanding the small family business* (pp. 46–57). London: Routledge.

Kuper, A. (2009). *Incest and influence: The private life of bourgeois England*. Cambridge, MA: Harvard University Press.

Kuratko, D. K., & Hodgetts, R. M. (2004). *Entrepreneurship: Theory, process and practice*. Mason, OH: Thomson South-Western.

Liang, X., Wang, L., & Cui, Z. (2014). Chinese private firms and internationalization effects of family involvement in management and family ownership. *Family Business Review, 27*(2), 126–141.

McDonogh, G. W. (1986). *Good families of Barcelona: A social history of power in the industrial age*. Princeton: Princeton University Press.

Moss, T. W., Payne, G. T., & Moore, C. B. (2014). Strategic consistency of exploration and exploitation in family businesses. *Family Business Review, 27*(1), 51–71.

Naldi, L., Nordqvist, M., Sjoberg, K., & Wiklund, J. (2007). Entrepreneurial orientation, risk taking and performance in family firms. *Family Business Review, 20*(1), 33–47.

Oswald, S. L., Muse, L. A., & Rutherford, M. W. (2009). The influence of large stake family control on performance: Is it agency or entrenchment? *Journal of Small Business Management, 47*, 116–135.

Oxfeld, E. (1993). *Blood, sweat and mahjong: Family and enterprise in an overseas Chinese community*. Ithaca: Cornell University Press.

Poza, E. J., Hanlon, S., & Kishida, R. (2004). Does the family business interaction factor represent a resource of a cost? *Family Business Review, 17*, 99–118.

Pukall, T. J., & Calabrò, A. (2014). The internationalization of family firms a critical review and integrative mode. *Family Business Review, 27*(2), 103–125.

Ramadani, V., Fayolle, A., Gerguri, S., & Aliu, E. (2013). The succession issues in family firms: Evidence from Macedonia, *5th E-LAB international symposium of entrepreneurship on family entrepreneurship: A new field of research*, EM Lyon Business School, Lyon, France.

Ratten, V. (2014). Developing a theory of sport-based entrepreneurship. In M. Weed (Ed.), Sport and leisure management. Sage, United Kingdom, pp. 293–307.

Robbins, S. P. (1998). *Organizational behavior* (8th ed.). New Jersey: Prentice Hall.

Singer, J., & Donahu, C. (1992). Strategic management planning for the successful family business. *Journal of Business and Entrepreneurship, 4*(3), 39–51.

Steier, L. P. (2003). Variants of agency contracts in family financed ventures as a continuum of familial altruistic and market rationalities. *Journal of Business Venturing, 18*, 597–618.

Steward, A., & Hitt, M. A. (2012). Why can't a family business be more like a non-family business?' Modes of professionalization in family firms. *Family Business Review, 25*(1), 58–86.

Tsui-Auch, L. S. (2004). The professionally managed family ruled enterprise: Ethnic Chinese business in Singapore. *Journal of Management Studies, 41*, 693–723.

Van Essen, M., Carney, M., Gedajlovic, E. R., Heugens, P., & Van Oosterhout, J. (2010) *Do US publicly listed family firms differ? Does it matter? A meta-analysis*, Paper presented at the 10th Annual Family Businesses Research Conference, Lancaster, England.

Ward, J. (1991). *Creating effective boards for private enterprises: Meeting the challenges of continuity and competition.* San Francisco: Jossey Bass.

Watson, R. S. (1985). *Inequality among brothers: Class and kinship in South China.* New York: Cambridge University Press.

Westhead, P. (1997). Ambitions, external environment and strategic factor differences between family and non-family companies. *Entrepreneurship and Regional Development, 9*, 127–157.

Westhead, P., & Cowling, M. (1997). Performance contrasts between family and non-family unquoted companies in the UK. *International Journal of Entrepreneurial Behavior and Research, 3*, 30–52.

Family Businesses in the Trade Sector: An Examination of a Case Study from Kosovo

Veland Ramadani, Gramos Gashi, Taki Fiti, and Betim Humolli

Abstract In this chapter is presented a successful story of family business from Kosovo. In this chapter are treated topics such as: history of Albi Group, its business entities, development over the years, governance and succession planning.

Keywords Albi Group • Succession issues • Governance • Planning • Kosovo

1 Introduction

Kosovo is located in southeastern Europe in the central Balkan Peninsula. The country covers 10,908 km^2, where the capital city is Prishtina and covers 572 km^2. Kosovo is bordered by four countries, namely Montenegro (border length 78.6 km) to the northwest, Serbia (border 351.6 km) to the north and northeast, Macedonia (border 158.7 km) to the south and Albania (border 111.8 km) to the west and southwest. Resident population is around 1.74 million. The real GDP growth in 2013 was 4.5 % and GDP per capital was 2,650.0 € (Ministry of Trade and Industry, 2013).

Over 60,000 SMEs were active in 2011; approximately 50 % of these were engaged in the trade sector. Republic of Kosovo offers excellent business environment. It has an excellent tax system and quick and easy business registration. In order to create an enabling environment for the stable development of the pure market, Kosovo's government has been working towards facilitating the free movement of goods and services throughout the country's borders. This makes it easier for small and medium enterprises operating as manufacturing companies, as

V. Ramadani (✉)
Faculty of Business and Economics, South-East European University, Tetovo, Republic of Macedonia
e-mail: v.ramadani@seeu.edu.mk

G. Gashi • B. Humolli
ALBI Group, Prishtina, Kosovo
e-mail: gramos.gashi@albicenter.com; betim.humolli@albicommerce.com

T. Fiti
Faculty of Economics-Skopje, Ss. Cyril and Methodius University, Skopje, Macedonia
e-mail: takifiti@eccf.ukim.edu.mk

© Springer International Publishing Switzerland 2015
L.-P. Dana, V. Ramadani (eds.), *Family Businesses in Transition Economies*,
DOI 10.1007/978-3-319-14209-8_16

well as for distribution companies. As a result, Kosovo currently enjoys free trade within the Central European Free Trade Agreement—CEFTA—enabling its producers to access the regional market comprising 28 million consumers, free of any customs duties. In 2012 the total export with CEFTA members was 102.6 million and import 844.6 million (Ministry of Trade and Industry, 2013).

In order to make improvement and creating a friendlier environment for the development of family businesses, the Kosovo government has undertaken a reform of all the rules, where the core of its enforcement measures consists in reducing administrative barriers and business costs. Kosovo Government is in the process of improving the conditions of doing business, by facilitating the registration of business and tax environment, which could increase the reliability of people for fair competition in the market.

Also in Kosovo, family businesses promote economic development, and this can be observed through their influence and contribution to employment and gross domestic product growth (GDP). Kosovo's Government recognizes the importance and role of small and medium enterprises for the economic development of the country, where most of them are family businesses. Responsible for developing strategy for these businesses is the ministry of trade and industry, through the agency to support SMEs. They have created a strategy for a 5-year period which began implementation from January 2012 (Gashi & Ramadani, 2013).

This project has four main components:

1. Improving the business climate;
2. Establishing public-private dialogue and donor coordination;
3. Improving the competitiveness of SMEs in Kosovo; and
4. Public information campaign (Ministry of Trade and Industry, 2013).

Kosovo's government has plans to make some things easier through this strategy for small and medium businesses. It plans to make ease of entry and exit of a business from the market, as it has profound impact on business growth and overall vitality of the private sector. If barriers to entry are high then this will discourage entrepreneurs from entering the market.

As in the most of countries in Europe, also in Kosovo the dominant form of business is Family Business. Despite this fact, there are very few studies in Kosovo for family businesses, on the organization and their functioning. This is the reason that pushed us to start this study on family businesses, because for a long time we are working in a business that is family business and we wanted to know more about these businesses and give our contribution in their study. Becoming part of the family business is a special sensation, after entering the family business world means giving the opportunity and sense of belonging and pride

Family business is the dominant form of business in Republic of Kosovo and is a major driver for job creation, economic growth and social stability. When family business is mentioned in Kosovo, the first though that comes to our minds is that these business are craft stores, confectionary, bakery or small manufacturing companies. In most cases these businesses are founded by the need, due to high rates of unemployment that has existed and exists in our country, and the foundation of this business is seen as the best way to ensure the existence (Gashi & Ramadani, 2013). A family business could never be called 'small', because how can be called small when from this business it depends the welfare of your family, where you have invest your all wealth and your toil.

These businesses demonstrate the highest level of loyalty, increasing community development, perspective on long-term vision, and motivation that comes from the feeling of wealth and reputation associated with the business.

Family business tends to think in a long term basis and not in the short term basis. They tend to think about their business over generations and not just only based on profits. The desire and dedication to grow the business is always present in every family member. Emotion plays a big role in family business. Family business has a build-in structure with emotional issues with unique values and personalities that are reflective of the family culture (Martin, 2003).

The strength and success of the family business sector is vital to the future of Kosovo's economy, community and culture. In family business the integrity and family reputation are more important than the individual success, money and growth. If family business wants to be healthy, the family members must have the ability to convey mutual respect, trust and support for each other. Family and non-family members should have freedom to express their thoughts and feelings.

In our case study we will analyze ALBI Group, which is one of the most successful family businesses in Republic of Kosovo. Our research will aim to study the history, founders, management, development of their business over years, success and the succession plans that this family business have so the business continue over generations.[1]

2 The History of ALBI Group

ALBI Group was established on 5th of December 1990, initially known as ALBI Commerce. Its founder, Tahir Humolli initially employed seven employees, whereas now the company employs over 800 employees. ALBI Group is one of the most successful private companies in the Kosovo which is comprised of seven business entities and it employs over 860 employees. It manages over 58 stores with a total area of 31,500 m^2 and it has loaned out over 15,000 m^2. All of these components create one of the big economic giants in the trade industry in Kosovo.

As is seen on this graph the employer rate was growing since 1990, where from only seven employees now are 869 employees (Fig. 1), and this fact show that ALBI Group are among the most important contributors to the creation of wealth and generating employment vacancies.

ALBI Group has a very young workforce, where the majority of employees are among the age 30 years. As in seen in this figure the 65 % of all employees are

---

[1] The data about this company are collected by interviewing ALBI GROUP owners.

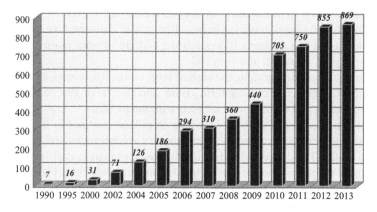

Fig. 1 Number of employees 1990–2013 (Source: Authors)

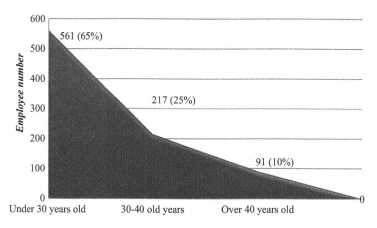

Fig. 2 Age structure of employees (Source: Authors)

among the age of 30 years old. 25 % are between 30 and 40 years old and 10 % are over 40 years old (Fig. 2).

3 ALBI Group Business Entities

ALBI Group has many business entities. We will try to explain with few words each of their business entities.

ALBI Commerce is one of the leading companies in product distribution in the Republic of Kosovo. Twenty years ago it started the production and distribution of Ceylon tea whereas in year 2003 it launched and registered internationally the brand Albred.

It distributes products of general consumption in all territory of Kosovo. It possesses two very modern distribution centers, one with an area of 5,000 m^2 and the other one with an area over 10,000 m^2. It is an exclusive representative for Kosovo in different products programs such as: Lactalis Group (President, Dukat, Galbani, Ideal Sipka), Kraš, Trevalli Cooperlat (Hopla), Johnson&Johnson, Werner&Mertz, Peros, etc.

ALBI Shopping—It is one of the biggest chains of retail stores in Kosovo. It is mainly focused on the most frequent locations in the Prishtina region. It aims to grow and expand in all territory of Kosovo. Their aim is to offer the customer the widest range of products and the lowest prices in the market so that consumers of all strata of society may find their selves and fulfill all their needs.

In 2006 ALBI Group opened its first shopping mall in the Prishtina outskirts, Veternik. The first Hypermarket, in the European levels, was opened by ALBI in the same shopping mall. ALBI Group added another outlet center and a big hypermarket in September 2010. This center operates based on the concept of outlet clothing. It is located in the industrial zone in Prishtina and it has an area of 7,500 m^2. Today ALBI shopping has five hypermarkets and nine markets, and has plans to expand with markets throughout the territory of Kosovo.

ALBI Mall—was established in 2006 and it is the biggest and the most modern shopping mall in Kosovo. It has an area of 35,200 m^2. This mall fulfills all the client requests and needs by offering a broad spectrum of goods and products for all ages and groups. Here you can find all you need for you and your family, you can have fun through various spaces for entertainment or you can sit for food, any coffee or dessert in restaurants that are located in this shopping center because the mall contains a modern hypermarket with a variety of fresh products, restaurants, cafeteria, the most well-known textile brands, different entertainment areas, children's playing areas, etc.

Albi & Fashion—ALBI Group in 2006 established Albi & Fashion Company. It represents famous textile brands such as: Okaidi, Timberland, Golden Point, Springfield, Bitsiani, Miss Sixty and Energie.

Sportina & Albi—In June 2008, ALBI Group along with the Slovenian company who is a leader in the region in textiles "Sportina", established the *Joint venture* named "Sportina & Albi". It is a representative of famous textile brands such as: Tom Tailor, Tally Weijl and Sportina, many stores with brands such as Vero Moda, Only, Jack&John, etc. When the expansion occurred at ALBI Mall, this company opened 13 other stores with different brands and 3 coffee bars Coffeeshop. The new brands from this company are: Esprit, Orsay, Tamaris, Parfois, Six, XWZ (Hugo Boss, Armani Jeans, Iceberg, Cerruti, Pimkie a famous French brand was opened in year 2012 in ALBI Mall. This company has also expanded its activities outside the shopping mall by positioning two stores, Tom Tailor and Tally Weijl in the heart of Prishtina.

Since year 2006 ALBI is an exclusive representative of the famous Italian brand Geox. It has opened four stores in Kosovo.

In 2010 ALBI opened the first store of the famous Turkish brand Özdilek. In 2011–2012, it was opened two other stores of the same brand. Other famous brands have joined the ALBI portfolio such as Motivi, Oltre, etc.

4   Development over the Years

The road to success was very difficult, with many challenges to face, which were successfully passed by hard work and shared ideas of members from this family.

ALBI Group has achieved success in all of its companies and it has become one of the leaders of private business in the economic development of the country. ALBI Group objective is growth and development, therefore the company has expanded the mall for 20,000 m^2 in the last 2 years and it has invested in building a new distribution center and growing the number of retail markets in Kosovo. At the same time it is continuously enriching its portfolio as a products distributor of general consumable good as well as being a representative of the most famous textile brands with competitive advantage in the market.

In December 2011, ALBI Group purchased 100 % of the shares from Mango in Kosovo and therefore became the exclusive representative of this brand. On 29th of September it opened the second Mango store in ALBI Mall. In October 2012, Sportina & ALBI opened the first store of the famous French brand Pimkie in ALBI Mall.

Photo 1   ALBI Mall in Prishtina, Kosovo *(Photographed by authors)*

Photo 2 ALBI Group in Lipjan, Kosovo *(Photographed by authors)*

ALBI Group has achieved to become famous even abroad. Business expansion, growth and development are obviously an objective of this company. Therefore the number of employees is expected to grow rapidly and considerably in the coming years.

During the enlargement process of ALBI Mall came out with the motto "Growing Bigger-Turning Better" which encompasses the philosophy of creating value for the consumers and fulfilling their needs and requests.

By being the biggest and the most modern shopping mall in the country, this center has achieved to fulfill the requests of all ages; all groups therefore the needs of all the citizens in Kosovo. This center has the food court, cafeteria and restaurants, home appliances, famous textile brands, children's playing area, bowling, etc. ALBI Mall's motto "Your Family's Place" best expresses the embodying of the Kosovo citizens with this center and it makes you feel as if you are in one of the most developed countries in Europe. Therefore, ALBI Mall is the first choice of Kosovo citizens to meet, to go for an outing, for entertainment, purchases, food and this shows the client's loyalty toward the company. Filling the needs and wishes of the consumers/clients in the long-term is one of the competitive advantages which differs ALBI from the others.

Successful management of world brands and excellent cooperation with local partners has made ALBI Commerce an important address through which international companies aim to penetrate in the Kosovo market.

5 Governance in Family Business

Governance refers to the ability to control and regulate the relations between family members, shareholders, managers and employers, in order that company can have the opportunity to flourish, and family promotes and protects their unit as for the sake of her family as well as for the sake of the company, considering that family unity is a source of values, which can return to competitive advantage (Lipman, 2010).

ALBI Group is managed by family members that are employed in the business. They have created a governance structure in the company in order to protect interests of shareholders in the long term growth and ensuring continuity of enterprise and promoting harmony and well-being of family.

Mr. Tahir Humolli is a man who loves life, loves his employees and loves his company. He has four sons and one daughter all involved in the business. The oldest son Sytki is CEO of the Company. The second son Nexhat is executive manager for Distribution Company. The third son Nehat is executive manager for retail stores and the youngest one Betim is executive manager for shopping mall textile brands, also the daughter Valbona is responsible for some brands that ALBI Group is representative for Kosovo. In this family business are respected different skills of each other, and they believe that they can compete and do their job in right way.

The father and his children are working hard together in evident harmony toward a common goal, customers lending massive support to an obviously successful business; and even distributors and suppliers, are unanimous in their praise, admiration and expressions of loyalty. They key strength are family values, culture, and the costumer focus. Their family values are being honest, working as a team, listening, caring and meet customer needs. These values have built a unique and strong culture to grow a flexible team.

6 Succession Planning

Family business continuity, generation after generation is very important for family businesses and for the economy in general. Generation to generation process is difficult and continuity is called as the last and most difficult test for family businesses. Succession "is not a single event that occurs when old leader retires and passes the torch to a new leader, but is a time-driven process development, which begins very early in the life of some families and continues through maturation and aging generations". Succession is the process of preparation and forecasting, which helps in better way to surrender the keys of leadership, regulation and adaptation of business (Gersick, Davis, Hampton, & Lansberg, 1997).

The purpose of succession planning is to achieve the transfer of control and responsibility of the family business in the best manner possible to next generation (Kaneff, 2011).

The succession planning should be the most important task of the leader of the family business and should be initiated at an early stage of the business life cycle. Succession includes two movements, successor which moves and takes office and leader who retire, and this motion is very important for the succession process that should be done after the selection of appropriate successor. Succession planning is like an insurance, which protects family from the destruction of the financial value (Hess, 2006).

As we mentioned the ALBI Group was founded by the Mr. Tahir Humolli. Years after years his sons joined the business and today they are part of the family business. Also in this family business are many family members employed and have managerial positions. Here are working: first generation (founder), second generation (the founder's sons and daughters) and the third generation (nephews of the founder). Three generations are part of this family business. Every founder dream is that one day he can pass to the children the business that he has created.

The founder of ALBI Group thinks that the successful planning of succession process requires time and can be successful only when it results from the creation of good relationships with the next generation and is based on responsibility, commitment and mutual respect.

For him, the role of the next generation is the crucial for the business success and their continuity across generations. Training and educating successor can be a challenge. This is an issue that request in depth consideration to work properly and the successor be ready for taking the baton. Every possible successor needs a support and training. The owner's experience in the business will enable a determination of which criteria are necessary for good training. Usually, an owner will want to assess a successor in the areas of decision-making, leadership, risk management, ability to deal with people, and how they handle stress.

The successors are all well educated. They are all working in the company and they are faced with daily challenges that a family business have. Over years they started to plan the succession. While undergoing training the successors have been introduced into the owner's outside and inside network of contacts. This can include the firm's customers, bankers, accountants, lawyers, other business associates and firms employers. These have given them time to get to know the successor and create some opportunities for the successor to spend time in those other businesses. The successors also have finished their studies in one of the best universities outside the country, and also some courses in business management. The use of strategic planning as training tool for successors can be very useful. Members of the next generation can get double benefits by participating in the strategic planning process. They acquire knowledge about the business, which the family member can use in order to avoid wrong direction of values and business norms also, learning and management tools to develop their professional skills. Success in family business for the successor to be successful requires careful planning. The succession process they have is adapted with the succession model based on business life cycle (Fig. 3).

The first phase of the management from owner is the stage where the owner is the only family member directly involved in the business, and its successor is not directly involved in the business. At this stage the founder has complete business direction and he use his skills trying to create organizational culture which on one hand is needed to run the daily affairs of the business and in the long term is beneficial for successful succession business. During this stage the founder learns to delegate.

The second phase is known as the training and development phases and is the stage where the successor is recognized and learned the business. At this stage

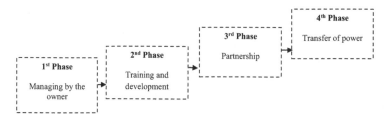

Fig. 3 Succession model based on the business life cycle. Source: Adapted from Churchill and Hatten (1987, pp. 51–64)

successor entered into organization and began to participate in daily chores. Here the successor learns and develops his skills to run the business and has ability to delegate power.

The third phase is the stage where the partnership is developed between ancestors and descendants. Here more authority remains descendants and is developing stronger relationship between the two. The succession process of ALBI Group is in this phase.

The fourth phase, which is the last stage where the current strength of the business is transferred under the responsibility of offspring. At this stage is the ability of the ancestors to seek new opportunities for his life which really simplifies the process of succession.

7 Conclusion

ALBI has over 24 year's tradition as a producer and distributor of goods and experience in the retail trade in the Republic of Kosovo. The success of the company is composed of the human, capital and information resources. The company has always adjusted to the changes in information technology by modernizing work processes and by being very efficient in offering services to consumers/clients. Investments in staff training and development, recruitment of professionals, advanced computer systems, management of the vehicles through online GPS, as well as the continued update of the database, has made ALBI one of the most competitive companies in Kosovo, in all business aspects.

References

Churchill, N. C., & Hatten, K. J. (1987). Non-market-based transfers of wealth and power: A research framework for family businesses. *Family Business Review, 10*(1), 53–67.
Gashi, G., & Ramadani, V. (2013). Family businesses in Republic of Kosovo: Some general issues. In V. Ramadani & R. C. Schneider (Eds.), *Entrepreneurship in the Balkans*. Heidelberg: Springer.

Gersick, K. E., Davis, J. A., Hampton, M. M., & Lansberg, I. (1997). *Generations to generations: Life cycles of the family business*. Boston: Harvard Business School Press.

Hess, E. D. (2006). *The successful family business: A proactive plan for managing the family and the business*. Westport: Praeger.

Kaneff, M. (2011). *Taking over: Insider tips from a third-generation CEO*. New York: Teen Eagles Press.

Lipman, F. D. (2010). *The family business guide, everything you need to know to manage your business from legal planning to business strategies*. New York: Palgrave Macmillan.

Martin, D. W. (2003). *The family business in transition*. http://www.ecmag.com/section/your-business/family-business-transition#sthash.kCcMyPrm.dpuf. Accessed 10 Mar 2014.

Ministry of Trade and Industry. (2013). *Private sector development strategy 2013–2017*. http://www.mti-ks.org/repository/docs/MTI_Strategjia_ZHSP_Eng_115534.pdf. Accessed 30 May 2014.

About the Editors

Léo-Paul Dana received BA and MBA degrees at McGill University and a PhD from HEC-Montreal. He is Professor of Entrepreneurship at Montpellier Business School and holds the honorary title of Adjunct Professor at the University of Regina, in Canada. He was earned tenure at the University of Canterbury and formerly served as Visiting Professor of Entrepreneurship at INSEAD and Deputy Director of the International Business MBA Programme at Nanyang Business School. He has published extensively in a variety of leading journals including the *Cornell Quarterly, Entrepreneurship and Regional Development, Entrepreneurship: Theory and Practice, Journal of Small Business Management, Journal of World Business*, and *Small Business Economics*. His research interests focus on cultural issues, including the internationalization of entrepreneurship. He is Editor *Emeritus* of the *Journal of International Entrepreneurship*. Among his books are *When Economies Change Hands: A Survey of Entrepreneurship in the Emerging Markets of Europe from the Balkans to the Baltic States*, published by Routledge in 2010 and the *World Encyclopedia of Entrepreneurship*, released in 2011.

© Springer International Publishing Switzerland 2015
L.-P. Dana, V. Ramadani (eds.), *Family Businesses in Transition Economies*,
DOI 10.1007/978-3-319-14209-8

Veland Ramadani is an Associate Professor at South-East European University, Republic of Macedonia, where he teaches both undergraduate and postgraduate courses in entrepreneurship and small business management. During the period 2012–2014, he served as Coordinator of Integrated Study Programme Department: Contemporary Enterprise Management, within South-East European University. He formerly served as Visiting Professor of Entrepreneurship at Universum College and AAB University, Republic of Kosovo. His research interests include entrepreneurship, small business management and venture capital investments. He authored or co-authored around 45 research articles and ten books. Among his recent books are *Entrepreneurship in the Balkans*, published by Springer, *Entrepreneurship*, published by South-East European University and *Female entrepreneurship in transitional economies: Trends and challenges*, published by Palgrave Macmillan. Veland also serves as a member of editorial and reviewer board of several international journals. He was engaged by the President of Republic of Macedonia as a member of experts' committee to analyse the economical, technological and juridical conditions for establishing techno-parks in the Republic of Macedonia. He has also delivered different trainings to the heads of departments in the Ministry of Economy of Macedonia.

About the Authors

Elena Aculai is a Leading Scientific Researcher and a scientific project's Director at the National Institute for Economic Research of the Republic of Moldova. Her scientific interests include SMEs' development policy in transition economies; identification of characteristics of women's entrepreneurship. She was the leader of more than 20 research projects, oriented to SMEs. She participated in elaboration of legislation and policy documents governing the development and support of SMEs in Moldova. She is the author of more than 70 publications, including participation in 8 collective monographs on various aspects of SMEs in countries with transition economies.

Egzona Aliu is International Training Consultant at LEORON Professional Development Institute, United Arab Emirates. Previously she has worked at the Government of Republic of Macedonia in the Secretariat for European Affairs, working in EU funds coordination. She also has managed with her father their own family business, Euro-Aktiva (Trading with construction materials, tires for any type of vehicles, security agency, gas station, service, markets, restaurants etc.). She received MA degree at City College-International Faculty of the University of Sheffield, Thessaloniki, Greece.

Přemysl Bartoš is concerned about the credit risk of small and medium-sized companies. He is the owner of a private company and also operates at Tomas Bata University in Zlín. The results of his scientific research have been published in proceedings at international scientific conferences, and in some scientific journals. He works in several scientific projects at Tomas Bata University in Zlín.

Jaroslav Belás is an expert in commercial banking, credit risk, and business environment. Previously he worked in the banking sector of Slovakia. In academic field has worked at the University of Economics in Bratislava, and the Banking Institutions of Prague. He is currently at Tomas Bata University in Zlín. He authored six monographs; the results of the research activities have been published in prestigious journals. He is a member of Scientific Council of Pan European

© Springer International Publishing Switzerland 2015
L.-P. Dana, V. Ramadani (eds.), *Family Businesses in Transition Economies*,
DOI 10.1007/978-3-319-14209-8

University in Bratislava and the Scientific Council of Georg Zilina publisher in Slovakia. Currently takes care and manages five scientific projects.

Valerija Bublić is a full time teacher at the University of Applied Sciences VERN', Entrepreneurship and Management Department in Zagreb, Croatia. She has been teaching both undergraduate and graduate courses in Entrepreneurial Management, Change Management and Business Plan. Her main fields of research interests include risk management, change management and entrepreneurial planning in the SMEs sector. She authored and co-authored several research papers. Her professional experience gathered while working in management jobs and executive positions in Croatian enterprises of all sizes; doing business internationally in the multicultural environment; being owner manager of a small enterprise; and her research; have added a great deal to her teaching and benefit all her students. She was also engaged in the project "Train the Trainers" which was launched by Croatian Ministry of Economy, Labour and Entrepreneurship as well as in several projects launched by NGOs.

Tullio Buccellato received his PhD in International Economics from the University of Rome Tor Vergata. His research focuses on the emerging markets and Russia in particular on corporate governance issues in the extraction sector. Tullio is presently with Ernst & Young in Paris, France, and has worked at Fondazione Manlio Masi, ECOPA, and as an Economic Adviser in the Office for National Statistics in the UK.

Gordana Ćorić is a Deputy Head of Undergraduate study program Entrepreneurial Economics and Senior Lecturer of Dynamic Entrepreneurship and Business Ethics at the University of Applied Sciences VERN', Zagreb, Croatia. She is also the owner-manager of consultancy and training company Festina lente (business services, counseling, consulting, training programs). She currently teaches at the University of Applied Sciences VERN' (Basics of Entrepreneurship, Dynamic Entrepreneurship, Business Ethics and Culture, Managing Growing Companies, etc.). Her previous work experience includes several years of coordination of various projects for fast-growing companies at the European Foundation for Entrepreneurship Research (EFER) in Amsterdam, and work for the American organization World Learning in projects of education of entrepreneurs and economic empowerment of women. She has published over 20 professional, scientific and review papers. Her teaching, mentoring and research interests include entrepreneurship (dynamic, women, rural, social, corporate, etc.), economic empowerment of marginalized groups, start-ups, growth strategies etc.

Léo-Paul Dana received BA and MBA degrees at McGill University and a PhD from HEC-Montreal. He is Professor of Entrepreneurship at Montpellier Business School and holds the honorary title of Adjunct Professor at the University of Regina, in Canada. He was earned tenure at the University of Canterbury and formerly served as Visiting Professor of Entrepreneurship at INSEAD and Deputy Director of the International Business MBA Programme at Nanyang Business School. He has published extensively in a variety of leading journals including the Cornell

Quarterly, Entrepreneurship and Regional Development, Entrepreneurship: Theory and Practice, Journal of Small Business Management, Journal of World Business, and Small Business Economics. His research interests focus on cultural issues, including the internationalization of entrepreneurship. He is Editor Emeritus of the Journal of International Entrepreneurship. Among his books are Léo-Paul Dana, When Economies Change Hands: A Survey of Entrepreneurship in the Emerging Markets of Europe from the Balkans to the Baltic States, published by Routledge in 2010 and the World Encyclopedia of Entrepreneurship, released in 2011.

Mojca Duh is an Associate Professor of Strategic Management at Faculty of Economics and Business at the University of Maribor where she teaches both undergraduate and postgraduate courses in strategic management and family business management. She is a head of the Department of Strategic Management and Business Policy. Her main research interests include strategic management and particularities of development and management of family businesses. She participated with research papers at several national and international conferences; she is (co)author of research articles, and chapters in several books. She serves as a member of editorial and reviewer board of several international journals.

Alain Fayolle is a professor of entrepreneurship at EM Lyon Business School, France and a founder and director of the entrepreneurship research centre. His research interests cover a range of topics in the field of entrepreneurship: education and training, corporate entrepreneurship, new venture creation process, family entrepreneurship, opportunity and necessity entrepreneurship, etc. Among them, entrepreneurship education issues take a great place. On this topic, Dr. Fayolle has notably edited three volumes of the Handbook of Research in Entrepreneurship Education (2007 and 2010, Edward Elgar Publishing). He has been also (or still is) acting as an expert for different governments and international institutions (OECD, EC). Alain published over 20 books and 100 articles in leading international and French-speaking scientific journals. Among his editorial positions, he is notably an Associate Editor of JSBM and an Editor of two leading French-speaking journals, Revue de l'Entrepreneuriat and Entreprendre & Innover.

Gian Fazio obtained his PhD in Economics and Econometrics in 2010 from the University College London's School of Slavonic and Eastern European Studies. He worked at the Office of the Fair Trading in the past. Currently he is the President at United Textiles and Components.

Taki Fiti is a full-time professor at the Faculty of Economics—Skopje, University "Ss Cyril and Methodius", and a member of the Macedonian Academy of Sciences and Arts. His scientific preoccupations are economics, economic growth and development, entrepreneurship, countries in transition, modern macroeconomic conceptions, and politics. He authored or coauthored over 230 scientific and professional articles (books, textbooks, scientific projects, articles, reviews, etc.) published in the country and abroad. He has realized scientific and professional stays in Italy, Germany, Great Britain, France, and other countries. Taki Fiti was

Dean of the Faculty of Economics in Skopje, a long-time President of the Association of Economists in Macedonia, Minister of Finance of the Republic of Macedonia (1996–1998), member of the Advisory Board of the Russian and East European Research Centre (University of Wolverhampton), consultant of OECD for projects in the field of small- and medium-sized enterprises and entrepreneurship, member of the counseling team of the Prime Minister of the Republic of Macedonia (2005–2006), member of the counseling board of the Governor of National Bank of Macedonia (2005–2008), cochairman of the Blue Ribbon commission for Macedonia, member of boards of directors of affirmed Macedonian enterprises and banks, etc.

Gramos Gashi is engaged as Import Manager at Albi-Mall in the Republic of Kosovo. His research interests include entrepreneurship, small business management and family business management, and succession process. He graduated in master degree for management in South East European University in Tetovo, Macedonia. He is certificated in European Business Competence License. Gramos has participated in many business fairs in Germany, Croatia and Netherlands. He is co-author in the book "Entrepreneurship in the Balkans: Diversity, Support and Prospects" (Edited by Veland Ramadani and Robert C. Schneider, published by Springer) with a chapter "Family Business in Republic of Kosovo, Some General Issues".

Shqipe Gërguri-Rashiti is an Assistant Professor at College of Business Administration, American University of Middle-East (Kuwait). Previously, she has taught at South East European University (Macedonia). Her research interests include management, strategic management, management information systems, etc. She authored research articles in journals such as Strategic Change: Briefings in Entrepreneurial Finance, Journal of Entrepreneurship and Small Business, Journal of Balkan and Near Eastern Studies and International Bulletin of Business Administration. Besides being a Lecturer, she has been also involved in managing UNDP projects within the South-East European University, Macedonia.

Radmila Grozdanić is Full University Professor at Faculty of Business Administration and Entrepreneurship in Belgrade, Serbia. She completed Faculty of Economy, Master degree and PhD in Economic Sciences. She has written more than 10,000 pages related to SMEs, entrepreneurship, female and family businesses, local and regional development and innovation ecosystems.

Roman Hlawiczka is an expert in banking and credit risk of SMEs in the Czech Republic. He has been working in the banking sector of the Czech Republic since 1991. He started in Komercni banka, a.s. as a Deputy Head of Department, held various offices in this bank from a Section Manager for bank services to Group Branch Manager and has advanced to positions up to a Superior Branch Manager. In academic field he has worked at the University of Economics in Ostrava as an external lecturer. The results of the research activities have been published in scientific journals.

Frank Hoy is the Paul R. Beswick Professor of Innovation and Entrepreneurship in the School of Business at Worcester Polytechnic Institute. He was most recently director of the Centers for Entrepreneurial Development, Advancement, Research and Support at the University of Texas at El Paso (UTEP), also serves as director of the Collaborative for Entrepreneurship & Innovation (CEI), WPI's nationally ranked entrepreneurship center. Hoy joined the WPI faculty in August 2009, and holds a BA from the University of Texas at El Paso, an MBA from the University of North Texas, and a PhD in management from Texas A&M University. He was a faculty member in the Department of Management at the University of Georgia for 10 years, where he founded and directed the Center for Business and Economic Studies, coordinated the entrepreneurship curriculum, and served as director of the Georgia Small Business Development Center. In 1991 he returned to Texas to join UTEP as a professor of management and entrepreneurship and dean of the College of Business Administration. Hoy is a past president of the United States Association for Small Business and Entrepreneurship and past chair of the Entrepreneurship Division of the Academy of Management. His research has appeared in the Academy of Management Journal, Academy of Management Review, Journal of Business Venturing, Family Business Review, and he is a past editor of Entrepreneurship Theory and Practice.

Maria Hudáková took the highest university education at the Faculty of Mechanical Engineering of the Zilina University in the field of Enterprise Management. She is a specialist assistant on Department of Crisis Management on Faculty of special engineering on University of Zilina. Her scientific-research activities are oriented on controlling as an early warning system in enterprise, risk management in enterprise and risks in quality management. She published articles on national and international level. She is a member of national and international science projects. She continuously enhances her knowledge through participating in various courses oriented on development of pedagogical and professional skills.

Betim Humolli is engaged as a Business Development Director at Albi Group (Kosovo), where in close cooperation with Albi senior Management team he is been working as a Transition/Business Model advisor. Betim graduated at Webster Graduate School, London for master degree in Business management and leadership. He was awarded with Outstanding Graduate Student Award, March 2008, at Webster University, London. For the period September 2009–May 2010 he was as First Assistant to Management field Professor at American University in Kosovo (AUK). Betim participated in many business fairs in Germany, Italy, France, Netherlands and Turkey.

Marina Letonja is a Senior Lecturer of Entrepreneurship at GEA College—Faculty of Entrepreneurship in Ljubljana, Slovenia. Her main research interest is in entrepreneurship, particularly family entrepreneurship and the questions of succession and innovation management. She published research findings on family businesses, as well on ethical entrepreneurship, bio-tech entrepreneurship in numerous research papers and articles. She is co-author of the book on Entrepreneurship

(2000) and of many study materials on the field of entrepreneurship (2005), business planning and macroeconomics. She is actively involved in numerous European projects (AISP-Tempus, ACROSSEE-SEE, COFFE) as researcher and/or project manager.

Predrag Ljubotina is an entrepreneur and manager of his own company Vedis Ltd. He graduated on master's level from GEA College in Ljubljana, Slovenia. His main field of activity is business consulting with the focus on marketing, market diversification and internationalization for SMEs. Throughout his entrepreneurial career, he gained experience in building family business and business development in multicultural environments. For 20 years he was a co-owner and marketing director in company Amba Ltd., where he successfully carried out the process of business internationalization. Recently he is involved in several projects concerning growing and internationalization of Slovenian small and medium sized companies with the objective to support and stimulate the process of professionalization and market diversification in those subjects. He is a PhD. student at University of Primorska researching entrepreneurial aspirations of young graduates through the spectrum of family business. He has been recently involved in several international researching projects.

Saša Petković is an Assistant Professor at University of Banja Luka, Faculty of Economics, Republic of Srpska, Bosnia and Herzegovina where he teaches both undergraduate and postgraduate courses in entrepreneurship and small business management. His research interests include entrepreneurship, economics and SMEs management and theoretical economics. He published 14 papers and 3 monographs (two monographs in English). Also, he serves as a member of editorial and reviewer board of several international journals. He is vice dean for student affairs and work part time as a project manager at CARE International Balkans.

Mirjana Radović-Marković is an Academician and Full University professor of Entrepreneurship. She holds BSc, MSc and PhD Degrees in Economics, as well as Post-Doctoral Studies in Multidisciplinary Studies. Recently she is elected as an Academician of Bulgarian Academy of Arts and Sciences (2013). Furthermore, she is a Fellow of the Academia European (EA), London, Royal Society of the Arts in the UK (the RSA) and a Fellow of the World Academy of Art and Science (WAAS). In addition, she is also academician of EMAAS, Greece and etc. She has written 34 books and more than 150 peer-reviewed articles.

Veland Ramadani is an Associate Professor at South-East European University, Republic of Macedonia, where he teaches both undergraduate and postgraduate courses in entrepreneurship and small business management. He is Coordinator of Integrated Study Programme Department: Contemporary Enterprise Management, within South-East European University. He formerly served as Visiting Lecturer of Entrepreneurship at Universum College and AAB University, Republic of Kosovo. His research interests include entrepreneurship, small business management and venture capital investments. He authored around 45 research articles and ten books. Veland also serves as a member of editorial and reviewer board of several international journals. He was engaged by the President of Republic of Macedonia as a member of experts' committee to analyse the economical, technological and juridical conditions for establishing techno-parks in the Republic of Macedonia. He has also delivered different trainings to the heads of departments in the Ministry of Economy of Macedonia.

Vanessa Ratten is an Associate Professor of Entrepreneurship and Innovation in the Department of Management, La Trobe Business School at La Trobe University, Melbourne, Australia. She teaches Entrepreneurial Business Planning, Managing Innovation in Organisations and Entrepreneurship. She has previously been on the business faculty of Duquesne University, the University of Queensland, Queensland University of Technology and Deakin University. She has won a Vice Chancellors award for community engagement with innovation and entrepreneurship programs. Her main research areas are entrepreneurship, innovation and sport.

Gadaf Rexhepi is an Assistant Professor at South-East European University, Republic of Macedonia where he teaches both undergraduate and postgraduate courses in Management, Game Theory and Strategic Management. His research interests include management and strategic management. He authored around 40 research articles and several text-books and monographs. Also, he serves as a member of editorial and reviewer board of several international journals. Besides theoretical background, he works as a consultant in Business Development Center at South East European University and as consultant for development Alma-M one of the biggest company in Macedonia. He also has been consultant of the Ministry of the Economy and is active as an expert in five commissions in ministries in Macedonia. From 2010 he is Vice-Dean for postgraduate studies.

Yulia Rodionova started her career in consulting and policy research and spent the past several years working in Higher Education. Yulia's areas of specialisation include small business enterprise, gender, corporate finance, international finance and econometrics. She is a Senior Lecturer at the Department of Accounting and Finance, De Montfort University, and has published in internationally-recognised journals and frequently presents at national and international academic conferences.

Iva Senegović is a Deputy Chair of Entrepreneurship and Management Department, student business incubator manager, and a full time teacher at the University of Applied Sciences VERN' in Zagreb, Croatia. She has been teaching both undergraduate and graduate courses in Entrepreneurship, Entrepreneurial Management, and she is a holder of Family Business course. Her main fields of research interest include family business, startup entrepreneurship, institutional support to the SMEs sector, and entrepreneurship education. Ms. Senegović is an author, co-author and mentor to several research papers on the concept of entrepreneurial university, transfer of ownership and leadership in the family business, education programs for dynamic and startup entrepreneurship, teaching entrepreneurship, entrepreneurial approach to rural development, etc.

Ralitsa Simeonova-Ganeva is an Associate Professor at the Faculty of Economics and Business Administration, Sofia University St. Kliment Ohridski, where she teaches both courses in economic statistics and econometrics. Her research interests include applied econometric analysis like modeling competitiveness, policy impact assessment, forecasting labour demand and supply, etc. She authored/co-authored over 50 publications, among which 14 journal articles and 18 books and economic reports. She was key expert/team leader in numerous analytical and forecasting assignments for the Council of Ministers, Ministry of Economy, Bulgarian SME Promotion Agency, Ministry of Finance, Ministry of Labour, the President of Republic of Bulgaria, etc.

Jelena Trivić is an Assistant Professor at Faculty of Economics University of Banja Luka, Republic of Srpska, Bosnia and Herzegovina, where she teaches undergraduate courses in International Economics. Her research interests include international trade and trade policy, international finances (exchange rate regimes, international capital flows and crisis), globalization, as well as the field of European integration process. Beside her work at the Faculty, she has been engaged in the various projects and activities financed mainly by EU funds in the field of research, education, European integration and development of small businesses. She authored around 25 research articles.

Jaka Vadnjal is Dean at GEA College of Entrepreneurship. He has been teaching there for the last 17 years and managed and participated in several research projects. He was visiting professor at a couple of foreign universities. He also teaches part time at Faculty of Economics of University of Ljubljana. Before joining GEA College for full time, he had been deputy director of the government's agency for promotion of entrepreneurship. He has extensive family business experience. For 10 years he was managing director of the second generation family firm established by his father. He quit because of several other professional challenges. Later he consulted more than 20 family businesses, mostly helping them with transition issues. He published more than hundred articles in popular press covering various topics in the fields of family business, entrepreneurship, venture capital and SME support policy. He presented more than 30 papers at most prominent research conferences worldwide. He published 33 papers in scientific journals and seven chapters in scientific books. He is also co-author of four text-books on entrepreneurship, also published outside Slovenia.

Natalia Vershinina is a Principal Lecturer at the Department of Strategic Management and Marketing, Leicester Business School, De Montfort University, Leicester, UK. She has co-authored the market-leading Management textbook with R. Daft and M. Kendrick. Her main teaching and research area is entrepreneurship and small firms with particular interest in ethnic minority entrepreneurship and effect of gender on women's enterprise.

Valentina Veverita is a Director of Small and Medium-Sized Enterprises Development Policies and Liberal Profession Department, the Ministry of Economy of the Republic of Moldova. Her research interests include entrepreneurship and

SMEs development policy. With her active participation, by the main legal documents governing the development and support of SMEs in the Republic of Moldova have been developed and adopted. She is also a professor at the State University of Moldova, lecturing the course in entrepreneurship for students and undergraduates. She is author of more than 20 publications on SMEs policy issues in the Republic of Moldova.

Natalia Vinogradova is a Leading Scientific Researcher at the National Institute for Economic Research of the Republic of Moldova. Her scientific interests include the research of SMEs' problems and entrepreneurship policy development in Moldova as well as some aspects of the greening of SMEs in the countries with transition economies. She was a member of a number of SMEs' oriented research projects, both national, implemented within the Academy of Sciences of Moldova, and international as well. She is the author of more than 20 scientific publications.

Zhelyu Vladimirov is teaching courses on Organisational Change and Development, HRM, and Small Business Management in the Faculty of Economics and Business Administration at the Sofia University St Kliment Ohridski. He had published in national and international journal on topics, related to the whole socio-political transformation in Bulgaria after 1989, agriculture and food industry development, implementation of quality standards in small food processing enterprises, ICT adoption by private and public organisations, and small and medium sized enterprises (SME) competitiveness. He took part in more than 20 national and international projects as an expert and principal coordinator. Currently he is a Marie Curie Fellow at the Faculty of Business, Economics, and Law at the University of Surrey, where he is working on the project devoted to the SME competitiveness, and particularly in the tourism sector.

Desislava Ivanova Yordanova is an Associate Professor at the Department of Business Administration of Sofia University "St Kliment Ohridski", where she is teaching both undergraduate and postgraduate courses in entrepreneurship. She authored around 45 articles, books, book chapters, and reports. She has published articles in various international journals, including Journal of International Management, International Journal of Entrepreneurial Behaviour & Research, Journal of Developmental Entrepreneurship, International Journal of Management, Service Business, and Journal of Applied Economic Sciences. Her research interests include entrepreneurship, small business management, and family business management.

Index

© Springer International Publishing Switzerland 2015
L.-P. Dana, V. Ramadani (eds.), *Family Businesses in Transition Economies*,
DOI 10.1007/978-3-319-14209-8

Lightning Source UK Ltd.
Milton Keynes UK
UKOW06n0131240415

2673UKAU00001B/5/P